WORKING WITH
EMOTIONAL
INTELLIGENCE

BY THE SAME AUTHOR

Emotional Intelligence

WORKING WITH

EMOTIONAL INTELLIGENCE

DANIEL GOLEMAN

BLOOMSBURY

First published in Great Britain 1998
This paperback edition published 1999

Copyright © 1998 by Daniel Goleman

The moral right of the author has been asserted

Bloomsbury Publishing Plc, 36 Soho Square, London W1D 3QY

A CIP catalogue record for this book is available from the British Library

ISBN 978 0 7475 4384 8

20 19 18 17 16 15 14

All papers used by Bloomsbury Publishing are natural,
recyclable products made from wood grown in well-managed forests.
The manufacturing processes conform to the
environmental regulations of the country of origin.

Printed in Great Britain by Clays Ltd, St Ives plc

www.bloomsbury.com/danielgoleman

Contents

····································

5

The Emotionally Intelligent Organization

Acknowledgments

The thinking that led to this book has many roots. One of the most important was an ongoing series of talks with my wife, Tara Bennett-Goleman, triggered by sitting through many frustrating business meetings together, particularly of boards of directors we sat on. I was often aware that, for some reason, things just were not working. Tara was able to tune in to the emotional currents beneath the surface of those meetings and identify the ones that diverted the group's focus and energy, keeping us from getting our business done.

Tara and I began working together on what eventually became the book *Emotional Intelligence.* Her thinking and work are bearing fruit in a book of her own, now in progress. She has been with me every step of the way on this intellectual journey.

Another main taproot of the thinking reflected here is my late friend David C. McClelland, formerly my professor at Harvard University. David's visionary sense of the nature of competence and his keen quest for truth have long been an inspiration for me, and a large portion of the evidence on which I build my case traces back to David's research. I was saddened to learn of David's death as I was finishing this book.

I was helped by many friends at the Boston office of Hay/McBer (the company David founded with David Berlew, now my business advisor): James Burrus, president; Mary Fontaine, vice president and general manager; Ruth Jacobs, senior consultant; and Jason Goldner and Wei Chen, researchers.

Richard Boyatzis, associate dean for executive education at the Weatherhead School of Management at Case Western Reserve University, a past president at Hay/McBer, a colleague of David McClelland, and a good friend since our graduate school days at Harvard, has been of enormous help. His books *The Competent Manager* and *Innovation in Education* are classic statements of the importance of emotional competencies and the best practices for cultivating them. Richard has generously shared his years of data on competence, as well as his wealth of insights and experience; I'm delighted to be working together with him in my new venture, Emotional Intelligence Services.

Lyle Spencer, director of research and technology worldwide at Hay/McBer, has been a font of data and wisdom about the competencies of star performance, and the value of stars for organizational performance. The book he coauthored, *Competence at Work,* remains definitive for professionals in the field.

Marilyn Gowing, director of the Personnel Resources and Development Center at the U.S. Office of Personnel Management, was especially helpful in sharing her groundbreaking research into the role of emotional competence in individual and organizational performance.

Particular gratitude goes to my other colleagues on the Consortium for Research on Emotional Intelligence in the Workplace: my cochair, Cary Cherniss, of the Graduate School for Applied Psychology at Rutgers University; Robert Caplan, professor of organizational psychology at George Washington University; Kathy Kram, director of the executive MBA program at Boston University School of Management; Rick Price, of the Institute for Social Research at the University of Michigan; and Mary Ann Re in Human Resources Governance at AT&T. Rob Emmerling and Cornelia Roche, researchers for the Consortium, provided invaluable assistance in scouring the research literature on training and development. Graduate students of Maurice Elias at Rutgers did an early background survey of the research terrain.

Deep appreciation goes to the Fetzer Institute for their support of the Consortium's work, and their ongoing interest in emotional intelligence initiatives.

My colleagues Rita and Bill Cleary, Judith Rodgers, Ken Rhee, and Thérèse Jacobs-Stewart at Emotional Intelligence Services have been instrumental in evolving the practical applications that flow from my analysis of working with emotional intelligence.

I owe an intellectual debt to Claudio Fernández-Aráoz of the Buenos Aires office of Egon Zehnder International, whose generosity of spirit, keen intellect, and prodigious energy enriched this book. And conversations with those at Egon Zehnder International, including the CEO, Daniel Meiland, Victor Loewenstein, the managing director, and Egon Zehnder himself—a pioneer in creating an emotionally intelligent organization—aided my case study.

Others who generously shared their thinking with me include Warren Bennis, Distinguished Professor of Business Administration at USC; John Seely Brown, chief scientist at Xerox Corporation; Rick Canada, director of leadership and organizational development for Motorola's Cellular Sector; Kate Cannon, director of leadership development, American Express

Financial Advisors; Richard Davidson, director of the Laboratory for Affective Neuroscience at the University of Wisconsin; Margaret Echols and Meg O'Leary, at Coopers & Lybrand; Susan Ennis, head of executive development at BankBoston; Joanna Foster, of British Telecom; Howard Gardner, professor at Harvard University; Robert E. Kelley, at Carnegie-Mellon University; Phil Harkin, president of Linkage; Judith Hall, psychologist at Northeastern University; Jed Hughes of Walter V. Clarke Associates; Linda Keegan, vice president for executive development at Citibank; Fred Kiehl, president of KRW Associates in Minneapolis; Doug Lennick, executive vice president at American Express Financial Advisors; Mark Loehr, managing director at Salomon Smith Barney; George Lucas, CEO, LucasFilm; Paul Robinson, director of Sandia National Laboratories; Deepak Sethi, executive education, AT&T; Erik Hein Schmidt, CEO of Rangjung Yeshe Publications; Birgitta Wistrand, of the Swedish Parliament; Nick Zeniuk, of Interactive Learning Labs; Dr. Vega Zagier of the Tavistock Institute, London; Shoshana Zuboff, of Harvard Business School; and Jim Zucco of Lucent Technologies.

Rachel Brod, my chief research assistant, tracked down the studies I needed to keep this book grounded in the most current findings. Miranda Pierce, my chief data analyst, analyzed hundreds of competence models to assess the potency of emotional intelligence in excellence at work. Robert Buchele, professor of economics at Smith College, performed a parallel analysis on federal employees and provided other helpful research in economics.

David Berman, computer consultant par excellence, offered timely crisis management and technical support. Rowan Foster, my assistant, kept my professional life running while writing consumed my time.

My deepest gratitude is to the hundreds of men and women from companies large and small around the world who have shared with me their experiences, stories, and thoughts. Many are cited by name in these pages, but many, many more are not. This book owes much to them for its insights into what it means to work with emotional intelligence.

1

Beyond Expertise

1

··········

The New Yardstick

The rules for work are changing. We're being judged by a new yard-stick: not just by how smart we are, or by our training and expertise, but also by how well we handle ourselves and each other. This yard-stick is increasingly applied in choosing who will be hired and who will not, who will be let go and who retained, who passed over and who promoted.

The new rules predict who is most likely to become a star performer and who is most prone to derailing. And, no matter what field we work in cur-rently, they measure the traits that are crucial to our marketability for future jobs.

These rules have little to do with what we were told was important in school; academic abilities are largely irrelevant to this standard. The new measure takes for granted having enough intellectual ability and technical know-how to do our jobs; it focuses instead on personal qualities, such as initiative and empathy, adaptability and persuasiveness.

This is no passing fad, nor just the management nostrum of the moment. The data that argue for taking it seriously are based on studies of tens of thousands of working people, in callings of every kind. The research distills with unprecedented precision which qualities mark a star performer. And it demonstrates which human abilities make up the greater part of the ingredi-ents for excellence at work—most especially for leadership.

If you work in a large organization, even now you are probably being evaluated in terms of these capabilities, though you may not know it. If you are applying for a job, you are likely to be scrutinized through this lens, though, again, no one will tell you so explicitly. Whatever your job, understanding how to cultivate these capabilities can be essential for success in your career.

If you are part of a management team, you need to consider whether your organization fosters these competencies or discourages them. To the degree your organizational climate nourishes these competencies, your organization will be more effective and productive. You will maximize your group's intelligence, the synergistic interaction of every person's best talents.

If you work for a small organization or for yourself, your ability to perform at peak depends to a very great extent on your having these abilities—though almost certainly you were never taught them in school. Even so, your career will depend, to a greater or lesser extent, on how well you have mastered these capacities.

In a time with no guarantees of job security, when the very concept of a "job" is rapidly being replaced by "portable skills," these are prime qualities that make and keep us employable. Talked about loosely for decades under a variety of names, from "character" and "personality" to "soft skills" and "competence," there is at last a more precise understanding of these human talents, and a new name for them: emotional intelligence.

A Different Way of Being Smart

I had the lowest cumulative grade point average ever in my engineering school," the codirector of a consulting firm tells me. "But when I joined the army and went to officer candidate school, I was number one in my class—it was all about how you handle yourself, get along with people, work in teams, leadership. And that's what I find to be true in the world of work."

In other words, what matters is a different way of being smart. In my book *Emotional Intelligence,* my focus was primarily on education, though a short chapter dealt with implications for work and organizational life.[1]

What caught me by utter surprise—and delighted me—was the flood of interest from the business community. Responding to a tidal wave of letters and faxes, e-mails and phone calls, requests to speak and consult, I found myself on a global odyssey, talking to thousands of people, from

CEOs to secretaries, about what it means to bring emotional intelligence to work.

Over and over I heard what became a familiar litany. People like the high-performing business consultant with the low GPA told me they found emotional intelligence, not technical expertise or book learning, to be what mattered most for excellence. My book, they said, made it safe to speak up about the business costs of emotional ineptitude, and to question a narrow, expertise-is-all view of capabilities. They felt they now had a new way to think about what they wished for in their own workplaces.

People spoke with extraordinary candor about matters far beyond the reach of corporate PR radar. Many detailed what is *not* working (such tales of emotional ineptitude are retold here without revealing the person's or organization's identity). But many others told success stories, confirming the practical value of working with emotional intelligence.

And so began the two-year inquiry that has culminated in this book. The effort has woven together several professional strands from my own life. From the outset, I've relied on the methods of journalism to delve into the facts and to narrate my conclusions. I've also gone back to my professional roots as an academic psychologist, conducting an exhaustive review of the research that illuminates the place of emotional intelligence in high performance for individuals, teams, and organizations. And I've performed or commissioned several new scientific analyses of data from hundreds of companies to establish a precise metric for quantifying the value of emotional intelligence.

This search has taken me back to research I participated in while a graduate student, and then faculty member, at Harvard University. That research was part of an early challenge to the IQ mystique—the false but widely embraced notion that what matters for success is intellect alone. This work helped spawn what has now become a mini-industry that analyzes the actual competencies that make people successful in jobs and organizations of every kind, and the findings are astonishing: IQ takes second position to emotional intelligence in determining outstanding job performance.

Analyses done by dozens of different experts in close to five hundred corporations, government agencies, and nonprofit organizations worldwide have arrived independently at remarkably similar conclusions, and their findings are particularly compelling because they avoid the biases or limits inherent in the work of a single individual or group. Their conclusions all point to the paramount place of emotional intelligence in excellence on the job—in virtually any job.

To be sure, these ideas are not new to the workplace; how people manage themselves and relate to those around them is central to much classic management theory. What's new is the data: We now have twenty-five years' worth of empirical studies that tell us with a previously unknown precision just how much emotional intelligence matters for success.

Another strand: In the decades since my own research in psychobiology, I have been tracking cutting-edge findings in neuroscience. This has allowed me to propose a foundation in brain science for the emotional intelligence model. Many businesspeople are traditionally skeptical of "soft" psychology and wary of the pop theories that come and go, but neuroscience makes crystal clear why emotional intelligence matters so much.

The ancient brain centers for emotion also harbor the skills needed for managing ourselves effectively and for social adeptness. Thus these skills are grounded in our evolutionary heritage for survival and adaptation.

This emotional part of the brain, neuroscience tells us, learns differently from the thinking brain. That insight has been pivotal in my development of this book—and leads me to challenge much conventional wisdom in corporate training and development.

I'm not alone in this challenge. For the last two years I have been working as cochair of the Consortium for Research on Emotional Intelligence in Organizations—a group of researchers from business schools, the federal government, and industry. Our research reveals deplorable weaknesses in how businesses train people in skills from listening and leadership to team building and handling change.

Most training programs have embraced an academic model—but this has been a drastic mistake, wasting millions of hours and billions of dollars. What's needed is an entirely new way of thinking about what it takes to help people boost their emotional intelligence.

Some Misconceptions

As I've toured the world talking and consulting with people in business, I've encountered certain widespread misunderstandings about emotional intelligence. Let me clear up some of the most common at the outset. First, emotional intelligence does not mean merely "being nice." At strategic moments it may demand not "being nice," but rather, for example, bluntly confronting someone with an uncomfortable but consequential truth they've been avoiding.

Second, emotional intelligence does not mean giving free rein to feelings—"letting it all hang out." Rather, it means managing feelings so that they are expressed appropriately and effectively, enabling people to work together smoothly toward their common goals.

Also, women are not "smarter" than men when it comes to emotional intelligence, nor are men superior to women. Each of us has a personal profile of strengths and weaknesses in these capacities. Some of us may be highly empathic but lack some abilities to handle our own distress; others may be quite aware of the subtlest shift in our own moods, yet be inept socially.

It is true that men and women as groups tend to have a shared, gender-specific profile of strong and weak points. An analysis of emotional intelligence in thousands of men and women found that women, on average, are more aware of their emotions, show more empathy, and are more adept interpersonally.[2] Men, on the other hand, are more self-confident and optimistic, adapt more easily, and handle stress better.

In general, however, there are far more similarities than differences. Some men are as empathic as the most interpersonally sensitive women, while some women are every bit as able to withstand stress as the most emotionally resilient men. Indeed, on average, looking at the overall ratings for men and women, the strengths and weaknesses average out, so that in terms of total emotional intelligence, there are no sex differences.[3]

Finally, our level of emotional intelligence is not fixed genetically, nor does it develop only in early childhood. Unlike IQ, which changes little after our teen years, emotional intelligence seems to be largely learned, and it continues to develop as we go through life and learn from our experiences—our competence in it can keep growing. In fact, studies that have tracked people's level of emotional intelligence through the years show that people get better and better in these capabilities as they grow more adept at handling their own emotions and impulses, at motivating themselves, and at honing their empathy and social adroitness. There is an old-fashioned word for this growth in emotional intelligence: *maturity*.

Emotional Intelligence: The Missing Priority

More and more companies are seeing that encouraging emotional intelligence skills is a vital component of any organization's management philosophy. "You don't compete with products alone anymore, but how well you use your people," a manager at Telia, the Swedish telecommunications company, put it to me. And Linda Keegan, vice president for executive development at Citibank, told me, "Emotional intelligence is the underlying premise for all management training."

It's a refrain I hear time and again:

- The president of a hundred-person job shop in the aerospace industry tells me that one of the main companies he supplies, Allied-Signal, required that he and all his employees be trained in the ubiquitous "quality circle" approach. "They wanted us to work better as a team, which was great," he says. "But we've found it hard—how can you be a team if you're not a group first? And to bond as a group we needed to boost our emotional intelligence."

- "We've been very effective at increasing profitability through methods like reengineering and speeding up the turnaround cycle for new products. But even with some big successes, our curve of improvement is flattening," a manager at Siemens AG, the German conglomerate, tells me. "We see the need to use our people better—maximize our human assets—to make the curve rise again. So we're trying to make the company more emotionally intelligent."

- A former project manager at Ford Motor Company recounts how he used the "learning organization" methods developed at MIT's Sloan School of Management in redesigning the Lincoln Continental. He says that learning about emotional intelligence was a kind of epiphany for him: "Those are exactly the abilities we had to build up to make us an effective learning organization."

A 1997 survey of benchmark practices among major corporations, done by the American Society for Training and Development, found that four out of five companies are trying to promote emotional intelligence in their employees through training and development, when evaluating performance, and in hiring.[4]

If so, why write this book? Because many or most organizations' efforts to encourage emotional intelligence have been poor, wasting vast amounts of time, energy, and money. For instance, the most systematic study ever done of the return on investment in leadership training (as we will see in Part 4) found that one well-respected week-long seminar for top-level executives actually had a slight *negative* effect on their job performance.

Businesses are waking up to the fact that even the most expensive training can go awry, and often does. And this ineptness comes at a time when emotional intelligence in individuals and organizations is emerging as a missing ingredient in the recipe for competitiveness.

Why This Matters Now

At a California biotech start-up, the CEO proudly enumerated the features that made his organization state-of-the-art: No one, including him, had a fixed office; instead, everyone carried a small laptop—their mobile office—and was wired to everyone else. Job titles were irrelevant; employees worked in cross-functional teams and the place bubbled with creative energy. People routinely put in seventy- and eighty-hour work weeks.

"So what's the downside?" I asked him.

"There is no downside," he assured me.

And that was the fallacy. Once I was free to talk with staff members, I heard the truth: The hectic pace had people feeling burned out and robbed of their private lives. And though everyone could talk via computer to everyone else, people felt that no one was truly listening to them.

People desperately felt the need for connection, for empathy, for open communication.

In the new, stripped-down, every-job-counts business climate, these human realities will matter more than ever. Massive change is a constant; technical innovations, global competition, and the pressures of institutional investors are ever-escalating forces for flux.

Another reality makes emotional intelligence ever more crucial: As organizations shrink through waves of downsizing, those people who remain are more accountable—and more visible. Where earlier a midlevel employee might easily hide a hot temper or shyness, now competencies such as managing one's emotions, handling encounters well, teamwork, and leadership, show—and count—more than ever.

The globalization of the workforce puts a particular premium on emotional intelligence in wealthier countries. Higher wages in these countries, if they are to be maintained, will depend on a new kind of productivity. And structural fixes or technological advances alone are not enough: As at the California biotech firm, streamlining or other innovations often create new problems that cry out for even greater emotional intelligence.

As business changes, so do the traits needed to excel. Data tracking the talents of star performers over several decades reveal that two abilities that mattered relatively little for success in the 1970s have become crucially important in the 1990s: team building and adapting to change. And entirely new capabilities have begun to appear as traits of star performers, notably change catalyst and leveraging diversity. New challenges demand new talents.

Churning and the New Dread

A friend at a Fortune 500 company, one that had just downsized, letting thousands of employees go, told me: "It was terrible—so many people I've known for years were booted out, demoted, or transferred. It was hard for everybody. I still have my job, but I'll never feel the same about this place.

"I've been here thirty years, and over that time we were given the sense that as long as we put in a decent work day, the company would stand by us. Then, out of the blue, we were told, 'No one is guaranteed a job here anymore.' "

It seems no one is guaranteed a job *anywhere* anymore. These are troubled times for workers. The creeping sense that no one's job is safe, even as the companies they work for are thriving, means the spread of fear, apprehension, and confusion.

One sign of this growing unease: An American headhunting firm reported that more than half of callers making inquiries about jobs were still employed—but were so fearful of losing those jobs that they had already started to look for another.[5] The day that AT&T began notifying the first of forty thousand workers to be laid off—in a year when its profits were a record $4.7 billion—a poll reported that a third of Americans feared that someone in their household would soon lose a job.

Such fears persist at a time when the American economy is creating more jobs than it is losing. The churning of jobs—what economists euphemistically call "labor market flexibility"—is now a troubling fact of work life. And it is part of a global tidal wave sweeping through all the leading economies of the developed world, whether in Europe, Asia, or the Americas. Prosperity is no guarantee of jobs; layoffs continue even amidst a booming economy. This paradox, as Paul Krugman, an MIT economist, puts it, is "the unfortunate price we have to pay for having as dynamic an economy as we do."[6]

There is now a palpable bleakness about the new landscape of work.

"We work in what amounts to a quiet war zone" is the way one midlevel executive at a multinational firm put it to me. "There's no way to give your loyalty to a company and expect it to be returned anymore. So each person is becoming their own little shop within the company—you have to be able to be part of a team, but also ready to move on and be self-sufficient."

For many older workers—children of the meritocracy, who were taught that education and technical skills were a permanent ticket to success—this new way of thinking may come as a shock. People are beginning to realize that success takes more than intellectual excellence or technical prowess, and that we need another sort of skill just to survive—and certainly to thrive—in the increasingly turbulent job market of the future. Internal qualities such as resilience, initiative, optimism, and adaptability are taking on a new valuation.

A Coming Crisis: Rising IQ, Dropping EQ

Since 1918, when World War I brought the first mass use of IQ tests on American army recruits, the average IQ score in the United States has risen 24 points, and there has been a similar rise in developed countries around the world.[7] The reasons include better nutrition, more children completing more schooling, computer games and puzzles that help children master spatial skills, and smaller family size (which generally correlates with higher IQ scores in children).

There is a dangerous paradox at work, however: As children grow ever smarter in IQ, their emotional intelligence is on the decline. Perhaps the most disturbing single piece of data comes from a massive survey of parents and teachers that shows the present generation of children to be more emotionally troubled than the last. On average, children are growing more lonely and depressed, more angry and unruly, more nervous and prone to worry, more impulsive and aggressive.

Two random samples of American children, age seven to sixteen, were evaluated by their parents and teachers—adults who knew them well. The first group was assessed in the mid-1970s, and a comparable group was surveyed in the late 1980s.[8] Over that decade and a half there was a steady worsening of children's emotional intelligence. Although poorer children started out at a lower level on average, the rate of decline was the same across all economic groups—as steep in the wealthiest suburbs as in the poorest inner-city slum.

Dr. Thomas Achenbach, the University of Vermont psychologist who did these studies—and who has collaborated with colleagues on similar assessments in other nations—tells me that the decline in children's basic emotional competencies seems to be worldwide. The most telling signs of this are seen in rising rates among young people of problems such as despair, alienation, drug abuse, crime and violence, depression or eating disorders, unwanted pregnancies, bullying, and dropping out of school.

What this portends for the workplace is quite troubling: growing deficiencies among workers in emotional intelligence, particularly among those newest to the job. Most of the children that Achenbach studied in the late 1980s will be in their twenties by the year 2000. The generation that is falling behind in emotional intelligence is entering the workforce today.

What Employers Want

A survey of American employers reveals that more than half the people who work for them lack the motivation to keep learning and improving in their job. Four in ten are not able to work cooperatively with fellow employees, and just 19 percent of those applying for entry-level jobs have enough self-discipline in their work habits.[9]

More and more employers are complaining about the lack of social skills in new hires. In the words of an executive at a large restaurant chain: "Too many young people can't take criticism—they get defensive or hostile when people give them feedback on how they're doing. They react to performance feedback as though it were a personal attack."

The problem is not just in new workers—it's true for some seasoned executives as well. In the world of the 1960s and 1970s, people got ahead by going to the right schools and doing well there. But the world is full of well-trained, once-promising men and women who have plateaued in their careers—or worse, derailed—because of crucial gaps in emotional intelligence.

In a national survey of what employers are looking for in entry-level workers, specific technical skills are now less important than the underlying ability to learn on the job. After that, employers listed:

- Listening and oral communication
- Adaptability and creative responses to setbacks and obstacles

- Personal management, confidence, motivation to work toward goals, a sense of wanting to develop one's career and take pride in accomplishments

- Group and interpersonal effectiveness, cooperativeness and teamwork, skills at negotiating disagreements

- Effectiveness in the organization, wanting to make a contribution, leadership potential[10]

Of seven desired traits, just one was academic: competence in reading, writing, and math.

A study of what corporations are seeking in the MBAs they hire yields a similar list.[11] The three most desired capabilities are communication skills, interpersonal skills, and initiative. As Jill Fadule, managing director of admissions and financial aid at the Harvard Business School, told me, "empathy, perspective taking, rapport, and cooperation" are among the competencies the school is looking for in those who apply.

Our Journey

My mission in writing this book is to act as a guide to the scientific case for working with emotional intelligence—as individuals, in groups, as organizations. At every step I have sought to validate the science with the testimony of people in jobs and organizations of all kinds, and their voices will be heard all along the way.

In Part 1 I make the case that emotional intelligence counts more than IQ or expertise for determining who excels at a job—*any* job—and that for outstanding leadership it counts for almost everything. The business case is compelling: Companies that leverage this advantage add measurably to their bottom line.

Part 2 details twelve specific job capabilities, all based on self-mastery—initiative, trustworthiness, self-confidence, and achievement drive among them—and describes the unique contribution each makes to star performance.

In Part 3 I turn to thirteen key relationship skills—such as empathy and political awareness, leveraging diversity, team capabilities, and leadership. These are the skills that let us, for instance, navigate the currents of an organization effortlessly while others founder.

Throughout, readers can get a rough sense of where they stand when it comes to working with emotional intelligence. As I will show in Chapter 3, star performance does not require us to excel in all these competencies, but rather that we be strong in enough of them to reach the critical mass for success.

Part 4 heralds the good news: Whatever competencies we may be weak in, we can always learn to be better. To help readers who want to improve their own emotional intelligence capabilities—and to avoid wasting time and money—I offer practical, scientifically grounded guidelines for the best ways of doing so.

Finally, Part 5 considers what it means for an organization to be emotionally intelligent. I describe one such company and show why such practices can help not just with business performance but also in making organizations satisfying and desirable to work for. I also show how companies that ignore the emotional realities of their employees do so at their own risk, while those organizations with emotional intelligence are best equipped to survive—and to do well—in the ever more turbulent years ahead.

Though my aim is to be helpful, this is not a self-help book. There are perhaps too many how-to books promising far too much about improving emotional intelligence. Though these books are no doubt well intended, they typically perpetuate misconceptions about what upgrading these most essential capacities truly demands. Instead of quick fixes, you will find here sound guidelines for the real work of becoming more emotionally competent. These guidelines represent a level-headed survey of new thinking, research findings, and model practices from organizations around the world.

We live in a time when our prospects for the future increasingly depend on managing ourselves and handling our relationships more artfully. My hope is to offer some practical guidance for the crucial personal and business challenges we all face in the coming century.

2

....

Competencies of the Stars

t was the dawn of the 1970s, at the height of worldwide student protests against the Vietnam War, and a librarian stationed at a U.S. Information Agency post abroad had received bad news: A student group was threatening to burn down her library. But the librarian had friends among the group of student activists who made the threat. Her response on first glance might seem either naïve or foolhardy—or both: She invited the group to use the library facilities for some of their meetings.

But she also brought Americans living in the country there to listen to them—and so engineered a dialogue instead of a confrontation.

In doing so, she was capitalizing on her personal relationship with the handful of student leaders she knew well enough to trust—and for them to trust her. The tactic opened new channels of mutual understanding, and it strengthened her friendship with the student leaders. The library was never touched.

The librarian exhibited the skills of a superb negotiator or peacemaker, able to read the currents of a tense, swiftly moving situation and manage a response that brings people together instead of setting them against each other. Her facility escaped the damage wreaked on other American outposts manned by those less adept at these human skills.

The librarian was among a group of young diplomats the State Department identified as "superstars," who were intensively interviewed by a team led by Professor David McClelland of Harvard.[1]

At the time, McClelland was my main advisor for my doctoral work, and he drew me into his research program. The results of his studies led McClelland to publish a paper that sparked a revolution in thinking about the roots of excellence.

In exploring the ingredients of superb job performance, McClelland was joining an enterprise that got its first scientific footing at the beginning of the twentieth century with the work of Frederick Taylor. Taylorist efficiency experts swept the world of work, analyzing the most mechanically efficient moves a worker's body could make. The measure of human work was the machine.

On the heels of Taylorism came another standard of evaluation: the IQ test. The correct measure of excellence, proponents argued, was the capacities of the human mind.

Then, with the rise of Freudian thinking, another wave of experts argued that in addition to IQ, personality was an ingredient in excellence. By the 1960s, personality tests and typologies—whether, for example, a person was outgoing or introverted, a "feeling" or "thinking" type—were part of the standard measures of work potential.

But there was a problem. Many of the personality tests had been designed for completely different reasons, such as diagnosing psychological disorders, and so were poor predictors of how well people actually performed on the job. IQ tests, too, were not infallible; people of high IQ often performed poorly at work, while those of moderate IQ did extremely well.

McClelland's 1973 paper "Testing for Competence Rather than Intelligence" shifted the terms of the debate. He argued that traditional academic aptitude, school grades, and advanced credentials simply did not predict how well people would perform on the job or whether they would succeed in life.[2] Instead, he proposed that a set of specific competencies including empathy, self-discipline, and initiative distinguished the most successful from those who were merely good enough to keep their jobs. To find the competencies that make for star performance at a given job, McClelland suggested, first look at the stars and determine what competencies they display.

His paper launched an entirely new approach to the measure of excellence, one that assesses people's competencies in terms of the specific job they are doing. A "competence," in this tradition, is a personal trait or set of habits that leads to more effective or superior job performance—in other words, an ability that adds clear economic value to the efforts of a person on the job.

That insight has, over the last quarter century, triggered research on hundreds of thousands of workers, from clerks to top executives, in organizations as vast as the U.S. government and AT&T, and as tiny as one-person enterprises. In all the findings, a common core of personal and social abilities has proven to be the key ingredient in people's success: emotional intelligence.

The Tuned-Out Programmer

Two computer programmers are explaining how they go about doing their job, designing programs to fill the pressing business needs of their clients. Recounts one: "I heard him say he needed all the data in a simple format that could fit on one page." So the programmer followed through to deliver just that.

The second, however, seems to have trouble getting to the point. Unlike the first programmer, he doesn't mention the needs of his clients. Instead he launches into a litany of technical talk: "The HP3000/30's BASIC compiler was too slow, so I went directly to a machine-language routine." In other words, he focuses on machines, not people.

The first programmer was identified as outstanding at his work, able to design programs that are user-friendly; the second is at best mediocre at this task—he has essentially tuned out his customers. The first computer programmer displays emotional intelligence; the other exemplifies its absence. Both were interviewed using a method developed by McClelland to detect the competencies that distinguish star performers in jobs of every kind.[3]

McClelland's original insight was rooted in work he had done for corporations and in organizations such as the U.S. State Department, where he had been asked to assess the capabilities of outstanding foreign-service officers, the young diplomats who represent America in other countries. Like sales staff or account managers in a large corporation, the real job of these officers is to "sell" America, to get people abroad to feel positively about the United States.

Selection for these diplomatic posts was a formidable hurdle, one only those with the best education could jump. The selection test gauged abilities higher officials in the State Department thought a diplomat needed—mainly a sound grounding in academic disciplines like American history and culture, language fluency, and specialized expertise in a field such as economics. The problem was that the exam reflected only how well candidates had done in their studies.

Their scores were a poor indicator of how adept these new diplomats were on their feet in Frankfurt, Buenos Aires, or Singapore.[4] In fact, their on-the-job performance ratings actually correlated *negatively* with how well they did on the very test used to select them; sheer mastery of academic topics was irrelevant (or worse, detrimental) to the competencies that count in that form of sales known as diplomacy.

What mattered, McClelland found, was another kind of competence altogether. When he interviewed the superstars—those the State Department had identified as their most brilliant and effective young diplomats—and compared them to peers who were mediocre, the most telling differences emerged in a set of basic human abilities that academic or IQ tests simply did not measure.

Among the radically different tests McClelland turned to was a clever assessment of the ability to read emotions, newly developed by a Harvard colleague. In this test people watch snatches of videotapes of people talking about emotional situations like going through a divorce or having an argument at work.[5] An electronic filter alters the sound, so what comes through is not the words themselves, but rather the tones and nuances that reveal what the person is feeling.

McClelland found that the stars scored much higher than the mediocre diplomats at accurately discerning the speakers' emotions. This translated into an ability to read emotional messages in people with backgrounds vastly different from their own, even when they couldn't understand the language being spoken—a competence crucial not only for diplomats but throughout today's work world for capitalizing on diversity.

Time after time in describing critical moments on the job, the foreign-service officers told tales of touchy situations similar to those of the peacemaking librarian. But for the less socially astute diplomats the stories more often ended with events blowing up in their faces because of their inability to read or handle the people they dealt with.

Domains of Excellence: The Limits of IQ

Two of the smartest people I ever knew (at least in the academic sense) followed strikingly different career paths. One was a friend during my freshman year in college who had perfect scores on his college admissions tests—a pair of 800s on the verbal and math sections of the SAT, and a 5 on each of three advanced placement tests. But he was unmotivated in school, often skipped class, and got papers in late. He dropped out for a while, finally graduating after ten years. Today he reports he is satisfied working as a one-man computer consulting business.

The other was a math prodigy who entered my high school at ten, graduated at twelve, and got his doctorate in theoretical mathematics from Oxford at eighteen. In high school he was a bit short for his age, which, because he was so young, made him about a foot shorter than most of us. He was also about twice as bright as everyone else—and many students resented him for it. He was often taunted and bullied. But despite his diminutive stature, he didn't back down. Like a little bantam rooster, he stood his ground against the biggest hulks in school. He had assertiveness to match his intellect—which may explain why, last I heard, he's now the head of one of the most prestigious mathematics departments in the world.

Given how much emphasis schools and admissions tests put on it, IQ alone explains surprisingly little of achievement at work or in life. When IQ test scores are correlated with how well people perform in their careers, the highest estimate of how much difference IQ accounts for is about 25 percent.[6] A careful analysis, though, suggests a more accurate figure may be no higher than 10 percent, and perhaps as low as 4 percent.[7]

This means that IQ alone at best leaves 75 percent of job success unexplained, and at worst 96 percent—in other words, it does not determine who succeeds and who fails. For example, a study of Harvard graduates in the fields of law, medicine, teaching, and business found that scores on entrance exams—a surrogate for IQ—had zero or negative correlation with their eventual career success.[8]

Paradoxically, IQ has the least power in predicting success among that pool of people smart enough to handle the most cognitively demanding fields, and the value of emotional intelligence for success grows more powerful the higher the intelligence barriers for entry into a field. In MBA programs or in careers like engineering, law, or medicine, where professional selection focuses almost exclusively on intellectual abilities, emotional intelligence carries much more weight than IQ in determining who emerges as a leader.

"What you learned in school distinguishes superior performers in only a handful of the five or six hundred jobs for which we've done competence studies," says Lyle Spencer Jr., director of research and technology worldwide and cofounder of what is now Hay/McBer, the consulting firm McClelland started.[9] "It's just a threshold competence; you need it to get in the field, but it does not make you a star. It's the emotional intelligence abilities that matter more for superior performance."

This paradoxical importance of emotional intelligence in cognitively demanding disciplines is a consequence of the difficulty of entering them in the first place. In professional and technical fields the threshold for entry is typically an IQ of 110 to 120.[10] The result of having to jump such a high initial entry barrier is that since everyone is in the top 10 percent or so of intelligence, IQ itself offers relatively little competitive advantage.

We do not compete in our careers with people who lack the requisite intelligence to enter and stay in our field—but rather against the much smaller group of those who have managed to jump the hurdles of schooling, entry exams, and other cognitive challenges to get into the field in the first place.

Since emotional intelligence is not nearly as great a factor as IQ in selection for entering such fields, there is more variation in this "soft" domain than there is in IQ among these professionals. The difference between those at the high and low ends of the emotional intelligence scale is very large, and being at the top confers a major competitive advantage. Thus "soft" skills matter even more for success in "hard" fields.

The Second Domain: Expertise

Here's the dilemma: You're a cultural affairs officer at a U.S. embassy in North Africa, and you get a wire from Washington telling you to show a film featuring an American politician greatly reviled in that country.

If you show it, the locals will find it offensive. If you don't, headquarters back home will be upset.

What do you do?

This is not a hypothetical situation; it was the predicament faced by one of the foreign-service officers McClelland studied. The officer recalled, "I knew that if I showed the film, this place would be burned down the next day by about five hundred angry students. Yet Washington felt the film was great. What I had to do was figure out how to show the film so the embassy could tell Washington we had done as they wished, and yet not offend people in the country."

His solution? He screened the movie on a holy day, when he knew no one could come.

That brilliant bit of common sense exemplifies practical intelligence, a combination of technical expertise and experience.[11] Apart from IQ, our practical skills, along with the technical abilities we master, determine how well we perform on an everyday basis. Whatever our intellectual potential, it is expertise—our total body of specialized information and practical skills—that makes us good enough to do a particular job.

The most competent doctors, for example, are those who keep expanding their knowledge base by keeping up with current findings and who have a vast reservoir of hands-on experience, and can draw on all this in making diagnoses and treating their patients. This continued drive to keep up-to-date matters far more in how well they can help their patients than their scores on the entrance exam for medical school.

In large part, expertise is a combination of common sense plus the specialized knowledge and skill we pick up in the course of doing any job. Expertise comes from in-the-trenches learning. It shows up as an insider's sense of the tricks of a trade—the real knowledge of how to do a job that only experience brings.

Such down-to-earth abilities have been extensively studied by Yale psychologist Robert Sternberg, an authority on intelligence and success.[12] In tests with managers at Fortune 500 companies, Sternberg discovered that practical intelligence seems to account for at least as much on-the-job success as does IQ.[13]

On the other hand, practical intelligence is rarely the main factor in a star's outstanding job performance. "In the hundreds of rigorous studies we've done comparing star performers with merely average ones in companies around the world, expertise just never made the difference," says Ruth Jacobs, a senior consultant at Hay/McBer in Boston.

"Expertise is a baseline competence. You need it to get the job and get it done, but how you do the job—the other competencies you bring to your expertise—determines performance," Jacobs adds. "Are you able to translate your expertise into something that's marketable, that stands out? If not, it makes little difference."

Supervisors of technical and professional workers, for example, need to have some degree of expertise in their area; it would be nearly impossible to manage such work without a reasonable understanding of what people are doing. But that expertise is a *threshold* requirement; the abilities that distinguish the outstanding supervisors in technical fields are not technical, but rather relate to handling people.[14]

So to a degree, experience and expertise, like IQ, matter—but there is much more to the story when it comes to excellence.

The Third Domain: Emotional Intelligence

Sternberg tells a cautionary tale about two students, Penn and Matt. Penn was a brilliant and creative student, an exemplar of the best Yale had to offer.[15] The trouble with Penn was that he knew he was exceptional—and so was, as one professor put it, "unbelievably arrogant." Penn, despite his abilities, put people off, especially those who had to work with him.

Even so, he looked spectacular on paper. When he graduated, Penn was highly sought after: All the top organizations in his field offered him interviews for jobs, and he was a universal first pick—at least on the basis of his résumé. But Penn's arrogance came across all too clearly; he ended up with only one job offer, from a second-tier outfit.

Matt, another Yale student in Penn's field, wasn't as academically brilliant. But he was adept interpersonally; everyone who worked with him liked him. Matt ended up with seven job offers out of eight interviews and went on to success in his field, while Penn was let go after two years at his first job.

Penn lacked—and Matt had—emotional intelligence.

Emotional intelligence skills are synergistic with cognitive ones; top performers have both. The more complex the job, the more emotional intelligence matters—if only because a deficiency in these abilities can hinder the use of whatever technical expertise or intellect a person may have. Take, for example, an executive who had just been brought in to run a $65 million, family-owned business, the first president from outside the family.[16]

A researcher, using an interview method to assess the executive's ability to handle cognitive complexity, determined his capacity was the very highest—a "level six," someone smart enough, theoretically, to be CEO of a global firm or head of a country.[17] But during that interview the conversation turned to why he had to leave his previous job: He had been fired because he had failed to confront subordinates and hold them responsible for their poor performance.

"It was still an emotional trigger for him," the researcher told me. "His face got red and flushed, he started waving his hands—he was clearly agitated. It turned out that his new boss—the owner of the company—had criticized him that very morning for the same thing, and he went on and on about how hard it was for him to confront low-performing employees, especially when they had been with the company for a long time." And, the researcher noted, "While he was so upset his ability to handle cognitive complexity—to reason—plummeted."

In short, out-of-control emotions can make smart people stupid. As

Doug Lennick, an executive vice president at American Express Financial Advisors, put it to me, "The aptitudes you need to succeed start with intellectual horsepower—but people need emotional competence, too, to get the full potential of their talents. The reason we don't get people's full potential is emotional incompetence."

The Great Divide

It was Super Bowl Sunday, that sacrosanct day when most American men are to be found in front of their televisions. A departing flight from New York to Detroit was delayed two hours, and the tension among the passengers—almost entirely businessmen—was palpable. When they finally arrived in Detroit, a mysterious glitch with the boarding ramp made the plane stop about a hundred feet from the gate. Frantic about being late, passengers leaped to their feet anyway.

One of the flight attendants went to the intercom. How could she most effectively get everyone to sit down so that the plane could finish taxiing to the gate?

She did *not* announce, in a stern voice, "Federal regulations require that you be seated before we can move to the gate."

Instead, she warbled in a singsong tone, suggestive of a playful warning to an adorable small child who has done something naughty but forgivable, "You're staaan-ding!"

At that everyone laughed and sat back down until the plane had finished taxiing to the gate. And, given the circumstances, they got off the plane in a surprisingly good mood.

The great divide in competencies lies between the mind and heart, or, more technically, between cognition and emotion. Some competencies are purely cognitive, such as analytic reasoning or technical expertise. Others combine thought and feeling; these I call "emotional competencies."[18]

All emotional competencies involve some degree of skill in the realm of feeling, along with whatever cognitive elements are at play. This stands in sharp contrast to purely cognitive competencies, which a computer can be programmed to execute about as well as a person. A digitized voice could have announced: "Federal regulations require all passengers be seated before we proceed to the gate."

But the stilted tones of a computerized voice would never have had the artful effect of that flight attendant's wit. People might grudgingly comply with a robotlike directive, but they would undergo nothing like the mood shift the attendant accomplished. She was able to hit exactly the right emotional note—something human cognition alone (or for that matter, computers) cannot do (at least not yet).[19]

Take competence in communication. As I type this, for example, I can ask my software program to check what I'm writing for grammatical accuracy. But I cannot ask it to check what I'm writing for its emotional power, its passion, or its ability to engage and influence readers. These other, crucial elements of effective communication depend on emotional capacities: being able to gauge an audience's reactions, to fine-tune a presentation to have meaningful emotional impact.

The most convincing, powerful arguments speak to the heart as well as the head. This tight orchestration of thought and feeling is made possible by what amounts to a superhighway in the brain, a bundle of neurons connecting the prefrontal lobes, behind the forehead—the brain's executive decision-making center—with an area deep in the brain that harbors our emotions.[20]

Damage to this crucial connection leaves people emotionally incompetent, even though their purely intellectual abilities are untouched. In other words, such people would still score well on IQ tests and other measures of cognitive ability. But on the job—and in life generally—they would fail at the emotional arts that make people like the flight attendant so effective.

Thus the divide between those competencies that are purely cognitive, and those that depend on emotional intelligence as well, reflects a parallel division in the human brain.

Emotional Competence

An emotional *competence* is a learned capability based on emotional intelligence that results in outstanding performance at work.[21] Take the finesse shown by the flight attendant. She was superb at influence, an important emotional competence: getting others to respond in a desired way. At the heart of this competence are two abilities: empathy, which involves reading the feelings of others, and social skills, which allow handling those feelings artfully.

Our emotional *intelligence* determines our potential for learning the practical skills that are based on its five elements: self-awareness, motivation, self-regulation, empathy, and adeptness in relationships. Our emotional *competence* shows how much of that potential we have translated into on-the-job capabilities. For instance, being good at serving customers is an emotional competence based on empathy. Likewise, trustworthiness is a competence based on self-regulation, or handling impulses and emotions well. Both customer service and trustworthiness are competencies that can make people outstanding in their work.

Simply being high in emotional intelligence does not guarantee a person will have learned the emotional competencies that matter for work; it means only that they have excellent potential to learn them. A person might be highly empathic, for example, and yet not have learned the skills based on empathy that translate into superior customer service, top-flight coaching or mentoring, or the ability to bring together a diverse work team. The parallel in music would be someone with perfect pitch, say, who also had lessons in singing, and so became a superb operatic tenor. Without the lessons, there would be no opera career, despite the potential—a Pavarotti who never had the chance to blossom.

Emotional competencies cluster into groups, each based on a common underlying emotional intelligence capacity. The underlying emotional intelligence capacities are vital if people are to successfully learn the competencies necessary to succeed in the workplace. If they are deficient in social skills, for instance, they will be inept at persuading or inspiring others, at leading teams or catalyzing change. If they have little self-awareness, they will be oblivious to their own weaknesses and lack the self-confidence that comes from certainty about their strengths.

Table 1 shows the relationship between the five dimensions of emotional intelligence and the twenty-five emotional competencies.[22] None of us is perfect on this scale; we inevitably have a profile of strengths and limits. But, as we shall see, the ingredients for outstanding performance require only that we have strengths in a given number of these competencies, typically, at least six or so, and that the strengths be spread across all five areas of emotional intelligence. In other words, there are many paths to excellence.

These emotional intelligence capacities are:

- *Independent:* Each makes a unique contribution to job performance.

- *Interdependent:* Each draws to some extent on certain others, with many strong interactions.

- *Hierarchical:* The emotional intelligence capacities build upon one another. For example, self-awareness is crucial for self-

TABLE 1

The Emotional Competence Framework

Personal Competence

These competencies determine how we manage ourselves.

Self-Awareness

Knowing one's internal states, preferences, resources, and intuitions
(see Chapter 4)

- *Emotional awareness:* Recognizing one's emotions and their effects
- *Accurate self-assessment:* Knowing one's strengths and limits
- *Self-confidence:* A strong sense of one's self-worth and capabilities

Self-Regulation

Managing one's internal states, impulses, and resources
(see Chapter 5)

- *Self-Control:* Keeping disruptive emotions and impulses in check
- *Trustworthiness:* Maintaining standards of honesty and integrity
- *Conscientiousness:* Taking responsibility for personal performance
- *Adaptability:* Flexibility in handling change
- *Innovation:* Being comfortable with novel ideas, approaches, and new information

Motivation

Emotional tendencies that guide or facilitate reaching goals
(see Chapter 6)

- *Achievement drive:* Striving to improve or meet a standard of excellence
- *Commitment:* Aligning with the goals of the group or organization
- *Initiative:* Readiness to act on opportunities
- *Optimism:* Persistence in pursuing goals despite obstacles and setbacks

Social Competence

These competencies determine how we handle relationships.

Empathy

Awareness of others' feelings, needs, and concerns
(see Chapter 7)

- *Understanding others:* Sensing others' feelings and perspectives, and taking an active interest in their concerns
- *Developing others:* Sensing others' development needs and bolstering their abilities
- *Service orientation:* Anticipating, recognizing, and meeting customers' needs
- *Leveraging diversity:* Cultivating opportunities through different kinds of people
- *Political awareness:* Reading a group's emotional currents and power relationships

Social Skills

Adeptness at inducing desirable responses in others
(see Chapters 8 and 9)

- *Influence:* Wielding effective tactics for persuasion
- *Communication:* Listening openly and sending convincing messages
- *Conflict management:* Negotiating and resolving disagreements
- *Leadership:* Inspiring and guiding individuals and groups
- *Change catalyst:* Initiating or managing change
- *Building bonds:* Nurturing instrumental relationships
- *Collaboration and cooperation:* Working with others toward shared goals
- *Team capabilities:* Creating group synergy in pursuing collective goals

regulation and empathy; self-regulation and self-awareness contribute to motivation; all the first four are at work in social skills.

- *Necessary, but not sufficient:* Having an underlying emotional intelligence ability does not guarantee people will develop or display the associated competencies, such as collaboration or leadership. Factors such as the climate of an organization or a person's interest in his or her job will also determine whether the competence manifests itself.

- *Generic:* The general list is to some extent applicable to all jobs. However, different jobs make differing competence demands.

The list offers a way to inventory our strengths and to pinpoint competencies we may want to bolster. Parts 2 and 3 of the book give more detail and insight into each of the competencies, showing how they look when displayed in full power—or when they are lacking. Readers may want to turn directly to the competencies most relevant to their interests; the chapters describing them do build on one another to an extent (as do the competencies they describe), but they need not be read in a fixed order.

The Best: What It Takes

The same competencies can make people excel in different jobs. For instance, at a Blue Cross health insurance division, successful customer service representatives exhibit high self-control, conscientiousness, and empathy. For successful retail store managers, the key competencies include the same triumvirate—self-control, conscientiousness, and empathy—plus a fourth competence, service orientation.[23]

The competencies one needs for success may change as one rises through the ranks; in most large organizations, senior executives need a greater degree of political awareness than middle managers.[24] And certain positions require specific competencies.[25] For the best nurses, it's a sense of humor; for bankers, respecting customers' confidentiality; for outstanding school principals, seeking out ways to get feedback from teachers and parents. At the Internal Revenue Service, the best tax collectors are strong not just in accounting, but also in social skills. Among law enforcement officers, using the least amount of force necessary is, understandably, a valued ability.

Furthermore, key competencies match a given organization's reality. Each company and each industry has its own emotional ecology, and the most adaptive traits for workers will differ accordingly.

Such specifics aside, close to three hundred different company-sponsored studies show that across a wide array of jobs the recipe for excellence gives far more weight to emotional competencies than to cognitive abilities.[26] That the most important competencies among stars stem from emotional intelligence is no surprise for, say, salespeople. But even among scientists and those in technical professions analytic thinking ranks third, after the ability to influence and the drive to achieve. Brilliance alone will not propel a scientist to the top unless she also has the ability to influence and persuade others, and the inner discipline to strive for challenging goals. A lazy or reticent genius may have all the answers in his head, but they amount to little if no one knows or cares!

Take the "techies of the techies," whose usual title is "corporate consulting engineer." These brilliant troubleshooters are kept on hand by high-tech firms to rescue projects in danger of going off the track; they are so highly valued that annual reports list them along with corporate officers. What makes the best technology gurus so special? "What made the difference was not their brain power—most everyone at these companies is just as smart—but their emotional competence," Susan Ennis, of BankBoston and formerly of DEC, says. "It's their abilities to listen, to influence, to collaborate, and to get people motivated and working together well."

To be sure, many people have gotten to the top despite flaws in emotional intelligence; that's long been a reality of organizational life. But as work becomes more complex and collaborative, companies where people work together best have a competitive edge.

In the new workplace, with its emphasis on flexibility, teams, and a strong customer orientation, this crucial set of emotional competencies is becoming increasingly essential for excellence in every job and in every part of the world.[27]

3

....

The Hard Case for Soft Skills

■ At Lucent Technologies, the teams that stock raw material for manufacturing need more than technical know-how—they need skills in listening and understanding, flexibility, and teamwork. They also need the ability to energize others, commitment, and confidence in those they work with.

■ At the University of Nebraska Medical Center, technical expertise and analytical skills are invaluable, but so are emotional competencies like interpersonal skills, innovation, effective leadership, building partnerships, and networking.

■ At Amoco, the giant petrochemical firm, for superior performance in engineering or managing information technology, expertise and analytic thinking are, again, on the list. But so are self-confidence, flexibility, an achievement drive, service orientation, teamwork and cooperation, wielding influence, and developing others.[1]

These portraits of competence, drawn from hundreds of hours of on-the-job interviews and assessments, summarize the nitty-gritty reality of thousands of people at work. Poring over hundreds of such summaries, it struck me to ask a question that no one had thought to ask before: Exactly how important for excellence is emotional competence compared to technical skills and intellect?

The Ratio of Excellence

I was lucky enough to have access to competence models for 181 different positions drawn from 121 companies and organizations worldwide, with their combined workforce numbering in the millions. The models showed what management in each organization agreed captured the particular profile of excellence for a given job.[2]

My analysis was straightforward: I compared which competencies listed as essential for a given job, role, or field could be classed as purely cognitive or technical skills, and which were emotional competencies. For instance, fifteen key competencies were listed for information technology project managers at Amoco. Of these, four were purely cognitive or technical, while the rest fell in the emotional competence category. Simple math yields the finding: 73 percent of the abilities identified by Amoco as key to superior performance in this job were emotional competencies.

When I applied this method to all 181 competence models I had studied, I found that *67 percent*—two out of three—of the abilities deemed essential for effective performance were emotional competencies. Compared to IQ and expertise, emotional competence mattered *twice* as much. This held true across all categories of jobs, and in all kinds of organizations.

To make sure my findings weren't a fluke, I turned to Hay/McBer and commissioned them to do an independent study. (See Appendix 2 for more details of this and other corroborating research.) They reanalyzed raw data from forty different corporations to determine how much more of a given competence star performers demonstrated compared to average—a slightly different way to answer my question.

The Hay/McBer analysis was based on some of the very best data available anywhere, the results of in-depth interviews and extensive testing and evaluation of hundreds of workers. Again, emotional competencies were found to be *twice* as important in contributing to excellence as pure intellect and expertise.

The Leadership Edge

E motional competence is particularly central to leadership, a role whose essence is getting others to do their jobs more effectively. Interpersonal ineptitude in leaders lowers everyone's performance: It wastes time, creates acrimony, corrodes motivation and commitment, builds hostility and apathy. A leader's strengths or weaknesses in emotional competence can be measured in the gain or loss to the organization of the fullest talents of those they manage.

A manager for business research at a global technology company is in charge of two hundred researchers worldwide. Among their critical tasks: to meet with technical experts who have developed new product ideas and decide if the concept should be brought to market; to prod managers of products whose market share is dropping; to guide researchers who are floundering and need direction.

"Feelings run high in these meetings," the manager tells me. "You've got to be reasonable, quell any tense situation, keep your cool. People can be highly excitable when they want to bring a product they've been developing to market, or when they're having problems. But you've got to keep your perspective and present yourself in such a way that you will be trusted and respected.

"Most of our people are MBAs; they've learned the analytic tools," he observes. "But when people come at them with all their fears and problems, they have to be able to take it in stride and take a global perspective. They have the technical tools, but they have to be able to seize the creative idea or offer an actionable, practical path that will turn an idea into a useful product."

Handling an emotional situation demands troubleshooting skills: being able to establish trust and rapport quickly, to listen well, and to persuade and sell a recommendation. As he puts it, "You need capacities like self-awareness, perspective taking, a sense of presence, so you're the person at the table everyone is going to rely on."

Robert Worden, director of business research at Eastman Kodak, agrees: "It's not enough to be able to do a conjoint analysis or sit at your computer excited about a fantastic regression analysis if you're squeamish about presenting those results to an executive group. The ability to relate, to speak up and be heard, to be comfortable with yourself—these are the kinds of abilities that make the crucial difference."

Other ingredients for excellence at Kodak are, in Worden's words: "How well can you present your case? Drive—are you just there eight A.M. to five P.M. and need prodding, or do you have high energy and are willing to make some personal sacrifices? Are you difficult to work with, or are you seen as

a natural leader? Then there's diplomacy—do you sense personal and organizational sensitivities? Are you able to take creative risks and adapt? Are
you combative, undermining other people's self-confidence, or do you inspire and guide other people? And finally, there's proactivity: Are you action-oriented, following up to impact the business?"

Many top managers at Kodak have come up via market research, including the president, who spent seven years there. But the feel for the market that research gives people is just a start. "Half the skills you need are
technical," says Worden. "But the other half are in that softer domain, emotional intelligence. And it's amazing how it's the latter that distinguishes the
top performers."

The Rule of Thumb

Worden's observation is borne out by data. In studying hundreds of companies, it became clear to me that the importance of emotional intelligence increases, the higher you go in the organization.

My hunch was borne out in a systematic study of one very large organization—the U.S. government, with more than two million employees. It's
one of the few organizations anywhere to have a detailed assessment of the
competencies necessary for effective performance in virtually every job.[3]
Working with Robert Buchele, a labor economist at Smith College, we
found that, indeed, the higher the level of the job, the less important technical skills and cognitive abilities were, and the more important competence
in emotional intelligence became.

But government might be a special case. So I again commissioned
Hay/McBer to reanalyze their database, this time to assess the importance of
emotional competence for executive and leadership positions in business.
Based on their research with hundreds of top executives at fifteen global
companies—including IBM, PepsiCo, and Volvo—the results were stunning.

Just one cognitive ability distinguished star performers from average:
pattern recognition, the "big-picture" thinking that allows leaders to pick out
the meaningful trends from the welter of information around them and to
think strategically far into the future.[4]

But with this one exception, intellectual or technical superiority played
no role in leadership success. At the top executive levels, everyone needs
cognitive skills, to a certain extent, but being better at them does not make
a star leader.

Rather, emotional competence made the crucial difference between mediocre leaders and the best. The stars showed significantly greater strengths in a range of emotional competencies, among them influence, team leadership, political awareness, self-confidence, and achievement drive. On average, close to *90 percent* of their success in leadership was attributable to emotional intelligence.

To sum up: For star performance in all jobs, in every field, emotional competence is twice as important as purely cognitive abilities.

For success at the highest levels, in leadership positions, emotional competence accounts for virtually the entire advantage.

The Value of Magic

Patrick McCarthy is working his retail magic again, this time with Donald Peterson, the retired chairman of Ford Motor Company. Peterson is looking for a certain kind of sport coat in size 43 long, which is difficult to get. He calls McCarthy, a salesman in men's clothing at Nordstrom's flagship store in Seattle, who searches their stock but can't find the jacket. So Peterson keeps asking around at other men's clothing stores, only to find that no one has the jacket.

But a few days later McCarthy calls Peterson: He was able to make a special appeal to his supplier, and so the jacket in the right size is on its way to him.

At a chain famous for customer service, McCarthy is a legend who reigned as the number one sales associate for over fifteen years.[5] McCarthy nurtures his personal customer base of about six thousand shoppers by going beyond merely giving helpful service when they are in the store: He routinely takes it upon himself to call specific customers when merchandise comes in that he thinks they will like. He even phones the family of customers with gift suggestions when the customer has an upcoming birthday or anniversary.

Given that emotional competencies make up two thirds or more of the ingredients of such a standout performance, the data suggests that finding people who have these abilities, or nurturing them in existing employees, adds tremendous value to an organization's bottom line. How much? McCarthy's annual sales of over $1 million compare with an industry average of around $80,000.

The best estimate of the economic value added by such standouts comes from a landmark analysis of thousands of people in jobs ranging from postal clerks to partners in corporate law firms.[6] The study, by the experts in this area, John Hunter (at Michigan State University), Frank Schmidt, and Michael Judiesch (both at the University of Iowa), compared the economic value of top performers like Patrick McCarthy—those in the highest 1 percent—with that of average or poor performers.

That value, they found, increases with the complexity of the job:

- For simpler jobs, like machine operators or clerks, those in the top 1 percent produced three times more output than those in the bottom 1 percent—that is, they were worth three times more.

- For jobs of medium complexity, like sales clerks or mechanics, a top performer was twelve times more productive than those at the bottom. That is, a single person in the top 1 percent was worth twelve people in the bottom 1 percent.

- A different comparison was made for the most complex jobs, like insurance salespeople, account managers, lawyers, and physicians. Those at the top were measured against average performers, rather than against those at the bottom. Even in this case, the added value of a performer in the top 1 percent was 127 percent more.[7]

Competence Pays Most at the Top

A CEO at a subsidiary of a South American conglomerate was promoted to another position, leaving six top managers vying to succeed him. The six fell into a competition that undermined their unity as a management team. The conglomerate called in a consultant to sort out the strengths and weaknesses of the six and thus help them come to a decision.

Manager #1 had the most experience and was the smartest of the bunch; he probably would have been the choice by traditional standards. But Manager #1 had a drawback: He was widely known to lack the personal and social qualities of emotional intelligence.

Manager #2 looked like a strong candidate, too—fairly high in experience, and in emotional intelligence, and very bright. And Manager #3 was a contender, too—highest in emotional intelligence, slightly behind the other two leading candidates in IQ and experience.

The choice?

Manager #3. A key reason was that one chief task of the new CEO was to head the management team and make it work again, a job that demanded a high degree of interpersonal effectiveness. Says the consultant, "The new CEO's very strong emotional intelligence made it easier for the other five managers, who had all been competing for the CEO position, to accept his promotion." Under the new CEO's direction, he adds, the company "has become the most profitable in the country in its sector, and has achieved its highest profitability ever."

To the degree emotional competence spurs such outstanding accomplishment, it understandably pays off most at the top. Because of their financial leverage, executives' performance has a much greater dollar consequence than does that of the clerks who work for them. At the extreme, a brilliant CEO can multiply the earnings of a large company by millions, while a blundering one can sink a company.

In the lower reaches of job complexity there is a more or less direct ratio between a person's cognitive ability and performance, in that a smarter clerk or machine operator will do better than one who is not so bright. But at the higher levels of job complexity—in executive or managerial ranks, or among engineers and scientists, for example—IQ and expertise, as we saw in Chapter 2, do not predict who will be the standout performers; rather, they are largely entry-level barriers.

The immense difference in economic value between top and bottom performers in high-complexity jobs, the Hunter analysis suggests, makes emotional intelligence not simply additive with cognitive ability, but multiplicative: arguably, the hidden ingredient in star performance.

What Exactly Is a Star Worth?

A small group of account managers at RCA were able to increase the size of their accounts each year for tens of millions of dollars more in sales. How? It wasn't because they had more technical expertise than other account managers—it was because they had better people skills.

This case is one of thousands collected by a McClelland protégé, Lyle Spencer Jr., director of research and technology worldwide at Hay/McBer in Boston.[8] The reason for the astounding success of the account managers?

"Just-average account managers were content to spend a minimal amount of time with their clients, just enough to make sure the customers were satisfied," Spencer told me. "But these stars spent lots of time with them, wooing them, going out drinking, telling them about new technologies and product possibilities that would improve their clients' products—so they didn't just keep the account steady, but made more sales. What mattered was relationship building, sensing the client's hot buttons and enthusiasms and knowing how to play to them, and making the match between the client's needs and desires and their product."

One of the more surprising job arenas where emotional intelligence makes a competitive difference is computer programming, where the rate at which the top 10 percent exceed average performers in producing effective programs is 320 percent. And those rare superstars, in the top 1 percent of programmers, produce a boggling 1,272 percent more than the average.[9]

"It's not just computing skills that set apart the stars, but teamwork," says Spencer. "The very best are willing to stay late to help their colleagues finish a project, or to share shortcuts they discover rather than keep them to themselves. They don't compete—they collaborate."

The payoff from top levels of competence can be spectacular. In a study of salespeople in forty-four Fortune 500 firms, including AT&T, IBM, and PepsiCo, Spencer asked sales heads how much better than average their very best salespeople performed. He found that the top 10 percent of the sales force toted up $6.7 million in sales per person, compared to the norm of $3 million—more than twice the average. Given that the typical salary of the sales force at the time was around $42,000, that meant the top performers' value added of $3.7 million was about eighty-eight times their salary![10]

The Tipping Point

Competencies come in clusters. For top performance a person must master a mix of competencies, not just one or two. David McClelland found that stars are not just talented in, say, initiative or influence—they have strengths across the board, including competencies from each of the five emotional intelligence areas: self-awareness, self-regulation, motivation, empathy, and social skills.

Only when they reach a critical mass from the full spectrum do they emerge as outstanding—something akin to a chemical reaction achieving the moment of catalysis. McClelland calls this critical mass the "tipping point."

"Once you reach the tipping point, the probability of your performance being outstanding shoots up," Mary Fontaine of Hay/McBer explained to me about studies with executives at IBM and PepsiCo. "The critical point may be due to how frequently you show the key competencies, or your level of sophistication in them, or how well you can manifest them."

At PepsiCo, those executives who had reached the tipping point—possessing strengths in at least six competencies from across the entire spectrum—were far more likely to perform in the top third as reflected in salary bonuses for performance of the divisions they led. Of those leaders who were strong in six or seven competencies, 87 percent were in the top third.[11]

The competencies predicted success not just at the company's branches in the United States, but around the world; those who reached the tipping point were in the top third 82 percent of the time in Europe and 86 percent of the time in Asia.

Weaknesses in these competencies were often fatal flaws. In Europe, for example, those who lacked strengths in the key competencies had outstanding performance only 13 percent of the time, in Asia just 11 percent, and in America 20 percent.

The emotional competencies that most often led to this level of success were:

- Initiative, achievement drive, and adaptability.

- Influence, team leadership, and political awareness.

- Empathy, self-confidence, and developing others.

Division leaders with these strengths outperformed their targets by 15 to 20 percent; those who lacked them underperformed by almost 20 percent.

The tipping point is important not just for executives; it operates at every level in an organization. One of the more dramatic demonstrations was found at a national insurance company. Those insurance sales agents who were very weak in specific emotional competencies such as self-confidence, initiative, and empathy sold policies with an average premium of $54,000. But those who were very strong in at least five of eight key competencies had remarkable success by comparison, with the average size of policies they sold $114,000.

When Turnover Bleeds the Bottom Line

Just as there is clear value added from emotional competence, a deficit in these competencies also carries a high price—in turnover. Lyle Spencer estimates that the real cost to a company from the turnover of an employee is the equivalent of one full year of pay. These hidden costs come not just from finding and training replacements, but in customer satisfaction and retention, and in lowered efficiency for everyone who works with the new hire.

When organizations lose many employees, even at low salary levels, the real costs can be substantial. Turnover rates in retail and insurance sales, for example, are estimated to exceed 50 percent per year, mostly among new hires.[12] When the employee who leaves is a highly placed executive, that expense can be enormous. The cost for a company to replace a derailed executive with someone from outside can run into the hundreds of thousands, even millions, of dollars.

At a global consumer beverage firm, when standard methods—which ignored emotional competence—were used to hire division presidents, 50 percent left within two years (most because they were performing poorly) at a total search cost of close to $4 million. But when the firm started to evaluate for competencies such as initiative, self-confidence, leadership, and the like, the retention rate was much greater, with only 6 percent of new division presidents leaving within two years.[13]

Consider three cases, all salespeople in very different kinds of industries.[14] At L'Oréal, the cosmetics giant, sales agents who were selected for their strengths in emotional competence had 63 percent less turnover during their first year than did those whose selection disregarded their competence profile. Among newly hired sales reps at a start-up computer company, those hired for emotional competence were 90 percent more likely to finish their training than those hired on other criteria. And at a national furniture retailer, salespeople hired because of strengths in key emotional competencies had half the dropout rate of those hired on the basis of other standards during their first year on the job.

The Case of the Derailed COO

After hearing me give a talk on emotional intelligence, the CEO of a company—one of the ten largest in its market—told me in confidence about why, instead of grooming his chief operating officer of many years to take his place as CEO, he fired him: "He was extraordinarily talented, brilliant conceptually, a very powerful mind. He was great on the computer, knew the numbers up, down, and backward. That's how he got to be chief operating officer.

"But he was not a brilliant leader, not even particularly likable. He was often brutally acerbic. In groups he was socially awkward; he had no social graces, or even a social life. At forty-five, he had nobody he was close to, no friends. He worked all the time. He was one-dimensional; that's why I finally let him go.

"But," the CEO added, "if he could have done just five percent of what you're talking about, he'd still be here."

This example fits well with the conclusions of a landmark study of top executives who derailed.[15] The two most common traits of those who failed:

- *Rigidity:* They were unable to adapt their style to changes in the organizational culture, or they were unable to take in or respond to feedback about traits they needed to change or improve. They couldn't listen or learn.

- *Poor relationships:* The single most frequently mentioned factor: being too harshly critical, insensitive, or demanding, so that they alienated those they worked with.

These traits proved fatal handicaps even to brilliant executives with strong technical expertise. One executive described a derailed colleague this way: "He's a great strategic thinker and he has high ethical standards, but he lashes out at people. He's very smart, but he achieves superiority through demeaning others. Many people have tried to help him work on this flaw, but it seems hopeless."[16]

The opposite of rigidity is adaptability. "Leadership agility, the ability to work with different styles and with people at all levels of the organization, from the sales rep on the street to top management, demands empathy and emotional self-management. You need agility in leadership and in learning," Patrick O'Brien, formerly vice president for North American sales at Johnson Wax, tells me. "We find an absence of this kind of agility is a top derailer for people we seek to develop."

Sharp differences emerged between the successful managers and those who derailed on most major dimensions of emotional competence.[17]

- *Self-control:* Those who derailed handled pressure poorly and were prone to moodiness and angry outbursts. The successful stayed composed under stress, remaining calm and confident—and dependable—in the heat of crises.

■ *Conscientiousness:* The derailed group reacted to failure and criticism defensively—denying, covering up, or passing on the blame. The successful took responsibility by admitting their mistakes and failures, taking action to fix the problems, and moving on without ruminating about their lapse.

■ *Trustworthiness:* The failures typically were overly ambitious, too ready to get ahead at the expense of other people. The successes had high integrity, with a strong concern for the needs of their subordinates and colleagues, and for the demands of the task at hand, giving these higher priority than impressing their own boss at any cost.

■ *Social skills:* The failures lacked empathy and sensitivity, and so were often abrasive, arrogant, or given to intimidation of subordinates. While some were charming on occasion, even seeming concerned about others, the charm was purely manipulative. The successes were empathic and sensitive, showing tact and consideration in their dealings with everyone, superiors and subordinates alike.

■ *Building bonds and leveraging diversity:* The insensitivity and manipulative manner of the failed group meant that they failed to build a strong network of cooperative, mutually beneficial relationships. The successes were more appreciative of diversity, able to get along with people of all kinds.

Talents for These Times: The Global View

Claudio Fernández-Aráoz, in charge of executive searches throughout Latin America from Egon Zehnder International's Buenos Aires office, compared 227 highly successful executives with 23 who failed in their jobs.[18] He found that the managers who failed were almost always high in expertise and IQ. In every case their fatal weakness was in emotional intelligence—arrogance, overreliance on brainpower, inability to adapt to the occasionally disorienting economic shifts in that region, and disdain for collaboration or teamwork.

Parallel analyses of successful and failed managers in Germany and Japan revealed the same pattern: Those who failed had their largest deficit in the emotional intelligence competencies, and their failure came despite strengths in expertise and cognitive abilities. In Germany, three quarters of failed managers showed a major deficit in emotional intelligence; in Japan a little more than half did so.[19]

In Latin America a deficit in emotional intelligence seems to imply almost certain failure. That is not so strongly the case in Germany or Japan—yet. As Fernández-Aráoz told me, "Latin America has seen a huge rate of change in recent years—hyperinflation, political turmoil, shifts from controlled to open economies. Things change radically, sometimes almost every day. Your experience is not as crucial as your adaptability. You need close contact with everybody you work with, your customers, your suppliers—everyone—just to keep track of what's going on. There are new forms of organization, new mergers and coalitions, new technologies, new rules. We've found that a lack of emotional intelligence in such an unstable environment means certain failure. And that's everyone's future."

Or, as summed up by Kevin Murray, director of communications at British Airways: "Organizations going through the greatest change are those who need emotional intelligence the most."

The Peter Principle:
Too Much College, Too Little Kindergarten

A young engineer who had earned straight A's in school came to work at an environmental engineering company but was fired within a relatively short period of time. The reason? "He was brilliant at his work," his manager told me, "but he couldn't take direction. His supervisor would tell him how to do a design, and he'd do it his own way. When his supervisor would point out how the design didn't conform to the specifications, he'd get defensive. He couldn't take feedback—he acted as though it were a personal criticism.

"When other engineers would ask him to help, he'd turn them down, saying he was too busy with his own part of the project. He created so much animosity that when he needed some help, no one wanted to give it to him."

High IQ and technical expertise can have a paradoxical effect among seemingly promising people who fail. In a study of once-successful managers who failed, most were technically brilliant.[20] And their technical skills were often the very reason they were promoted into management in the first place.

But once they reached higher positions, their technical strength became a liability: Arrogance led some to offend their peers by acting superior, others to micromanage subordinates—even those with better technical expertise.

This is the Peter Principle at work: People are promoted to their level of incompetence. A person who is promoted because of expertise ("He's great with the numbers") finds himself at a new level, where many or most duties revolve around managing people—not technical skill. This means the working world is peppered with bad bosses.

The Peter Principle does much to explain why so many people who are abrasive, thoughtless, and otherwise interpersonally inept are in so many positions of power in organizations everywhere. The classic mistake is assuming that if someone has a special expertise, it necessarily means they also have the ability to lead. "I call it the Michael Jordan effect," Paul Robinson, director of Sandia National Laboratories, tells me. "I see it all the time in science labs: A top executive leaves and you immediately turn to the best scientist as the replacement.

"But it's as if the Chicago Bulls lost a coach and appointed Michael Jordon to replace him. He's a brilliant basketball player, of course, but the game comes so naturally to him that he may not be very good at coaching other players—he probably never even thinks about how he does what he does. So how well are the Bulls going to do as a team when Michael Jordan is on the bench, not on the court? It's the same with us—we need those outstanding scientists in the lab, not in the office."

To avoid the problem, "We set up two tracks, recognizing that some people are excellent technical professionals and like their work, but terrible managers and dislike management as a career," Ira Stepanian, retired CEO of BankBoston, told me. "Without the people skills they would never succeed at the top levels of management. We tried to spare them the failure of the Peter Principle by keeping them in a professional track."

Again, the principle applies to jobs of every sort. Take, for example, Patrick McCarthy, the star sales associate at Nordstrom. Early in his career McCarthy was promoted to department manager—a post he left after a year and a half to return to sales.[21] As he put it: "Sales was what I was good at and felt comfortable with."

The Computer Nerd: Trained Incapacity

People in information technology are notorious for having high levels of technical skills, but not getting along with people so well," an executive at Hitachi Data Systems told me. "They tend to lack certain skills, like empathy and social abilities. Folks in information tech divisions are famous in our industry for not getting along with people in other parts of their companies."

I used to think that such pronouncements reflected a cultural misperception, a negative stereotype of the "computer nerd." Underlying my assumption was my belief that emotional intelligence and IQ were essentially independent.

But a friend on the faculty at MIT argues that at the extreme high end of the IQ scale, there is often a lack of social skills. "Trained incapacity" is the term used by Stephen Rosen, himself a theoretical physicist, and now head of a project to study why some scientists' careers founder.[22] "The smarter they are, very often the less competent they are emotionally and in handling people. It's as though the IQ muscle strengthened itself at the expense of muscles for personal and social competence."

Mastery of these technical pursuits demands long hours spent working alone, often beginning in childhood or the early teen years—a period of life when, ordinarily, people learn vital social skills from interacting with friends. Self-selection plays a role, too. People who are attracted to fields typified by very high levels of cognitive effort, like computer science or engineering, are sometimes drawn "in part because you don't have to deal with your emotions," points out Robert E. Kelley, a psychologist at Carnegie-Mellon University. "This is why nerds are drawn to fields like engineering—you can be reclusive, get by with few social graces, as long as you do well on the cognitive side."

This does not mean, of course, that all high-IQ scientists are socially incompetent. But it does mean that emotional intelligence abilities will pay off with special strength in such careers, where the pool of potential standout managers—people with both high science skills and high social skills—may be relatively small.

In an unusual study begun at the University of California at Berkeley in the 1950s, eighty Ph.D. students in science went through an intensive battery of IQ and personality tests, as well as extensive interviews with psychologists who evaluated them on such qualities as emotional balance and maturity, integrity, and interpersonal effectiveness.[23]

Forty years later, when the former students were in their early seventies, researchers tracked them down again. In the 1994 follow-up, estimates were made of each person's career success on the basis of résumés, evaluations by experts in their own field, and sources like *American Men and Women of Science*. The result: Emotional intelligence abilities were about *four times* more important than IQ in determining professional success and prestige— even for these scientists.

As an engineer who formerly worked at Exxon told me, "What made the difference there wasn't your grade point average—everyone there had done well in school. The difference was in personal qualities like perseverance, finding a mentor, being willing to put in more hours and try harder." Or, as Ernest O. Lawrence, the Nobel laureate who founded the labs at Berkeley that bear his name, put it, "In scientific work, excellence is not about technical competence, but character."[24]

Help Wanted: Techies with Passion and Intuition

Such realizations have spurred a growing movement among graduate schools to ensure that budding engineers and scientists come into the working world with stronger emotional intelligence skills. Phil Weilerstein, director of the National Collegiate Inventors and Innovators Alliance, told me, "The skills engineers will need in the future are different from what they have been trained for: to sit in a cubicle at General Dynamics and design propeller blades. They need to be nimble enough to change jobs every three, four, five years. They need to know how to develop and execute ideas as a part of a team, how to sell an idea, take criticism and feedback, adapt. Engineering education has ignored this range of skills in the past. It can't afford to in the future."

As John Seely Brown, director of Xerox Corporation's Silicon Valley R&D facility, said to me, "I raise eyebrows when I tell people that we don't go out of our way to hire the brightest people—in all the years here, I've never looked at anyone's university transcript. The two competencies we look for the most are grounded intuitions and a passion for making an impact. We want people who are bold but grounded."

But what does it mean to be intuitive, passionate, bold but grounded— to display emotional intelligence? What *are* the human capabilities that matter most for on-the-job effectiveness?

Answering these questions in precise detail will be the next stop in our exploration of what it means to work with emotional intelligence.

2

Self-Mastery

4

···················

The Inner Rudder

A good friend, a physician, was once offered a business proposition: If he would leave his practice to become medical director of a fledgling condominium health resort and invest $100,000 of his own capital in the venture, his projected share of the business would amount to $4 million within three years. Or so the business plan promised.

My friend liked the vision of a resort where people could improve their health as they vacationed; coupled with the lure of a possibly fantastic pay-off, he couldn't resist. He sold his medical practice, invested in the resort, and became its medical director. But during that start-up year he found that there was no medical program to direct yet—he ended up spending his days essentially as a salesman, trying to interest people in buying time-share condos at the resort.

One day, as he was driving to work at his new job, he found himself—to his astonishment—pounding the dashboard of his car and yelling, "I can't do this! I can't do this!" Pulling over, my friend took a few moments to get a grip on his tumultuous feelings, calmed down, and drove on to work.

A year later the resort was bankrupt—and so was he.

He admits now that he had a gut feeling from the outset that there was something wrong with the proposition, that the projections in the business plan were too rosy, and that the scheme was really about real estate development, not preventive medicine. But at the time he had been craving a change. And the financial incentives looked so promising that he buried his misgivings—much to his later regret.

Life more often than not presents us with murky decisions, nothing like the clear, neat "if this, then that" matrices taught in classes on risk analysis and decision making. That approach is oversold as a way to make the real, day-to-day choices we face at work: which person to promote, which company to merge with, what marketing strategy to follow, or whether a proffered business deal should be accepted. When it comes to decisions like these, our gut feelings—our deepest sense of what *feels* right and what is "off"—provide critical information that we must not ignore, lest we regret our choices a month or a year down the road.

Beyond the Pros and Cons

The deal my friend accepted looked good—on paper. But far more important than the financial projections were intangibles such as the trustworthiness and abilities of the people he was allying himself with. Though there are no easily quantifiable ways of measuring such important aspects of a decision, we do nevertheless have an immense amount of relevant "data" in the form of hunches. And, as my friend did, we ignore such data at our own risk.

Of sixty highly successful entrepreneurs connected with companies having revenues ranging from $2 million to $400 million, just one said his business decisions were made using only the classic decision-tree methods—and even he added that his final decision was still made intuitively.[1] The others all either used their feelings to confirm (or disconfirm) a rational analysis or let their emotions guide them at the outset and subsequently looked for data or a rationale that supported their gut hunch.

One entrepreneur told me, "The first step is to work it out step by step, consciously and deliberately, very analytically . . . but at the same time the emotional side is doing something. I think you need both."

Another pointed to the fallacy of trying to make decisions purely rationally, what he called the "yellow pad theory": "When you do that and you're completely objective . . . all you really have are cold statistics. But inside, it's almost as if you had a meter that measures all of that data. . . . The needle is measuring feeling. Sometimes the brain says, 'Well, that's going to make a lot of people ticked off,' or whatever, and yet this sixth sense says, 'Yeah, but it feels right.' And I have learned to trust that."

The Source of Gut Feeling

The ability to read such subjective currents has primordial roots in evolution. The brain areas involved in gut feelings are far more ancient than the thin layers of the neocortex, the centers for rational thought that enfold the very top of the brain. Hunches start much deeper in the brain. They are a function of the emotional centers that ring the brain stem atop the spinal cord—most particularly an almond-shaped structure called the amygdala and its connected neural circuitry. This web of connectivity, sometimes called the extended amygdala, stretches up to the brain's executive center in the prefrontal lobes, just behind the forehead.[2]

The brain stores different aspects of an experience in different areas—the source of a memory is encoded in one zone, the sights and sounds and smells in other areas, and so on. The amygdala is the site where the emotions an experience evokes are stored. Every experience that we have an emotional reaction to, no matter how subtle, seems to be encoded in the amygdala.[3]

As the repository for everything we feel about what we experience, the amygdala constantly signals us with this information. Whenever we have a preference of any kind, whether for ordering the risotto rather than the sea bass special, or a compelling sense that we should dump our shares in a stock, that is a message from the amygdala. And via the amygdala's related circuitry, particularly nerve pathways that run into the viscera, we can have a somatic response—literally, a "gut feeling"—to the choices we face.

This capacity, like other elements of emotional intelligence, can grow stronger with the accumulating experiences life brings us. As one successful entrepreneur in a University of Southern California study described it: "It's a *kinesthetic* feel that some people have. I think that there are fewer people with strong intuitions at a young age than old, because life experiences add up. . . . It's like your gut tells you things and there's a chemical reaction that's going on in your body, which is triggered by your mind, and tightening your stomach muscles, so your gut is saying, 'This doesn't feel right.' "

The classic term for this strengthening of our guiding sensibility is *wisdom*. And, as we shall see, people who ignore or discount messages from this repository of life's wisdom do so at their peril.

The Lawyer Who Couldn't Decide

Dr. Antonio Damasio, a neurologist at the University of Iowa, had a patient who was a brilliant corporate lawyer. Some years earlier, this man had been diagnosed with a small tumor in his prefrontal lobes. Surgery was successful—except that the surgeon accidentally cut the circuits connecting the lawyer's prefrontal lobes with the amygdala. The results were puzzling—and dramatic. On the one hand, the lawyer had no discernible cognitive deficits. On the other, he became inept at work, lost his job, and was unable to keep another. He ended up out of work; his wife left him; he lost his house.[4]

The lawyer went to Damasio for help. Looking over the results of his neuropsychological tests, which were all normal, Damasio was baffled at first. Then one day he noticed that when he asked the innocent question, "When should we have our next appointment?" the lawyer was capable of giving him the rational pros and cons for every possible hour for the next two weeks—but had no idea which of those hours was best.

Damasio realized the flaw: The lawyer had no *feelings* about his thoughts, and so no preferences. Damasio's conclusion was that our minds are not designed like a computer, to give us a neat printout of the rational arguments for and against a decision in life based on all the previous times we've faced a similar situation. Instead, the mind does something much more elegant: It weighs the *emotional* bottom line from those previous experiences and delivers the answer to us in a hunch, a gut feeling.

This sense of rightness or wrongness deep in the body is part of a steady background flow of feeling that continues throughout the day. Just as there is a stream of thought, there is a parallel stream of feeling. The notion that there is "pure thought," rationality devoid of feeling, is a fiction, an illusion based on inattention to the subtle moods that follow us through the day. We have feelings about everything we do, think about, imagine, remember. Thought and feeling are inextricably woven together.

Such fleeting feelings are typically subtle, but important. Not that gut feeling outweighs the facts—but it should be weighed in *with* the facts. Attunement to feelings offers us crucial information for navigating through life. This sense of "rightness" or "wrongness" signals that what we are doing either does or does not fit our preferences, guiding values, and life wisdom.

The Power of Intuition: The First Thirty Seconds

redit managers must sense when a deal might go bad even if the numbers look fine; executives have to decide whether a new product is worth the time and money it takes to develop; people must make an educated guess about who among a field of candidates for a job will have the best chemistry in a working group. All such decisions demand the capacity to fold into the decision-making process our intuitive sense of what is right and wrong.

Indeed, among three thousand executives in a study of decision making, those at the top in a wide range of fields were most adept at utilizing intuition in reaching their decisions.[5] As one highly successful entrepreneur put it, "An intuitive decision is nothing but a subconscious logical analysis. . . . Somehow the brain goes through these calculations and comes up with what we would call a weighted conclusion—it seems more right to do it this way than that way."[6]

Intuition may play its biggest role in work life when it comes to people. Bjorn Johansson, head of a Zurich executive search firm specializing in placing top-level executives with multinational firms, told me, "This business is intuition from A to Z. First you have to assess a company's chemistry—size up the CEO, his personal qualities and expectations, the tone he sets, and the resulting culture of the corporation. I have to understand how the management team works, how they deal with each other. There's what you might call a 'smell' to every corporation, a distinctive quality you can sense."

Having registered that "smell," Johansson then sizes up prospective job candidates accordingly. The key judgment is intuitive: "I know within thirty seconds of meeting someone whether this person's chemistry fits with my client. Of course I need to also analyze his career, his references, and the like. Still, if he doesn't pass the first barrier, my intuitive sense, I don't bother. But if my brains, heart, and gut all say this is the right person, that's who I recommend."

That fits with data from studies at Harvard: People can sense intuitively in the first thirty seconds of an encounter what basic impression they will have of the other person after fifteen minutes—or half a year. For instance, when people watch just thirty-second snatches of teachers giving a lecture, they can assess each teacher's proficiency with about 80 percent accuracy.[7]

Such instantaneous intuitive astuteness may be the remnant of an essential early warning system for danger, one that lives on today in feelings such as apprehension. Gavin deBecker, a specialist in security arrangements for celebrities, calls apprehension a "gift of fear."[8] This radar for danger alerts us with a primal feeling that something is "off."

Intuition and gut feeling bespeak the capacity to sense messages from our internal store of emotional memory—our own reservoir of wisdom and judgment. This ability lies at the heart of self-awareness, and self-awareness is the vital foundation skill for three emotional competencies:

- *Emotional awareness:* The recognition of how our emotions affect our performance, and the ability to use our values to guide decision making

- *Accurate self-assessment:* A candid sense of our personal strengths and limits, a clear vision of where we need to improve, and the ability to learn from experience

- *Self-confidence:* The courage that comes from certainty about our capabilities, values, and goals

■ EMOTIONAL AWARENESS ■

Recognizing One's Emotions and Their Effects

People with this competence

- Know which emotions they are feeling and why

- Realize the links between their feelings and what they think, do, and say

- Recognize how their feelings affect their performance

- Have a guiding awareness of their values and goals

He's a candidate to become a partner at a huge Wall Street investment banking firm. And he's in trouble.

"He's made it by virtue of conquering everything and everyone in his way," said the psychiatrist his company had him consult. "But he uses this warrior's ruthlessness when it just doesn't apply. He gets irritated way too easily, without any sense that his anger is making him treat people in an abrasive way. No one wants to work with him or for him. He just doesn't have any awareness at all of how his emotions are pushing him around."

That awareness—of how our emotions affect what we are doing—is the fundamental emotional competence. Lacking that ability, we are vulnerable, like the investment banker, to being sidetracked by emotions run amok. Such awareness is our guide in fine-tuning on-the-job performance of every kind, managing our unruly feelings, keeping ourselves motivated, tuning in with accuracy to the feelings of those around us, and developing good work-related social skills, including those essential for leadership and teamwork.

Perhaps it's no surprise that outstanding counselors and psychotherapists demonstrate this skill. "It's a focusing ability, knowing the internal meters and subtle signals that tell you what you're feeling, and using them as an ongoing guide to how you're doing," says Richard Boyatzis, who studied self-awareness in counselors.

The same skill comes into play in most jobs, particularly those that involve dealing with people about any sort of sensitive matter. For instance, at American Express Financial Advisors, financial advisors' awareness of their own emotions is a competence central to excellent performance in that job.[9] The interaction between a planner and client is delicate, dealing not only with hard questions about money, but also, when life insurance comes up, the even more sensitive issue of mortality.

The company found these interactions rife with feelings of distress, uneasiness, and distrust, all too often ignored in the haste to make a sale. American Express realized they would have to help their financial advisors tune in to this sea of feeling and handle it effectively in order to better serve their clients.

As we'll see in Chapter 11, when financial advisors at American Express were trained to be more emotionally self-aware and to have more empathy for their clients, they were better able to build long-term, trusting relationships. And those relationships translated into higher sales per customer.

Emotional awareness starts with attunement to the stream of feeling that is a constant presence in all of us and with a recognition of how these emotions shape what we perceive, think, and do. From that awareness comes another: that our feelings affect those we deal with. For financial planners, this means knowing that their own emotions can reverberate in the interaction with clients—for better or worse (more on this in Chapter 7).

A person excelling in this competence is aware of her emotions at any given moment—often recognizing how those emotions feel physically. She can articulate those feelings, as well as demonstrate social appropriateness in expressing them.

American Express Financial Advisors recognized that their planners needed not just an awareness of feelings, but also an ability to sense whether their own work-life, health, and family concerns are in balance, as well as the capacity to align work with personal values and goals—all, as we shall see, abilities that build on self-awareness.

The Stream of Feeling

Our background stream of feeling runs in perfect parallel to our stream of thought. We always feel some mood or other, though we typically do not tune in to the subtle moods that ebb and flow as we go through our daily routine: the sullen or cheery feeling we wake up with, the slight irritation that a frustrating commute to work triggers, the hundreds or even thousands of large and small emotions that come and go with the day's ups and downs.

In the rush and pressure of our work days, our minds are preoccupied by the stream of thought—planning the next thing, immersion in our present task, preoccupation with things undone. It takes a mental pause to become sensitive to the subterranean murmur of mood—a moment we rarely take. Our feelings are always with us, but we are too seldom with them. Instead, we typically become aware of emotions only when they build up and boil over. But if we are attentive, we can experience them at subtler levels long before they emerge so strongly.

The rhythm and pace of modern life give us too little time to assimilate, reflect, and react. Our bodies are geared to a slower rhythm. We need time to be introspective, but we don't get it—or don't take it. Emotions have their own agenda and timetable, but our rushed lives give them no space, no airtime—and so they go underground. All of this mental pressure crowds out a quieter inner voice that offers an inner rudder of conviction we could use to navigate through life.

People who are unable to know their feelings are at a tremendous disadvantage. In a sense, they are emotional illiterates, oblivious to a realm of reality that is crucial for success in life as a whole, let alone work.

For some, emotional "tone deafness" takes the form of obliviousness to the messages their bodies are trying to send—in the form of chronic headaches, lower back pain, anxiety attacks—that something is amiss. At the other extreme are those with alexithymia, the psychiatric term for people with a confused awareness of their own feelings. For such people, the outer world is clearer and more detailed than their own inner universe. Such people blur distinctions among emotions, whether benign or unpleasant, and have a constricted emotional range, particularly sparse in positive moods like happiness. For them the nuances of emotion are elusive, and so they are unable to use a gut sense to guide their thinking and action.

But self-awareness can be cultivated. Edward McCracken, former CEO of Silicon Graphics, who affirms the ability to include the intuitive in decision making, says, "In our industry very often we don't have time to think. You have to do all your homework, but then you have to go with your intuition without letting your mind get in the way." McCracken's method of allowing his intuitive feelings space? He's been meditating daily for a decade.[10]

His approach is a time-honored way to get in touch with our deeper, quieter voice of feeling: taking time out to "do nothing." Doing nothing productively means not only not working, but also not filling the time with idle time wasters: watching TV, say, or, even worse, doing something else while watching TV. Instead it means putting aside for the time being all other goal-oriented activities and doing something that opens our minds to a deeper, quieter sensibility.

Living by the Inner Rudder

Richard Abdoo has a resolution: No matter how busy his work gets, he reserves eight hours a week for solitary reflection.[11] As CEO of Wisconsin Energy, a $2-billion-a-year utility company, that resolution takes some effort. A devout Catholic, Abdoo often uses those hours for long walks. Or sometimes his contemplative time takes other forms, like working in his home shop—or riding his Harley. "You have to force yourself to spend some time away from the hustle and bustle of your job in order to get down to reality again," Abdoo explains. "If you don't spend enough time doing that, you can lose hold of the reins and get into all kinds of trouble."

What kind of trouble? Drifting away from our guiding values, for one. Personal values are not lofty abstractions, but intimate credos that we may never quite articulate in words so much as *feel*. Our values translate into what has emotional power or resonance for us, whether negative or positive.

Self-awareness serves as an inner barometer, gauging whether what we are doing (or are about to do) is, indeed, worthwhile. Feelings give the essential reading. If there is a discrepancy between action and value, the result will be uneasiness in the form of guilt or shame, deep doubts or nagging second thoughts, queasiness or remorse, and the like. Such uneasiness acts as an emotional drag, stirring feelings that can hinder or sabotage our efforts.

Choices made in keeping with this inner rudder, on the other hand, are energizing. They not only feel right but maximize the attention and energy available for pursuing them. In a study of "knowledge workers" (in this case, engineers, computer programmers, and auditors), the star performers made career choices that let them work with their own sense of meaning intact or enhanced, where they felt a sense of accomplishment and believed they made a contribution.[12]

While average workers were content to take on whatever project they were assigned, superior performers thought about what project would be invigorating to work on, which person would be stimulating to work under, which personal idea would make a good project. They knew intuitively what they did best and enjoyed—and what they did not. Their performance excelled because they were able to make choices that kept them focused and energized.

People who follow their inner sense of what is worthwhile minimize emotional static for themselves. Unfortunately, too many people feel that they cannot speak up for their deep values at work, that such a thing is somehow impermissible.

The silence about values skews the collective sense of what motivates people, making money alone seems to loom much larger than it actually is for many of us. In the University of Southern California study of sixty highly successful entrepreneurs, ostentatious displays of wealth were rare. What motivated these successful entrepreneurs more than money, the report concluded, were things like the excitement and challenge of starting a business, the freedom of being the boss, the chance to be creative, and the opportunity to help others by helping themselves.

Except for the financially desperate, people do not work for money alone. What also fuels their passion for work is a larger sense of purpose or passion. Given the opportunity, people gravitate to what gives them meaning, to what engages to the fullest their commitment, talent, energy, and skill. And that can mean changing jobs to get a better fit with what matters to us.

Managing Your Career

The drive to establish ourselves and make our mark in the world is most urgent in our twenties and thirties, and into our forties. But by our mid-forties or early fifties people typically reevaluate their goals, because they often come to the radical realization that life is limited. With this acknowledgment of mortality comes a reconsideration of what really matters.

"By midlife, there are many, many corporate executives and lawyers pulling down seven-figure salaries who wish instead they were doing social work or running a restaurant," says Stephen Rosen, who counsels professionals who are trying to find more fulfilling livelihoods—or who have no choice, having lost a job.

A consultant who has assessed top executives at firms such as General Electric, DEC, and Mobil Oil tells me that many at midlife are "highly excited about pet projects—being on a school board, a small business they're running on the side. But they're bored by their own job." One highly successful entrepreneur who had started a series of businesses found himself running one he hated: "This company is at the point where it controls me. I'm stuck. . . . I don't like what I'm doing. I'm much happier fixing the engine on my boat or something, but not this."[13]

As the saying goes, "If you don't know where you're going, any road will get you there." The less aware we are of what makes us passionate, the more lost we will be. And this drifting can even affect our health; people who feel their skills are not being used well on the job, or who feel their work is repetitive and boring, have a higher risk of heart disease than those who feel that their best skills are expressed in their work.[14]

Self-awareness offers a sure rudder for keeping our career decisions in harmony with our deepest values. "Some women executives have suppressed their self-awareness to get where they are," Kathy Kram, a professor of management at Boston University, told me. "These are high-achieving women who end up in senior management, but who suffer from relationship deprivation. Their connections are instrumental, goal-oriented—the pattern more typical of men. The cost for them is that their personal lives wither."

This problem is by no means limited to women. "Many executives, especially males, have never really thought it important to educate themselves about their interior landscape," Michael Banks, a New York–based executive coach with KRW International, tells me. "They never made the connection between how they behave under stress and their ability to retain loyalty and talent or meet the bottom line. They may be moving into their late forties and get an inkling that something's been missing. It might be triggered by a marriage falling apart or by finding they're making mistakes because of their inner turmoil." But these can be fruitful crises: "It starts to crack open their hard veneer—they start to feel emotions they never let themselves feel before, and to take a new look at that side of their lives."

Attention: Our Most Precious Resource

H e was the managing partner of a prosperous corporate law firm, wealthy and accomplished. But at fifty, something was gnawing at him.

"He had always believed by the time he was fifty he would have more freedom and flexibility in his life," Shoshana Zuboff, a psychologist and professor at the Harvard Business School, told me about the lawyer. "But instead he saw himself a slave to billable hours, to the needs of his partners and demands of his clients. His success was his own prison."

That reality came home to him as he made the journey through Odyssey, a unique program of self-reflection.[15] Developed by Zuboff, the program was first offered only to alumni of the Harvard Business School, but by virtue of its popularity, it is now available to other businesspeople and professionals at midlife. The enthusiasm for Odyssey stems in large part from the chance it gives people to closely examine their lives by using their deepest feelings to find answers to questions like "Who am I?" "Where am I going?" and "What do I want?"

The people who participate, says Zuboff, tend to be very successful, having achieved the goals they set for themselves in their twenties and thirties. But they're looking forward to two or three decades more of productive work life and are asking, "What's next?"

The standard approach to that question "encourages us to look at our work lives from the outside—how to make yourself a more attractive commodity, how to market yourself—and to think in terms of external variables, like what's the salary or position or city a job is in, how am I doing compared to my peers? We take the opposite approach, looking from the inside out at our changing sense of self and what constitutes fulfillment," Zuboff says.

For many of those in Odyssey, their careers have become like a train—pulling them along without giving them the time or space to decide if they really want to be going down that track. Odyssey gives people a chance to look within and reflect on their journey. The first week of the program helps focus people on paying attention to their inner world, and how they feel about what they are doing or would like to do—followed by three weeks off, to further digest and reflect, and then another week where they and their spouse come back to work out a plan for the future.

"People have to stop thinking of their feelings as irrelevant and messy, and realize they are in fact highly differentiated, nuanced patterns of reaction, knowable sources of information," Zuboff explains. "We only will know what to do by realizing what feels right to us. Attention is our most precious resource. Feelings are the body's version of the situation; everything we want to know about our situation is revealed in our feelings. The big switch for businesspeople comes when they realize what they thought was soft is hard, and what they thought was hard is often arbitrary. In this sense, feelings are guides to the big issues, like 'Where am I going?'"

For the disgruntled lawyer, the week of reflection led to the realization, recounts Zuboff, that he no longer needed the law firm in the way he once did, though his partners still derived their main sense of identity from it. He was living for other people's expectations. His real pleasure came from a cattle-trading business he ran on the side with his son. Though the enterprise had started as a hobby, he found it engrossing, challenging, and fun.

With this self-knowledge, he resolved to reduce his billable hours by 50 percent over the course of two or three years and spend the other half of his time trading cattle. The result: Two years later he had done just that, plus started up two other businesses—and he made more from cattle sales in six months than he had in two years at the law firm.

More important, said Zuboff, "He's happy. He'd been someone who dreaded getting up in the morning and going to work. Now he's excited, reenergized, renewed."

■ ACCURATE SELF-ASSESSMENT ■

Knowing One's Inner Resources, Abilities, and Limits

People with this competence are

- Aware of their strengths and weaknesses
- Reflective, learning from experience
- Open to candid feedback, new perspectives, continuous learning, and self-development

■ Able to show a sense of humor and perspective about
themselves

■■

Mort Meyerson's awakening started when he accepted an invitation to become CEO of Perot Systems, a computer services company. In the first six months at his new job he began to realize that, compared to the organizational world he had known years earlier as CEO of the computer services giant EDS, everything was different—not just the technology, the market, and the customers, but also the people who worked for him and their reasons for working.

He realized that he too must change. As he wrote about it in a surprisingly revealing and introspective article, "Everything I thought I knew about leadership was wrong. My first job as a leader was to create a new understanding of myself."[16]

Meyerson went through what he describes as a time of "intense self-examination," wrestling with questions that went to the heart of the leadership style he had prided himself on. He came to see that during his years running EDS, he had been both extremely successful and extremely ruthless. To be sure, under his stewardship EDS saw profits climb every quarter without exception, making many employees with equity wealthy, but in looking back, Meyerson also saw that he had created immense personal misery for his employees even as he made them rich. At EDS eighty-hour work weeks were typical, people were shuffled from place to place without a second thought about the disruptions it might cause in their lives—and no questioning was tolerated. The employees' term for assignments there was "death march"; the cultural tone was, as Meyerson put it, "young, male, and military."

While at EDS, Meyerson headed a fifty-person team designing the federal system for processing Medicare claims, with everyone working eighteen-hour days in order to meet a deadline. One day, despite a heavy snow, every member of the team made it in to work except for one, Max Hopper. Meyerson, furious, called him up and bawled him out. Hopper left the company at the first opportunity—and went on to revolutionize the airline reservation industry with his invention of the SABRE computerized reservation system.

Recalling his alienation of Hopper, a brilliant, talented employee, Meyerson admitted he was too quick to make harsh judgments, too slow to see things from other people's perspectives. Reflecting on the human cost of his old style years later, Meyerson came to realize that what he had considered strengths were now more clearly identifiable as weaknesses. For example, at EDS his communications with employees were in the old hierarchical model: "I showed up onstage every six months and delivered a pep rally speech." His memos went only to the top dozen people; he had virtually no contact with the rest of his employees.

With the realization that a leader today needs to be receptive to honest, direct messages from anywhere and everywhere in a company, Meyerson changed his ways. He got an e-mail address that received thousands of messages a month—all of which he read—from all over the company. He even fired off a congratulatory e-mail to a team that made a competitive sale— and did so within an hour of their victory.

"Before you can lead others, before you can help others, you have to discover yourself," says Joe Jaworski, formerly with Royal Dutch/Shell's scenario planning group.[17] "If you want a creative explosion to take place, if you want the kind of performance that leads to truly exceptional results, you have to be willing to embark on a journey that leads to an alignment between an individual's personal values and aspirations and the values and aspirations of the company."

Blind Spots

Harry was a top manager at a company that had begun a major campaign to flatten the corporate hierarchy and give employees the authority to make critical decisions. Harry had all the right rhetoric about "sharing power" and delegating authority—he just couldn't do it when any hint of a crisis arose.

When things were going well, Harry was actually fairly good about handing down responsibility to his staff, who were extremely competent. But at the least whiff of an emergency, Harry grabbed the reins, rebuffing anyone else's advice or efforts. This not only undermined the company's initiative to push power down the line, but it damaged the self-confidence of Harry's staff. And his incessant talk about the virtues of sharing power while actually taking it back corroded his credibility.

"Unfortunately, Harry couldn't see the contradiction, even when a subordinate had the nerve to point it out to him," says Robert E. Kaplan, formerly of the Center for Creative Leadership.[18] "The first step in improving one's performance is to identify a need for improvement, but, as in Harry's case, such self-knowledge can be extremely difficult to come by."

Being blind to our problem areas can put our career at risk. In a comparison of executives who derailed and those who did well, *both* groups had weaknesses; the critical difference was that those who did not succeed failed to learn from their mistakes and shortcomings.[19] The unsuccessful executives were far less open to acknowledging their own faults, often rebuffing people who tried to point them out. This resistance meant they could do nothing to change them.

Among several hundred managers from twelve different organizations, accuracy in self-assessment was a hallmark of superior performance, something poorer performers lacked.[20] It's not that star performers have no limits on their abilities, but that they are *aware* of their limits—and so they know where they need to improve, or they know to work with someone else who has a strength they lack.

Our Strengths—and Our Weaknesses

He was promoted to the top tier of a large manufacturing company, bringing with him a reputation as a kick-ass turnaround artist because of the ruthless reengineering and job cutting he had conducted in the past. "He never smiled—there was a scowl on his face all the time," Kathryn Williams, an executive coach with KRW International, told me. "He was always impatient and quick to anger. When people brought bad news, he would attack the messenger, so people stopped telling him things. He had no idea he frightened people. His gruff, intimidating demeanor may have worked while he was the turnaround artist, but now it was undermining him."

Williams was called in to consult with the executive. She videotaped him in action and then replayed the tape for him, pointing out the effect his habitual forbidding facial expression had on people. It was a revelation: "When he realized how he was coming across, he got tears in his eyes," Williams remembers.

That was the beginning of positive change for the once-gruff executive. But that is not always the case: People in high positions too often view their need to change as a sign of failure or weakness. The competitive striving that got them to the top can also stop them from admitting shortcomings, if only out of fear of their competitors in organizational politics.

We all share this tendency toward denial, an emotionally comfortable strategy that protects us from the distress that acknowledging the harsh truth would bring. Defensiveness takes many forms: minimizing the facts, filtering out crucial information, rationalizations and "good excuses"—anything to rob the facts of their emotional truth.

And people around us may tend to collude with our denial. Among the more difficult kinds of information to get in organizational life is honest, constructive feedback about how we are doing, especially about our lapses. Coworkers, subordinates, and bosses have an easier time complaining to each other out of earshot of a person than having an honest and open talk with that person about what's wrong. There is a Faustian bargain in this collusion to act as though everything is fine when in fact it is not, for we buy the illusion of harmony and effectiveness at the cost of the truth that could open the way to genuine improvement.

Whenever someone consistently mishandles a given situation, that is a sure sign of a blind spot. In the lower reaches of an organization, such problems can more easily be dismissed as "quirks." But at higher levels these problems are magnified in consequence and visibility; the adverse effects matter not just to the person who has them, but to the group as a whole.

Here is a list of some of the more common—and costly—blind spots from a study of forty-two otherwise highly successful executives studied by Robert E. Kaplan.[21] Those studied ranged from department heads to CEOs, but similar problems can arise in any position.

- *Blind ambition:* Has to win or appear "right" at all costs; competes instead of cooperates; exaggerates his or her own value and contribution; is boastful and arrogant; sees people in black-and-white terms as allies or enemies

- *Unrealistic goals:* Sets overly ambitious, unattainable goals for the group or organization; is unrealistic about what it takes to get jobs done

- *Relentless striving:* Compulsively hardworking at the expense of all else in life; runs on empty; is vulnerable to burnout

- *Drives others:* Pushes other people too hard, burning them out; micromanages and takes over instead of delegating; comes across as abrasive or ruthless and insensitive to the emotional harm to others

- *Power hungry:* Seeks power for his or her own interests, rather than the organization's; pushes a personal agenda regardless of other perspectives; is exploitative

- *Insatiable need for recognition:* Addicted to glory; takes credit for others' efforts and puts blame on them for mistakes; sacrifices follow-through in pursuit of the next victory

- *Preoccupation with appearances:* Needs to look good at all costs; is overly concerned with public image; craves the material trappings of prestige

- *Need to seem perfect:* Enraged by or rejects criticism, even if realistic; blames others for his or her failures; cannot admit mistakes or personal weaknesses

Such blind spots can actually motivate people to avoid self-awareness, since by knowing themselves they would have to admit to failings they cannot bear to acknowledge. This need to deny makes such people resistant to any and all feedback—and can make them a nightmare to work with and for.

All workplace competencies are *learned habits*—if we are deficient in one or another, we can learn to do better. The arrogant and impatient person *can* learn to listen and take other views into account; the workaholic *can* slow down and find more balance in life. But those improvements will never happen without the first step, which is to become aware of how these habits damage us and poison our relationships. With no glimmer of what these behaviors do to us and others, we have no motive to change them. As the head of executive development at a Fortune 500 company told me, "The biggest problem around here is the lack of self-awareness."

Among 184 midlevel managers in a leadership program at the Center for Creative Leadership, there were telling discrepancies between how managers rated themselves on abilities like listening and adaptability and how their peers rated them. In general, when there are such discrepancies, how our peers see us is the more accurate predictor of our actual job performance.[22] For the most part such discrepancies averaged out, with managers rating themselves more leniently than peers on some competencies, more harshly on others.

But some managers had only a rosy view of themselves—if they rated themselves significantly better on abilities such as being considerate and flexible, they would also see themselves as trustworthy and credible. At the extreme, this is the self-view of the narcissist, who admits no flaws, exaggerates his own abilities, and dodges feedback, not wanting to hear about any of his own deficiencies.

Roads to Improvement

A college professor tells about a small, inventive step he took to help himself become a more effective communicator.[23] One day a student was brave enough to tell him about what amounted to a verbal tic that distracted and confused his listeners: He ended sentences with the words "on it," much as some people pointlessly insert "you know" into sentences.

The professor was shocked when he started monitoring his own lectures—"on it" came up time and again without his having intended it or even realizing he was speaking the words. He had been utterly oblivious to this disquieting habit. But now, determined to change, he took a bold step, asking his students to raise their hands whenever they heard the words. And, he says, "With three hundred hands making me fully conscious of this habit, I changed in no time."

Superior performers intentionally seek out feedback; they *want* to hear how others perceive them, realizing that this is valuable information. That may be part of the reason people who are self-aware are also better performers.[24] Presumably their self-awareness helps them in a process of continuous improvement.

And self-awareness in itself is an invaluable tool for change, especially if the need to change is in line with the person's goals, sense of mission, or basic values—including the belief that self-improvement is good.

Knowing their strengths and weaknesses, and approaching their work accordingly, was a competence found in virtually every star performer in a study of several hundred "knowledge workers"—computer scientists, auditors, and the like—at companies including AT&T and 3M. Says Robert Kelley of Carnegie-Mellon University, who did the study with Janet Caplan, "Stars know themselves well."[25]

▪ SELF-CONFIDENCE ▪

A Strong Sense of One's Self-Worth and Capabilities

▪▪

People with this competence

▪ Present themselves with self-assurance; have "presence"

▪ Can voice views that are unpopular and go out on a limb for what is right

▪ Are decisive, able to make sound decisions despite uncertainties and pressures

▪▪

While he would never say so, his job performance was a profile in courage.

Brought in to head a privately owned airline in a small Latin American country, he found the business a quagmire. The falling revenues were due to a legacy of cronyism and favoritism: The main sales agent for the airline was a close friend of the owner, and his contract was far more favorable than his competitors', though his agency was weak in sales. The excessively generous contract for the pilots, who were part of one of the most politically powerful unions in the country, was a major cash drain for the company. Their pay was far above the industry standard.

What's more, two of the company's planes had crashed on the way to a resort, and the bad publicity cut their market share from 50 percent to 20 percent within days.

People cautioned the new head of the airline not to take on the union; people who did such things sometimes found their families threatened or their own lives in danger. But he waded in. He told the pilots that the company would go bankrupt and be out of business if they didn't renegotiate their contract. The pilots listened and upped the hours they worked without demanding more pay.

Then he went to the owner of the airline, bluntly detailing how the owner's close friend, the head of the ticket agency, was incompetent and didn't produce the revenue he should. "Get rid of that agency or I'm leaving," he said. The owner listened too, and canceled his crony's contract.

As a friend who knew this courageous executive put it, "He was willing to confront even when his own job or safety was at stake."

Such self-confidence is the sine qua non of superior performance—without it, people lack the conviction that is essential for taking on tough challenges. Self-confidence gives us the requisite self-assurance for plunging ahead or stepping in as a leader.

For those who lack self-confidence, every failure confirms a sense of incompetence. The absence of self-confidence can manifest itself in feelings of helplessness, powerlessness, and crippling self-doubt. Extreme self-confidence, on the other hand, can look like arrogance, especially if the person lacks social skills. And self-confidence is not to be confused with brashness; to have a positive impact, self-confidence must be aligned with reality. For this reason a lack of self-awareness is an obstacle to realistic self-confidence.

Self-confidence can reveal itself in a strong self-presentation, a projection of "presence." Highly self-confident people can seem to exude charisma, inspiring confidence in those around them. Indeed, among supervisors, managers, and executives, higher levels of self-confidence set apart the best performers from average ones.[26]

People with self-confidence typically see themselves as efficacious, able to take on challenges and to master new jobs or skills. They believe themselves to be catalysts, movers, and initiators, and feel that their abilities stack up favorably in comparison to others'. From such a position of inner strength, they are better able to justify their decisions or actions, staying unfazed by opposition. One trait of outstanding auditors, for example, is not being intimidated or easily pressured.

Self-confidence gives the strength to make a tough decision or follow a course of action one believes in despite opposition, disagreement, or even explicit disapproval from those in authority. People with self-confidence are decisive without being arrogant or defensive, and they stand by their decisions. As Lee Iacocca, who rebuilt Chrysler into a world-class auto company, put it, "If I had to sum up in one word the qualities that make a good manager, I'd say that it all comes down to decisiveness. . . . In the end you have to bring all your information together, set up a timetable, and act."[27]

Having Talent—and Believing It

When I was around nine or ten, I decided I wanted to earn money during the summer by mowing lawns. I lined up a mower, got my parents to agree to pay for the gas, and even had flyers printed. But when it came time for me to go door-to-door to solicit business, I lacked the confidence to approach even one house."

That poignant memory comes from a student as an explanation for why, having returned to an executive MBA program after a few years as a manager, he is determined to increase his self-confidence.[28] Even now, as an adult, he finds that "one of the most difficult things for me to do is to approach someone, on the phone or in person, to discuss opportunities in which I am interested—I lack the self-confidence."

This story ends happily: Over the course of several months of systematic efforts to be more assertive, he grew in self-confidence. While some people seem born with a natural self-assurance, even those who are shy and timid can become more bold with practice.[29]

Closely related to self-confidence is what psychologists call "self-efficacy," the positive judgment of one's own capacity to perform. Self-efficacy is not the same as the actual skills we have, but rather our *belief* about what we can do with the skills we have. Skill alone is not enough to guarantee our best performance—we have to *believe* in our skills in order to use them at their best.

Albert Bandura, the Stanford University psychologist who pioneered the study of self-efficacy, points out the contrast between those who doubt themselves and those who believe in their abilities when it comes to taking on a difficult task.[30] Those with self-efficacy gladly step up to the challenge; those with self-doubt don't even try, regardless of how well they might actually do. Self-confidence raises aspirations, while self-doubt lowers them.

Among 112 entry-level accountants studied, it was those with the highest sense of self-efficacy who ten months later were rated by their supervisors as having the best job performance. Their level of self-efficacy was a stronger predictor of job performance than the actual level of skill or training they had received before being hired.[31]

There is a tight link between self-knowledge and self-confidence. We each have an inner map of our proclivities, abilities, and deficiencies. For example, one young man who viewed himself as skilled at personal public relations, able to carry off a job interview or sales call with style, felt shy in his personal life, whether at a party or on a date.[32] Our sense of self-efficacy, then, is domain-specific: How well we think we can do on the job does not necessarily match how well we believe we might do in a parallel activity elsewhere in life.

Workers who believe in their abilities do better in part because that belief motivates them to work harder and longer and to persist through difficulties. We typically avoid situations or fields in which we fear we might fail; even if we actually have the abilities it takes to succeed at a job, if we lack the belief that we can handle its challenges, we can start to act in ways that doom us. The thought "I can't do this" is crippling.

One of the more common traits found in workers who lack self-confidence is the paralyzing fear of seeming inept. Another is too easily giving up on their own opinions and judgments—even their good ideas—when challenged. Others include chronic indecisiveness, especially under pressure; shying away from even the smallest risk; and failing to voice valuable ideas.

In a decades-long study of managers at AT&T, self-confidence early in a person's career predicted promotions and success in higher management years later.[33] And in a sixty-year study of more than a thousand high-IQ men and women followed from childhood through retirement, those most self-confident in their early years were most successful as their careers unfolded.[34]

The Courage to Speak Out

It was out-of-control blood pressure—a result of neglecting to take his hypertension medication—that had led the elderly man to suffer a massive stroke. Now he was in intensive care in a hospital that specialized in brain injury, and the next few days would tell whether he would live or die. Frantic treatments focused on assessing the amount of brain damage and trying to control any further bleeding.

His visitor, a close friend who was a registered nurse working in the same hospital, happened to see the man's medical chart and noticed that of the many medications he was being given, none was for controlling blood pressure. Concerned, she asked the neurology resident poring over the results of a brain scan at her friend's bedside, "Is he taking his blood pressure medication?"

Irritated at the interruption, the brain specialist snapped, "We only treat them from the neck up here," and stalked out of the room.

Now alarmed that a medication crucial for her friend's recovery seemed to have been overlooked, the nurse marched into the office of the hospital's chief of medicine. She waited for him to finish a phone call, apologized for the interruption, and explained her concern. The order to resume the patient's blood pressure medication came immediately.

"I knew I was going outside proper channels by going to the chief of medicine," the nurse explained to me. "But I'd seen stroke patients die because their blood pressure wasn't properly controlled. It was too urgent to let protocol get in the way."

The attitude that the rules and standard procedures can be bent, and the courage to do so, are hallmarks of self-confidence. Indeed, in a study of 209 nurses at a large university hospital, those who had the strongest sense of self-efficacy were most likely to speak out when confronting inadequate or medically risky situations.[35] Nurses high in self-confidence would confront the physicians directly or, if that failed to correct things, go to their superior.

Such a confrontation or protest is an act of courage, especially given the low status of nurses in the hospital hierarchy. The self-confident nurses believed that if they dissented, their opinions would carry weight in changing the problem for the better. The nurses who lacked self-confidence had another inclination: Rather than protest or make efforts to right the wrong, they said they would quit.

Nursing may be a special case, because nurses as a rule are highly employable. In occupations where the job market is tighter—teaching, social work, or middle management, for instance—it may take a particularly high level of self-confidence to see a similar degree of courageous, open dissent. But no matter the kind of job or organization, it is those with the greatest self-confidence who will be most willing to take the risk of speaking up and pointing out problems or injustices that others only grumble about—or quit over.

5

....

Self-Control

Banish fear.
—W. Edwards Deming

t's every public speaker's worst nightmare. My friend, a psychologist,
had flown from the East Coast to Hawaii to address a convention of police chiefs. Delayed planes and missed connections made him lose a
night's sleep, leaving him both exhausted and jet-lagged, and his speech was
first thing the next morning. My friend had been apprehensive about the talk
to begin with, since he was taking a controversial stand. Now exhaustion
was rapidly converting that apprehension to outright panic.

My friend began by telling a joke—but stopped just before the punch
line. He had forgotten it. He froze, his mind a blank. Not only couldn't he
remember the punch line, he couldn't remember his speech. His notes suddenly made no sense, and his attention fixed on the sea of faces, riveted on
him. He had to apologize, excuse himself, and leave the podium.

Only after several hours' rest was he able to compose himself and give
his lecture—including the complete joke—to great applause. Telling me
later about his initial bout of panic, he said, "All I could think of was all
those faces staring at me—but I couldn't for the life of me remember what
I was supposed to say."

The single most striking finding from brain studies of people under
stress—like giving a talk in front of a critical audience—shows the emotional brain at work in ways that undermine the workings of the brain's executive center, the prefrontal lobes, located just behind the forehead.

The prefrontal area is the site of "working memory," the capacity to pay attention and keep in mind whatever information is salient. Working memory is vital for comprehension and understanding, planning and decision making, reasoning and learning.

When the mind is calm, working memory functions at its best. But when there is an emergency, the brain shifts into a self-protective mode, stealing resources from working memory and shunting them to other brain sites in order to keep the senses hyperalert—a mental stance tailored to survival.

During the emergency, the brain falls back on simple, highly familiar routines and responses and puts aside complex thought, creative insight, and long-term planning. The focus is the urgent present—or the crisis of the day. For my friend, this emergency mode paralyzed his ability to recall his speech, while focusing his attention on the "threat" at hand—all those rapt faces in the audience waiting for him to speak.

While the circuitry for emergencies evolved millions of years ago, we experience its operation today in the form of troubling emotions: worries, surges of anxiety, panic, frustration and irritation, anger, rage.

The Three-Million-Dollar Amygdala Hijack

When Mike Tyson became enraged and bit off a chunk of Evander Holyfield's ear during their 1997 heavyweight boxing title match, it cost him $3 million—the maximum penalty that could be taken from his $30 million purse—and a year's suspension from boxing.

Tyson was, in a sense, a victim of the brain's alarm center. Located in the ancient emotional brain, the alarm circuitry centers on a series of structures that ring the brain stem, which are known as the limbic system. The structure that plays the key role in emotional emergencies—that makes us "snap"—is the amygdala.

The prefrontal area, the executive center, links to the amygdala through what amounts to a neural superhighway. These neural links between amygdala and prefrontal lobes act as the brain's alarm, a setup that has had immense survival value during the millions of years of human evolution.

The amygdala is the brain's emotional memory bank, repository for all our moments of triumph and failure, hope and fear, indignation and frustration. It uses these stored memories in its role as a sentinel, scanning all incoming information—everything we see and hear from moment to moment—to assess it for threats and opportunities by matching what's happening now to the stored templates of our past experiences.[1]

For Tyson, a head-butting by Holyfield flooded him with angry memories of Holyfield's doing the same eight months earlier, in a match that Tyson also lost—and about which he had complained vociferously. The upshot for Tyson was a classic amygdala hijack, an instantaneous reaction with disastrous consequences.

In evolution, the amygdala most likely used its memory templates to answer questions crucial for survival, such as "Am I its prey, or is it mine?" The answers to such questions required astute senses to take in the situation, and formulate an instantaneous, ready response. Not helpful: Pausing to reflect deeply or mull things over.

The brain's crisis response still follows that ancient strategy—it heightens sensory acuity, stops complex thought, and triggers the knee-jerk, automatic response—though this can have dramatic drawbacks in modern work life.

When Emotions Boil Over

I can't help but overhear the conversation of the woman on the phone next to me at O'Hare Airport—she's yelling. It's clear she's in the middle of a messy divorce, and that her ex is being difficult. "He's being a bastard about the house!" she shouts into the phone. "My lawyer beeped me out of a meeting to tell me we have to go back to court now. And I have to give a presentation this afternoon. . . . This is the worst possible time for this bullshit!" She slams down the receiver, gathers her bags, and stalks off.

It's always "the worst possible time" for the hassles and pressures that put us over the edge—or so it seems. When stresses pile one on top of the other, they are more than additive—they seem to *multiply* the sense of stress, so that as we near a breaking point, each additional burden seems all the more unbearable, the last straw. This is so even for small hassles that ordinarily wouldn't faze us but suddenly can seem overwhelming. As poet Charles Bukowski put it, "It's not the big things that send us to the madhouse, not the loss of a love, but the shoelace that breaks when there's no time left."

To the body, there is no division between home and work; stress builds on stress, no matter the source. The reason a small hassle can drive us over the brink if we are already overwrought is biochemical. When the amygdala hits the brain's panic button, it induces a cascade that begins with the release of a hormone known as CRF and ends with a flood of stress hormones, mainly cortisol.[2]

The hormones we secrete under stress are enough for a single bout of fight or flight—but once secreted, they stay in the body for hours, and each successive upsetting incident adds more stress hormones to the levels already there. The resulting buildup can make the amygdala a hair trigger, ready to hijack us into anger or panic at the least provocation.

One impact of stress hormones is on blood flow. As the heart rate shoots up, blood is shunted away from the brain's higher cognitive centers to other sites more essential for emergency mobilization. Levels of blood sugar available for fuel jump, less relevant body functions slow down, and heart rate climbs to prepare the body to fight or run. The overall impact of cortisol on brain function is to enforce that primitive strategy for survival: heightening the senses, dulling the mind, and doing what's most well rehearsed, even if that habit is yelling or freezing in panic.

Cortisol steals energy resources from working memory—from the intellect—and shunts them to the senses. When cortisol levels are high, people make more errors, are more distracted, and can't remember as well—even something they've just recently read.[3] Irrelevant thoughts intrude, and processing information becomes more difficult.

If stress is sustained, the likely end state is burnout or worse. When lab rats are put under constant strain, cortisol and related stress hormones reach toxic levels, actually poisoning and killing neurons. If the stress continues for a significant part of their lifespan, the effect on their brain is dramatic: an erosion and shrinkage of the hippocampus, a key center for memory.[4] Something similar goes on with people.[5] It's not just that acute stress can make us momentarily inept; sustained stress can have a lasting, dulling effect on intellect.

Of course stress is a given; it's often impossible to avoid the situations or people that swamp us. Take the message explosion. A study of workers at major corporations found that each received and sent an average of 178 messages a day; they were interrupted by a message three times or more an hour, each one with its (usually false) air of urgency.[6]

E-mail, instead of reducing information overload, has added to the total amount of messages coming by phone, voice mail, fax, letter, and so on. Being flooded with intermittent messages puts people in a reactive mode, as though they are continually putting out small brush fires. The biggest impact is on concentration: Each message serves as a distraction, making it all the harder to return with full focus to the interrupted task at hand. The cumulative effect of the message deluge is chronic distractedness.

Indeed, a study of daily productivity in jobs like engineering found that one major cause of low performance was frequent distractions. One outstanding engineer, though, found a strategy that let him stay focused: He wore headphones while working away at his keyboard.[7] Everyone thought he was listening to music, but he was actually listening to nothing—the headphones were just to keep the phone and coworkers from breaking his concentration! Such strategies may work to some extent, but we also need the inner resources to handle the feelings that stress triggers within us.

The Just-Say-No Neurons

The prefrontal lobes ordinarily keep the amygdala's urges in check, bringing to this raw impulse judgment, an understanding of the rules of life, and a sense of what response is most skillful and appropriate.[8] These "just-say-no" circuits reassure the frantic amygdala that we are not, in fact, in danger, and that a less desperate mode of response will do.

The basic design of the brain is built around a simple opposition: Some neurons initiate action, others inhibit that same action. From the finely tuned orchestration of these counterposed tendencies comes smooth execution, whether it be the delivery of a persuasive pitch or the precise incision made by a skilled surgeon. When people are too impulsive, the trouble seems to be in the operation of the prefrontal inhibitory circuitry for impulse rather than in the amygdala—such individuals are not overly eager to act so much as unable to stop once they've started.[9]

Because the amygdala is the brain's alarm, it has the power to override the prefrontal lobes within a split second to meet the emergency it proclaims. The prefrontal lobes, on the other hand, cannot quickly and directly override the amygdala. Instead, the prefrontal lobes have an array of "inhibitory" neurons capable of stopping the directives the amygdala so frantically sends—much like punching in the secret code that shuts down a home security system's false alarm.

Richard Davidson, the director of the Laboratory for Affective Neuroscience at the University of Wisconsin, conducted a landmark series of brain imaging studies that tested two groups of people: one identified as highly resilient to life's ups and downs, the other easily upset by them. Davidson tracked their brain function as they performed stressful tasks, such as writing about the most upsetting experience in their lives or performing difficult math problems under time pressure.

The resilient people had a remarkably rapid recovery from stress, with their prefrontal areas starting to calm the amygdala—and them—within seconds. The more vulnerable people, by contrast, saw a continued escalation of their amygdala's activity, and their distress, for several minutes after the stressful activity ended.

"The resilient people had already started to inhibit the distress during the stressful encounter," Davidson says. "These are optimistic, action-oriented people. If something goes wrong in their lives, they immediately start to think about how to make it better."

This inhibitory circuit between prefrontal lobes and amygdala underlies many of the self-regulation competencies, especially self-control under stress and the ability to adapt to change, both of which allow calm in the face of those existential facts of work life: crisis, uncertainty, and shifting challenges. The prefrontal lobes' ability to inhibit the amygdala's message preserves mental clarity and keeps our actions on a steady course.[10]

To go from the laboratory to reality, consider the cost to a business when a manager, the chief decision maker and people handler, does poorly at this most basic emotional skill. A study of store managers at a large American retail chain found that the managers who were most tense, beleaguered, or overwhelmed by job pressures ran stores with the worst performance, as measured four ways: by net profits, sales per square foot, sales per employee, and per dollar of inventory investment. And those who stayed most composed under the same pressures had the best per-store sales records.[11]

The Marshmallow Kids Grow Up and Go to Work

Six friends, all in college, were drinking and playing cards late into the night when an argument broke out. Mack and Ted's disagreement got louder and angrier until Mack flew into a rage, yelling and screaming—at which point Ted became noticeably cool and reserved. But Mack's temper was now out of control; he stood up and challenged Ted to a fight. Ted responded to Mack's goading very calmly, saying he'd consider fighting Mack, but only if they finished playing the card game.

Mack, though boiling with rage, agreed. During the several minutes it took to play out the game, everyone else took Ted's lead and finished the game as though nothing much had happened. This gave Mack time to settle down and collect his thoughts. At the end of the hand Ted calmly told Mack, "Now if you would like to discuss this further, I'll step outside." But Mack, who by now had had time to quiet down and think things over, apologized for his temper, and there was no fight.

They met again twenty years later, at their school reunion. Ted had a successful career in commercial real estate, while Mack was out of work and struggling with drugs and alcohol.[12]

The contrast between Mack and Ted is telling testimony of the benefits of being able to say no to impulse. The key circuitry here is an array of inhibitory neurons in the prefrontal lobes that can veto the impulsive messages that come from the emotional centers, primarily the amygdala, in moments of rage and temptation. For Ted, that circuit apparently operated well; for Mack, it too often failed.

The tale of Mack and Ted parallels neatly the life trajectory of two groups of children I wrote about in *Emotional Intelligence* who were part of an experiment at Stanford University known as the "marshmallow test." Briefly, four-year-olds in the Stanford preschool were brought into a room one by one, a marshmallow was put on the table in front of them, and they were told, "You can have this marshmallow now if you want, but if you don't eat it until after I run an errand, you can have two when I return."

Some fourteen years later, as they were graduating from high school, the children who ate the marshmallow right away were compared with those who waited and got two.[13] Those who grabbed, compared to those who waited, were more likely to fall apart under stress, tended to become irritated and pick fights more often, and were less able to resist temptation in pursuit of their goals.

Most surprising to the researchers, though, was a completely unanticipated effect: Those children who had waited for the marshmallow, compared to those who hadn't, had scores averaging a remarkable 210 points higher (out of a possible 1,600) on the SAT, the college entrance exam.[14]

My best guess as to why impulsivity should diminish learning ability harks back to the link between amygdala and prefrontal lobes. As the source of emotional impulse, the amygdala is the font of distraction. The prefrontal lobes are the site of working memory, the capacity to pay attention to what is on our mind at the moment.

To the extent we are preoccupied by emotionally driven thoughts, we have that much less attentional space left in working memory. For a schoolchild, this means less attention to pay to the teacher, to a book, to homework. If this persists over years and years, the result is the deficiency in learning that was revealed by the lower SAT scores. The same is true for someone at work—the cost of impulsivity and distractedness is a hampered ability to learn or adapt.

As the children in the Stanford study grew into adulthood and joined the workforce the differences became even more pronounced.[15] In their late twenties, those who had resisted the marshmallow in childhood were still more intellectually skilled, more attentive, and better able to concentrate. They were better able to develop genuine and close relationships, were more dependable and responsible, and showed better self-control in the face of frustration.

By contrast, those who grabbed the marshmallow at four were now, in their late twenties, less cognitively adept and strikingly less emotionally competent than those who had restrained themselves. They were more often loners; they were less dependable, more easily distracted, and unable to delay gratification in pursuing their goals. When stressed, they had little tolerance or self-control. They responded to pressure with little flexibility, instead repeating the same futile and overblown response time and again.

The story of the marshmallow kids holds larger lessons about the costs of out-of-control emotions. When we are under the sway of impulse, agitation, and emotionality, our ability to think—and work—suffers.

The Managed Heart

Emotional self-regulation includes not just damping down distress or stifling impulse; it can also mean intentionally eliciting an emotion, even an unpleasant one. Some bill collectors, I'm told, prime themselves for calls on people by getting themselves worked up into an irritable, ill-tempered state. Physicians who have to give bad news to patients or their families put themselves in a suitably somber, dour mood, as do morticians meeting with bereaved families. In retail and service industries, exhortations to be friendly to customers are virtually universal.

One school of thought argues that when workers are ordered to display a given emotion, they have to perform an onerous "emotional labor" in order to keep their job.[16] When the dictates of the boss determine the emotions a person must express, the result is an estrangement from one's own feelings. Retail clerks, flight attendants, and hotel staff are among the workers prone to such attempted management of the heart, which Arlie Hochschild, a sociologist at the University of California, Berkeley, calls a "commercialization of human feelings" that amounts to a form of emotional tyranny.

A closer look reveals this perspective to be only half the story. Critical in determining whether emotional labor is onerous or not is how much the person identifies with the job.[17] For a nurse who sees herself as a caring, compassionate person, taking a few moments to console a patient in distress represents not a burden but what makes her job more meaningful.

The notion of emotional self-control does not mean denying or repressing true feelings. "Bad" moods, for instance, have their uses; anger, sadness, and fear can become sources of creativity, energy, and connectedness. Anger can be an intense source of motivation, particularly when it stems from the urge to right an injustice or inequity. Shared sadness can knit people together. And the urgency born of anxiety—if not overwhelming—can prod the creative spirit.

Emotional self-control is not the same as *over*control, the stifling of all feeling and spontaneity. In fact, there is a physical and mental cost to such overcontrol. People who stifle their feelings, especially strong negative ones, raise their heart rate, a sign of increased tension. When such emotional suppression is chronic, it can impair thinking, hamper intellectual performance, and interfere with smooth social interactions.[18]

By contrast, emotional competence implies we have a choice as to *how* we express our feelings. Such emotional finesse becomes particularly important in a global economy, since the ground rules for emotional expression vary greatly from culture to culture. What is appropriate in one country may appear an unseemly outburst in another. For example, executives from emotionally reserved cultures, like those in northern Europe, can be seen as "cold" and aloof by Latin American business partners.

In the United States, being emotionally unexpressive often communicates a negative message, a sense of distance or indifference. One study of nearly two thousand supervisors, managers, and executives in American companies showed a strong link between lack of spontaneity and poor performance.[19] While superior managers were more spontaneous than their mediocre peers, executives as a group were more controlled in expressing their personal feelings than managers at lower levels; the executives apparently gave more consideration to the impact of expressing the "wrong" feeling in a given situation.

That measured approach in the top tiers speaks to the sense in which the workplace is a special case when it comes to emotions, almost a "culture" apart from the rest of life. Within the intimate zone of friends and family, we can bring up and mull over whatever weighs on our heart—and should. At work, a different set of emotional ground rules more often prevails.

■　■　■

Self-regulation—managing impulse as well as distressing feelings—depends on the working of the emotional centers in tandem with the brain's executive centers in the prefrontal areas. These two primal skills—handling impulse and dealing with upsets—are at the core of five emotional competencies:

- *Self-control:* Managing disruptive emotions and impulses effectively

- *Trustworthiness:* Displaying honesty and integrity

- *Conscientiousness:* Dependability and responsibility in fulfilling obligations

- *Adaptability:* Flexibility in handling change and challenges

- *Innovation:* Being open to novel ideas, approaches, and new information

■ SELF-CONTROL ■

Keeping Disruptive Emotions and Impulses in Check

People with this competence

- Manage their impulsive feelings and distressing emotions well

- Stay composed, positive, and unflappable even in trying moments

- Think clearly and stay focused under pressure

"Bill Gates is pissed. His eyes are bulging and his oversized glasses are askew. His face is flushed and spit is flying from his mouth. . . . He's in a small, crowded conference room at the Microsoft campus with 20 young Microsofties gathered around an oblong table. Most look at their chairman with outright fear, if they look at him at all.

"The sour smell of sweaty terror fills the room."

So begins the narrative of a demonstration of the high art of handling emotions.[20] While Gates continues his angry tirade, the hapless programmers fumble and stutter, trying to persuade or at least placate him. All to no avail. No one seems to be able to get through—except a small, soft-spoken Chinese-American woman, who seems to be the only person in the room who is unfazed by his tantrum. She looks him in the eye while everyone else avoids eye contact.

Twice she interrupts his tirade to address him in quiet tones. The first time, her words seem to calm him a bit before his shouting resumes. The second time, he listens in silence, thoughtfully gazing down at the table. Then his anger suddenly vanishes and he tells her, "Okay—this looks good. Go ahead." With that he ends the meeting.

What the woman said was not much different from what the others had been saying. But her unflappability may well have allowed her to say it better, to think clearly rather than being swamped by anxiety. Her manner was certainly part of her message, sending the signal that the tirade did not intimidate her, that she could take it without becoming unhinged, that there was no real reason to be so agitated.

This skill is, in a sense, largely invisible—self-control manifests largely in the *absence* of more obvious emotional fireworks. Signs include being unfazed under stress or handling a hostile person without lashing out in return. Another mundane example is time management: Keeping ourselves on a daily schedule demands self-control, if only to resist seemingly urgent but actually trivial demands, or the lure of time-wasting pleasures or distractions.

The ultimate act of personal responsibility at work may be in taking control of our own state of mind. Moods exert a powerful pull on thought, memory, and perception. When we are angry, we more readily remember incidents that support our ire, our thoughts become preoccupied with the object of our anger, and irritability so skews our worldview that an otherwise benign comment might now strike us as hostile. Resisting this despotic quality of moods is essential to our ability to work productively.

When Work Is Hell

...ny years ago I had a newly promoted boss who struck me as vastly
... ambitious. His strategy for looking good in his new post was to hire
fresh writers—"his people"—and make sure their work got prominent display in the publication. He would spend a great deal of time with the new
folks, while studiously ignoring us old hands.

Perhaps my boss was under pressure from *his* boss—I never knew his
motivation. But one day, to my surprise, he asked me to have a cup of coffee with him in the company cafeteria. There, after a few words of perfunctory small talk, he abruptly informed me that my work was not up to
standards. Exactly how I didn't meet standards was vague—under a former
boss my work had been nominated for major awards. But the consequence
was clear: If I didn't improve, he would fire me.

Needless to say, that caused me tremendous, relentless anxiety. Over my
head in debt and with children heading for college, I desperately needed that
job. Worse, writing itself demands high levels of concentration, and those
worries kept intruding, distracting me with vivid fantasies of career and financial catastrophe.

What saved my sanity was a relaxation technique I had learned years before, a simple meditation practice that I had done on and off for years.
Though I had been lackadaisical in using it, now I became fanatical, allowing myself a half hour or even a full hour of calming centeredness every
morning before I started my day.

It worked; I kept myself together and sane, doing my best to turn out
workmanlike articles on demand. And then came relief: My unbearable boss
got his promotion—to another department.

People best able to handle distress often have a stress management technique they call on when needed, whether it's a long bath, a workout, or a
yoga session—as I did with meditation. Having such a relaxation method in
our repertoire does not mean that we won't feel upset and distressed from
time to time. But regular, daily practice of a relaxation method seems to reset the trigger point for the amygdala, making it less easily provoked.[21] This
neural resetting gives us the ability to recover more quickly from amygdala
hijacks while making us less prone to them in the first place. The net result
is that we are susceptible to distress less often, and our bouts are shorter.

A Sense of Helplessness

The feeling of helplessness about work pressures is in itself per~
Among small-business owners and employees, those with a stro~
sense that they control what happens to them in life are less likely to becom~
angry, depressed, or agitated when faced with conflicts and strains on the
job. But those who feel little control are more prone to getting upset or even
quitting.[22]

In a study of 7,400 men and women in London civil service jobs, those
who felt they had to meet deadlines imposed by someone else and had little
say in how they did their work or with whom they did it had a 50 percent
higher risk of developing symptoms of coronary heart disease than those
with more job flexibility.[23] Feeling little control over the demands and pressures of the work we have to do holds as great a risk of heart disease as risk
factors like hypertension.[24] That is why, of all the relationships we have at
work, the one with our boss or supervisor has the greatest impact on our
emotional and physical health. When volunteers at a British colds research
unit were exposed to a cold virus and followed for five days to see who
would get sick, it turned out that those entangled in social tensions were the
most susceptible.[25] An isolated tough day at the office was not a problem, but
having persistent trouble with a superior was stressful enough to lower immune resilience.

In the newly discovered anatomical links between brain and body that
connect our mental state with physical health, the emotional centers play the
critical role, with the richest web of connection to both the immune system
and the cardiovascular system. These biological ties explain why distressing
feelings—sadness, frustration, anger, tension, intense anxiety—double the
risk that someone with heart disease may experience a dangerous decrease
in blood flow to the heart within hours of having these feelings. Such de-
creases can sometimes trigger a heart attack.[26]

It is no news to working mothers that they bear a unique physiological
burden as ordinary work pressures are compounded by the mental strain of
being "on call" for unexpected family problems, like a sick child. Single and
married mothers alike who hold midlevel jobs where they have little control
have substantially higher levels of cortisol, the stress hormone, than do their
counterparts at work who do not have children at home.[27]

At low levels, cortisol can help the body fight a virus or heal damaged
tissues, but when too much cortisol flows, it diminishes the effectiveness of
the immune system.[28] As one researcher at the National Institute of Mental
Health put it, "If you're sitting there watching the stock market crash, your

cortisol from the psychological stress is going to be up. Then, if someone coughs in your face, you're going to be susceptible to getting the flu."[29]

How Self-Awareness Pays Off

A college professor with heart problems was given a portable heart rate monitor to wear, because when his heart rate exceeded 150 beats per minute, too little oxygen reached his heart muscle. One day the professor went to one of the regular, seemingly endless departmental meetings, which he felt were a waste of time.

But he learned from the monitor that, while he thought he was cynically detached from the discussions, his heart was pounding away at dangerous levels. He had not realized until then how emotionally upset he was by the daily tussle of departmental politics.[30] Self-awareness pays off as a key skill in handling stress. Without careful attention, we can—like the college professor—be surprisingly oblivious to just how stressful our work life really is.

Simply bringing simmering feelings into awareness can have salutary effects. When sixty-three laid-off managers participated in a study at Southern Methodist University, many were, understandably, angry and hostile. Half were told to keep a journal for five days, spending twenty minutes writing out their deepest feelings and reflections on what they were going through. Those who kept journals found new jobs faster than those who didn't.[31]

The more accurately we can monitor our emotional upsets, the sooner we can recover from distress. Consider an experiment in which people watch a graphic anti-drunk-driving film depicting bloody automobile accidents.[32] During the half hour after the film, viewers report feeling distressed and depressed, with their thoughts repeatedly going back to the troubling scenes they've just witnessed. The quickest to recover are those with the greatest clarity about their feelings. Emotional clarity, it seems, enables us to manage bad moods.

Unflappability, however, does not necessarily mean we have done the job. Even when people seem unflappable, if they are actually seething inside, they still need to handle their troubled feelings. Some cultures, particularly those in Asia, encourage this pattern of masking negative feelings. While this may keep relationships tranquil, it can have a cost to the individual. A psychologist teaching emotional intelligence abilities to flight attendants in Asia said, "Imploding is the problem there. They don't explode—they hold it in and suffer."

Emotional implosion has several drawbacks: Imploders often fail to take any action to better their situation. They may not show outward signs of an emotional hijack, but they suffer the internal fallout anyway: headaches, edginess, smoking and drinking too much, sleeplessness, endless self-criticism. And they have the same health risks as those who explode, and so need to learn to manage their own reactions to distress.

Self-Control in Action

It's a classic Manhattan street scene: A man stops his Lexus in a No Stopping zone on a busy street, hurries into a shop, makes a few purchases, and rushes out—only to find a traffic cop has not only written out a ticket, but also called a tow truck, to which his Lexus is now being hitched.

"Goddamn!" the man explodes in rage, screaming at the traffic cop. "You are the lowest form of human slime!" he yells, pounding the hood of the tow truck with his fist.

The cop, visibly ruffled, somehow manages a calm response: "It's the law. If you think it's wrong, you can appeal." And with that, he turns and walks away.

Self-control is crucial for those in law enforcement. When facing someone who is in the throes of an amygdala hijack, like the abusive motorist, the odds of the encounter ending in violence will escalate rapidly if the officer involved gets hijacked by his amygdala, too. Indeed, Officer Michael Wilson, who teaches at New York City's police academy, says these situations make many officers struggle to handle their visceral response to disrespect, an attitude they see not just as an idle threat, but as signaling a shift in power in the interaction, which could pose a danger to their life.[33] As Wilson puts it, "Initially, when someone gives you major grief, your body wants to react. But there is this little person inside your head saying, 'It's not worth it. I put my hands on this person, I lose.' "

The training of police (at least in the United States, which, sadly, has one of the highest levels of violence in the world) requires a careful titration of the use of force in amounts that correspond to the situation at hand. Threats, physical intimidation, and drawing a gun are last resorts, since each of these is itself likely to incite an amygdala hijack in the other person.

Competence studies in law enforcement organizations find outstanding officers use the least force necessary, approach volatile people calmly and with a professional demeanor, and are adept at de-escalation. A study of New York City traffic cops found that those who managed a calm response even when faced with angry motorists had the fewest incidents escalate into outright violence.[34]

The principle of remaining calm despite provocation applies to anyone who routinely faces obnoxious or agitated people on the job. Among counselors and psychotherapists, for example, superior performers respond calmly to a personal attack by a patient.[35] So do outstanding flight attendants faced with disgruntled passengers.[36] And among managers and executives, superior performers balance their drive, ambition, and assertiveness with self-control, harnessing their personal needs in the service of the organization's goals.[37]

Resilience—Thriving on Stress

Compare two executives at one of America's regional telephone companies, a company where stress has soared as the entire industry undergoes wrenching changes. One of the executives is plagued by tension: "My life seems like a rat race. I'm always trying to catch up, meet deadlines imposed on me, but most aren't even important. They're just routine. So even though I'm nervous and tense, I'm also bored a lot of the time."

The other executive says, "I'm almost never bored. Even when there's something I have to do that doesn't strike me as interesting at first, usually once I get into it, I find it worthwhile in a way that teaches me something. I'm always out there straining to make a difference, to shape a productive work life for myself."

The first executive was identified as low in—and the second high in—a quality called "hardiness," the ability to stay committed, feel in control, and be challenged rather than threatened by stress. The study found that those who react to stress with hardiness, seeing work as strenuous but exciting and change as a chance to develop rather than as an enemy, bear the physical burden of stress much better, coming through with less illness.[38]

A paradox of work life is that a situation can be seen by one person as a devastating threat but by another as an invigorating challenge. With the right emotional resources, what seems threatening can be taken instead as a challenge, and met with energy, even enthusiasm. There is a crucial difference in brain function between "good stress"—the challenges that mobilize and motivate us—and "bad stress," the threats that overwhelm, paralyze, or demoralize us.

The brain chemicals that generate enthusiasm for a challenge are different from those that respond to stress and threat. They are at work when our energy is high, our effort maximal, and our mood positive. The biochemistry of these productive states revolves around activating the sympathetic nervous system and the adrenals to secrete chemicals called catecholamines.

The catecholamines, adrenaline and noradrenaline, arouse us to action in a more productive way than the frantic urgency of cortisol. Once the brain goes into its emergency mode, it starts pumping out cortisol as well as vastly elevated levels of catecholamines, but we do our best work at a lower level of brain arousal, when only the catecholamine system is engaged. (And it doesn't take a threat to our job or a negative comment from the boss to activate cortisol; boredom, impatience, frustration, even tiredness will do it.)

In a sense, then, there are two kinds of stress—good and bad—and two distinct biological systems at work. There is also a balance point when the sympathetic nervous system is pumping (but not too much), our mood is positive, and our ability to think and react is optimal. Here lies our peak performance.

■ TRUSTWORTHINESS AND CONSCIENTIOUSNESS ■

Maintaining Integrity and Taking Responsibility for Personal Performance

People with this competence

For Trustworthiness

■ Act ethically and are above reproach

■ Build trust through their reliability and authenticity

■ Admit their own mistakes and confront unethical actions in others

■ Take tough, principled stands even if they are unpopular

For Conscientiousness

■ Meet commitments and keep promises

■ Hold themselves accountable for meeting their objectives

■ Are organized and careful in their work

■■■

The inventor of a promising new product, a two-chamber air mattress that had the competitive advantage of preserving body heat, tells of talking to a businessman who offered to manufacture and sell the mattresses, giving the inventor a royalty. The businessman, over the course of their conversation, revealed with some pride that he never paid any taxes.[39]

"How do you do it?" the inventor asked, incredulous.

"I keep two sets of books," the businessman replied smugly.

"So which set of books will you use to record the sales of my mattresses to compute the royalty you owe me?" the inventor asked.

To that question there was no reply. End of deal.

Credibility stems from integrity. Stars know that trustworthiness at work translates into letting people know one's values and principles, intentions and feelings, and acting in ways that are reliably consistent with them. They are forthright about their own mistakes, and confront others about their lapses.

Workers with integrity are frank, even acknowledging their feelings—"I was getting a little nervous about that"—which contributes to their aura of authenticity. By contrast, those who never admit a lapse or imperfection or who "hype" themselves, their company, or a product undermine their credibility.

Integrity—acting openly, honestly, and consistently—sets apart outstanding performers in jobs of every kind. Take those in sales roles that depend on the strength of ongoing relationships. In such a job, someone who hides crucial information, breaks promises, or fails to fulfill commitments undermines the trust so vital to repeat business.

"Of the general managers for sales who've worked for me and washed out, the single thing they lacked most was trustworthiness," a senior vice president at a division of Automatic Data Processors told me. "In sales, it's trade-offs—I'll give you this if you give me a concession on that. It's an ambiguous situation, where you have to take someone's word for it. A field like finance—that's more science than art, it's more clear-cut. But in sales it's grays, so being trustworthy is all the more important."

Douglas Lennick, executive vice president of American Express Financial Advisors, concurs: "Some people have the mistaken impression you can succeed in business by cheating people or pressuring them into buying something they don't need. That may work for you in the short term, but it will undermine you in the long run. You'll be far more successful if you stay in alignment with your personal values."

When Business Is Business

I met her on a plane, my seatmate for a few hours on a flight out West. We'd been chatting for a while when she found out I was writing about emotions at work. Then her story spilled out: "We do safety testing for the chemical industry, assessing their materials and how they handle them for risks like combustibility. We verify that their procedures for handling these substances meet federal safety standards. But my boss doesn't care if the report is accurate; he just wants it done on time. His motto is, Get the job done quick as you can and get the money.

"I recently found that the calculations for one job were wrong, so I redid them. But the boss gave me grief about it because it took more time than he wanted. I have to do what this guy tells me, even though I know he's incompetent. So I'm always redoing calculations at home, on my own time. Everyone's unhappy that the boss pushes us this way."

Why does she put up with it?

She tells me about a messy divorce, having to take care of her two children on her own, being stretched. "I'd leave if I could, but I need the work. Jobs are tight just now. . . ."

After a long, reflective silence, she continues. "He signs all the work, even what we do. At first it bothered me that he was taking all the credit, but now I'm relieved—I don't want my name on those reports. It doesn't feel right to me. There haven't been any accidents, like fires or explosions, but there might be someday."

Shouldn't she speak up, report what's going on?

"I've thought about saying something to someone, but I can't say anything because I signed a secrecy agreement when I was hired. I'd have to leave the company and then be able to prove in court what I said—that would be a nightmare."

As our plane taxis in for a landing, she seems at once relieved and nervous about what she's revealed—so anxious, she won't tell me her name or that of her company. Still, she takes my name and number, saying she has more to say. She'll call me.

She never does.

The Ethics Officers Association commissioned a survey of 1,300 workers at all levels in American companies, and what they found is startling: About half admitted to engaging in unethical business practices.[40]

For the most part, breaches of trust or codes of morality were relatively minor, such as calling in sick when they want time off, or taking home supplies from the company cabinet. But 9 percent admitted lying or deceiving a customer, 6 percent have falsified numbers in reports or documents, and 5 percent have lied to superiors on serious matters or withheld critical information. And 4 percent admitted to having taken credit for someone else's work or idea. Some of the breaches are extremely serious: 3 percent have engaged in a copyright or software infringement, and 2 percent have forged someone's name on a document. One percent have reported false information when filing government forms, such as tax returns.

By contrast, a study of outstanding accountants at one of America's largest firms discovered that one distinction was a competence called "courage": They were willing to stand up to their clients and against pressures at their own accounting firms, to risk losing an account, to insist people do what was right. And the best accountants had the courage to speak up against even massive resistance to be sure the rules were followed—a stance requiring immense integrity and self-confidence. (There was a good news/bad news edge to this finding: The good news was that their best accountants had this kind of courage; the bad news was that most of their accountants did not.)

Impulse Control: An Emotional Fault Line

■ A corporate comptroller was fired because he sexually harassed the women who worked for him. He was also intensely aggressive in dealing with people generally.

■ An executive at another company was by nature outgoing, talkative, friendly, and spontaneous—but also had little self-restraint. He was fired for leaking company secrets.

▪ The head of a small industrial company was charged with criminal behavior in managing his company's funds. He had selected a chief financial officer (an accomplice) who shared with him both a lack of conscience and little apprehension about the consequences of what they were doing.

These case studies of wrecked careers come from the files of a consulting company that assessed each of these executives in the course of testing 4,265 people, from company heads to blue-collar workers.[41] They all had a lack of impulse control, with little or no ability to delay gratification. With self-restraint, people can think through the potential consequences of what they are about to do and assume responsibility for their words and deeds.

The consulting firm that did the study of self-restraint in professions, recommends that, in general, "When selecting people for industrial jobs—at all levels—it is wise to reject candidates who are low or very low" in self-restraint, since "the odds of them creating problems of some kind are extremely high." (It does note, though, that people can be helped to handle their impulsivity better—poor impulse control need not be a sentence to a dead-end career.)

Even among football players, whose very role would seem to demand a certain level of spontaneous aggressiveness, restraint pays. In a study of more than seven hundred pros, NFL draft choices, and college players, those with higher levels of restraint were rated by their coaches as being more motivated, having better abilities as football players, being better leaders, and being easier to coach.[42] On the other hand, those with low levels of restraint were rated as showing little respect for teammates and coaches and were unwilling to listen or take direction. They were cavalier about their agreements or contracts, used insulting "trash talk" with opponents, and indulged in show-offish end-zone dancing. Take two football players with very low levels of restraint: One was found to be using drugs, and the other was a troublemaker who punched and knocked out a teammate during practice.

Quiet Virtue: The Conscientious

By contrast, the everyday signs of conscientiousness—being punctual, careful in doing work, self-disciplined, and scrupulous in attending to responsibilities—are hallmarks of the model organizational citizen, the people who keep things running as they should. They follow the rules, help out, and are concerned about the people they work with. It's the conscientious worker who helps orient newcomers or updates people who return after an absence, who gets to work on time and never abuses sick leaves, who always gets things done on deadline.

Conscientiousness is a taproot of success in any field. In studies of job performance, outstanding effectiveness for virtually all jobs, from semi-skilled labor to sales and management, depends on conscientiousness.[43] It is particularly important for outstanding performance in jobs at the lower levels of an organization: the mailroom clerk who never misplaces a package, the secretary whose message taking is impeccable, the delivery truck driver who is always on time.

Among sales representatives for a large American appliance manufacturer, those who were most conscientious had the largest volume of sales.[44] Conscientiousness also offers a buffer against the threat of job loss in today's ever-churning market, because employees with this trait are among the most valued. For the sales reps, their level of conscientiousness mattered almost as much as their sales in determining who stayed on.[45]

There is an aura of sorts around highly conscientious people that makes them seem even better than they actually are. Their reputation for reliability biases supervisors' ratings of their work, giving them higher evaluations than objective measures of their performance would predict.

But conscientiousness in the absence of empathy or social skills can lead to problems. Since conscientious people demand so much of themselves, they can hold other people to their own standards, and so be overly judgmental when others don't show the same lofty levels of exemplary behavior. Factory workers in Great Britain and the United States who were extremely conscientious, for example, tended to criticize coworkers even about mundane lapses that seemed trivial to those they criticized, which strained their relationships.[46]

When conscientiousness takes the form of a relentless conformity to expectations, it can put a damper on creativity. In creative callings like art or advertising, openness to wild ideas and spontaneity are at a premium. Success in such occupations calls for a balance, however; without enough conscientiousness to follow through, people become mere dreamers, with nothing to show for their imaginativeness.

▪ **INNOVATION AND ADAPTABILITY** ▪

Being Open to Novel Ideas and Approaches, and Being Flexible in Responding to Change

▪▪

People with this competence

For Innovation

▪ Seek out fresh ideas from a wide variety of sources

▪ Entertain original solutions to problems

▪ Generate new ideas

▪ Take fresh perspectives and risks in their thinking

For Adaptability

▪ Smoothly handle multiple demands, shifting priorities, and rapid change

▪ Adapt their responses and tactics to fit fluid circumstances

▪ Are flexible in how they see events

▪▪

It was a subtle signal. Sometime in the mid-1970s there was a shift in how Intel managers were treated by their peers in Japan. Where before they had been shown lavish respect, now they came back with the vague feeling that they were being viewed with a newfound derision. Something had changed.

That report from the front lines was a harbinger of the coming Japanese supremacy in the market for computer chips, at the time Intel's main business. The story is told by Andrew S. Grove, Intel's chairman, as an example of how hard it can be for executives to adapt to shifts in an industry.[47]

It took Intel's top management, Grove confesses, several more years to realize that Japanese companies had used their strength in precision manufacturing to beat Intel at its own game, making and selling memory chips.

Such moments, when changing circumstances turn a winning strategy sour, are crucial in the history of any company. These moments amount to what Grove calls a "valley of death": If a company is not nimble enough to rethink its strategy while it still has the assets and strength to change and adapt, it is doomed to wither or die.

In facing such make-or-break moments, the emotional capabilities executives bring to bear make a crucial difference. The ability to be flexible, to take in new, even painful, information without tuning out in self-protection, and to respond nimbly is essential.

Too often corporate inertia takes over instead, with top management failing to read the signs of the coming sea change—or fearing to act on the implications—even as the rules of the game are mutating.

At Intel the dominant assumption into the 1980s was that they were a "memory company," selling chips, even though by then their share of that market had shrunk to around 3 percent. Barely noticed was the sideline work that would become their new core business: microprocessors, or what we all now know as "Intel Inside."

The high-tech industry, perhaps the fastest-changing of all, is littered with the remains of companies whose management failed to adapt to market shifts. An engineer who had worked at Wang Laboratories during its heyday in the 1980s, when the company surged to $3 billion in sales—and was there to see the company fail—said, "I've seen what success does—it breeds arrogance. You stop listening to your customers and employees. You get complacent about your business, and finally get leapfrogged by competitors."

Change Is the Constant

Grove contends a company's ability to survive such a looming valley of death depends on one thing: "How the top management reacts emotionally." When their very status and well-being—and that of their company—face a great threat, when their most cherished assumptions about their mission and their business are being undermined, what emotions take over?

At Intel adaptability was crucial in facing two major crises: the loss of the memory chip market and, more recently, the disaster when a flaw in the company's then-new Pentium processor made millions of computer owners lose faith in the product. While the latter corporate drama took only about a month to unfold, beginning to end, that short period telescoped a classic management adaptation to challenging new realities: a cycle of initial denial followed by unavoidable facts, followed by a flood of distress, all of which was resolved when Grove and his top executives came to grips with reality and finally made a wrenching, costly concession—the promise to replace Pentium processors for all who asked, even though it would cost the company $475 million.

The half a billion dollars the replacements cost the company was the price for establishing Intel as a commercial brand name. The "Intel Inside" campaign was intended to make computer buyers perceive that the microprocessor inside the computer *is* the computer. This built customer loyalty to Intel that went beyond whatever brand of PC they might buy.

For any organization to reinvent itself, basic assumptions, visions, strategies, and identities have to be questioned. But people hold emotional attachments to all these elements of their work life, making change all the harder.[48] Consider the disaster at the Schwinn bicycle company, America's number one manufacturer of bicycles from the mid-1950s through the 1970s.[49] A family-owned company, Schwinn failed to spot the motocross and mountain-biking trends of the 1980s and was slow to match competition from abroad for the booming market in upscale bikes for adults. Top management, oblivious to the changing tides of bikers' tastes, was far too slow in rethinking their marketing strategy. One sales manager even dismissed the new, lightweight bikes with the derisive comment, "Are you gonna ride it or carry it?"

Its overseas suppliers—including Giant Bicycles of Taiwan, which Schwinn had inadvertently helped build into a bicycle manufacturing titan—were among the creditors that eventually forced Schwinn into bankruptcy in 1992.

Such changes in market realities, of course, are an inevitable part of competition in business large and small. An executive at a company that processes data for auto dealers tells me, "One of our main competitors made four hundred million dollars a year supplying forms to auto dealers. Then we introduced a way for auto dealers to use computers and laser printers to do away with the forms. We grew to sixty million dollars per year, all business taken from that competitor. Just this month they finally woke up and introduced a computerized system competitive to ours—but it took them four years and cost them a huge piece of their business."

Surviving Change: The Emotional Prerequisites

He was brilliant, no question about it: a CPA who also had a master's in economics, an MBA, and additional advanced course work in finance, all from an Ivy League university. He had been a standout as a credit officer and risk manager for a major global bank for many years.

And now he was being fired.

The reason: He could not adjust to his new job. His success had won him a place on a team the bank had put together to find promising companies to invest in. Their mandate was to recoup the value of government bonds in countries where they had been devalued up to 80 percent. Within the countries themselves, the bonds could still be invested at full face value. But instead of helping his team think through the *positive* scenarios that might make a company a good buy, this former risk manager simply continued with his old naysaying approach.

"He kept insisting on analyzing for weakness, for what the downside might be—killing businesses instead of building them," I was told by the executive recruiter he saw when he lost his job. "His boss finally got fed up and fired him. He just couldn't adapt to the new goal."

At work these days, the constant is change. "We used to be very rigid in how we operated. You did it by the book, A, B, C, D—no other way," an advertising sales rep for a major publication told me. "But now we make those decisions ourselves; there's no set formula for how you work. We're encouraged to take risks, work as teams. The atmosphere has changed. But some people seem at a loss. They just have a hard time with the new way of doing things."

People who lack adaptability are ruled by fear, anxiety, and a deep personal discomfort with change. Many managers are having trouble adapting to the trend toward diffusing responsibility and decision making throughout organizations. As an executive at Siemens AG, the German conglomerate, explained, "People have old habits of authority. The new model empowers individuals to make decisions themselves, delegating responsibility downward in the hierarchy, closer to the customer. But when things go poorly—say, profitability is down for a month—some managers panic, fall back on their old ways, and tighten up control again. When they do, it undermines the new way of doing things."

If there is any competence these times call for, it is adaptability. Stars in this competence relish change and find exhilaration in innovation.[50] They are open to new information and—like the management team at Intel—can let go of old assumptions, and so adapt how they operate. They are comfortable with the anxiety that the new or unknown often brings and are willing to take a gamble on a new way of doing things.

Adaptability requires the flexibility to take into account multiple perspectives on a given situation. This flexibility depends, in turn, on an emotional strength: the ability to stay comfortable with ambiguity and remain calm in the face of the unexpected. Another competence that supports adaptability is self-confidence, particularly the sureness that allows someone to quickly adjust their responses, even dropping everything without reservation as realities shift.

The openness to change that typifies adaptability ties this competence to another that is increasingly prized in these turbulent times: innovation.

The Innovators

Levi Strauss, the huge garment manufacturer, faced a dilemma regarding two sewing subcontractors in Bangladesh who were using child laborers. International human rights activists were pressuring Levi Strauss to stop allowing contractors to use underage workers. But company investigators discovered that if the children lost their jobs, they would be impoverished and maybe driven into prostitution. Should the company fire them, in a principled stand against child labor? Or keep them on, to protect them from a worse fate?

The creative solution: neither. Levi Strauss decided to keep the children on the payroll while they went to school full time, and then, when they reached fourteen—the local age of maturity—hire them back.[51]

That innovative response offers a model of creative thinking for multinationals seeking to be socially responsible. Coming to such an original resolution demands entertaining ideas that may seem too radical or risky at first glance, yet having the courage to pursue them anyway.

The emotional foundation of the innovator at work is taking pleasure in originality. Creativity on the job revolves around applying new ideas to achieve results. People who have this knack can quickly identify key issues and simplify problems that seem overwhelmingly complex. Most important, they can find original connections and patterns that others overlook.

People who lack a flair for innovation, by contrast, typically miss the larger picture and get enmeshed in details, and so deal with complex problems only slowly, even tediously. Their fear of risk makes them shy away from novel ideas. And when they try to find solutions, they often fail to realize that what worked in the past is not always the answer for the future.

Deficits in this competence can go beyond mere lack of imagination. People who are uncomfortable with risk become critics and naysayers. Defensive and cautious, they may constantly deride or undermine innovative ideas.

The creative mind is, by its very nature, a bit unruly. There is a natural tension between orderly self-control and the innovative urge. It's not that people who are creative are out-of-control emotionally; rather, they are willing to entertain a wider range of impulse and action than do less adventurous spirits. That is, after all, what creates new possibilities.

Self-control—in the sense of following the rules—predicts outstanding performance in large organizations, especially where a bureaucratic sense of doing the right thing is rewarded. But in entrepreneurial companies and in creative jobs like advertising, being *overly* controlled predicts failure.

A German venture capitalist decries the lack of support in his country for the innovative thinking and risk taking at the heart of entrepreneurial ventures. I hear the same concern voiced in Japan. The German venture capitalist tells me, "Many countries, like my own, are worrying about how to encourage the entrepreneurial skills that create jobs." Risk taking and the drive to pursue innovative ideas are the fuel that stokes the entrepreneurial spirit.

Old and New Paradigms for Innovation

The act of innovation is both cognitive and emotional. Coming up with a creative insight is a cognitive act—but realizing its value, nurturing it, and following through calls on emotional competencies such as self-confidence, initiative, persistence, and the ability to persuade. And throughout, creativity demands a variety of self-regulation competencies, so as to overcome the internal constraints posed by emotions themselves. As Yale psychologist Robert Sternberg observes, these involve fluctuations in emotions from depression to elation, apathy to enthusiasm, and distractedness to focus.[52]

The nineteenth-century mathematician Jules-Henri Poincaré proposed a model of the basic four stages of the creative act that more or less holds true today. The first stage is *preparation*—immersing ourselves in the problem, gathering a broad range of data and information. This first stage more often than not leads to a sometimes frustrating impasse: lots of possibilities, but no insights.

In the next phase, *incubation,* the information and possibilities simmer on a mental back burner. We let the mind play: daydreaming, free-associating, brainstorming, harvesting ideas as they float up. Then, with some luck, comes the third phase, *illumination*—that "aha!" moment where the breakthrough insight comes. This is a thrilling moment, a culmination. But illumination is not enough: The working world is littered with promising ideas never pursued. The final phase is *execution,* following through with action. This demands a dogged persistence despite all the objections, setbacks, trials, and failures that typically arise with any innovation.

"There's a huge difference between someone who actually invents something and makes it real, and someone who just dreams about it," says Phil Weilerstein, director of the National Collegiate Inventors and Innovators Alliance. Those who can follow through and execute their ideas, he tells me, "tend to have a high emotional intelligence level. They see that a variety of elements—most of them human—have to come together to make something new happen. You've got to communicate with people and persuade them, solve problems with them, collaborate."

Ray Kurzweil, an inventor of voice recognition software, agrees: "Courage is essential if you're going to get a creative project off the ground," he told me. "And not just courage, but salesmanship."

Today the very paradigm of invention, even in science, is changing its focus from the individual to collaboration. "In fields of complex modern technology and business we are clearly in an era where the ideas of a single person seldom lead to significant progress," I heard Alex Broer, vice chancellor of Cambridge University and a former director of research at IBM, tell a London briefing on emotional intelligence for British Telecom.

"The ideas of an individual must fit into a matrix of innovation that spreads across a group of researchers around the world," Dr. Broer added. "You have to *talk* to everybody. So today you need more emotional intelligence than before to know how and from whom to get relevant ideas," let alone to form the coalitions and collaborations that will bring those ideas to fruition.

Angel's Advocates and Voices of Doom

New ideas are fragile and all too easily killed by criticism. Sir Isaac Newton is said to have been so sensitive to criticism that he withheld the publication of a paper on optics for fifteen years, until his main critic died. Managers who work with creative groups can help nurture these tendrils of new possibility by protecting them from too-withering criticism that comes too early.

"We have a standing rule that whenever someone offers a creative idea, the people who speak up about it first have to be angel's advocates, people who support and defend it," Paul Robinson, director of Sandia National Laboratories, told me. "Only then can we hear the inevitable criticisms that otherwise might kill an idea in the bud."

Marvin Minsky, the pioneer in artificial intelligence at MIT, observes that the problem in capitalizing on creativity is not just creating ideas, but choosing the ones to bet on. He told me that in the late 1970s Xerox had created six prototypes of the laser printer, the first of their kind, and loaned one to his group at MIT to try out. As Minsky recalls it, "We at MIT said, 'This is fabulous'—and some vice president at Xerox ignored our opinion and decided not to pursue the technology. Canon was the first to bring it to market, and Xerox lost a crucial head start on a billion-dollar market."

Just as chilling as the voice of doubt is its close cousin, the voice of indifference. Engineers have a term for it: NIH, "not invented here"—if it's not our idea, we're not interested. Teresa Amabile, a psychologist at the Harvard Business School, describes four "creativity killers," each of which constricts working memory, the mental space in which brainstorms occur and creativity flourishes, and squelches risk taking:[53]

- *Surveillance:* Hovering and constant scrutiny. This stifles the essential sense of freedom needed for creative thinking.

- *Evaluation:* A critical view that comes too soon or is too intense. Creative ideas should be critiqued—not all are equally good, and promising ones can be refined and honed by helpful criticism—but evaluation is counterproductive when it leads to a preoccupation with being judged.

- *Overcontrol:* Micromanaging every step of the way. Like surveillance, it fosters an oppressive sense of constriction, which discourages originality.

■ *Relentless deadlines:* A too-intense schedule that creates panic.
   While some pressure can be motivating, and deadlines and goals
   can focus attention, they can kill the fertile "off time" where
   fresh ideas flourish.

Collective Creativity

A dapting nimbly to shifting market realities requires a collective creativity, a comfort with uncertainty at every level of a company. Consider
SOL, a highly successful industrial cleaning business in Finland. When it
was spun off from a larger family-owned conglomerate in 1992, it had two
thousand employees, fifteen hundred customers, and annual revenues of $35
million. Just four years later it had doubled its customer base, almost doubled its employees, and reached revenues of $60 million.[54]

Employees there have extraordinary freedom in how they do their work.
It's a workplace with no titles, individual offices, executive perks, or even
secretaries. Nor are there set working hours, a radical innovation for Finland,
where an eight-to-four work day is almost universal. SOL has freed its employees to be creative about how they do their business—and what business
they do.

This autonomy has allowed SOL to shine for its nimble innovation in an
otherwise stodgy, low-end business. At some hospitals, for instance, SOL
cleaners saw a niche and so have taken on some night nursing duties, like
helping patients get to the bathroom or notifying doctors about emergencies.
At several grocery chains, SOL cleaners use their nighttime hours to stock
shelves.

Creativity tends also to be enhanced in organizations that, like SOL,
have less formality, allow more ambiguous and flexible roles, give workers
autonomy, have open flows of information, and operate in mixed or multi-
disciplinary teams.[55]

Just as with creativity in individuals, there are several stages to the
flourishing of innovation in organizations. Two crucial ones are *initiation,*
coming up with the bright idea in the first place, and *implementation,* getting the idea enacted.

In an organization, the idea generators and those who champion the innovation are typically different people, from different groups. A study of
thousands of people in the R&D arms of engineering firms shows that the
idea generators tend to have strengths in a narrow range of expertise and

find pleasure when immersed in abstract ideas.[56] They also prefer to work alone.

By contrast, those who are effective champions of the resulting innovations are particularly adept at influence and political awareness: selling the ideas and finding support and allies. While it goes without saying that the relevant technical expertise is vital to generating innovative ideas, when it comes to putting those ideas to practical use, navigating the web of influence that permeates an organization makes all the difference. So an organization that values innovation needs to support both kinds of competence in its key people.

6

....

What Moves Us

Joe Kramer can fix anything. A welder who helps assemble railroad cars in a South Chicago plant, Joe is the guy everyone calls on when any piece of machinery breaks down.

Joe loves the challenge of finding out what makes a machine work. He started as a boy, fixing his mother's toaster, and he continues to seek out new mechanical challenges. When he decided to put in a sprinkler system at home, he couldn't find one that had a mist fine enough to make rainbows. So he designed his own and built it on his basement lathe.

Joe also knows every aspect of how the plant operates, and he can fill in for any of the two hundred or so others who work there. Almost sixty, Joe has been doing his job for close to forty years, and he still loves what he does. "If I had five more like Joe," the manager says, "I'd have the most efficient railroad shop in the business."

Joe is an example of people who find their work exhilarating—and who perform at their best. The key to that exhilaration is not the task itself—Joe's job is often routine—but the special state of mind Joe creates as he works, a state called "flow." Flow moves people to do their best work, no matter what work they do.

Flow blossoms when our skills are fully engaged and then some—say, by a work project that stretches us in new and challenging ways. The challenge absorbs us so much we lose ourselves in our work, becoming so totally concentrated we may feel "out of time." In this state we seem to handle everything effortlessly, nimbly adapting to shifting demands. Flow itself is a pleasure.[1]

Flow is the ultimate motivator. Activities we love draw us in because we get into flow as we pursue them. Of course, what gives people such pleasure varies: a machinist may love the challenge of a difficult weld; a surgeon gets contentedly absorbed in a complex operation; an interior designer finds delight in the creative play of pattern and color. When we work in flow, the motivation is built in—work is a delight in itself.

Flow offers a radical alternative to the widely held ideas about what motivates people at work. This is not to say that incentives don't matter; they are key as prods or ways to "keep score." There is, of course, value in reviews and promotions, stock options and bonuses—as there is with basic salary. But the most powerful motivators are internal, not external.

For instance, when people kept a journal of how they felt while they performed a range of tasks throughout the day, one result was clear: They felt better doing work they loved rather than work they did only because they were rewarded for it. When doing a task for the pleasure of it, their mood was upbeat, both happy and interested. When doing something simply for the pay, they were bored, disinterested, even mildly irritated (and most unhappy if the tasks were stressful and onerous). It feels better to do what we have passion for, even if the rewards are greater elsewhere.

When all is said and done and a job has been pursued to its end, what are the ultimate sources of satisfaction? That question was asked of more than seven hundred men and women in their sixties, most of whom were nearing the end of successful careers as professionals or business executives.[2] Most rewarding was the creative challenge and stimulation of the work itself, and the chance to keep learning. The next three sources of reward: pride in getting things done, work friendships, and helping or teaching people on the job. Much lower on the list came status, and even lower was financial gain.

Traditional incentives miss the point when it comes to getting people to perform at their absolute best. To reach the top rung, people must love what they do and find pleasure in doing it.

Motive and *emotion* share the same Latin root, *motere,* "to move." Emotions are, literally, what move us to pursue our goals; they fuel our motivations, and our motives in turn drive our perceptions and shape our actions. Great work starts with great feeling.

Loving What Pays Off

People in flow often make the difficult look easy, an external appearance that mirrors what is happening in their brain. Flow poses a neural paradox: We can be engaged in an exceptionally demanding task, and yet our brain is operating with a minimal level of activity or expenditure of energy. The reason seems to be that when we are bored and apathetic, or frenzied with anxiety, our brain activity is diffused; the brain itself is at a high level of activation, albeit poorly focused, with brain cells firing in far-flung and irrelevant ways. But during flow, the brain appears efficient and precise in its pattern of firing. The result is an overall lowering of cortical arousal—even though the person may be engaged in an extremely challenging task.[3]

And work is the main arena in life that gives people the chance for flow. Mihalyi Csikzentmihalyi, the University of Chicago psychologist who pioneered the study of flow, outfitted 107 people in positions from management and engineering to the assembly line with a beeper that periodically reminded them to note what they were doing and how they felt. The results were surprising.[4] They reported, on average, being in flow about half the time while on the job—and less than 20 percent of the time during their leisure hours. The most common emotional state reported during leisure time was apathy!

But there was also a wide variation in just how much of the time people were in flow at work. Those with complex, challenging jobs, who had more flexibility in how they approached each task, were most likely to be in flow. Managers and engineers had more flow time than those in routine jobs. More control means more opportunity to maximize flow. Control can take many forms—even putting something off until the last minute as a way to up the challenge, creating a pressured "rush" period that adds adrenaline to an otherwise easy task.

For top performers, there is an especially tight calibration of flow and task; flow occurs in the work that is most critical to their goals and productivity, rather than in fascinating diversions or irrelevancies.[5] For the stars, excellence and pleasure in work are one and the same.

Psychological Presence

A project manager at an architectural firm notices a draftsman struggling over a simple aspect of a blueprint. The project deadline looms, and they are all under tremendous pressure. As she approaches her colleague, the project manager notices that her hands are clenched, her thoughts are fixed on angry feelings about the difficult deadline, and she feels frustrated because the draftsman is not further along.

She relaxes a bit and asks the draftsman, "What's going on—is something wrong?" His response is a litany of frustrations of his own—about not having enough information to finish the drawing, about how much he was asked to do in so little time.

Sympathetic, the project manager asks the draftsman more detailed questions about what he's up against. Her speech is lively, animated, her gaze direct. She lets him know she feels overwhelmed by the pressure, too.

Her line of questioning leads him to see that he actually has more information than he thought, and that he can, in fact, finish the drawing. He is buoyed, eager again to get back to the task. The project manager even makes a joke about how everyone was missing some data on this project—especially the vice president who had made such a crazy commitment in the first place. They both laugh and get on with the work at hand.

What did the project manager do that was so right? She was *present.*

This encounter, though nothing extraordinary, exemplifies the quality of being emotionally present at work. When people are present in this sense, they are fully attentive and completely involved in their work—and so perform at their best. Others experience them as accessible and engaged, and they contribute their creative ideas, energy, and intuitions fully.

The opposite, a psychological absence, is all too familiar from people who go through their work routines by rote, obviously bored, or otherwise disconnected. In a sense, they may as well not have shown up. The receptionist at the same architectural firm, who hates her job, puts it like this: "Sitting up here in front and smiling and typing and being friendly, it's all bullshit. It's just a role, and there isn't any satisfaction in it for me. This eight or nine hours is a waste."

Being present requires "not being disabled by anxiety, and so being open to others rather than closed," says William A. Kahn, the psychologist at Boston University School of Management who cites the project manager as a model.[6] Such presence shares a key attribute of flow: a total attention to, or immersion in, the task at hand. In contrast, the enemies of presence (and of flow) are the twin afflictions of apathy and anxiety.

Presence begins with self-awareness. The project manager, in Kahn's analysis, was attuned to her feelings; her clenched hands cued her to the anger she was feeling about the situation. And her empathy made her receptive to picking up the draftsman's sense of frustration without taking it as a reflection on herself.

The project manager's ability to be comfortable with these distressing feelings let her deal with them effectively rather than avoid them. Instead of dismissing the draftsman's frustration or preemptively criticizing his performance, she drew him out. And she was able to highlight information that transformed the frustration to enthusiasm, ending the encounter with a joke that put the onus where they both felt it to be—an emotional judo move that tightened the bond between them.

When fully present, we are more attuned to those around us and to the needs of the situation, and we fluidly adapt to what is needed—in other words, we are in flow. We can be thoughtful, funny, or self-reflective, drawing on whatever capacity or skill we need at the moment.

Getting Better and Better

A college professor describes why she loves her job: "I enjoy the fact that in the position I'm in, I'm continuously learning new things. It's continuous stimulation. I have to keep on my toes because things are always changing. You have to keep up."[7]

Our learning edge is at the point that most fully engages our maximum skill—and that precisely matches the zone of flow. Flow naturally propels self-improvement, for two reasons: People learn best when they are fully engaged in what they are doing, and the more people practice a task, the better they get. The result: continual motivation (enjoying flow) to master new challenges.

When a job lacks flow, even success can bring a curious malaise: What was once exciting can become boring. When a job has been mastered, the danger of stagnation rises sharply. That may explain why midlife is a notorious time for career changes.

"You get restless in midlife and midcareer, and that restlessness can have huge repercussions for your career," says a psychologist who counsels executives. "You start answering calls from headhunters even though you don't really want a new job. You start devoting your time and attention to a small business you start on the side. Or you get irritable and grouchy, or start collecting something like sports cars, or have affairs."

A main cause of such boredom is that people are no longer finding a ge to their abilities; their work, so familiar and easy, has gone stale. psychologist adds, "A healthy response might be to take on a new, challenging project within the company, because you need to find a way to keep yourself engaged in your work."

Good Stress: The Engaged Challenge

Remember the stormy tirade by Bill Gates that the unflappable woman handled so well? One school of thought holds that the well-timed use of such controlled outbursts can be motivating—that they can be a way of raising the temperature of a group. Gates is famous for his confrontational, explosive style; at Microsoft it's a kind of badge of honor to be a target of his attacks.

As one friend told me, "My boss knew who could take it; he never yelled at me. He'd do it in a meeting where everyone was low-energy. He'd suddenly tear into someone and everyone would wake up."

Flow occurs in that middle zone between boredom and immobilizing anxiety. A *moderate* amount of anxiety in the air, a sense of urgency, mobilizes us. Too little urgency and we are apathetic; too much and we are overwhelmed. The message "This matters" can be compelling.

Eustress, or "good" stress, refers to the pressure that mobilizes us to action. Its neurochemistry is revealing. When we are positively engaged by a challenge, our brain is being soaked in a bath of catecholamines and other substances triggered by the adrenal system. These chemicals prime the brain to stay attentive and interested, even fascinated, and energized for a sustained effort. Intense motivation is, literally, an "adrenaline rush."

A German study shows this relationship between motivation and the brain chemistry of eustress rather neatly.[8] Volunteers were given a taxing mental challenge, 120 arithmetic problems that they had to solve in an ever-shorter span of time, until they were wrong one in every four times. Whenever they felt confident that their answers were correct, they were checked; if right, they got a cash reward, and if wrong, they were penalized the same amount.

Those volunteers highest in hope of success—a variant of the need to achieve—were best able to keep their mobilization at a level that produced mostly catecholamines, rather than letting it rise to the emergency mode, where cortisol kicks in. But those who were motivated by a fear of failure were swamped with cortisol.

This proved to be a self-reinforcing effect. Those with lower levels of cortisol were better able to think and pay attention during the math challenge. Their heart rates showed they were no more anxious during the challenge than before it started; they stayed alert, calm, and productive. The effect on their performance was dramatic: They won more than twice as much as their peers.

Affiliation: The People Motive

Eugenia Barton, in her twelfth year as a high-school teacher, still adores her students: "I think I like them more every year. As I get to know them and have them in two or three classes, I become very close to them."

In an evaluation of a large group of teachers, Barton rated among the most compassionate and caring.[9] The pleasure she gets from her connection with her students bespeaks the many avenues people have for getting into flow.

There is a saying in India, "When a pickpocket meets a saint, all he sees are the pockets." Our motives shape how we see the world; all attention is selective, and what matters to us most is what we automatically scan for. Someone who is motivated to get results notices ways to do better, to be entrepreneurial, to innovate, or to find a competitive advantage. People like Barton, who is motivated by the pleasure of her relationships with her students, seek out opportunities for connection.

The need for achievement is one of the most frequently occurring competencies in star performers. The need for *affiliation,* by contrast, shows up less often, except in the helping professions, like nursing, medicine, and teaching. But affiliative interest—a genuine appreciation and enjoyment of other people—is also a key element of success not just for top nurses and teachers, but also for client-relations managers.[10]

Affiliation as a motive becomes an end in itself—a goal, if you will—not a means to something else. This sounds quite positive, but when it is excessive or the main motivator, it can be detrimental to managerial performance. For instance, successful managers and supervisors often have relatively low affiliative needs—and so are freer to refuse requests or set limits, despite objections.[11]

Too high an affiliative drive can become distracting, even a hindrance.[12] "Affiliation—liking people—is fine when it serves to strengthen relationships in the course of getting the task done," Richard Boyatzis, who studied affiliation in managers, told me. "If you're too caught up with personal relationships at work, you can lose sight of the manager's task."

Affiliation as a motive may play its most basic role in determining one's career choice. Those with high affiliation needs gravitate toward "people" jobs, like teaching and nursing. In this way, it operates as a threshold competence and can set people on very fulfilling career paths, where relating—not managing and delegating—is a top priority.

The Neurology of Motivation

Different motives presumably involve differing mixes of brain chemicals, though we don't know which.[13] We *do* know that the amygdala houses the general brain circuitry that undergirds motivation. The emotional learning that predisposes someone to take pleasure in one set of activities rather than another, as well as the repertoire of memory, feelings, and habits associated with those activities, is stored in the emotional memory banks of the amygdala and its related circuits.

One frustration for computer scientists trying to build robotlike devices that can see and hear like humans is that computers lack the guiding hand of emotion.[14] Without an emotional memory bank that can instantly recognize what matters to us—what data arouses *feeling*—computers haven't a clue. They give equal value to all they see and hear, and so fail to pick out what in each moment is most salient. Computers lack the guiding force that our emotions and motivations allow us.

Our motives guide our awareness toward the opportunities they seek out. The amygdala is part of a "neural doorway" through which whatever we care about—whatever motivates us—enters and is weighed in terms of its value as an incentive.[15] A guide to what matters most to us, it is the clearinghouse for our priorities in life.

People who suffer brain diseases or trauma that deprive them of their amygdala (but leave the rest of the brain intact) suffer from a disorder of motivation. They are unable to distinguish between what matters most to them and what is irrelevant, between what moves them and what leaves them cold. Every act is of the same emotional valence, and so neutral. The result is paralyzing apathy, or an indiscriminate, uncontrollable indulgence in appetites.

This motivational circuitry—our navigator through life—connects to the prefrontal lobes, the brain's executive center, which brings a sense of

context and appropriateness to the amygdala's surges of passi
The prefrontal area houses an array of inhibitory neurons tha
tone down the amygdala's impulses, adding caution to the circu
vation: While the amygdala wants to leap, the prefrontal lobes v
first.

Three motivational competencies typify outstanding performers:

- *Achievement drive:* Striving to improve or meet a standard of excellence

- *Commitment:* Embracing the organization's or group's vision and goals

- *Initiative and optimism:* Twin competencies that mobilize people to seize opportunities and allow them to take setbacks and obstacles in stride

■ ACHIEVEMENT DRIVE ■

Striving to Improve or Meet a Standard of Excellence

People with this competence

- Are results-oriented, with a high drive to meet their objectives and standards

- Set challenging goals and take calculated risks

- Pursue information to reduce uncertainty and find ways to do better

- Learn how to improve their performance

"There are three hundred American companies selling auto insurance, and we're the sixth largest," Peter Lewis, CEO of Progressive Insurance, told me when I visited his Cleveland headquarters. "Our objective is to triple in size and be number three by the year 2000." And Progressive just may do it: Only fifteen years ago it was ranked forty-third. Their rapid climb has been marked by the introduction of several innovations that have raised the bar for the rest of what has traditionally been a stodgy, risk-averse industry.

For example, Progressive promises to get one of its people to an accident scene within two hours of being notified. And the agents, using laptop computers to price replacement parts and estimate repair costs, write a check on the spot. No other major insurer offers this swift, on-the-scene claims service.

Even more radical is 1–800–AUTOPRO, a twenty-four-hour toll-free service that quotes auto insurance rates—Progressive's and those of the top three other insurers in the local market—for people shopping around. Progressive's rates often, though not always, come out lowest. This open, easy comparison of rates is unheard-of in the industry (and came about at the suggestion of a college classmate of Lewis's, consumer advocate Ralph Nader).

Another sign of the company's success: Progressive is one of the few insurance companies that is profitable just from its premiums.

Lewis is blunt about his drive to do even better, to capture a larger and larger market share, and what that means for the people who work for him: "We demand a very high standard, but the rewards can be great—people can earn up to double their salary in bonuses. It's an aristocracy of performers: We pay the best, but we demand the most—and we fire people who don't produce."

Despite this perform-or-leave policy, the company has a turnover rate of around 8 percent, about par for the industry. The reason: Those who gravitate to the company share Lewis's commitment to achievement. As Lewis put it, "One of our core values is doing better than you did before. It's an enormous challenge, but these are people who love it."

Progressive's statement of core values reads in part like a credo for the achievement competence: *"Excellence.* We strive constantly to improve in order to meet and exceed the highest expectations of our customers, shareholders and people."

Success demands this drive to achieve. Studies that compare star performers in executive ranks to average ones find the stars show the following signs of the achievement competence: They talk about and take more calculated risks; they urge and support enterprising innovations and set challenging goals for their employees; and they throw their support behind others' entrepreneurial ideas. The need to achieve is the single strongest competence that sets apart star from average executives.[16]

For those at higher levels of management, the obsession with getting results can express itself through the working of an entire department or company—Progressive Insurance is the vehicle for Peter Lewis's competitive drive no less than Microsoft is for Bill Gates's.[17] A study of the hundred wealthiest Americans throughout history—including Gates and John D. Rockefeller—shows that what they all share is their competitive drive: a single-minded passion for their business.[18]

The Calculated Risk

It seems like an innocent enough challenge: Toss a ring over an upright peg. The catch is that the farther away the peg is, the more points you make, and you get to set the peg yourself. People who are too grandiose in their thinking typically set the peg beyond their throwing range. Those who are too cautious set the peg too close and score too few points.

The ring-toss game is a metaphor for calculated risk taking in life. It was used by David McClelland, then my professor at Harvard, to assess the ability to set risky but manageable challenges. Entrepreneurial drive demands that people be comfortable taking risks but know how to calculate them carefully. This skill at taking smart risks is a mark of the successful entrepreneur.

McClelland found outstanding performers set more challenging goals for themselves; they routinely calculated a placement for the peg that brought them around a 50 percent success rate.

This risk strategy in high achievers alerts them to specific performance benchmarks; they can tell you, "When I took over, efficiency was 20 percent—now it's 85 percent." Their decisions are often based on a careful cost-benefit analysis that frees them to take calculated risks.

High achievers—those willing to commit to something new—are restless in positions that stifle that urge. "When we trained assembly line workers at Ford to raise their need to achieve, most ended up leaving and starting their own business," Lyle Spencer Jr., a longtime colleague of McClelland, tells me. "The same thing happened with a group of computer engineers at IBM."

What seems absurdly risky to others will seem possible to entrepreneurs. When Leif Lundblad, the Swedish inventor of an automatic cash dispensing device for tellers, made a deal with Citibank to deliver the first batch of machines, he felt perfectly confident he could fulfill the order—his first ever. But, Lundblad told me, after he had met the delivery date "the people at Citibank told me that they thought there was only a ten percent chance that I would succeed."

The drive to do better shows up as a constant theme in entrepreneurs' thoughts, and a continuous improvement in performance. Consider a study of fifty-nine entrepreneurs, most of them research scientists, each of whom had taken advantage of an innovative technology to found a high-tech firm.[19] Five years after establishing their firms, those who were highest in achievement traits (like seeking out feedback on their performance and setting goals) were the most likely to have flourished—they had an average increase in sales of $1 million a year, increased the number of employees by fifty or more, or sold their company for a substantial profit.

By contrast, those founders who were low in achievement competence had done poorly. They had four or fewer employees, had sold the business for a loss—or had simply given up.

A Passion for Feedback

When a major customer of the Donnelly Corporation, which supplies glass to the auto industry, kept rejecting large numbers of their products for being substandard, three Donnelly production workers drove four hundred miles to learn why the customer was unhappy with their product.

Their startling discovery: The customer was offering its own employees a bonus for finding less-than-perfect parts from Donnelly. Rising to this challenge, the Donnelly workers raised their own quality control standards, being sure to ship only perfect parts.[20]

Those enterprising workers at Donnelly exemplify the spirit of striving to improve that lies at the heart of the achievement motive. Whenever a working group meets regularly to find ways to improve performance, they embody a collective drive to achieve.

By contrast, when it comes to setting goals or standards for themselves, people low in achievement competence are lackadaisical or unrealistic, seeking work that is either too easy or unrealistically ambitious. Likewise, supervisors who lack this skill create a work climate where goals are fuzzy and people are unsure about their own responsibilities, the limits of their authority, and even their job objectives. They don't give employees feedback on how they're doing or what is expected of them.

Those driven by the need to achieve seek ways to track their success. For

many, this means money—though they often say that money is less important for what it can buy than as feedback on how well they are doing. As one
California entrepreneur put it, "Money was never a big issue with me; it was
just a way of keeping score." Another called it "a report card."[21]

Even those with moderate levels of achievement competence rely on
performance measures like sales quotas or company quality standards. They
may create their own measures of performance, setting goals like outper-
forming peers, doing a job more quickly, or beating some competitor.

In a small business such as a restaurant, performance feedback comes
daily; those who manage stock portfolios get it almost by the minute. But
for many people getting performance feedback can be frustratingly difficult
because of the unquantifiable nature of their work. Such people have to develop a strong self-critical sense, to provide the feedback themselves. And
top performers seek out the feedback they need at the point when it is most
useful to them.

The Pursuit of Information and Efficiency

Nathan Myhrvold, Microsoft's chief technology officer, is a prodigious
reader, a collector of knowledge for its own sake, a tracker of data of
every sort.[22] He has to be. As Microsoft's in-house visionary, he never
knows what random bit of data will be the seed of the next billion-dollar
idea. He typifies the information addict, someone whose thirst for knowledge is limitless and feeds into a keen sense of innovativeness—and competitiveness.

In the chaotic modern world of work, the sheer volume of data—and the
queasy feeling that we are falling behind in tracking it—can be a source of
gnawing anxiety. One way to alleviate that anxiety is to monitor relentlessly
what's going on, like Myhrvold—and so reduce the level of uncertainty.[23]
People with an intense need to achieve are voracious in seeking out new
ideas and information, particularly as it pertains (even peripherally) to their
goals. They regularly call on others to get their perspective, and recruit others into an ongoing network of informants to get fresh intelligence and essential feedback.

People who lack this competence settle for whatever information comes
their way or consult only the obvious and readily available sources of data.
For executives this need to know can take the form of "management by
walking around" or encouraging impromptu contacts or informal meetings

with people at all levels. Such wide information gathering minimizes unpleasant surprises and maximizes the likelihood of spotting and seizing potential opportunities.

The craving for data runs in parallel to an urge to make things ever more efficient. When this tendency takes the form of obsessive, rule-bound, by-the-book supervision, it signifies poor performance. When high-level executives exhibit too much concern for detail and order, it can be a sign that they are focused on a smaller scale than their job demands. This is the micromanager who bird-dogs subordinates while paying too little attention to the bigger picture.

However, this drive to handle uncertainty can also foster meticulous attention to the details that matter. Superior performers are adept at putting into place systems that track progress or ensure a better quality and flow of data. One sales manager, frustrated by the long interval between reports from his large sales team, developed an automated phone system that beeped every salesperson at the end of the day, prompting them to punch in the sales they had made. This meant he had vital information not in two weeks but in eight hours!

▪ COMMITMENT ▪

Aligning with the Goals of a Group or Organization

▪▪

People with this competence

▪ Readily make sacrifices to meet a larger organizational goal

▪ Find a sense of purpose in the larger mission

▪ Use the group's core values in making decisions and clarifying choices

▪ Actively seek out opportunities to fulfill the group's mission

▪▪

On learning that the American Airlines national office was about to become their neighbor, enterprising employees at a Dallas branch of Herman Miller, the office furniture company, wrote a letter asking the airline to consider furnishing their new office with Herman Miller products.

Their initiative paid off in a sizable order. But the week before the airline office opened, the employees who went over to check that the order had been delivered properly found that the packing crates had crushed the plush on the fabric of hundreds of chairs. So the employees formed teams to work around the clock and over the weekend to raise the plush with steam irons.[24]

The essence of commitment is making our goals and those of our organization one and the same. Commitment is emotional: We feel a strong attachment to our group's goals when they resonate strongly with our own. Those who value and embrace an organization's mission are willing not just to make an all-out effort on its behalf, but to make personal sacrifices when needed. These are the staff who choose to work late into the night or over a weekend to get a project done on deadline, and the managers willing to leave town on a few hours' notice when an urgent mission comes along.

Commitment can even express itself in unpopular decisions that are made to benefit the larger group, even if these decisions rouse opposition or controversy. The truly committed are willing to make short-term sacrifices if they are for the larger good of the group. In short, the committed are the "patriots" of a company, natural boosters.

Among the competencies that Johnson Wax seeks to instill in its award-winning sales team is an unselfish strategic vision—doing what's right for the long term, even if there are no immediate rewards. "It might take the organization two or three years to catch up with what you are doing and reward you fully for it, but if it's right for the long term, you go ahead and trust that management will support you," an executive there tells me.

High levels of commitment are, of course, more likely in companies where people see themselves as "shareholders" (or actually *are* shareholders) rather than simply as employees. But workers who are inspired by a shared goal often have a level of commitment that is greater than any financial incentive. As Patricia Sueltz, an IBM vice president who is leading a drive to make her company a major presence on the Internet, puts it, "I get called by headhunters all the time. They say, 'We can make you very rich.' But they don't get it. I am going to change the world with this. I'm making a difference."[25]

Companies or organizations that lack a well-formulated mission—or whose mission statements are little more than public-relations ploys—offer people little to commit to. Employees need a clear sense of an organization's core values to form an allegiance to them.

Self-awareness is a building block of commitment. Employees who know their own guiding values or purpose will have a clear, even vivid sense about whether there is a "fit" with an organization. When they feel a match, their commitment is spontaneous and strong.

I remember a woman who sold advertising space for *The New York Times* telling me about an after-hours conversation among people in her department: "We realized that we in advertising provide the diesel fuel for the rest of the *Times* to work, that we're crucial to the paper's mission. We were talking about the time the paper ran a pictorial editorial on the crisis in Rwanda, triggering a flood of news coverage, and how the U.S. government sent aid over right afterward. That made us all feel really good about what we do."

Organizational Citizenship

The committed are the model citizens of any organization. They go the extra mile. And like pebbles in a pond, committed workers send ripples of good feeling throughout an organization.

Employees who feel strong organizational commitment will put up with highly stressful job conditions if need be—long hours, deadline pressure, and the like—out of devotion to collective goals. High levels of commitment allow employees to thrive under challenges and pressures that those who feel no particular loyalty to the organization find only stressful and onerous. At one federal agency, those administrators who felt the greatest organizational commitment suffered the least from the high stress typical of their jobs and reported the most satisfaction with their work.[26]

But if employees are not treated fairly and respectfully, no organization will gain their emotional allegiance. The more support employees feel from their organization, the more trust, attachment, and loyalty they will feel, and the better organizational citizens they will be.[27]

Organizational commitment grows from such emotional bonding. In a study of workers like teachers, clerks, insurance reps, and police officers, the key to how much effort they put into their work was how *emotionally attached* they felt to their organization—how proud to work there, how large their job figures in their sense of identity, how much they feel "part of the family."[28]

The Uncommitted

I set it up so they got the credit—it really motivated the team, and our unit did quite well," a manager reports about how he got his team to surpass their goal.

By contrast, a consultant boasts, "I made sure I got the juiciest assignment, did it well, and got the kudos. The others were envious, which is their problem."

The manager used his position of power to share credit and so boost the morale of—and motivate—his team; the consultant could care less about the impact of his self-serving manipulation on his peers or the organization—he just wants the glory.[29]

Employees who see themselves as visitors rather than organizational residents show little commitment. But the same attitude can be found among workers who may have been in an organization for years. Employees who feel bitter about being underpaid or otherwise taken advantage of by an organization are certain to feel little commitment to its overall goals. So do those who see themselves as isolated and disconnected from decisions that impact their work.

These disaffected people are most prone to using the resources of the organization solely for their own benefit. The opportunistic among them see their current position mainly as a step on the way to somewhere else. Those who feel disconnected aren't even interested in moving up; instead their dissatisfaction manifests itself as a lack of integrity (doctoring expense accounts, for example, or stealing supplies).

An attitude of self-interest is, understandably, growing more common among once-committed employees who now confront downsizing and other changes that make them feel their organization is no longer loyal to *them*. This sense of betrayal or distrust erodes allegiance and encourages cynicism. And once lost, trust—and the commitment that stems from it—is hard to rebuild.

Tom Peters points to an emerging balance between people's needs to manage their own career and to commit to shared goals at work.[30] As he puts it, the emerging nature of loyalty balances allegiance to one's own goals and to the web of one's working relationships. This variety of loyalty, he says, "isn't blind loyalty to the company. It's loyalty to your colleagues, loyalty to your team, loyalty to your project, loyalty to your customers, and loyalty to yourself."

▪ INITIATIVE AND OPTIMISM ▪

Displaying Proactivity and Persistence

▪▪

People with this competence

For Initiative

- Are ready to seize opportunities

- Pursue goals beyond what's required or expected of them

- Cut through red tape and bend the rules when necessary to get the job done

- Mobilize others through unusual, enterprising efforts

For Optimism

- Persist in seeking goals despite obstacles and setbacks

- Operate from hope of success rather than fear of failure

- See setbacks as due to manageable circumstance rather than a personal flaw

▪▪

On several college campuses across America booths appeared selling snow cones with a difference—and a message. Instead of the standard heaps of colorful, sweetly flavored crushed ice, these snow cones came only in black—a political protest against oil drilling in Alaska's Arctic Wildlife Refuge. The snow cones were the brainchild of Adam Werbach, whose first political action came when he was just seven: He circulated a petition to his fellow second-graders urging the ouster of then Secretary of the Interior James Watt, an antienvironmentalist. By high school Werbach was organizing a drive to buy a truck for recycling the school's trash, and in his senior year Werbach founded the Sierra Student Coalition, an organization of young environmental activists which, through his college years, he built into a thirty-thousand-member organization. He gave the environmentalist message a new immediacy for city dwellers by making lead poisoning of children the group's signature issue. And he organized "dorm-storming" activists to sweep through college dormitories, encouraging students to use their computers to e-mail their legislators about environmental issues. At twenty-four, Werbach was elected the youngest-ever president of the Sierra Club, America's largest environmentalist group.[31]

Initiative often takes this form of being unusually enterprising. Take the shipping clerk who realized his company did enough business with Federal Express to get not just a volume discount, but a dedicated computer to track shipping orders. The clerk took it on himself to approach the CEO as he was leaving work and pitch the idea—and saved the company $30,000.[32]

At PNC Bank in Pittsburgh, a credit supervisor did a back-of-the-envelope calculation of the amount of electricity being eaten up by the bank's hundreds of personal computers left on by people after they had gone home. Those sixteen hours of idle time, he calculated, cost the bank $268,000 each year.

But when he went to higher-ups with his bright idea, they put him off, saying that switching computers on and off would decrease the life of the PCs. Undaunted, he did more research, finding that most business computer systems became obsolete and were routinely replaced years before the components wore out. The bank finally bought the idea—at a savings that would have required about $2 million in new revenues to have the equivalent bottom-line impact.[33]

Ways to Seize the Day

Those with initiative act before being forced to by external events. This often means taking anticipatory action to avoid problems before they happen, or taking advantage of opportunities before they are visible to anyone else. And the higher up the executive ladder, the larger the window of anticipation; for a midlevel supervisor or manager, it may mean being able to see days or weeks ahead; a visionary corporate leader sees years or even decades ahead.[34]

Possessing this farsightedness may mean taking steps when no one else sees the need to. This takes a certain courage, especially when others object. Star performers in federal research agencies, for example, plead with a skeptical Congress for basic research funds that, far into the future, might pay off with new cures for diseases.[35]

Constantly reacting to events rather than being prepared for them marks those who lack initiative. The failure to anticipate what's coming means operating in crisis mode. Such workers tend to fall behind and are continually forced to handle emergencies they did not foresee. All of this—as well as procrastination and not taking action in a timely way—indicates a basic failure to plan for or anticipate what lies ahead.

In contrast, proactivity pays off. Real estate agents can simply wait for the phone to ring, or they can scour classified ads for houses being sold by owners and approach them to list the house with their agency. They can screen prospective buyers to ensure they spend their time with those most serious about purchasing a house. Such acts of initiative result in a greater number of listings, a greater number of houses sold, and larger commissions.[36]

Seizing new opportunities is crucial for success in fields like consulting, where there is no revenue without initiative. At Deloitte & Touche Consulting, star performers stay alert to opportunities for "add-ons" that might extend a short-term project into a larger one, and take advantage of serendipity and unexpected opportunities to develop new business.[37]

Sometimes initiative simply means sheer hard work. One salesman with initiative said, "I was up at two o'clock this morning finishing my proposal—I'm calling stores during the day and preparing my programs and presentations at night."[38] Or take the tale of two trust officers: One exhibited high levels of initiative by selling an account to his doctor while he was in the hospital for a severe illness, while the other asked the researcher at the end of their interview if he had a will, since to the trust officer *everyone* was a potential client!

Hope and Perseverance

My seatmate seems right at home in the first-class cabin on our flight to Houston. A well-dressed, thirtyish organic chemist with an MBA, he's an account manager for a top chemical company.

But he tells me something surprising: "I grew up in Newark, New Jersey, on welfare. My parents had divorced, and I lived with my grandparents in a neighborhood where more kids went to jail than to college. I went back to visit there last month and saw one of my old friends—he's just been sentenced to three and a half years for dealing drugs. He told me, 'That's all we knew how to do.' And it's true. We never had any models for a way out."

So what made the difference between this account manager and his drug-dealing old buddy? "I was lucky. After high school my grandparents sent me to Texas to live with an aunt. I got a part-time job helping out with some research. And I started to see that these Ph.D.s I was working for weren't much different from me. I thought, 'I could do this, too.' So I started to go to night school, and finally got my B.A. in chemistry. Once you know what you want and see that it's feasible, you can figure out the steps you have to take. Then it's just persistence that gets you there."

And his old friends? "Those other kids gave up on themselves. They thought they didn't have what it takes to go to college. The only way they knew how to get respect was with a handgun."

A lack of initiative typifies those who feel a certain hopelessness—that their best efforts won't really make a difference. So, like the chemist's childhood friends, they don't push themselves. They see themselves as victims or passive pawns in the game of life, rather than master of their fate. The chemist's resilience may have owed more than he realized to the character lessons learned from his grandparents and aunt, but whatever its roots, those with initiative feel their own actions determine their future. These attitudes, in turn, determine how well we can deal with hardships and vicissitudes on the job. For example, among midlevel managers at a large corporation, those who saw themselves as masters of their fate were less fazed by difficult challenges and more positive in the face of stresses than were those who saw their destiny as being outside their control.[39]

Those who lack initiative are most likely to give up on themselves—and their jobs. This attitude can be seen in workers who need someone to direct them in performing their assignments. When it comes to going the extra mile—for example, staying late to get a priority project finished on time, or putting their own work aside to help someone else—such workers will often take a "not-my-job" line of resistance.

Too Much Initiative

While initiative is generally laudable, it needs to be balanced with social awareness in order to avoid unintended negative consequences.

Take the vice president of marketing at a large consumer products company, who discovered that one of his sales reps was unable to close a sale with a large national account.[40] The VP had made many presentations to that same account in the past, and so on his own initiative he called and set up a meeting there. Then he phoned the sales rep with instructions to meet him at the account's office the next day.

One result of the VP's initiative was that they made the sale. Another, unintended result was that the sales rep was deeply humiliated.

Feeling he had been made to look foolish and incompetent in front of his client, the rep protested, and his two bosses—the regional and the national sales managers—fired off irate memos to the vice president, claiming he had stepped out of bounds in going over their heads and humiliating their staffer.

But the warning had no effect. The same pattern continued for two years, with the VP acting high-handedly with other sales reps, until the president of the company, worried about a slump in sales, blamed it on the VP's demoralization of the company's sales force. The net result: The president gave the VP a choice—leave the company or step down to take a regional sales job.

Bosses who micromanage—who take control over small details best left to subordinates—may *seem* to have initiative, but they lack a basic awareness of how their actions affect other people. Initiative without empathy—or a sense of the bigger picture—can be destructive and typifies managers who perform poorly.[41]

Persisting—and Bouncing Back

Two executives were both refused a promotion because of negative evaluations from a superior.[42] One reacted to the setback with rage and fantasies of killing his boss; he complained to anyone who would listen and he went on a drinking binge. "It seemed like my life was over," he said later.

He avoided his boss, lowering his head when they passed in the hall. "Even though I was angry and felt cheated," he adds, "deep down I feared that he was right, that I am sort of worthless, that I had failed, and there was nothing I could do to change that."

The other passed-over executive was also stunned and angry. But he had a more open-minded perspective: "I can't say I was surprised, really. He and I have such different ideas, and we've argued a lot."

This executive went home and talked over the setback with his wife to figure out what had gone wrong and what he could do about it. Engaging in some introspection, he realized he hadn't been giving his maximum effort. With that knowledge his anger faded, and he resolved to talk with his boss. The result: "I had some discussions with him and things went very well. I guess he was troubled about what he had done, and I was troubled about not working up to potential. Since then, things have been better for both of us."

The key competence here is optimism, which hinges on how we *interpret* our setbacks. A pessimist, like the first executive, sees a setback as confirming some fatal flaw in himself that cannot be changed. The net result of such a defeatist attitude is, of course, hopelessness and helplessness: If you're doomed to fail, why try?

Optimists, by contrast, see a setback as a result of factors they have the power to do something about, not some flaw or deficiency in themselves. Like the second executive, optimists can deal with a setback by finding a positive response.

Consider how optimism helps people recover from failure.

Anne Busquet, once head of American Express's Optima Card division, was demoted in 1991 when five of her employees were revealed to have hidden $24 million in bad debt. Busquet, though not responsible, was accountable, and so lost her position as general manager of the division. Though devastated by the setback, Busquet felt a basic confidence in her abilities and rallied to another challenge she was offered at a lower level: salvaging merchandising services, a failing division of American Express.[43]

Optimists can more readily make a realistic assessment of a setback and admit how they contributed to it. Busquet, for example, reexamined her perfectionist, sometimes overly critical management style—even considering that it might have cowed her employees into hiding losses. She underwent executive coaching to soften her style, becoming more patient and a better listener. And under her direction, the failing merchandising services division reached profitability within two years.

Or take Arthur Blank, whose personality clashes with his boss at Handy Dan's, a Los Angeles hardware chain, led to his being fired in 1978. Blank's mother had kept the mail-order drug company his father had founded going after his death when Blank was young, and Blank himself, having witnessed how she overcame adversity, learned to keep trying instead of giving up when things went badly in life. So when an investor approached him, he jumped at the chance to found Home Depot, the no-frills, high-service, huge-selection home improvement chain that has grown to be a retailing giant.

Arthur Blank didn't give up; he reacted like an optimist, using the insider's expertise he had acquired in his years at Handy Dan's to invent a business that could outcompete his former employer. He saw himself as having the ability to change things for the better. For an optimist, a failure is just a lesson to learn from for the next round.

"Mistakes are treasures," as a German manager put it to me, "a chance to improve." But he added, "many managers have to realize they should be more tolerant of people's mistakes—not punish them for it, but help them learn from it."

Optimism and Hope

Classic studies of how optimism bolstered sales productivity at MetLife, an insurance company, were done by Martin Seligman, a University of Pennsylvania psychologist.[44] Seligman found that optimists sold 29 percent more insurance in the first year than did their more pessimistic peers, and 130 percent more their second year.

The value of an optimistic outlook has been proven in many organizations. At American Express Financial Advisors, a pilot test of optimism training helped produce a rise in sales after just three months, big enough to convince the company to make it a standard part of training. Other studies of superior managers show that they look at their failures as due to a correctable mistake and take steps to ensure that the problem won't crop up again.[45]

The near cousin of optimism is hope: knowing the steps needed to get to a goal and having the energy to pursue those steps. It is a primal motivating force, and its absence is paralyzing. Competence studies show that top performers in the human services—everything from health care and counseling to teaching—express hope for those they seek to help.[46]

The power of hope was shown in a study of caseworkers whose task it is to help people with the most severe mental disabilities—chronic schizophrenia, severe retardation—carve out a life for themselves in supervised homes.[47] The first year in such jobs is the toughest: Clients don't get better, things go wrong, people can be ungrateful, caseworkers burn out and quit. But those caseworkers who were the most hopeful—optimistic about their clients' potential for improvement and their own ability to help—fared the best. After a year on the job, those who began with high levels of hope survived with the most satisfaction, were less emotionally exhausted, and were most likely to stay in their jobs.

In jobs like these, where stress is high and frustrations common, a rosy outlook may get better results. Hopefulness is crucial when anyone undertakes a tough task; positive expectations may be especially beneficial in the toughest jobs, where high optimism may be a pragmatic job strategy.[48]

A caveat: There is something very American about these upbeat competencies. They reflect a frontier ideology that does not translate to all other cultures. In research done among top executives in a global food and beverage company, for instance, optimism was found to predict star performance in America—but not in Asia or Europe.

"In many Asian countries, like Japan, Taiwan, and India, the can-do attitude is seen as too bold or too individualistic," Mary Fontaine, managing director of the Hay/McBer Innovation and Research Center, told me. "In those cultures optimism typically manifests in more low-key ways, with the attitude, 'This is a very difficult challenge, and I'm trying, even though I may not be able to do it.' You don't hear people saying, 'I know I can do it, I know I'm good.' And in Europe, what Americans see as optimism can simply seem like arrogance."

3

···················

People
Skills

7

······················

Social Radar

The major account was underperforming, baffling the sales team at Johnson Wax: Why were the sales on a key product far softer there than at other retailers'?

The sales rep responsible for the account thought he knew the reason: The chain's buyer wanted to place bigger orders, but he was powerless: A battle between managers of two different departments at the retailer meant that the product was being sold in the wrong part of the stores—and so faring poorly. The department manager who was selling the product refused to give it up to the other department, and the buyer did not have the power to break the deadlock.

To solve the problem, Johnson Wax's sales team called for the retail equivalent of a bilateral diplomatic commission: a meeting with three levels of executives above the sales rep and the buyer. At that meeting, Johnson Wax shared data with the executives from the chain showing that if they handled the product differently, it could bring them $5 million more in profits annually. That hit home.

"When they saw they were passing up a five-million-dollar opportunity because of battles between departments, they decided they had to break down the walls," says Patrick O'Brien, then vice president for North American sales. "All three levels got behind the buyer. It had taken a year to have the discussion—but once they saw they wanted to do it, it took just days to make the change."

That sales strategy exemplifies one of the marks of empathy: being able to see a sales situation from the standpoint of the customer in order to help *the customer* succeed. Such sensitivity demands being able to read the political currents and realities of someone else's organization.

"The best approach is to have a deep understanding of a buyer's business needs and objectives, and work toward that end," O'Brien comments. "The key is probing and listening to hear what's important for that person's success. It's been one of the fundamentals of sales success for the last century."

When I spoke with O'Brien, he was flush with two triumphs: His sales team had just been named Vendor of the Year by both Wal-Mart and Target, two of America's largest retail chains.

One of the changing barometers for retail sales is "category management," where retailers at a grocery store, for example, will treat all their snacks or air fresheners as a single category, and make judgments on which brands to carry collectively, rather than on a one-by-one basis. Paradoxically, this by-the-numbers approach has made personal relationships between sales reps and category managers all the more important.

"Our sales stars have the ability to balance the world of fact with the interpersonal world," O'Brien notes. "The sales profession has gone from rapport selling to number-based sales; the field has been shifting from the traditional social skills of sales to a model of managers who work their numbers, not their contracts; but you have to balance these. You need the interpersonal side because these are still individual decisions."

Empathy takes many forms. One is the kind of astute awareness the people at Johnson Wax had of their client's needs. But it also can be seen in the company that has a realistic, accurate sense of its own people, its customers and clients, its competitors and market, and other stakeholders, from unions to shareholders. Being able to see reality from their perspective, to sense how they are reacting to the company's actions, offers a powerful set of readings for effective management.

The head of a private bank in Switzerland tells me, "My job is something like a family priest or doctor. You can't be in private banking without using your emotional intelligence, especially empathy. You have to sense what your client hopes for, fears—even if he can't express it in words."

Empathy Begins Inside

As Freud observed, "Mortals can keep no secret. If their lips are silent, they gossip with their fingertips; betrayal forces its way through every pore." The nervous fidgeting of a negotiator belies her deadpan expression; the studied disinterest of a customer dickering over prices in an auto showroom is contradicted by the excited way he gravitates toward the convertible he covets. Being able to pick up on such emotional clues is particularly important in situations where people have reason to conceal their true feelings—a fact of life in the business world.

Sensing what others feel without their saying so captures the essence of empathy. Others rarely tell us in words what they feel; instead they tell us in their tone of voice, facial expression, or other nonverbal ways. The ability to sense these subtle communications builds on more basic competencies, particularly self-awareness and self-control. Without the ability to sense our own feelings—or to keep them from swamping us—we will be hopelessly out of touch with the moods of others.

Empathy is our social radar. A friend tells me about her early sense of a colleague's unhappiness: "I went to my boss and said, 'Something's up with Kathleen—she's not happy here.' She wasn't making eye contact with me, she stopped sending me her usual witty e-mails. Then she announced she was leaving for another job."

Lacking such sensitivity, people are "off." Being emotionally tone deaf leads to social awkwardness, whether from misconstruing feelings or through a mechanical, out-of-tune bluntness or indifference that destroys rapport. One form this lack of empathy can take is responding to other people as stereotypes rather than as the unique individuals they are.

At the very least, empathy requires being able to read another's emotions; at a higher level, it entails sensing and responding to a person's unspoken concerns or feelings. At the highest levels, empathy is understanding the issues or concerns that lie behind another's feelings.

The key to knowing others' emotional terrain is an intimate familiarity with our own, shown in research by Robert Levenson at the University of California at Berkeley.[1] Levenson has married couples come into his physiology lab for two discussions: a neutral "How was your day?" talk and a fifteen-minute discussion of something the couple disagrees about. During this small battle Levenson records their responses in every way, from heart rate to changes in their facial expression.

After the disagreement, one partner leaves. The one who stays then watches a replay of the talk while narrating the hidden dialogue of what he or she was actually feeling but did not express. Then that partner leaves, and the other returns to narrate the same scene from the *other* partner's perspective.

Partners adept at empathizing do something quite extraordinary physiologically: Their own body mimics their partner's while they empathize. If the heart rate of the partner in the videotape goes up, so does the heart rate of the partner who is empathizing; if the heart rate slows down, so does that of the empathic spouse.[2] This mimicry involves a biological phenomenon called entrainment, a sort of intimate emotional tango.[3]

Such highly attuned rapport demands we put aside our own emotional agendas for the time being so that we can clearly receive the other person's signals. When we are caught up in our own strong emotions, we are off on a different physiological vector, impervious to the more subtle cues that allow rapport.[4]

Charles Darwin proposed that the twin abilities to send and read feelings have played an enormous role in human evolution, both in creating and maintaining the social order. In evolution, negative emotions—fear and anger— no doubt had immense survival value, impelling a threatened animal to fight or flee. In a sense this evolutionary holdover is still with us today; during our own amygdala hijacks, we read and respond more strongly to someone else who is also in a bad mood than to someone in a good one. This can be a recipe for emotional disaster, creating a feedback loop of negativity or rage.

The prerequisite for empathy is self-awareness, recognizing the visceral signals of feelings in one's own body. Among counselors, for instance, the most effective and empathic were best able to tune in to their body's own signals for emotion—an essential for any job where empathy matters, from teaching to sales and management.[5]

A Subtle Dance

We had a woman who could clear a room in minutes," the marketing manager of a California-based educational software firm tells me. "She wouldn't listen first and then join the conversation. She'd launch into a monologue—some complaint or attack that had nothing to do with what was being talked about—and she'd go on and on, oblivious to the yawns. She didn't know when to stop. She didn't have a clue."

The smoothness in any social interaction depends to a great extent on spontaneous entrainment. When two people start to talk with each other, they immediately begin to fall into a subtle dance of rhythmic harmony, synchronizing their movements and postures, their vocal pitch, rate of speaking, and even the length of pauses between one person's speaking and the other's response.[6]

This mutual mimicry goes on outside conscious awareness, and seems to be controlled by the most primitive parts of the brain. These mechanisms kick in with breathtaking rapidity, as quickly as a fiftieth of a second. If this automatic coordination is missing, we feel slightly uncomfortable.

One of the main mutual adjustments is in facial expression. When we see a happy face (or an angry one), it evokes the corresponding emotion in us, albeit subtly.[7] To the degree we take on the pace, posture, and facial expression of another person, we start to inhabit their emotional space; as our body mimics the other's, we begin to experience emotional attunement.[8]

Our nervous system is automatically set to engage in this emotional empathy (again, the amygdala plays the key role in this attunement).[9] But how well we use this capacity is largely a learned ability that depends on motivation. Animals—and people—who have been raised in extreme social isolation are poor at reading emotional cues in those around them not because they lack the basic circuitry for empathy but because, lacking emotional tutors, they have never learned to pay attention to these messages and so haven't practiced this skill.

Our first lessons in empathy begin in infancy, when we are held in our mother's or father's arms. These primary emotional bonds lay the groundwork for learning how to cooperate and be welcomed into a game or group. The extent to which we master this emotional curriculum determines our level of social competence. Take children on the playground who don't pick up the crucial cues for smooth interaction; when they want to join a game, they'll often just wade in and thereby disrupt it.

More socially skilled children, on the other hand, wait and watch awhile. They tune in to the game first and then enter seamlessly at a natural opening. It's the same with adults: Picking up the social rhythm and timing of those we work with is essential.

Because of differences in how well we have learned the basic skills of social awareness, there are corresponding differences among us in workplace competencies that build on empathy. Empathy represents the foundation skill for all the social competencies important for work. These include:

- *Understanding others:* Sensing others' feelings and perspectives, and taking an active interest in their concerns

- *Service orientation:* Anticipating, recognizing, and meeting customers' needs

- *Developing others:* Sensing others' development needs and bolstering their abilities

- *Leveraging diversity:* Cultivating opportunities through diverse people

- *Political awareness:* Reading the political and social currents in an organization

■ UNDERSTANDING OTHERS ■

Sensing Others' Feelings and Perspectives, and Taking an Active Interest in Their Concerns

People with this competence

- Are attentive to emotional cues and listen well

- Show sensitivity and understand others' perspectives

- Help out based on understanding other people's needs and feelings

An assistant at a large design firm describes the poisonous feelings emanating from a temperamental partner like this: "With a glance he became a closed door; he put up this don't-bother-me sign, so I knew to stay away from him. But if I have to deal with him at some of those times, I keep it short. I don't joke or anything—I did once and he went nuts. So I get monotonic, almost moronic, with him."[10]

The key phrase here is "with a glance he became a closed door"; that was the cue that told the assistant how to act around the temperamental design partner. At work we constantly pick up such emotional cues and adjust our behavior accordingly. Lacking such radar, we are vulnerable to shipwreck in the shoals created by the rocky emotions of those we work with.

Empathy is essential as an emotional guidance system, piloting us in getting along at work.

Beyond mere survival, empathy is critical for superior performance wherever the job focus is on people. Whenever an artful reading of a person's feelings matters, from sales and organizational consulting to psychotherapy and medicine, as well as leadership of every kind, empathy is crucial to excellence.

Medicine is a field newly awakened to the benefits of empathy, in part for some compelling economic reasons. In a day of heightened competition for patient loyalty, those physicians who are better at recognizing emotions in their patients are more successful in treating them than their less sensitive colleagues.[11] Physicians, of course, need to sense the anxiety and discomfort of their patients so they can treat them effectively, but a study found how rarely they listen. Patients usually had an average of four questions in mind to ask, but during the visits they were able to ask just one or two. Once a patient started speaking, the first interruption by the physician occurred, on average, within eighteen seconds.[12]

Physicians who don't listen get sued more—at least in the United States. Among primary-care physicians, those who had never had a malpractice suit were shown to be far better communicators than their lawsuit-prone peers. They took time to tell their patients what to expect from a treatment, to laugh and joke, to ask the patients' opinion and check their understanding, and to encourage the patients to talk.[13] And the time needed for a doctor to be successfully empathic? Just three minutes.

Empathic Design

Empathy has come to R&D. Researchers watch customers use a company's products—at home or at work—much as an anthropologist might observe another culture.[14] This peek into the customer's world offers a fuller understanding than can be gained through the typical round of focus groups and market surveys.

Such intimate exploration into a customer's life, combined with a company's openness to change, is a potent mix for innovation. When Kimberly-Clark sent observers to watch parents and toddlers use diapers, they realized that toddlers needed a first step toward "grown-up" dressing. That insight led to the creation of Huggies Pull-Ups, which toddlers can pull on themselves—and to $400 million in annual sales before competitors caught up.

The ability to read customers' needs well comes naturally to the best managers of product development teams. Being able to read what the market wants means empathizing with customers and then developing a product that suits their needs.[15]

At Ford Motor Company, empathic design was used in a makeover of the Lincoln Continental. The engineers, for the first time, were given intensive contact with owners of the car they were all trying to reinvent.

Instead of the old method, where market researchers would lead focus groups of car owners and distill the results, engineers spent a week talking to people who had bought Continentals. Their task: Get a sense of what owners loved about the car.

"Customers sense and feel distinctive qualities they value in a product," Nick Zeniuk, then one of the project managers, told me. "So we had to tune in to our customers' feelings. To do this, we had to be empathic. I told the design managers, 'Forget about the data you've seen from market research. Go out and talk to the people we're building this for. Listen, feel, sense. Look into their eyes, get a gut sense of what they want.' "

This personal approach brought a strong sense of the customer into the room with the automotive engineers as they created their specifications. Zeniuk remembers, "They'd come back with a video of a customer and say, 'You can't see it, but right here he was feeling very strongly about what he was saying.' We had to first get a sense of how all this needed to feel, and then figure out what that would look like in engineering terms—the technical specifications that would make the car feel comfortable or more responsive."

The Art of Listening

When you're desperate to make a sale you don't listen as well," the director of sales at a Wall Street brokerage firm told me. "There's nothing better in selling than when someone objects to something and you can say, 'You're absolutely right—we should consider that.' You do much better if you can listen and sympathize with their viewpoint."

A finely tuned ear is at the heart of empathy. Listening well is essential for workplace success. The U.S. Department of Labor estimates that of the total time we spend in communication, 22 percent is devoted to reading and writing, 23 percent to speaking—and 55 percent to listening.[16]

Those who cannot or do not listen come across as indifferent or uncaring, which in turn makes others less communicative. And listening is an art.

The first step is giving the sense that one is open to listening in the first place; managers with an "open door" policy, who appear approachable or go out of their way to hear what people have to say, embody this competence. And people who seem easy to talk to are those who get to hear more.

Listening well and deeply means going beyond what is said by asking questions, restating in one's own words what you hear to be sure you understand. This is "active" listening. A mark of having truly heard someone else is to respond appropriately, even if that means making some change in what you do. But just how far we should go in adjusting our actions based on what another says is itself a matter of some controversy.

In sales circles some view empathy quite narrowly, arguing that taking the customer's perspective will kill sales of products or services customers don't really want or need.[17] This, of course, implies a somewhat cynical or naïve view of the salesperson's task, as though it is only about making the sale, not building or improving a relationship with the customer.

A more enlightened view of sales, though, sees the task as being able to listen well and understand what the customer or client needs, and then find a way to meet those needs. This lesson, that empathy is at the heart of effective selling, was borne out by a survey of a random sample of buyers for both large and small American retailers, who were asked about apparel sales reps.[18]

The old stereotype that sales go to the highly affable, outgoing salesperson did not hold up. It wasn't enough to be a fast-talking extrovert; the buyers' consensus favored the reps who were most empathic—who cared about their needs and concerns.[19] That was especially true if the empathy went hand in hand with the sense that the sales rep could be trusted.

When Empathy Lacks Integrity

I want to assure you at the outset that the most important thing is the kids— they come first. I know some of you are worried. But if we find anything that might harm the kids, we'll stop."

So began the warm, reassuring presentation of the president of an outfit that specialized in recovering metals from the ash left by industrial burning. He had come to talk to the parents and teachers of a grammar school in the small town where his company was relocating; the plant would be down the street from the school, pending final approval by the town government.

As the company president ran through what would go on at the plant—the jobs it would bring, the benefits for the local economy—his sincerity and concern for the well-being of the children and their community were winning over his audience. He seemed so understanding, so empathic.

But then came the question-and-answer period. One of the parents, a chemist, asked, "But aren't you going to be processing ash that contains dioxin? And isn't dioxin highly carcinogenic? How will you protect our children from that?"

With that question, the president became flustered, defensive, even antagonistic—especially when other parents, now not so trusting, challenged him on why he had failed to mention this unsettling fact earlier.

The meeting ended with the parents deciding to consult an expert on industrial toxins and to ask the town manager to hold public hearings before approving the plant.

Empathy can be used as a tool for manipulation. This manifests frequently as pseudoempathy, a social pose that disintegrates quickly if recognized. A friend complained to me about the salespeople in a pricey clothing store she likes to browse in: "They always say how nice it is to see me, and follow me around trying to make small talk. I just want them to leave me alone until I have a question." Then one day, in an unguarded moment, one of the salespeople confessed that her boss had instructed them to strike up a friendly conversation with customers who had made expensive purchases before. But this forced friendliness just didn't ring true—it actually put off my friend.

We may have natural safeguards against such artificial empathy—the capacity to sense, as my friend did, when empathy is not sincere. And researchers who have assessed manipulative people find that those who are most motivated by a Machiavellian urge to use people for their own gain tend to be poorest at empathy. By contrast, those who are trusting—who believe that people are basically good—tend to be more highly attuned to feelings.[20]

Empathy Avoidance

S am was emotionally tone deaf. He picked up the phone, heard a sobbing voice ask to speak with his wife, Marcy, and handed her the phone with a cheery, "Marcy, it's for you!"

Elaine Hatfield, the University of Hawaii psychologist who knows him, says, "Sam was oblivious to emotional messages because he couldn't care less."[21]

It's not enough to have the potential to empathize—we have to care. But some people who seem to lack empathy may actually be doing so strategically and intentionally; they may avoid caring in order to hold to a hard line and to resist the urge to help.[22] And in the right measure, this is not necessarily a bad thing in the workplace.

Managers who go overboard in focusing on relationships or catering to people's emotional needs at the expense of organizational requirements perform poorly.[23] In situations where the perceived cost of empathy is thought to be too high—for example, in a negotiation over wages—people on both sides of the issue may have to blunt their sympathy. Lawyers, too, are notorious for their studied indifference to the concerns of the other side during litigation (though, as we shall see in Chapter 8, an extreme shutdown of empathy is not a fruitful negotiation strategy).

There may be some wisdom in tempering empathy, particularly when it comes to allocating tight resources in an organization. When we identify too strongly with someone else's need, we are more prone to go to extremes in helping them, even when that decision harms the collective good.[24]

By the same token, the head alone, without the heart, can make decisions that will backfire—as has been the case with many companies that ruthlessly downsized, then found themselves loathed or distrusted by the dispirited employees who were left. And some managers tune out the feelings of those they work with simply to avoid having to take those feelings into account—a tactic that can make them seem imperious or cold.

A lack of empathy may account for what happened with the surgeon who was going to treat a friend of mine for a blood clot in her leg. When he explained to her that one risk of the surgery was that she might lose her leg, my friend burst into tears.

His response: "If you're going to cry, you'll have to find another physician to treat you."

So she did.

Empathy Distress

S he had been a pediatric nurse for seven years, but now she was asking for a transfer to a different service at the medical center. Why?

"I just can't take holding another little kid who is going to die of cancer. It's too hard on me."

The nurse's anguish offers a case study in "empathy distress," where one person "catches" another person's upset. Instead of helping the children out of their pain and distress, the nurse found herself joining it.

Empathy distress is most common when we find ourselves deeply upset that someone we care about is in pain. For example, concern for a troubled friend—say, a coworker who fears being laid off—may stir the same troubling feelings in us. This phenomenon occurs when someone who is highly empathic is exposed to another person's negative moods and doesn't have the self-regulation skills to calm their own sympathetic distress.

Medical residents "toughen" themselves to handle empathy distress; their joking about patients near death as "crispy critters" or "goners" is part of this emotional shell, a way to deal with their own sensitivities. The danger, of course, is that they will end up like the insensitive surgeon who drove my friend away. A new generation of medical school programs has begun to teach students ways to manage their own distress more effectively without forfeiting empathy.

Workers such as customer service representatives, who regularly deal with people in bad moods, are also in danger of empathy distress. This problem often plagues people in the helping professions, who are exposed day after day to people in dire circumstances. The alternative is to stay open to feelings, but to be adept in the art of emotional self-management, so that we are not overwhelmed by the distress we catch from those we deal with.

The Politics of Empathy

T here is a politics of empathy: Those with little power are typically expected to sense the feelings of those who hold power, while those in power feel less obligation to be sensitive in return. In other words, the studied lack of empathy is a way power-holders can tacitly assert their authority.

During the days of the civil rights movement, Martin Luther King Jr. expressed surprise at how little insight whites had into the feelings of blacks; blacks, he said, had to be much more sensitized to how whites felt, if only to survive in a racist society. A parallel argument holds that to the degree women are oppressed in a society, they have had to be more empathic than men (for a review of the data on gender differences in empathy, see Appendix 3).

Research in the 1970s and 1980s suggested a negative correlation between being in positions of power and empathic abilities.[25] But that may hold less true today, since organizations are becoming more team-oriented and less stiffly hierarchical. The demands of modern leadership now include competence at empathy; the authoritarian style of the past just doesn't work as well as it once did.

Those who still dismiss empathy as out of place in business, or as too "soft," do so mainly because of two common misunderstandings. One is confusing empathy with psychologizing; the other is the mistaken belief that empathizing with people is the same as *agreeing* with them.

Richard Boyatzis told me, "At a major computer manufacturer I was assessing managers for empathy by asking them to describe a time they had helped someone with a problem. I found that some people would tell about deeply exploring the other person's psychological state and explaining it to them in terms of its childhood roots or some pop-psych theory like codependency. But that is psychologizing, not empathy—you're actually *dismissing* the problem by talking about its supposed causes."

Psychologizing, Boyatzis found, was related to mediocre performance in managers. The top performers listened and understood the others' feelings, and offered advice, without imposing their own "diagnosis" of what was behind the problem. Such psychological theorizing may be of interest, even helpful, over a cup of coffee between friends—but it is not appropriate at work. And while it may masquerade as empathy, it is not the same.

Similarly, understanding someone's point of view or perspective—knowing why they feel as they do—does not inevitably mean embracing it. Particularly in business dealings, understanding how someone feels need not lead to giving in, but to more skillful negotiation and management. As a result, tough decisions may generate less resentment and lasting ill will.

I remember talking with leaders of management teams at Lockheed Martin, an aerospace company that had gone through a period of major cutbacks. Many of the managers had laid off hundreds of workers—a process some described as the hardest thing they had ever had to do. I mentioned that some managers fear empathy will make them too softhearted to make the hard decisions of business life, and I asked them if they thought empathy mattered. "Absolutely," was one reply. "When you have to let thousands of people go, everyone else who stays is watching." They had to go through with the layoffs despite the pain—but, they told me, if they hadn't gone about the process with empathy, it would have demoralized or antagonized everyone.

Consider how employees were treated when plants closed at two companies. At GE, workers had two years' notice that the plant would be closed, and the company made an intense outplacement effort to help them find other jobs. The other company announced the closing with just one week's notice, and made no effort to help workers locate other employment.

The results? Almost a year later, the majority of the former GE workers said it had been a good place to work, and 93 percent lauded the transition services offered them.[26] At the other company, only 3 percent said it had been a good place to work. GE preserved a large pool of goodwill, while the other firm left a legacy of bitterness.

▪ DEVELOPING OTHERS ▪

Sensing Others' Development Needs and Bolstering Their Abilities

▪▪

People with this competence

- Acknowledge and reward people's strengths and accomplishments

- Offer useful feedback and identify people's needs for further growth

- Mentor, give timely coaching, and offer assignments that challenge and foster a person's skills

▪▪

It was a small lesson, but one with lasting impact. As a high-profile, fast-track editor at a national magazine, she had a problem: "I was prone to snap decisions, committing to projects in a moment of enthusiasm, then having to suffer through a torturous series of rewrites with authors that ended in their articles being killed. It was emotionally draining for me, and it created too much animosity and just plain pain.

"But then," she told me, "my editor in chief taught me a phrase that has helped immensely."

What was the phrase?

" 'I'll think about it.' "

That simple bit of advice exemplifies coaching, which lies at the heart of developing others. Excellence in this competence is emerging as second only to team leadership among superior managers.[27] For sales managers, developing others is even more important—the competence most frequently found among those at the top of the field.[28]

This is a person-to-person art; the heart of coaching and developing is the act of counseling. And the effectiveness of counseling hinges on empathy and the ability to focus on our own feelings and share them.[29]

In a study of supervisors, managers, and executives in twelve large organizations, the impact of developing others was greatest among supervisors, suggesting that this skill is crucial in managing those involved in front-line work—salespeople, line workers, and the like.[30] As the realm of a manager or executive's influence increases, the direct opportunities for developing others may diminish, while other competencies, like leadership, may emerge as more relevant.

Even so, "The head of an organization is essentially a teacher," Harry Levinson, a pioneer in consulting psychology, tells me. He adds, "People these days need to have the sense they are getting increasingly competent as they go on—or else they won't stay."

Strong coaching or mentoring helps employees perform better, enhances loyalty and job satisfaction, leads to promotions and pay increases, and lowers rates of turnover.[31]

An open, trusting relationship is the foundation of success in on-the-job coaching. That was the clear conclusion when fifty-eight top managers, all vice presidents or above at companies with annual sales of $5 billion or more, were asked about their own experiences.[32] These executives focus on helping people they see as having high potential. As one high-level executive puts it, "I'm nice to those whom I just expect to do their jobs, but I really lean on the talented ones—I push them to transcend themselves."

They spent most of their coaching time trying to boost performance, mainly by giving feedback and offering tips on developing needed skills. By and large their comments were positive; they spent only about 5 percent of their time confronting poor performance.

The key to success as coaches? The best coaches show a genuine personal interest in those they guide, and have empathy for and an understanding of their employees. Trust was crucial—when there was little trust in the coach, advice went unheeded. This happened also when the coach was impersonal and cold, or the relationship seemed too one-sided or self-serving. Coaches who showed respect, trustworthiness, and empathy were the best. But when employees resisted change or were difficult, then the experience was so unrewarding for the coaches that they tended to drop the effort.

"In retrospect, one of my biggest failures in business was not looking for coaching in my early years," a vice president at a large media conglomerate told me. "I was so afraid to seem inadequate that I didn't ask for advice on how to handle things. So I shut down many potential coaching relationships. Now a young associate of mine will appear in my doorway asking me to coach her on how to approach our president about something, or how to handle some situation. She's being smart."

The standard image of coaching or mentoring is a seasoned hand helping a favored younger person along. But people who are gifted at helping others can do so with anyone—even superiors. Managing upward—helping a superior do a better job—is part of this art. A chief petty officer in the U.S. Navy, for example, recounted how he had to "teach junior officers how to lead me. I tell them, 'You're running the ship and I'm watching all this equipment for you; you've got a right to know how it's running. Ask me. And ask me to help you when I can.' "[33]

The Art of the Critique

When it comes to giving feedback, perhaps no one is better than Shirley DeLibero, head of the New Jersey Transit Authority, which under her direction emerged as the most efficient transit company in America. De-Libero shows people she appreciates them, while giving them a consistent stream of positive and constructive performance feedback. "I spend lots of time praising people—I send personal notes to people throughout the company when they do a good job," DeLibero told me. "But I also let people know when they goof up. You do a disservice to people if you don't evaluate their performance honestly. You have to let them know *what* they need to improve."

Like DeLibero, the helpful coach gives specific information about what is wrong, combined with corrective feedback and a positive expectation of the person's ability to improve. By contrast, the worst way to give feedback is during an amygdala hijack, when the result is inevitably a character attack.

While that has a pernicious effect, so does another common failing: neglecting to give any performance feedback at all.

In a study of the effects of performance feedback on self-confidence, MBA students either were praised, were criticized, or received no feedback on their performance in a simulation of creative problem solving. They had been told that their efforts would be compared with how well hundreds of others had done on the same task. Those who heard nothing about how well they did suffered as great a blow to their self-confidence as those who were criticized.[34] The report cautions that "when organizations deprive employees of specific job-related information, they may unknowingly inhibit their performance."

People hunger for feedback, yet too many managers, supervisors, and executives are inept at giving it or are simply disinclined to provide any. And in some cultures—especially in Asia and Scandinavia—there is a tacit prohibition against expressing criticism openly, particularly in front of others. An executive at a Saudi company told me, "We have twenty-seven different nationalities working together in our organization. Most come from countries where people were brought up not to say bad things about the people they work with. So it's hard to get honest performance feedback."

On the other hand, giving brutal feedback can be a cover for pure competitive aggression—an attack disguised as "helpfulness." An executive at a bank in the Netherlands says, "Some people here give feedback to score in a macho game of one-upmanship; they pay no attention to the impact on the person receiving it, they're far too blunt. But it's not authentic help—it's part of a game. They need more empathy."

The Power of Pygmalion

They were a burden to their shipmates—sailors who were constantly in trouble, or simply did not do their jobs. "Undermotivated problem sailors" was the term the U.S. Navy used for them; the military acronym was "LP," for "low performer."

But their supervisors were given a set of tactics to change the LPs' behavior. The supervisors were taught something new: to expect the best of these low performers despite their abominable histories.

The supervisors let the LPs know they believed in their ability to change, and they treated them more like winners. That positive expectation proved powerful: The LPs began to do better on every front, receiving fewer punishments, showing better overall performance, even improving their personal appearance.[35] It was the Pygmalion effect in action: Expecting the best from people can be a self-fulfilling prophecy.

Athletic coaches and good managers alike have long known they can boost a person's performance by giving them a suitable challenge coupled with a vote of confidence.

One way to promote positive expectations is to let others take the lead in setting their own goals, rather than dictating the terms and manner of their development. This communicates the belief that employees have the capacity to be the pilot of their destiny, which is a core tenet held by those who take initiative.

Another technique that encourages people to perform better is to point to problems without offering a solution; this implies they can find the solution themselves. Outstanding tutors use this strategy with their students. They initiate what amounts to a Socratic dialogue, leading the person through a series of questions. This lets students find their own way to the answers, which will bolster their confidence in decision making.[36]

At a higher level of development, the coach or mentor arranges an ongoing assignment that will give the person needed training, experience, or challenges. This might take the form of delegating responsibilities, or putting the person in charge of a project that will call forth new skills. Doing this well demands a sensitivity to the readiness of the person being coached—if the assignment is too easy, little will be learned; if it's too difficult, the person may experience a setback. The skill lies in arranging successful "stretch" experiences that increase capability and confidence. The ultimate support comes in the form of promoting employees to appropriate positions—as a genuine acknowledgment of their newly achieved level of competence, and a new proving ground for yet another level of skill.

Still, the urge to help develop someone's abilities can go overboard, conflicting with the better interests of the organization. Putting too much emphasis on coaching and development at the expense of other needs is a danger. Supervisors and managers who devote too much time and effort to coaching and too little to leading or managing end up doing a mediocre job at best.[37]

▪ **SERVICE ORIENTATION** ▪

Anticipating, Recognizing, and Meeting Customers' Needs

People with this competence:

▪ Understand customers' needs and match them to services or products

▪ Seek ways to increase customers' satisfaction and loyalty

▪ Gladly offer appropriate assistance

▪ Grasp a customer's perspective, acting as a trusted advisor

To visit Stéphane & Bernard, a clothing boutique on the island of St. Barts, is to experience customer service as high art. The eponymous owners attend visitors with a combination of Gallic charm, wit, and undivided attention.

For two hours one lazy January afternoon, my wife and I luxuriated in that attention. My wife and Bernard talked about her life and her clothes, with Bernard running back and forth to the racks to find her the perfect piece. But he also took twenty minutes to carefully annotate a map of the island for me while regaling me with highlights of its restaurants, beaches, and snorkeling spots.

"My business is first of all to make people feel good here, to make everyone comfortable," Bernard explains, indicating their store, which crams clothes from fifteen top designers into just 450 square feet. Their tiny shop earns five times more per square foot than other such retailers—most of it in the four winter months of the tourist season.

The key to this success lies in their philosophy of customer service. "I have to know my customers to help them—how they like to dress, what they like to do, what part of their body they're dissatisfied with," Stéphane tells me.

They eschew the commission approach to sales, "where the salespeople don't care if it looks good or not. They just want to make the sale, so they tell you that whatever you've picked is perfect." Stéphane continues, "If I don't like how something looks on a customer, I tell her so—and why. I don't want to sell her something that's not right for her. I act as an advisor to my customers."

That is exactly what they are to their three hundred or so regular customers. These clients are so familiar to them that when Stéphane and Bernard travel on buying trips, many purchases are made with a specific customer in mind. "We build relationships," says Bernard. "We keep a complete file on each customer, follow what they bought, what they're looking for, and over the years we help them build a wardrobe."

Stéphane and Bernard exemplify the highest level of customer service, which means being able to identify a client's real, underlying—and often unstated—needs, and then matching them to one's products or services. It also means taking a long-term perspective and so sometimes trading off immediate gains in order to protect and preserve the relationship.

The service ideal of top performers transcends the ordinary customer service model altogether. Sales or continued patronage is no longer the sole goal of the relationship, but rather a natural by-product of servicing the client's needs.

Superlative customer service entails being a trusted advisor, as Stéphane and Bernard realize. This stance can mean occasionally taking a position that runs against the immediate interests of one's own organization but is the correct action for the client. This kind of trust-based relationship will only grow over time.

At the ultimate level of service, one acts as the client's advocate. This can lead to benefits in the long run—for example, advising a client not to overextend credit on purchases may mean fewer sales in the short term, but it ensures that the account will stay viable into the future. It might even mean on occasion suggesting a competitor's product, which may lose an immediate sale but cement a long-term relationship.

A Broader View

In the modern organization, everyone has "customers." Any colleague we need to assist or whose needs our own job affects is a client of sorts. Star performers go out of their way to make themselves available to serve their clients, especially during crucial moments. Stars also help their clients look good: for example, doing something that creates a visible success for the client (or coworker).

For those in the compensation and benefits arm of Sandoz Pharmaceuticals, outstanding customer service took forms like spending extra hours working closely with the head of sales to determine incentive targets, or giving a home phone number to a department head going through a critical period of reorganization, being available day or night to help out.[38] It also meant occasionally letting another person take credit for a job well done.

To shine at service we need to monitor the satisfaction of customers, not waiting to hear complaints but freely offering information that might be helpful without self-interest motivating the gesture. This lays the groundwork for a trusting relationship, one where the client or coworker will feel a positive regard and start to see us as a source of reliable and helpful information—elevating the relationship above one simply of buyer and seller.

That, of course, takes empathy. Consider the results from a study of the sales force of an office supply and equipment company that sells to industrial organizations and government agencies. The most successful members of the sales force were able to combine taking the customer's viewpoint with appropriate assertiveness to steer them toward a choice that satisfied both their needs.[39]

If a salesperson takes too much control, it can lead to resentment. Successful salespeople empathize at the outset of the interaction, sensing the buyer's viewpoint, and fine-tuning their sense of what the buyer wants as the interaction continues—for instance, noting signs of discomfort in response to a suggestion, and expressing empathic concern before going on.

The shift toward making the customer's needs the center of the relationship goes hand in glove with having a friendly emotional tone. This is crucial in handling disgruntled customers. "A customer was having some difficulty getting a refund check," a manager in a large retail store recalls.[40] "She came to me because she said our operations manager was rude to her. I'm sure that was just a misunderstanding, but I apologized, helped her get the check, and sent her on her way. It took only a few minutes to straighten out the problem, and she left feeling better than when she came in."

That last line bears repeating: "She left feeling better than when she came in." How customers *feel* when they interact with an employee determines how they feel about the company itself. In a psychological sense, the "company" as experienced by the customer *is* these interactions. Loyalty is lost or strengthened in every interaction between a company and its customers. To paraphrase business maven Peter Drucker, the purpose of business is not to make a sale, but to make and keep a customer.

The Costs of Cost-Cutting

Nancy Cohen walked into a Pier 1 store intending to buy a new set of kitchen chairs. The store had the chairs, but she walked out empty-handed and furious.

"I was presold," she told a colleague of mine.[41] "But I couldn't get anyone to help me. The sales help were too busy chatting among themselves. I said to the woman who finally faced me, 'I am interested in the chairs in the window. Do you have any in stock and do you have any other colors?' "

The reply: a vague gesture to a corner of the store filled with glassware, and the even vaguer, almost mystifying response, "I think it comes in that color."

And with that, the saleswoman walked away—from an $800 sale.

That salesclerk was absolutely incompetent at customer service, the critical ability for anyone who works at the interface between a company and its clientele.[42] And such incompetence is on the rise in American department and discount stores; a 1996 survey of four thousand consumers by Yankelovich Partners rated such retailers eleventh out of twenty consumer services, behind telephone companies, restaurants, and even the U.S. Post Office.[43] One villain seems to be too-sharply reduced staffing on sales floors; another, curtailing training; the American retail industry now spends less on training salespeople than any other business.

One of the worst signs of incompetence at customer service is an us-against-them mind-set, where the customer or client is targeted as an enemy and viewed only as someone to be manipulated. This stance hampers salespeople's effectiveness at selling because they don't really see the customer. This can lead to a misguided hard sell, where a salesperson comes on too strong in a way that is utterly at odds with the customer's needs.

▪ LEVERAGING DIVERSITY ▪

Cultivating Opportunities Through Different Kinds of People

People with this competence

▪ Respect and relate well to people from varied backgrounds

- Understand diverse worldviews and are sensitive to group differences

- See diversity as opportunity, creating an environment where diverse people can thrive

- Challenge bias and intolerance

■■

I often tell the story about my encounter with an outgoing bus driver in New York City who managed to keep up an upbeat patter with his passengers as he navigated the streets of the city. By the time people got off that bus, their bad moods had been lifted by exposure to his sheer exuberance. It was a breathtaking demonstration of social adeptness.

I used to describe the bus driver as "a black man around sixty." But after one lecture, an African-American woman came up and challenged me: "Why did you mention he was black? Would you have mentioned it if he had been Jewish or Japanese?"

I was stunned by her question. Thinking it over, I realized that, for me, mentioning the bus driver's race was implicitly part of a rejoinder I was making to the book *The Bell Curve,* which had argued that IQ is the key to life success and that African-Americans had a disadvantage relative to other groups in this area. In my analysis the book was based on flawed data, and besides, IQ was but one part of a spectrum of factors that led to life success, with emotional intelligence playing a major role.[44] I wanted to make the point that this African-American man was gifted in that domain.

But the woman retorted that I hadn't made any of that explicit, and to her ears I seemed to be describing someone who gets along by being overly eager to please white people. At any rate, his race was irrelevant, she argued.

And she was right. In the context in which I told the story, the man's race *was* irrelevant. To call attention to his race was to raise a difference that was beside the point. I dropped any mention of his race from then on.

Calling attention to someone's group affiliation when that identity is irrelevant can invoke a stereotype about that group in the minds of all concerned. And group stereotypes can have an *emotional* power that negatively affects performance.

The destructive power of stereotypes—particularly for members of minority groups in an organization—has been revealed in an elegant series of studies by Claude Steele, a psychologist at Stanford University. Steele should know: He's one of very few African-American members of that university's mostly white faculty.

While Steele's experiments dealt with academic performance, the implications for the workplace are direct: Negative stereotypes can cripple work performance. To be successful on a job, people need to feel they belong there and are accepted and valued, and that they have the skills and inner resources needed to achieve, even prosper. When negative stereotypes undermine these assumptions, they hamper performance.

"Stereotype threat" is the term Steele coined to refer to a kind of emotional land mine, an expectation of low performance that, though unspoken, permeates an organization, creating an atmosphere that negatively affects someones work abilities.[45] Such expectations have the potential to cause levels of anxiety that seriously impair cognitive ability. As we saw in Chapter 5, the aroused amygdala can shrink the space available in working memory, and stereotype threat is certainly capable of activating the amygdala.

A Threat in the Air

The test Steele devised was straightforward enough: College men and women who were strong in math were asked to solve problems taken from the qualifying exam for graduate school. They took the test in two groups. The first group was told that the test usually showed differences in ability between men and women. The others were told nothing.

The women's scores on the test were appreciably lower than the men's—but *only* when they had been told the test was sensitive to gender differences. The women who had not been reminded about gender issues did just as well as the men!

The same performance-lowering effect occurred when black test takers were given a similarly threatening message. Steele's experiments offer dramatic evidence of the power of even suggesting stereotypes. The active ingredient in lowering the women's scores, Steele found, was debilitating anxiety. Though they had the potential to perform well, the anxiety triggered by the threatening stereotype impaired their performance.

Steele contends that this anxiety is worsened by the interpretive framework the stereotype creates. The usual anxieties of a challenging task are seen as confirming that they cannot perform, which amplifies their own anxieties so they do, indeed, perform poorly.

Those most likely to feel the effects of stereotype threat are those at the *vanguard* of a group—the first women to become jet pilots, say, or the first minority group member to enter a law firm or brokerage house. Despite having the skills and self-confidence to enter this new territory, once there they can feel the full effect of stereotype threat and so, for the first time, may experience emotionally induced performance lapses.

Women who are at the higher reaches of executive ranks offer a case in point. A survey of women—and their CEOs—revealed that the CEOs believed women's lack of management experience and tenure was what prevented them from advancing to corporate leadership positions. The women executives, though, named as the number one and two reasons stereotyping and exclusion from informal networks in the organization.[46]

The stereotype threat for women executives seems to come into play in specific circumstances. A review of sixty-one studies on workplace prejudice against women managers found that bias comes into play most when women work in jobs that traditionally have been held by men, or are evaluated by men rather than women.[47]

How Stereotypes Threaten

Steele argues that stereotype threat may be one reason women are underrepresented in math, engineering, and the physical sciences. While American girls show no difference from boys in math abilities through elementary and middle school, once they enter high school their scores on math tests start to lag, and the gap widens through college and graduate school. At the start of their college careers, women drop out of math, science, and engineering programs at two and a half times the rate of men. American women earn just 22 percent of college degrees in these fields and only 13 percent of the Ph.D.s—and hold just 10 percent of the jobs (where, incidentally, they earn only three quarters of the salary paid to men in comparable positions).[48]

This failure to perform has nothing to do with skill. It has much to do with the presence of disabling stereotypes. Steele points to instances of underperformance by blacks and women despite high test scores as evidence of the role of emotional threat once people enter a domain where a threatening stereotype exists. At that point, he argues, people are particularly vulnerable to doubting their own abilities, questioning their talents and skills—thus undermining their own sense of capability. Their anxiety acts as a spotlight, both for themselves and (at least in their minds) those who are watching to see how well—or how poorly—they will do.

Black students, for example, are affected by "rumors of inferiority," such as those put forth in the book *The Bell Curve*. That same kind of wrong thinking afflicts oppressed minorities around the world. Through long exposure, such negative social stereotypes take hold, Steele argues, and so intimidate those who belong to such groups. That intimidation becomes emotionally potent and destructive in the workplace.

Success Through Others

One of the watchwords at the Harvard Business School these days is "Success through others who are different from yourself." There is strength in difference, and this makes the ability to leverage diversity an increasingly crucial competence.

The vastly greater variety of people working in organizations of every kind demands a greater awareness of the subtle distortions that stereotypes and bias bring to working relationships. Among managers, for example, being able to read people accurately, without the distortions of emotionally laden stereotypes, sets superior performers apart from average.[49]

We generally have difficulty reading the subtle nonverbal signals of emotion in those who belong to groups very different from our own—whether a different gender, race, nationality, or ethnic group.[50] Every group has its own norms for expressing emotion, and to the extent we are unfamiliar with those norms, empathizing grows more difficult. As we have seen, a failure of empathy can throw any interaction off-key, making both people uncomfortable and creating an emotional distance, which in turn encourages us to view the other person through the lens of a group stereotype rather than see him or her as an individual.

The missing ingredient in many diversity programs is that they fail to take advantage of diversity by using it to help participants learn how to do their business better. It's all well and good to make people of diverse backgrounds feel comfortable and welcome at work, but we can go further, *leveraging* diversity to heighten performance across the board.

Beyond zero tolerance for intolerance, the ability to leverage diversity revolves around three skills: getting along well with people who are different, appreciating the unique ways others may operate, and seizing whatever business opportunity these unique approaches might offer.

These principles point the way to what David Thomas and Robin Ely contend, in a *Harvard Business Review* article, can be the potential benefits of leveraging diversity: heightened profitability, enhanced organizational learning, flexibility, and rapid adaptation to shifting markets.[51]

To go that extra step requires questioning the widespread assumption that the only goal of diversification is simply to raise the numbers of different kinds of people in a workforce, channeling them to jobs specializing in dealing with customers like themselves. This assumes, Thomas and Ely argue, that the main special contribution minority group members can make to a company is in using their insider's sensibility to help the company market better to members of their group.

That is a decent goal so far as it goes, but it fails to reap the true benefits of diversity. Thomas and Ely propose that diverse people "bring different, important, and competitively relevant knowledge and perspectives about how to actually *do work*—how to design processes, reach goals, frame tasks, create effective teams, communicate ideas, and lead."[52] And this knowledge can improve an organization.

Consider the case of a public-interest law firm in the northeastern United States. In the 1980s, the law firm's all-white staff became concerned that their main clients, women in workplace disputes, were also all white. They felt obligated to diversify their client base.

So the firm hired a Hispanic lawyer, hoping she would bring in Hispanic clients. But something *more* happened: She brought in a new way of thinking about the basic business of the law firm itself. One result was that the firm expanded its practice beyond women's issues, also pursuing precedent-setting litigation challenging English-only policies.

As the firm began to take on more nonwhite lawyers, says one of its principal partners, "it affected our work by expanding our notions of what are relevant issues and framing them in creative ways that would have never been done with an all-white staff. It's really changed the substance—and in that sense enhanced the quality—of our work."[53]

When leaders of organizations value the insights brought to work by people of diverse backgrounds, it can lead to organizational learning that boosts competitiveness. Take a financial services company whose sales model had focused on rapid-fire cold calls, until it realized that its most successful salespeople were women who used a sales approach more in keeping with their gender style: the slow, sure building of relationships. This company now takes a more flexible approach to sales, encouraging and rewarding the differing styles that work better for salespeople of different backgrounds. The company was able to use the insight offered by the women's success to question its own assumptions, learn, and change—and so do better by leveraging diversity.

▪ POLITICAL AWARENESS ▪

Reading Social and Political Currents

▪▪

People with this competence

- ▪ Accurately read key power relationships

- ▪ Detect crucial social networks

- ▪ Understand the forces that shape views and actions of clients, customers, or competitors

- ▪ Accurately read organizational and external realities

▪▪

An outstanding diplomat tells of being posted to an oil-rich African nation and quickly learning that it was "the prime minister's executive assistant's mistress's nephew" who actually called the shots on that nation's petroleum policy. So the diplomat immediately arranged to get invited to a party where he could meet, befriend, and eventually lobby the nephew.[54]

The ability to read political realities is vital to the behind-the-scenes networking and coalition building that allows someone to wield influence—no matter what their professional role. Mediocre performers lack such social acumen and so betray a distressingly low level of political savvy.

A director of training and development at a Fortune 500 company asked me to help design a program for managers there, because, as she candidly put it, "You can describe many of the managers here as practically unconscious, oblivious to what's going on around them."

Every organization has its own invisible nervous system of connection and influence. Some people are oblivious to this below-the-radar world, while others have it fully on their own screen. Skill at reading the currents that influence the *real* decision makers depends on the ability to empathize on an organizational level, not just an interpersonal one.

People who maintain rich personal networks in an organization typically are savvy about what is going on, and this social intelligence extends to understanding the larger realities that affect the organization. For example, knowing how to read the currents in the client organization typifies people outstanding in corporate sales. One politically savvy star performer gave this example: "An executive VP who was relatively new on the board was a rising star and a 'favorite son' of the president of the corporation we sell to. He was really the decision maker: He had carte blanche from the president. We found that fostering a relationship with him was very much to our benefit and the key to the sale."[55]

Outstanding performers in most organizations share this ability. Among managers and executives generally, this emotional competence distinguishes superior performers; their ability to read situations objectively, without the distorting lens of their own biases or assumptions, allows them to respond effectively—and the further up the organizational ladder, the more this matters.[56]

Executives continually are put in the predicament of having to balance seemingly conflicting points of view or interests, whether from within or from the world at large. Without this political astuteness, managers are at a loss to balance the multitudinous perspectives of peers, bosses, subordinates, customers, and competitors.

People who do this well are able to distance themselves a bit, setting aside their own emotional involvement in events to see with more objectivity. For example, when faced with a conflict within their organization, they can take multiple perspectives, describing with some accuracy the position of each person involved. This is true despite the fact that all of us encounter few events—especially emotionally loaded ones—about which we have no opinion or feeling. This emotional competence builds on both emotional self-control and empathy, allowing people to see clearly rather than be swayed by their own point of view.

Political Savvy

The vice chairman of a large American oil company went to China during the rule of Deng Xiaoping. While there, he gave a talk to a small group of Chinese officials and made some comments critical of President Clinton.[57]

His audience sat listening in a frozen silence, and when he finished, no one said a word. The next day someone came to the offices of the oil company to apologize, saying with some delicacy, "We are sorry we were not able to carry on a conversation in a more interactive way yesterday. But you understand that many of the topics your vice chairman brought up are foreign to us."

The employee who received the message said later, "I considered them very gracious. What they did not say to my face was, 'Your vice chairman can criticize Clinton and feel that's okay. But if one of us did the same thing to our head of state, he'd probably be in jail the next day.' "

The oil company vice chairman lacked sensitivity to the ground rules of the culture he was dealing with. And as with national cultures, every organization has its implicit ground rules for what is acceptable and what is not. Empathizing at the organizational level means being attuned to the climate and culture of an organization.

The inevitable politics of organizational life create competing coalitions and power struggles. A sensitivity to these political fault lines of alliance and rivalry makes a person more understanding of the underlying issues and better able to address what really matters to key decision makers. At an even higher level of competence, this awareness extends to the larger forces in the world—competitive or regulatory pressures, technological opportunities, political forces, and the like—that determine the global opportunities and constraints of the organization.

A caution: While "political animals," those who live to play the game of organizational politics in pursuit of their own interest and advancement, eagerly study the invisible web of power, their weakness lies in the fact that their motive for doing so is pure self-interest. They ignore information that does not bear on their personal agenda, and this can create blind spots. It also means they tune out the feelings of those around them except when pertinent to their own ambition—and so political animals often come across as uncaring, insensitive, and self-centered.

Disdain of (or disinterest in) organizational politics is also a liability. Whatever the reason, those who lack political astuteness more often blunder in trying to mobilize others to their cause because their attempts at influence are misdirected or inept. An accurate understanding of the formal structure of the organizational chart is not enough; what's needed is a keen sense of the informal structure and the unspoken power centers in the organization.

8

....

The Arts of Influence

The merger of Salomon Brothers and Smith Barney created one of the world's largest financial firms. In the business press the event was heralded as a crowning achievement of Smith Barney's CEO, Sanford ("Sandy") Weill, who engineered the merger (and who, months later, would go on to yet another, with Citicorp).

Within weeks of the announcement, a series of meetings were held throughout the two firms, detailing just how the two heavyweight companies would morph into a single giant. As is usually the case in such mergers, hundreds of employees would lose their jobs, since many functions were duplicated between the companies.

But how can that news be delivered without rendering this already worrisome reality all the more so?

One department head did it the worst way. He gave a gloomy, even menacing, speech, saying essentially, "I don't know what I'm going to do, but don't expect me to be nice to you. I have to fire half the people here, and I'm not exactly sure how I'm going to make that decision, so I'd like each of you to tell me your background and qualifications so I can start."

His counterpart at the other company did much better. His message was upbeat: "We think this new company will be a very exciting platform for our work, and we're blessed with talented people from both organizations to work with. We'll make our decisions as quickly as we can, but not until we're positively sure we've collected enough information to be fair. We'll update you every few days on how we're doing. And we'll decide both on the basis of objective performance data plus qualitative abilities, like team-work."

Those in the second group, Mark Loehr, a managing director at Sa-lomon Smith Barney, told me, "became *more* productive, because they were excited about the potential. And they knew even if they didn't end up with a job, it would be a fair decision."

But in the first group, he observed, "Everyone was unmotivated. They heard 'I'm not being treated fairly,' and it triggered a collective amygdala at-tack. They were bitter, demoralized. People were saying, 'I don't know if I even *want* to work for this jerk anymore, let alone the company.' Head-hunters connected with his people and recruited some of the best away—but not those in the other group."

Said Loehr, "When Lehman didn't fully integrate Shearson when they merged, there was a massive failure. But when Smith Barney took over Shearson, they were able to make it work. It's how you treat people imme-diately after the merger that makes all the difference. It allows the roots of trust between the two cultures to start growing. Sandy Weill's genius is his ability to integrate firms quickly so they don't die."

The art of influence entails handling emotions effectively in *other* peo-ple. Both department heads were, in this sense, influential—but in opposite ways. Star performers are artful at sending emotional signals, which makes them powerful communicators, able to sway an audience—in short, leaders.

Emotions Are Contagious

All these abilities take advantage of a primal fact: We influence each other's moods. Influencing another person's emotional state for better or worse is perfectly natural; we do it constantly, "catching" emotions from one another like some kind of social virus. This emotional exchange constitutes an invisible interpersonal economy, part of every human interaction, but it is usually too subtle to notice.

Even so, the transmission of mood is remarkably powerful. When three strangers, all volunteers for a study of mood, sat quietly in a circle for two minutes, the most emotionally expressive person transmitted his or her mood to the two others over the course of the two minutes.[1] In every such session, the mood the most expressive person had going in was also the mood the other two felt coming out—whether happy, bored, anxious, or angry.

Emotions are contagious. As the Swiss psychoanalyst C. G. Jung put it, "In psychotherapy, even if the doctor is entirely detached from the emotional contents of the patient, the very fact that the patient has emotions has an effect upon him. And it is a great mistake if the doctor thinks he can lift himself above it. He cannot do more than become conscious of the fact that he is affected. If he does not see that, he is too aloof and then misses the point."

What holds in the intimate exchange of psychotherapy is no less true on the shop floor, in the boardroom, or in the emotional hothouse of office life. We transmit moods among us with such ease because they can be vital signals for survival. Our emotions tell us what to focus on, when to be ready to act. Emotions are attention grabbers, operating as warnings, invitations, alarms, and the like. These are powerful messages, conveying crucial information without necessarily putting that data into words. Emotions are a hyperefficient mode of communication.

In a primitive human band, emotional contagion—the spread from person to person of fear—presumably acted as an alarm signal, quickly focusing everyone's attention on an imminent danger, like a stalking tiger.

Today that same collective mechanism operates whenever word spreads of an alarming drop in sales, a coming wave of layoffs, or a new threat from a competitor. Each person in the chain of communication activates the same underlying emotional state in the next, and so passes on the message to be alert.

Emotions as a signaling system need no words—a fact evolutionary theorists see as one reason emotions may have played such a crucial role in the development of the human brain long before words became a symbolic tool for humans. This evolutionary legacy means that our radar for emotions attunes us to those around us, helping us interact more smoothly and effectively.

The *emotional* economy is the sum total of the exchanges of feeling among us. In subtle (or not so subtle) ways, we all make each other feel a bit better (or a lot worse) as part of any contact we have; every encounter can be weighted along a scale from emotionally toxic to nourishing. While its operation is largely invisible, this economy can have immense benefits for a business or for the tone of organizational life.

The Group Heart

A group of managers are negotiating how to distribute a limited amount of bonus money. Each presents a worthy candidate from his or her own department, making the arguments for what size bonus each candidate will get. It's a discussion that can turn acrimonious or end in harmony, depending.

Depending on what? It turns out that what makes the difference are the *moods* that spread among the managers as they talk. The moods people catch from each other at work are a crucial—yet often unnoticed—ingredient in how *well* they work.

One dramatic scientific demonstration of how the emotions rippling through a group can impact performance was done by Sigal Barsade, a professor at the Yale University School of Management.[2] A group of volunteers from the business school were brought together to act the part of managers allocating bonuses. Each volunteer had two goals: to get as large a bonus as possible for their candidate, and to help the committee as a group make the best use of the pool of funds for the company as a whole.

What they did not know was that among them was a plant who had been coached by Barsade. A trained actor, this manager always went first, and always made identical arguments. But he did it in one of four emotional keys: with cheerful, ebullient enthusiasm; with a relaxed, serene warmth; with a depressed sluggishness; or with an unpleasant and hostile irritability. His real role was to infect the group with one or another of these emotional states, like spreading a virus among unknowing victims.

The emotions *did* spread like a virus. When the actor argued with cheerfulness or warmth, those feelings rippled through the group, making people more positive as the meeting went on. And when he was irritable, people felt grumpier. (Depression, on the other hand, spread little, perhaps because it manifests as a subtle social withdrawal—indicated, for instance, by little eye contact—and so has little amplification.)

Good feelings spread more powerfully than bad ones, and the effects were extremely salutary, boosting cooperation, fairness, collaboration, and overall group performance. The improvement was more than just a glow from good feelings: Objective measures showed the groups were more effective—in this case, better able to distribute the bonus money fairly and in ways that would most benefit the company.

In the world of work, no matter the business at hand, emotional elements play a crucial role. Emotional competence requires being able to pilot through the emotional undercurrents always at play rather than being pulled under by them.

Handling the Other Person's Emotions

It's the end of a long, tiring, muggy day at Walt Disney World, and a bus-load of parents and children are starting the twenty-minute ride back to their hotel. The children are overstimulated and cranky, and so are the parents. Everyone is whiny.

It's a bus ride from hell.

Then, rising above the miasmic drone of complaining children and parents, comes a thin, persistent warble: The bus driver has started to sing the song "Under the Sea," from the movie *The Little Mermaid*. Everyone begins to quiet down and listen. Eventually a little girl chimes in, then several more children. By the end of the ride everyone is singing "The Circle of Life" from the movie *The Lion King*. The bus ride from hell has become the pleasurable, song-filled end to a full day.

That bus driver knew just what he was doing. In fact, the singing drivers are part of an intentional strategy to help keep customers mellow. I still remember (with some delight) the driver of a Mickey Mouse bus breaking into the theme song for the then-popular *Mickey Mouse Club* TV show when I visited Disneyland as a child way back in the 1950s; it remains my most vivid memory of that holiday trip.

This strategy takes clever advantage of emotional contagion. We are all part of each other's emotional tool kits, for better or worse; we continually prime others' emotional states, just as they do ours. This fact offers a powerful argument against the uninhibited expression of toxic feelings at work: They poison the well. On the flip side, our positive feelings about a company are to a large extent based on how the people that represent the organization make us feel.

The most effective people in organizations know this innately; they naturally use their emotional radar to sense how others are reacting, and they fine-tune their own response to push the interaction in the best direction. As Tom Pritzker, president of Hyatt Hotels, told me, "The lady at the front desk who wins over the customer with her smile can't be quantified, but you can sense the advantage." (It happens that smiles are the most contagious emotional signal of all, having an almost irresistible power to make other people smile in return. And smiling in and of itself primes positive feelings.)[3]

The same brain mechanisms that underlie empathy and allow for emotional attunement also create the pathway for emotional contagion. But in addition to the circuitry emanating from the amygdala, the basal areas (including the brain stem), which regulate reflexive, automatic functions, are also involved. These areas operate to create a tight loop of biological connectedness, re-creating in one person the physiological state of the other—and this seems to be a pathway emotions follow in traveling from one person to another.[4]

This is the system at work when someone is skilled at swaying an audience. As Howard Friedman, a psychologist at the University of California at Irvine, observes, "The essence of eloquent, passionate, spirited communication seems to involve the use of facial expressions, voices, gestures and body movements to transmit emotions." Friedman's research shows that people who have this emotional adeptness are better able to move and inspire others, and to captivate their imagination.[5]

In a sense, emotional display is like theater. We all have a backstage, the hidden zone where we feel our emotions, and a stage front, the social arena where we present the emotions we choose to reveal. This private split between our public and private emotional lives is analogous to the concept of the front of the store and the back office. Emotional displays are more often carefully stage-managed when interacting with customers, and less well managed backstage, and this discrepancy can be unfortunate. As one organizational consultant put it, "Many an executive who appears highly charismatic out of the office comes back and acts like a jerk with his employees." Or as the director of a large Sunday school complained to me about her minister, "He's just too impassive, completely unexpressive. He's so hard to read, I don't know how to take much of what he says to me—it's very difficult to work with him." Being poor at managing and appropriately expressing emotions can be a major handicap.

Social skills, in the essential sense of handling *another person's* emotions artfully, underlie several competencies. These include:

- *Influence:* Wielding effective tactics of persuasion
- *Communication:* Sending clear and convincing messages
- *Conflict management:* Negotiating and resolving disagreements
- *Leadership:* Inspiring and guiding
- *Change catalyst:* Initiating, promoting, or managing change

■ INFLUENCE ■

Wielding Effective Tactics for Persuasion

▪▪

People with this competence

■ Are skilled at winning people over

■ Fine-tune presentations to appeal to the listener

■ Use complex strategies like indirect influence to build consensus and support

■ Orchestrate dramatic events to effectively make a point

▪▪

A representative of an American company in Tokyo was taking his visiting boss to a series of meetings with their Japanese counterparts. On the way to the first meeting the representative, who spoke Japanese fluently, advised his American boss not to ask him to translate in front of the Japanese, but to rely instead on the translator. His boss readily agreed.[6]

Why?

"They'll think I'm just a mouthpiece to send things back to New York. I wanted to make sure they saw me as having real power to make decisions on the spot. I wanted to be seen as the person who did most of the talking. I had the answers, not New York."

That sensitivity to the impact of such a seemingly trivial matter bespeaks competence at influence. At the most basic level, influence and persuasion hinge on arousing specific emotions in the other person—whether that be respect for our power, passion for a project, enthusiasm for outdoing a competitor, or appropriate outrage over some unfairness.

People adept at influence are able to sense or even anticipate their audience's reaction to their message and can effectively carry everyone along toward an intended goal. Star performers at Deloitte & Touche Consulting, for example, know that a simple good argument may not be enough to win clients over, and they have the ability to sense what kinds of other appeals will persuade key decision makers.[7] Critical in these skills is being able to notice when logical arguments are falling flat and when appeals that are more emotional may add impact.

This emotional competence emerges over and over as a hallmark of superior performers, particularly among supervisors, managers, and executives.[8] At every level, however, a sophisticated understanding of influence is called for. "In entry-level positions, being too highly power-driven and overly concerned with having an impact can trip you up, especially if you try to put on airs and take on the trappings of power," Richard Boyatzis tells me. "If you were just made sales manager and you try to impress people by imposing distance or by feigning status—you start wearing expensive three-piece suits or tell subordinates to stop calling you by your first name, for example—you can alienate people."

The stratagems used by top performers include impression management, appeals to reason and facts, dramatic arguments or actions, building coalitions and behind-the-scenes support, emphasizing key information—and on and on. For instance, one outstanding manager was put in charge of quality control at a large manufacturer. The first thing he did was to change the name to quality *services,* a subtle but crucial shift of emphasis: "The image I wanted to create was that it's not just a policeman organization, but it provides technical input, too. Now we have an iron grip on tracking down quality complaints from customers, and the production people don't get defensive right away."[9]

Dramatic action can capture attention and arouse emotion; if well done, this is among the most effective of influence strategies. "Dramatic" does not necessarily mean having flashy visuals in presentations; sometimes the effect is felt through the most prosaic means. One outstanding salesman wowed a prospective account by spending the better part of a day with his sleeves rolled up, using one of his products to fix a piece of equipment—equipment that had been purchased from a competitor!

What got him the account was his dramatic demonstration of the level of service his prospective client could expect.[10] As he put it, "They were amazed."

First, Build Rapport

Empathy is crucial for wielding influence; it is difficult to have a positive impact on others without first sensing how they feel and understanding their position. People who are poor at reading emotional cues and inept at social interactions are very poor at influence. The first step in influence is building rapport.

For a business analyst at a global American oil company, that meant changing the way he approached the representatives of a South American bank.[11] He said, "I have a lot of funds going back and forth and the bank plays an important role, and in South America friendship ties mean a lot when you're doing business. I wanted to be able to call a commercial rep and say, 'Hey, I've got a problem,' and have them be willing to work with us to get our work done." His tactic: a long, leisurely meeting over coffee with several key representatives, where they talked about themselves, their families, their lives—not just business.

Similarly, a manufacturer's rep told me, "When you walk into a customer's office, the first thing you do is scan the room to pick up on something he's enthusiastic and excited about—that's where you start the conversation." His approach takes for granted that building rapport necessarily precedes persuasion. As one outstanding salesman put it, "Sometimes it means I go in without a briefcase and say, 'Hey, how ya doin' today? Want a hot dog from the guy across the street? Let's go out and get it together.' And I know that if I'm going to call on the man in the jeans and the flannel shirt, I won't wear my three-piece suit."[12]

Similar persuasion skills are seen in the executive who is trying to recruit someone to take a job that requires moving to another city. He knows the prospect loves sailing, and so shows her the local marina. Or he capitalizes on the prospect's spouse's love of riding by introducing him to friends who are equestrians, so that he will be on board for the move, too.

Persuasion is lubricated by identifying a bond or commonality; taking time to establish one is not a detour but an essential step. An announcement made by a remote and largely invisible CEO may have less immediate persuasive power than the same message delivered by someone workers have day-to-day contact with. One strategy for spreading change in a large and far-flung organization, then, is to use networks of local leaders, the individuals within a working group that everyone knows, likes, and respects.[13]

At the highest levels of effectiveness, the influential rely on indirect strategies, so that their hand is virtually invisible. They have a third party make the crucial argument, establishing chains of influence; they set up effective behind-the-scenes coalitions for support, or shape the presentation of information in subtle ways so that everyone easily and fluidly arrives at the desired consensus.

The rule of thumb is that consensus building is crucial, but this is ignored to a surprising degree. In a study of strategic decisions at 356 American companies, more than half were never adopted, were implemented only partially, or were abandoned at the outset.[14]

The single most common reason for the failure of these plans was that the lead executives were imperious, trying to impose their ideas instead of building a supporting consensus. When the imperious approach was employed, 58 percent of the time the result was failure. But when executives first conferred with colleagues to rethink their long-term priorities, strategic plans were adopted 96 percent of the time. As Paul McNutt, the Ohio State University professor of management who did the study, says, "If you involve people in at least some of the steps of the process, they will become missionaries for you."

The Failure to Convince

The benefit was for a good cause—a new preschool for children of poor, single working mothers. A local artist of some national prominence had invited about a hundred friends to a special show of her newest work and a buffet dinner contributed by several local restaurants. After the meal, the hostess gathered everyone together on the lawn and introduced the head of the organization that ran the preschool, who began with a detailed rundown of the events in her life that had led her to take her present job. Then she gave a blow-by-blow account of how the preschool got started. After that she proceeded to run through the entire history of the preschool, in what turned out to be excruciating detail.

A talk that might have been effective had it lasted for ten minutes went on for almost an hour. And she hadn't even introduced some mothers and teachers, each of whom was going to say a few words.

The audience, all sympathetic at the beginning, began to drift off. Dusk had arrived, and with it swarming mosquitoes.

Finally the hostess's husband, a somewhat cantankerous older gentleman, got up conspicuously, ambled straight for the cake table, and bellowed, "Too much detail! The cakes are falling!"

With that, all semblance of an attentive audience collapsed, and everyone headed for dessert.

People who, despite their good intentions, fail to connect emotionally with their audience fall at the bottom of the influence competence hierarchy: They may mean well, but they lack the means to get their message across. The blunt critique by the hostess's husband captured the mood of the audience at that moment far better than the speech by the long-winded school head.

Those who rely too heavily on the persuasive effects of aids such as elaborate overhead projections or elegant statistical analyses of data also can miss the boat. An audience must be emotionally engaged, but mediocre presenters rarely go beyond the same dry litany of facts, however flashily displayed, and never take into account the emotional temperature of the audience. Without an accurate reading of how a listener is taking in an idea, that idea is in danger of falling on deaf, indifferent, or even hostile ears.

No matter how intellectually brilliant we may be, that brilliance will fail to shine if we are not persuasive. That is particularly true in fields where entry has high hurdles for cognitive abilities, like engineering and science, medicine and law, and executive ranks in general. As the director of research at one of Wall Street's largest brokerage firms put it to me, "To get into our business you need to be highly adept at numbers. But to make things happen, that's just not enough—you have to be able to persuade."

Signs of weakness in the ability to persuade include:

- Failure to build a coalition or get "buy-in"

- Overreliance on a familiar strategy instead of choosing the best one for the moment

- Bullheaded promotion of a point of view, no matter the feedback

- Being ignored or failing to inspire interest

- Having a negative impact

The Machiavellian Manipulator

For him, appearance was all. He married a woman from a noble family, and he himself was extremely polished socially. As a highly placed manager in a German industrial dynasty, he was in charge of a division with revenues of more than $1 billion annually. But on the job he focused all his considerable charm upward, toward his own boss, and outward, to impress those who met him. When it came to those who reported to him, he was a petty tyrant mistreating his serfs.

"When you met him he could be quite beguiling, but people who worked for him were afraid of him," I was told by an outside consultant who was hired to do an impartial appraisal of the manager. "He had no respect for the people under him. If there was low performance, he shouted at people; if high, he said nothing. He demoralized his subordinates. His CEO finally asked him to leave—but, because he makes such a good first impression, he landed another high-level job immediately."

The slick German manager exemplifies a type who can thrive in organizations that are more politically oriented than performance oriented. Such people are "effective upward, but poor downward, because they don't really care," the consultant told me. "They are often self-centered, don't like people, and feel an obligation only to themselves, not to the organization."

Charm and social polish in themselves do not add up to competence at influence; social skill in the service of oneself, and to the detriment of the group as a whole, is sooner or later recognized as a charade. True influence as a positive competence is very different from a Machiavellian drive for personal success at all costs. The power exhibited in the influence competence is socialized and harmonious with the collective goal, rather than exclusively for selfish gain.

As one analyst of influence in close to three hundred organizations put it, "We have not found the best performers pursuing their own status, prestige, or gain at the expense of others or of the organization."[15]

▪ COMMUNICATION ▪

Listening Openly and Sending Convincing Messages

People with this competence

- Are effective in give-and-take, registering emotional cues in attuning their message

- Deal with difficult issues straightforwardly

- Listen well, seek mutual understanding, and welcome sharing of information fully

- Foster open communication and stay receptive to bad news as well as good

For Bill Gates at Microsoft, it's an e-mail address; for Martin Edelston, president of the Boardroom, Inc., it's an old-fashioned suggestion box. And for Jerry Kalov, CEO of Cobra Electronics, it's a phone extension known only to his employees. Any call on that confidential number is a priority; he picks it up whenever it rings.

Each of these conduits of communication represents one way of resolving every boss's dilemma: "Are they telling me only what they want me to hear instead of what I need to know?" Kalov got the idea for his phone line long before he became an executive.[16] "Very often I had things I wanted to say, but my immediate boss didn't let me, because he wanted to take the credit," Kalov remembers. "Or maybe he didn't agree with it. So I felt like I had good ideas or things to say but I couldn't get through. . . . Who knows where the next brilliant idea is going to come from?"

The phone line, Kalov adds, works better than management by walking around, because people may be intimidated to be seen talking to the chief executive or may be too shy even to approach him. The phone line offers discretion and confidentiality, which adds to open—even daring—communication.

Such open channels pay. A note in Edelston's suggestion box from a low-level employee—someone who ordinarily would never speak to him—saved the company half a million dollars a year. The suggestion from a shipping clerk was to keep company mailings under a four-pound postal rate limit. By reducing by one eighth the size of the books the company mailed out, the cumulative savings were hugely significant.

Creating an atmosphere of openness is not a trivial gesture. The biggest single complaint of American workers is poor communication with management; two thirds say it prevents them from doing their best work.[17]

"I'd say you're unlocking the value of a person when you communicate openly with them," Mark Loehr, a managing director at Salomon Smith Barney, observed to me. "When you communicate openly, you open the possibility of getting the best out of people—their energy, creativity. If you don't, then they just feel like cogs in a machine, trapped and unhappy."

Mood and Meaning

My boss withholds her emotions," an advertising account manager at a $2-billion-a-year media company complains to me. "She never praises anything I do. I just convinced a really big account to go from around three hundred thousand dollars a year in billings to almost double that. Her response when I told her wasn't 'You did a great job' but 'Sure they took your offer—it's a great deal.' There was no feeling whatsoever in her voice, no warmth or enthusiasm. Then she just walked away. When I told other sales managers about my coup, they complimented me. It was the biggest sale I'd ever made, and my boss just didn't acknowledge all the work I'd done to get the deal."

The account manager continues: "I started to feel that something must be wrong with me, but lots of other people feel the same about her: She never shows any positive feelings or gives any encouragement—not with little things, not with big things. . . . Our team is productive, but there's no sense of any bond with her."

Being an adept communicator is the keystone of all social skills. Among managers, communications competence strongly distinguishes star performers from average or poor ones; the lack of this ability, as seen in the account manager's boss, can torpedo morale.

Listening well, the key to empathy, is also crucial to competence in communicating. Listening skills—asking astute questions, being open-minded and understanding, not interrupting, seeking suggestions—account for about a third of people's evaluations of whether someone they work with is an effective communicator.[18] Understandably, listening is among the most frequently taught business skills.

Being in control of our own moods is also essential to good communication. A study of 130 executives and managers found that how well people handled their own emotions determined the degree to which those around them preferred to deal with them.[19] In dealing with peers and subordinates, calmness and patience were key. Bosses likewise preferred dealing with employees who were not overly aggressive with them.

It doesn't matter what mood we're in—the challenge is to stay cool and collected. Aiming for a neutral mood is the best strategy in anticipation of dealing with someone else, if only because it makes us an emotional clean slate and allows us to adapt to whatever the situation calls for.[20] It's like putting a car into neutral so that you can more readily shift into reverse, low, or high gear, as the emotional terrain demands. A neutral mood leaves us ready to be more fully involved, present rather than emotionally removed.

Keeping Cool

Being caught up in a strong consuming mood is a roadblock to smooth interaction. If we enter into a conversation while preoccupied by a strong mood, the other person is likely to experience us as being unavailable, or what the sociologist Irving Goffman has called "away"—just going through the motions of the conversation while obviously distracted.[21]

The ability to "keep cool" helps us to put preoccupations aside for the time being, staying flexible in our own emotional responses. This trait is admired worldwide, even in cultures that prefer agitation over calm in certain situations.[22] People who can stay collected in an emergency or in the face of someone else's panic or distress have a reassuring sense of self-control, enter smoothly into a conversation and stay effectively involved. In contrast, people who are burdened by their emotions are much less available for whatever the present moment demands.

A study of middle- and upper-level managers found that those rated best as communicators shared the ability to adopt a calm, composed, and patient manner, no matter what emotional state they were in.[23] They were able to put aside the imperatives of their own feelings, even when turbulent, in order to make themselves fully available for the person they were with. As a result, these managers were able to take the time needed to gather essential information and find a way to be helpful, including giving constructive feedback. Instead of being dismissive or attacking, they tended to be specific about what went right, what went wrong, and how to keep the good things going while fixing what was off. They exercised emotional control, keeping cool so as to stay open to what they were hearing, fine-tuning their responses instead of taking a one-size-fits-all approach.

Being socially outgoing and extroverted is not in itself a guarantee of being skilled at communication. And what constitutes effective communication in one culture or social setting can fail miserably in another.

Sometimes effective interaction means underplaying one's presence. Among the staff at an elite resort in the southwestern United States, effectiveness correlated *negatively* with being highly extroverted. In such a posh setting, those who were too loquacious and outgoing were experienced by guests as being intrusive. The guests were there for privacy, so the resort required its staff to be friendly and helpful as needed, but otherwise to be utterly inconspicuous.[24]

▪ CONFLICT MANAGEMENT ▪

Negotiating and Resolving Disagreements

People with this competence

- ▪ Handle difficult people and tense situations with diplomacy and tact

- ▪ Spot potential conflict, bring disagreements into the open, and help de-escalate

- ▪ Encourage debate and open discussion

- ▪ Orchestrate win-win solutions

"A banker wanted to sell a copper company to investors, and he needed a research person expert in mining to write about it so he could convince people in sales to pitch the deal. But the researcher refused outright, upsetting the banker. I was director of research, so the banker complained to me," says Mark Loehr, of Salomon Smith Barney.

"I went to the researcher, who told me he was overwhelmed. He was already working seventy to eighty hours a week, had to finish analyses of eighteen companies by the end of the month, make a hundred phone calls, run off to meetings in Boston—and this report would have taken him another forty hours to do. After we talked, he went back to the banker and explained how swamped he was, but added, 'If you want me to do it, I will.'

"Once the banker understood the researcher's predicament, he decided to find another way to get the job done. But there could have been a blowup. Everyone is so busy and overwhelmed, their listening abilities dwindle to nothing. And they tend to just assume that no one is as busy as they are, so they make imperious demands.

"It's so hard to get people to take the time to be good listeners. It's not just about being nice—until you're a good enough listener, until you can sense what the other person is going through, you won't be able to make a reasonable suggestion, to come up with something they'll buy."

One talent of those skilled at conflict resolution is spotting trouble as it is brewing and taking steps to calm those involved. Here, as Loehr points out, the arts of listening and empathizing are crucial: Once the investment banker understood the researcher's perspective, he became more accommodating—and the conflict ended.

Such diplomacy and tact are qualities essential for success in touchy jobs like auditing, police work, or mediation—or *any* job where people depend on each other under pressure. One of the competencies sought in tax auditors by the U.S. government is the ability to present an unpopular position in a way that creates little or no hostility and preserves the other person's sense of dignity. The word for this skill is *tact*. At American Express, the ability to spot potential sources of conflict, take responsibility for one's own role, apologize if need be, and engage openly in a discussion of each person's perspective is prized in their financial advisors.

Reading the Signs

Charlene Barshefsky had finally gotten the Chinese government, after months and months of negotiation, to agree to clamp down on the piracy of American movies, compact discs, and computer software. How? Barshefsky had refused to accept their "final" offer, just another in an ongoing series, all of which she felt were inadequate. But this time, the head of the Chinese delegation thanked her for her work, told her he would respond at a later date, and then moved his shoulders back in a slight shrug. That simple and subtle gesture indicated she had won their cooperation.

Barshefsky had been closely studying the faces across the table from her that day, and she had sensed far less acrimony than before in the endless, tedious meetings. That day, reactions were muted and questions few—a striking change from the combative, sharply challenging dialogue that had marked the early rounds of the negotiations.

Barshefsky's reading of those subtle signals proved right: That was the day the Chinese delegation stopped fighting and started moving toward the trade agreement the countries later signed.[25]

The ability to read the feelings of the opposition during a negotiation is critical to success. As one of my lawyers, Robert Freedman, says about negotiating contracts, "It's mainly psychological. Contracts are emotional—it's not just what the words say, but how the parties think and *feel* about them, that matters."

Those who have mastered the art of the deal realize the emotionally charged nature of any negotiation. The best negotiators can sense which points matter most to the other party and gracefully concede there, while pressing for concessions in points that do not carry such emotional weight. And that takes empathy.

Skill at negotiation obviously matters for excellence in professions like law and diplomacy. But to some extent everyone who works in an organization needs these abilities; those who can resolve conflict and head off trouble are the kind of peacemakers vital to any organization.

In a sense, a negotiation can be seen as an exercise in joint problem solving, since the conflict belongs to both parties. The reason for the negotiation, of course, is that each side has its own competing interests and perspective and wants to convince the other to capitulate to its wishes. But the very act of agreeing to negotiate acknowledges that the problem is a shared one and that there may be a mutually satisfying solution available. In this sense negotiation is a cooperative venture, not just a competitive one. Indeed, as Herbert Kelman, a Harvard psychologist who specializes in negotiations, points out, the process of negotiation itself restores cooperation between conflicting parties. Solving their problems together transforms their relationship.[26]

That resolution requires that each side be able to understand not just the other's point of view, but their needs and fears. This empathy, Kelman observes, makes each side "better able to influence the other to their own benefit, by being responsive to the other's needs—in other words, to find ways in which both parties can win."

Negotiating Channels

Negotiations, mostly informal, happen all the time. Take the negotiation between a manufacturer and the retail stores that sell its products, like this one: "I've been cut off from carrying one of our main lines of women's jewelry," a boutique owner explained. "I wanted to negotiate a better deal with the distributor—we've been a good outlet for them. But he got a better offer from a store across town. So I made a counterproposal. But the other store got the account—and the company only wants one outlet in a town this size. So now I'm out of luck."

Such channels of distribution are essential for manufacturers' very survival, just as the retailers depend on the manufacturers for their stock. But each party has an array of choices. The result is an ongoing negotiation over such issues as how large markups will be, the terms of payment, and timeliness of deliveries.

Most "channel relationships" are long-term and symbiotic. And in any long-term relationship, problems simmer and boil to the surface from time to time. When they surface, those involved on either side of manufacturer-retailer disputes typically use one of three styles of negotiation: problem solving, in which both parties try to find the solution that works best for each side; compromise, where both parties give in more or less equally regardless of how that serves their needs; and aggression, where one party forces unilateral concessions from the other side.

In a survey of retail buyers in department store chains, each of whom handled merchandise worth $15 million to $30 million, the style of negotiating was an accurate barometer of the health of the manufacturer-retailer relationship.[27] Predictably, when negotiations were typically aggressive, revolving around threats and demands, it boded poorly for the future of the relationship; buyers ended up embittered and dissatisfied and often dropped the product line. But for those relationships in which aggressiveness was ruled out in favor of problem solving or compromise, the longevity of the relationship increased.

Threats and demands poison the waters of negotiation. As the survey showed, even when one party is far more powerful than the other, a magnaminous spirit may be a winning strategy in the long run, particularly when the parties will have continued dealings. And this is why even when a retailer was completely dependent on a single manufacturer, negotiations were most often noncoercive; given the desire for a long-term relationship and their mutual dependence, a spirit of cooperation always worked best.

Resolving Conflict—Creatively

One evening Linda Lantieri was walking down a desolate, dangerous block lined with abandoned, boarded-up buildings when suddenly, out of nowhere, she was surrounded by three boys about fourteen years old. One pulled out a knife with a four-inch blade as they pressed in around her.

"Give me your purse! Now!" the boy with the knife hissed.

Though frightened, Lantieri had the presence of mind to take some deep breaths and reply coolly, "I'm feeling a little uncomfortable. You know, guys, you're a little into my space. I'm wondering if you could step back a little."

Lantieri studied the sidewalk—and, to her amazement, she saw three pairs of sneakers take a few steps back. "Thank you," she said, then continued, "Now, I want to hear what you just said to me, but to tell you the truth, I'm a little nervous about that knife. I'm wondering if you could put it away."

After what seemed an eternity of silence and uncertainty, the knife went back into a pocket.

Quickly reaching into her purse, Lantieri took out a $20 bill, caught the eye of the one with the knife, and asked, "Who should I give it to?"

"Me," he said.

Glancing at the other two, she asked if they agreed. One of the two nodded.

"Great," she said, handing the leader the $20 bill. "Now here's what's going to happen. I'm going to stay right here while you walk away."

With puzzled looks on their faces, the boys slowly started to walk away, glancing over their shoulders at Lantieri—and then they broke into a run. *They* were running from *her*.

In a sense, that small miracle of turning the tables is no surprise: Lantieri is the founder and director of the New York City–based Resolving Conflict Creatively Program, which teaches these skills in schools. Lantieri has immersed herself in the crafts of negotiation and handling conflict amicably.[28] While she learned her trade as a teacher—for a while in a Harlem school not far from that desolate block—she now trains others in more than four hundred schools throughout the United States.

Lantieri does more than just promote education in conflict resolution—she first convinces skeptical school boards to approve her program. In fact, when the school board of one California town was paralyzed by two bitterly bickering factions, both sides were so impressed by her negotiating skills they asked Lantieri to come in and help them heal the split.

Lantieri's maestro performance on the street illustrates some classic moves for cooling down conflicts:

- First, calm down, tune in to your feelings, and express them.

- Show a willingness to work things out by talking over the issue rather than escalating it with more aggression.

- State your own point of view in neutral language rather than in an argumentative tone.

- Try to find equitable ways to resolve the dispute, working together to find a resolution both sides can embrace.

These strategies parallel those espoused for win-win solutions by experts at Harvard's Center for Negotiation. But while following these strategies may seem simple, implementing them as brilliantly as Lantieri did requires the prerequisite emotional competencies of self-awareness, self-confidence, self-control, and empathy. Remember, empathy need not lead to sympathetically giving in to the other side's demands—knowing how someone feels does not mean agreeing with them. But cutting off empathy to hold a hard line can lead to polarized positions and deadlocks.

■ LEADERSHIP ■

Inspiring and Guiding Individuals and Groups

People with this competence

■ Articulate and arouse enthusiasm for a shared vision and mission

■ Step forward to lead as needed, regardless of position

■ Guide the performance of others while holding them accountable

■ Lead by example

Here's an extraordinarily instructive contrast in leadership: Ronald W. Allen, former CEO of Delta Air Lines, and Gerald Grinstein, a former CEO of Western Airlines and the Burlington Northern railway.[29]

Grinstein, a lawyer by training, is a virtuoso at establishing rapport with his employees and using that emotional attunement to persuade. As CEO of Western Airlines, an ailing company when he took it over in 1985, he spent hundreds of hours in cockpits, behind check-in counters, and in the baggage-handling pits getting to know his employees.

The rapport he built was crucial in convincing Western Airlines' workforce to agree to concessions on work rules and to take pay cuts, all for his promise of a solvent company in which they would have a bigger stake. With those concessions in hand, Western Airlines landed solidly in the black, and Grinstein was able to sell the airline to Delta for $860 million after just two years.

In 1987 he became CEO of Burlington Northern, another money-losing company, and again Grinstein worked his interpersonal magic. He flew a selected group of maintenance workers, secretaries, and train crews from all over the country to company headquarters in Fort Worth to dine with him. He rode the railroad's routes and talked with crews, all the while working—successfully—toward convincing them to buy into his cost-cutting plans.

A close friend of Grinstein observed of his leadership style, "You don't have to be an SOB to be tough."

Though the railroad was laden with $3 billion of debt when he took it over, Grinstein turned it around. And in 1995 he created the largest U.S. rail network when Burlington Northern bought Santa Fe Pacific.

Now let's look at Ronald W. Allen, who was fired by his board as CEO of Delta Air Lines in April of 1997, even as the company was enjoying record profits.

Allen had moved up through the ranks to become CEO in 1987, taking the helm just as the airline industry was deregulated. His strategic plan was to become more globally competitive; in 1991 he bought just-bankrupt Pan American World Airways, for access to its European routes. That turned out to be a miscalculation, loading Delta with a huge debt burden just as the industry saw profits plummet. Delta, always profitable in the past, plunged $500 million more into debt over each of the three years following the Pan Am purchase.

However, it was not this disastrous financial decision that cost Allen his job. Allen reacted to the hard times by becoming a tough, almost ruthless boss. He gained a reputation for humiliating underlings by berating them in front of other employees. He silenced opposition among top executives, even moving to replace the chief financial officer, the one person who had openly disagreed with him on the acquisition of Pan Am. Another top executive (with whom Allen had competed to become CEO) announced he was leaving to become president of Continental Airlines, and Allen is said to have responded by demanding the keys to the executive's company car on the spot, leaving him to find another way home.

Such pettiness aside, Allen's main failing was his heartless downsizing. Allen hacked away twelve thousand jobs, about a third of the total Delta workforce—some positions fat, no doubt, but many others the muscle, sinew, and nerves of the organization. With the deep cuts came a precipitous drop in the airline's once-enviable customer service ratings. Complaints about Delta suddenly skyrocketed—everything from dirty planes and late departures to missing baggage. Allen had squeezed the spirit out of the company along with the fat.

Delta employees were in shock; the company had never treated them so harshly before. Insecurity and anger were rampant. Even after the cuts put the airline into the black again, a company-wide survey of the twenty-five thousand remaining employees revealed a skeptical, frightened workforce, half of them hostile to Allen's leadership.

In October 1996 Allen publicly admitted that his draconian cost-cutting campaign had had devastating effects on Delta's workforce. But his comment was, "So be it." And that became the battle cry for the employees' protest; pins with the phrase "So be it" sprouted on the uniforms of pilots, flight attendants, and mechanics alike.

With Allen's contract up for renewal, the Delta board looked beyond the numbers to the overall health of the company. Delta's reputation for outstanding service was tarnished; talented managers were leaving the company. And, worst of all, morale among employees was abysmal.

So the board—led by none other than Gerald Grinstein—acted. Allen, the man whose power had once been so great that he held the titles of chairman, CEO, and president, was out at age fifty-five, largely because he was killing the company's soul.

Leadership as Giving Energy

The twin tales of Robert W. Allen and Gerald Grinstein demonstrate that the art of leadership lies in *how* a person implements change, not just in the change itself. Both men went through the painful process of cutting costs, but one did so in a way that kept employees' loyalty and spirits high, while the other demoralized and alienated an entire workforce.

The artful leader is attuned to the subtle undercurrents of emotion that pervade a group, and can read the impact of her own actions on those currents. One way leaders establish their credibility is by sensing these collective, unspoken feelings and articulating them for the group, or acting in a way that tacitly shows they are understood. In this sense, the leader is a mirror, reflecting back to the group its own experience.

However, the leader is also a key *source* of the organization's emotional tone. The excitement emanating from a leader can move an entire group in that direction. As Birgitta Wistrand, the CEO of a Swedish company, put it, "Leadership is giving energy."

This transmission of emotional energy lets leaders be the pilots of an organization, setting its course and direction. For example, when Lou Gerstner was brought in as CEO of IBM, he knew he had to transform the culture of the company to save it. And that, Gerstner said, "is not something you do by writing memos. You've got to appeal to people's emotions. They've got to buy in with their hearts and bellies, not just their minds."[30]

The ability of leaders to get that buy-in hinges in part on how emotions flow within a group. We've already seen how emotions spread from the most expressive person in a group. But this ability to transmit emotions is amplified for leaders, since people in groups spend more time looking at the leader than at anyone else. This attention magnifies the impact of the leader's mood on the group; a small change in the facial expression or tone of voice of a powerful figure can have more impact than dramatic shows of feeling by someone in a lesser position of power.

People not only pay more attention to leaders, they also tend to mimic them. Lore has it that at Microsoft people rock back and forth as they are pondering or arguing a point in a meeting, a nonverbal homage to Bill Gates's habit. Such mimicry is an unconscious way of showing allegiance and attunement to the most powerful person in a group.

During his presidency Ronald Reagan was known as "the Great Communicator." A professional actor, the emotional power of Reagan's charisma was shown in a study of how his facial expressions affected those of his listeners during an election debate with his opponent, Walter Mondale. When Reagan smiled, people who watched him—even on videotape—tended to smile, too; when he frowned, so did viewers. Mondale, who lost the election, had no such emotional impact, even on viewers who were sympathetic to his views.[31]

The ease with which emotions spread from a leader through the group has a downside, too. As the old saying holds, "A fish rots from the head down." Brutish, arrogant, or arbitrary leadership demoralizes a group. Birgitta Wistrand uses the term "emotional incontinence" for the leakage of destructive emotions from the top down: "With disturbing emotions a leader saps other people's energy by making them anxious, depressed, or angry," she says.

On the other hand, extremely successful leaders exhibit a high level of positive energy that spreads throughout the organization. And the more positive the mood of a group leader, the more positive, helpful, and cooperative are those in the group.[32]

In general, emotional charisma depends on three factors: feeling strong emotions, being able to express those emotions forcefully, and being an emotional sender rather than a receiver. Highly expressive people communicate through their facial expression, their voice, their gestures—their whole body. This ability allows them to move, inspire, and captivate others.[33]

The ability to convey emotion convincingly, from the heart, requires that a leader be sincere about the message being delivered; truly believing the emotional message is what separates the charismatic leader from the self-serving, manipulative one. Manipulative leaders may be able to play-act for a time, but they can less readily convince followers of their sincerity. Cynicism undermines conviction; to be a charismatic messenger, the leader must act from authentic belief.[34]

The Leader's Competence Tool Kit

Each emotional competency interacts with others; this applies to the leadership competence more than most. The task of the leader draws on a wide range of personal skills. My analysis of myriad jobs found that emotional competence makes up about two thirds of the ingredients of star performance in general, but for outstanding *leaders* emotional competencies—as opposed to technical or cognitive cues—make up 80 to 100 percent of those listed by companies themselves as crucial for success.[35]

Mathew Juechter, chairman of the American Society for Training and Development, agrees. "Leadership is almost all emotional intelligence, especially in distinguishing between what managers do and what leaders do—things like taking a stand, knowing what's important to you, pursuing your goals in partnership with others."

For the most effective CEOs, there are three main clusters of competence. The first two fall under the emotional intelligence heading; the first includes personal competencies like achievement, self-confidence, and commitment, while the second consists of social competencies like influence, political awareness, and empathy. This broad band of capabilities typified high-performing CEOs in Asia, the Americas, and Europe, suggesting that the traits of outstanding top leaders transcend cultural and national boundaries.[36]

The third cluster of competencies in the CEOs was cognitive: They think strategically, seeking out information with a broad scan, and apply strong conceptual thinking. As with the analysis of leaders in fifteen major corporations in Chapter 2, what distinguished standouts was the ability to see the big picture, to recognize telling patterns amidst the clutter of information, and to think far into the future.

But great leaders go a step further, integrating emotional realities into what they see, and so instilling strategy with meaning and resonance. Their emotional intelligence allows the blending of all of these elements into an inspired vision.

The best leaders, says Robert E. Kaplan of the Center for Creative Leadership, "have an almost magical ability to turn a phrase and articulate their agenda for the organization graphically, compellingly, memorably."[37] In other words, leadership entails exciting people's imaginations and inspiring them to move in a desired direction. It takes more than simple power to motivate and lead.

Nice Guys Finish First

An analysis of the power of a leader to set a positive—or negative—emotional tone in an organization was undertaken within the U.S. Navy, where the standards for superior performance are cut-and-dried: Annual awards are given to the most efficient, safest, and most prepared squadrons.[38] In an extensive comparison of superior and just-average commands, a striking difference in the *emotional* tone the commanding officers set was revealed. The very best commands, it turned out, were run not by Captain Ahab types who terrorized their crews, but by, well . . . nice guys.

The superior leaders managed to balance a people-oriented personal style with a decisive command role. They did not hesitate to take charge, to be purposeful, assertive, and businesslike. But the greatest difference between average and superior leaders was in their emotional style. The most effective leaders were more positive and outgoing, more emotionally expressive and dramatic, warmer and more sociable (including smiling more), friendlier and more democratic, more cooperative, more likable and "fun to be with," more appreciative and trustful, and even gentler than those who were merely average.

By contrast, the mediocre navy leaders reflected the classic stereotype of the military taskmaster. They were legalistic, negative, harsh, disapproving, and egocentric. Compared to the superior commanders, the average ones were more authoritarian and controlling, more domineering and tough-minded, more aloof and self-centered, and needed to show they were right more often. They led by the book, through the rules and the assertion of the raw power of their position. And it did not work, *even in the military,* where this emotional style might seem to find its natural home.

The Leadership Ripple Effect

he emotional tone set by any leader ripples downward with remarkable precision.[39] When successive levels from top to bottom of an organization are analyzed, the effect is very much like a set of Russian dolls, one stacked inside the other, with the leader containing all the rest.

This is most easily seen in military hierarchies, where—as was found in the navy study—the most effective leaders were warm and outgoing, emotionally expressive, democratic, and trusting—and so were leaders on down through the ranks, though not to the same extent as the top commander. By contrast, less effective officers were harsher and more disapproving, distant and irritable, legalistic and uncooperative—and so their subordinates were also.

While average leaders tend to be invisible, the best leaders frequently walk around and strike up conversations with their staff, asking about their families and other personal matters. They also let it be known that they want to be informed, creating an atmosphere of openness that makes it easier for communication to take place. This two-way channel encourages people at all levels to keep their superiors informed.

In mediocre military commands, junior-level people were reluctant to send news upward, especially bad news, because the top commanding officers so often "went ballistic" when given bad news, and, instead of delegating authority to the lowest possible level, stepped in to micromanage.

To be sure, the best officers were highly task-oriented and firm in swiftly reprimanding people whose actions threatened performance standards. But they were flexible when it came to trivial rules. The mediocre commanders made no distinction between meaningful and trivial regulations, holding instead to a legalistic, inflexible standard that did nothing to boost morale or performance.

Realizing that unity and cohesiveness are built from personal bonds, the best officers organize downtime events like softball games and awards celebrations—and make a point of attending themselves. From this shared downtime, with the attendant in-jokes and warm social climate, comes a strong sense of shared identity, which in turn pays off in superior on-the-job performance. By contrast, the mediocre officers are more concerned with whether the equipment is functioning than they are with their people.

When to Be Tough

T o be sure, leadership does demand a certain toughness—at times. The art of leadership entails knowing when to be assertive—for example, confronting someone directly about their performance lapses—and when to be collegial and use less direct ways to guide or influence.

Leadership demands tough decision making: Someone has to tell people what to do, hold people to their obligations, be explicit about consequences. Persuasion, consensus building, and all the other arts of influence do not always do the job. Sometimes it comes down to simply using the power of one's position to get people to act.

A common failing of leaders, from supervisors to top executives, is the failure to be emphatically assertive when necessary. One obstacle to such assertiveness is passivity, as can happen when someone is more concerned with being liked than with getting the job done right, and so tolerates poor performance rather than confronting it. People who are extremely uncomfortable with confrontation or anger are also often reluctant to take an assertive stance even when it is called for.

Incompetence here can show up in something as commonplace as failing to take the helm in a meeting and so letting it meander rather than steering it directly to key agenda items. Another deficiency in leadership in this area is the inability to be clear and firm. This results in workers not knowing what's expected of them.

One sign of an assertive leader is the ability to say no firmly and definitively. Another is to set an expectation of high standards for performance or quality and insist people meet them, even publicly monitoring performance if necessary.

When people fail to perform, the leader's task is to give helpful feedback rather than let the moment—and the lapse—go unnoted. And when someone consistently performs poorly, despite all attempts at helpful feedback and development, the lapse has to be confronted directly and openly.

Take the manager who says, "My predecessor didn't establish any discipline about meetings. The first meeting I ran, people straggled in late and weren't prepared. So when it happened a third time I put my foot down. I said, 'Ladies and gentlemen, I can't accept this behavior. I'm postponing this meeting for two days. Be on time and be prepared, or there'll be hell to pay.' "[40]

This does not describe the petty tyrant or office bully, however. This is a strategy that comes into play only when other, less severe approaches have failed—not as a first response. If the tone described above typifies a manager's everyday style, then there is something wrong with his abilities to build rapport and influence people. In other words, constant toughness is a sign of weakness, not a sign of strong leadership.

The glorification of leaders who are oafish, arrogant, and brash ignores the cost to the organization. To be sure, a certain decisiveness in making hard decisions is necessary, but if that decision is carried out with imperious ruthlessness, the boss who did it will end up hated—and a failure as a leader.

During hard times, leaders need to call on whatever reserve of goodwill they may have built up over time. This is when the Attila the Huns are often undone. "At our company one manager was pushy and abrasive, even resented by his people—but he got things done," Muhammad-Amin Kashgari, an executive vice president at the Savola Company, Saudi Arabia's largest food manufacturer, told me. "But when things changed and the market got tougher, and we all had to work harder to maintain our market share," he added, "that manager's autocratic style defeated him." The star manager that emerged then was someone people liked and who inspired everyone to work harder. "But the imperious manager just kept pushing in the same old way—and his people abandoned him."

Having the ability to keep raw, unrestrained lust for power under control is one mark of a mature leader. A classic long-term study at AT&T found that, particularly in large organizations, managers who combined self-control with the ability to have a high impact were promoted as time went on, while those who had great impact but lacked the basics of self-control foundered.[41] In top-performing managers and executives, the drive of personal ambition is held in check by strong self-control, and focused toward collective goals.[42]

The Virtual Leader

It's a fogged-in, desperate day at the San Francisco airport. Flight after flight is being canceled, and the lines at the airlines' service desks are snaking out of sight. Tension has been building by the hour, with people sniping at the airline representatives—and at each other. David Kolb, a professor of management at Case Western Reserve University, who tells this story, decided to try to change the mood of the mob—at least of those near him. So he announced, "I'm going to get some coffee—anyone else want some?"

He took down orders from a building chorus of frustrated fellow passengers, trundled off, and returned with a stack of drinks. And that was enough to trigger a rippling cascade of good feeling.

Kolb, at that moment, emerged as the natural leader of this inchoate group. His spontaneous rise speaks to the fluid nature of leadership itself.

Someone's formal position on the organizational chart and her actual role as leader don't always match up. People may come forward to take a leadership role for a time, as some special need arises—it can be in something as small as taking a supplier to task for a sloppy job—then fade back into the group. Such assertiveness can also be directed upward, as when a lower-level employee challenges a higher-level one on difficult issues or truths vital to the well-being of the organization.

For instance, higher-ups at an oil company that was establishing offices in a South American city chose to rent space in a brand-new high-rise tower in the most expensive part of town. But the manager of that branch, when talking with a local minister, was told sarcastically, "That sounds like something a company like yours would do."

Puzzled, the manager asked around and finally realized that locating their offices in that part of town had sent a message that the company was more interested in making an impression than in doing business. With that information in hand, he took it upon himself to abandon the original plan and look for offices in a growing business district, a location that would send the signal they were serious. Then he called his bosses back in the United States and told them what he had done and why.

His bosses' response: "We disagree with you, but we're not down there—you decide what's best."

Such a move, of course, requires self-confidence and initiative, both emotional competencies essential to leadership. The surfacing of such virtual leaders is becoming a standard mode of operating in high-tech fields, where very junior people may be very senior in terms of newly emergent areas of expertise.

At Finland's Nokia Telecommunications Group, about 70 percent of the employees are engineers, with an average age of thirty-two. A large percentage of these engineers are fresh out of university and are more familiar with newer technologies than are their fortyish bosses. Veli-Pekka Niitamo, head of competence management and recruitment there, says, "We've redefined the nature of leadership. Everyone has leadership—a young engineer takes leadership as necessary. Our model is that you are your own boss inside the Nokia world. The old static structure of managers and subordinates is outdated."

Indeed, all static structures are outdated in today's business climate. Which gets us to the next competence: leading change.

■ CHANGE CATALYST ■

Initiating or Managing Change

People with this competence

- Recognize the need for change and remove barriers
- Challenge the status quo to acknowledge the need for change
- Champion the change and enlist others in its pursuit
- Model the change expected of others

The personal epiphany came late in 1993 for John Patrick. And it took him just twenty-four months to transform that inspired insight into company policy.

The company is IBM; 1993 marked the year Lou Gerstner came to the helm and began the organization's turnaround. But massive, deep change happens not just from the top down; in Patrick's case, his minirevolution was a grassroots victory.

It all revolved around the Internet. That day in 1993, Patrick, then a senior strategist for the company, was fiddling with a program called Gopher, an Internet software utility. As he tells it, "I became captivated by the idea of sitting at home and cruising around in someone else's computer. Being remotely connected was hardly a new idea at IBM. But being *inside* someone else's computer, no matter what kind of computer either of us had—a light went off."[43]

At that point, IBM was a company focused on computer hardware. The burgeoning Internet was beneath its radar, and the company had virtually no products or plans for the Web. Gerstner was about to change that—but it was people like Patrick, dispersed throughout the company, who made it reality.

Patrick created the manifesto "Get Connected," in which he argued that Internet-like connections would reinvent the nature of organizations, industries, and work. He offered some practical suggestions to buttress his idea: Give an e-mail address to everyone in the organization, encourage newsgroups within the company in order to build communities of mutual interest, and put up an IBM website.

While those ideas are widely accepted now, at the time—and especially at IBM—they were radical. But the audience was there, spread throughout the company. As soon as he distributed his manifesto, Patrick started hearing from people by fax, e-mail, and phone, from every corner of IBM. So Patrick started a mailing list and used it to stitch together a kind of virtual organization within IBM that cut across its formal groups.

The members of this new group were from around the world. They had no formal status, authority, or budget. And though they were still undetected by the organizational radar, they got things done. Their first project was up and running by May 1994. It involved putting up IBM's company website, one of the first such by any major corporation.

That same month, Patrick committed the company to participate in the next Internet World forum—without permission from IBM. This moment of risk taking took courage and vision—and perhaps a bit of simple faith as well.

That faith paid off. Patrick approached various divisions of the company for funding, collecting $5,000 here, $5,000 there, and by the time Internet World rolled around, fifty-four people from twelve different units had signed on to represent IBM. The effort still had no formal status within the company, nor any budget.

But with this momentum, IBM developed a formal Internet strategy, convened a task force, and created its Internet division. That division came into being on December 1, 1995. Its task, defining and pursuing the company's Internet initiatives, was to be led by John Patrick, vice president in charge and chief technology officer. What was once a loose-knit virtual team was now a formal division with six hundred people.

One of its projects was a wildly successful website for the 1996 Olympics in Atlanta; the site averaged eleven *million* hits each day. The IBM team, using software in development to handle all that traffic, found the experience a natural R&D opportunity. They realized that they had developed software that could handle massive amounts of traffic, and rolled it over into what became commercial software—one of many product lines for the Net that are the fruit of Patrick's original epiphany.

The Change Catalyst: Key Ingredients

Today, organizations are reshuffling, divesting, merging, acquiring, flattening hierarchies, going global. The acceleration of change through the 1990s has made the ability to lead it a newly ascendant competence. In earlier studies in the 1970s and 1980s, being a change catalyst was not highly valued. But as we approach the millennium, more and more companies are putting a premium on people who can lead through change.

What are the qualities that make someone an effective change catalyst? "When we work with a company to help them transform their business, the personal abilities of the leader of their team count immensely," John Ferreira, a partner at Deloitte & Touche Consulting, tells me. "Say we're helping them cut the time it takes to fill orders. To do that, you have to work across the separate silos of the organization, and you need someone who's not at too high a level—not a theorist, but someone with enough hands-on expertise that they're close enough to what's going on that they can cut across all the functions involved and see the real situation. It's often a second-level manager."

Beyond technical expertise, the change catalyst needs a host of other emotional competencies. "You want the kind of second-level manager who has the ability to go into a vice president's office and lay on the table what that VP needs to do, without being intimidated by the fact that he's just a second-line manager," Ferreira adds.

For example, at a large financial services company going through the turmoil of deregulation and a newly competitive market, the leaders who were most confident in their abilities led divisions that flourished despite the changes.[44]

In addition to high levels of self-confidence, effective change leaders have high levels of influence, commitment, motivation, initiative, and optimism, as well as an instinct for organizational politics. As Ferreira puts it: "You need someone who takes this as a mission, not just a job—who is passionate about the change, gets up in the morning thinking about it. It's something like the difference between a renter and an owner—owners are dedicated. That's crucial, because it also takes perseverance—you get lots of smoke screens thrown up, lots of resistance. You need to know how to use us, the consultants, to help make your case to the right people at the right time. And you have to keep presenting your case, building coalitions of support, until you reach a critical mass that gets it over the top."

The Transformational Leader

C hange *leaders* are not necessarily *innovators*. While leaders recognize the value of a new idea or way of doing things, they often are not the ones who originated the innovation. For organizations riding the waves of change (and what organization is *not* these days?), traditional management is not enough. In times of transformation, a charismatic, inspiring leader is called for.

The model of "transformational leadership" goes beyond management as usual; such leaders are able to rouse people through the sheer power of their own enthusiasm. Such leaders don't order or direct; they inspire. In articulating their vision, they are intellectually and emotionally stimulating. They show a strong belief in that vision, and they excite others about pursuing it with them.[45] And they are committed to nurturing relationships with those they lead.

Unlike more rational modes of leadership, in which leaders use standard rewards like pay and promotions to encourage their workers, the transformational leader goes to another level, mobilizing people for organizational change by arousing their emotions about the work they do. In doing so, such leaders appeal to people's sense of meaning and value. Work becomes a kind of moral statement, a demonstration of commitment to a larger mission that affirms people's sense of sharing a valued identity.[46]

Doing this requires the leader to articulate a compelling vision of the new organizational goals. Even though the goals may be somewhat utopian, committing to them can be emotionally satisfying in itself. Arousing people's emotions in this way and harnessing them in pursuit of lofty or noble goals gives a leader a powerful force for change. Indeed, studies show that this kind of leadership brings greater efforts and better performance from subordinates, making their work more effective.[47]

The Emotional Craft

A test of this transformational leadership style came at a large Canadian financial services company that was struggling with immense market turbulence and high levels of uncertainty brought on by deregulation.[48] What had once been a staid and successful company in a protected market now had to be nimble to keep a place in a market it had once dominated.

A group of senior managers from the company's top four levels were followed for a year as they led their units through these chaotic times. At the end of that period each was evaluated in terms of productivity improvement, premium income, and salary-to-budget ratio. There was a wide range of success: Some leaders met as little as 17 percent of the targeted goals, while others achieved up to 84 percent of the targets.

Those who relied on the transformational style had the greatest success. Indeed, those who practiced standard management were seen as trying to control and restrict workers.

The successful leaders were rated by people who worked for them as highly charismatic and flexible. They seemed to spread their own sense of confidence and competence, and they inspired people to be more imaginative, adaptive, and innovative.

This study echoes what John Kotter, a Harvard Business School leadership expert, cites as the difference between "management" and "leadership."[49] In the way he uses the words, *management* refers to the ways complex enterprises are kept orderly, nonchaotic, and productive. *Leadership,* by contrast, refers to effectively handling the changes that the competitiveness and volatility of the times have wrought.

As Kotter puts it, "Motivation and inspiration energize people, not by pushing them in the right direction as control mechanisms but by satisfying basic human needs for achievement, a sense of belonging, a feeling of control over one's life, and the ability to live up to one's ideals. Such feelings touch us deeply and elicit a powerful response." Leadership of this kind, then, is an emotional craft.

9

....

Collaboration, Teams, and the Group IQ

None of us are as smart as all of us.

—Japanese proverb

I t was a seminal moment in the early history of Silicon Valley. At a 1982 meeting of the Silicon Valley Computer Club, with hundreds of engineers packing the room, a writer for the *San Jose Mercury* asked the assembly, "How many of you plan to start your own companies?"

Two out of three hands shot up.[1]

Since then thousands of companies, including Silicon Graphics, Oracle, and Cisco Systems, have popped up. The common theme of all these enterprises is the conviction that a great idea or innovative technology can make a difference. But there is something else that's needed if a great idea is to become the seed of a great business: collaboration.

The quest for superb teams represents a modern grail of sorts for business. "In the world today there's plenty of technology, plenty of entrepreneurs, plenty of money, plenty of venture capital. What's in short supply is great teams." So says John Doerr, a legendary Silicon Valley venture capitalist who has backed industry-changing start-ups from Lotus and Compaq to Genentech and Netscape.[2]

Doerr's company, Kleiner Perkins Caulfield and Byers, gets twenty-five hundred business plans each year from hopeful entrepreneurs. Of these, they pick about a hundred to consider seriously, and they invest in about twenty-five. Says Doerr, "A team thinks it's selling us on the technology and the product or service. But actually we're thinking about *them*—the team members. We want to understand who they are, how they will work together." During his meetings with prospective start-ups, he probes the group's dynamic: how they might manage themselves, agree on priorities, measure whether they're doing their jobs well, handle someone who isn't working out. "I'm checking their instincts, their navigation system, their values."

Crucial to such a team is the right mix of intelligence and expertise—or what Doerr calls "really smart people"—and (though he doesn't use the phrase) emotional intelligence. Doerr cautions the two must be balanced— not all brilliance and experience, nor just drive, energy, and passion. "Getting that mix right is the difference between ventures that achieve greatness and start-ups that are merely successful, or worse."

Survival of the Social

Humans are the primordial team players: Our uniquely complex social relationships have been a crucial survival advantage. Our extraordinarily sophisticated talent for cooperation culminates in the modern organization.

Some evolutionary thinkers see the key moment for the emergence of interpersonal skills as the point when our ancestors moved from treetops to life on the broad savannas—when social coordination in hunting and gathering paid huge dividends. Learning the essential skills for survival meant children needed "schooling" in that critical period, up to age fifteen or so, during which the human brain becomes anatomically mature. Cooperation provided this advantage, and with it came a complex social system—and a new challenge to human intelligence.[3]

This view of the crucial role of cooperation in evolution is part of a radical rethinking of just what the famous phrase "survival of the fittest" means.[4] In the late nineteenth century social Darwinists seized on that phrase to argue that "fitness" meant the strong and ruthless would inevitably triumph over the weak. They used that as a rationale to celebrate unbridled competition and to ignore the plight of the poor and disenfranchised.

Today that idea has been overturned in evolutionary theory by the simple insight that evolutionary fitness is measured not by toughness, but by reproductive success: how many of one's children survive to pass on one's genes to future generations. That genetic legacy is the true sense of "survival" in evolution.

From that perspective, the *group* working together—foraging for food, nurturing children, fending off predators—has been the key to human survival, not the ruthlessness of lone rogues. And, indeed, Darwin himself first proposed that human groups whose members were ready to work together for the common good survived better and had more offspring than those whose members were self-serving, or those who were not part of any group at all.

Even today the benefits of a close-knit band are evident in the few remaining human groups that subsist as hunters and gatherers, the mode of living throughout the millions of years during which our brain took on its present architecture. In such groups, one of the main determinants of children's health is whether they have a living grandmother or other elderly relative who can supplement the mother and father's efforts to garner food.[5]

One modern legacy of this past is the radar for friendliness and cooperation most of us have; people gravitate to those who show signs of these qualities. We also have a strong early-warning system that alerts us to someone who may be selfish or untrustworthy. An experiment at Cornell University had groups of strangers mix and meet for thirty minutes and then rate each other on how selfish or cooperative the others were. Those ratings held up when compared with how the people actually performed in a game where they could choose selfish or cooperative strategies for winning. Likewise, people are drawn to others who are as cooperative and friendly as they are; groups made up of cooperative strangers are as altruistic and helpful to each other as are members of the same family.[6]

Socializing Shapes the Brain

One great anatomical legacy of the human need to band together is the neocortex, the brain's topmost layers, which gives us the capacity to think.

The adaptive challenges that matter most to the survival of a species are what lead to evolutionary changes in that species. Operating in a coordinated band—whether it be a working corporate team or a roving group of protohumans—demands a high level of social intelligence, skill in reading and handling relationships. If the more socially intelligent have the greatest number of surviving offspring—and therefore are the most "fit"—then nature would select for changes in the human brain that better handle the complexities of living in groups.[7] In evolution, as today, group members had to balance the advantages of cooperation in fending off enemies, hunting and foraging, and caring for children with the disadvantages of competition within the group for food, mates, or other limited resources, particularly in times of scarcity. Add to that having to compute hierarchies of dominance, social and kinship obligations, and quid pro quo exchanges, and the result was a staggeringly large amount of social data to track and use well.

Therein lies the evolutionary pressure to develop a "thinking brain" with the capacity to make all these social connections instantly. In the animal kingdom, only mammals have a neocortex at all. Among primates (including us humans), the ratio of neocortex to total brain volume increases in direct proportion to the size of the group typical of that species.[8] For early humans, that group could number in the dozens or hundreds (and in today's organizational life it can be in the thousands).

In this view, social intelligence made its appearance well before the emergence of rational thought; the abstract thinking abilities of the human species piggybacked later onto a neocortex that had initially expanded to deal with the immediate interpersonal world.[9] The neocortex, however, evolved from more ancient structures in the emotional brain, like the amygdala, and so is heavily laced with circuitry for emotion.

The neocortex, with its sophisticated understanding of group dynamics, must interpret its data in attunement with emotional signals. Indeed, every mental act of recognition ("That's a chair") has embedded within it an emotional reaction (". . . and I don't like it").

This same brain circuitry lets us know immediately, for instance, whom among those standing near us in an elevator we should greet and whom not ("The boss looks like she's in a bad mood today—I think I won't bother her"). And it forges every detail of the cooperative working relationships that are the key to survival in today's organizations.

Even as we pass the driest information back and forth, our neural monitors for emotional nuance are reading innumerable tacit cues—tone of voice, choice of words, subtleties of posture, gesture, timing—for the textured messages that give that information its emotional context. These emotional signals have the power to keep the conversation—or the group—on track or not. Smooth coordination depends on this emotional channel as much as on the explicit, rational content of what is said and done.

The Art of Collaboration

John Seely Brown, chief scientist at Xerox Corporation and a cognitive theorist himself, points out that the crucial nature of social coordination is perhaps nowhere more evident than in today's scientific enterprises, where cutting-edge knowledge grows through orchestrated, collaborative efforts.

Brown explains, "Many theorists think of learning from a purely cognitive viewpoint, but if you ask successful people to reflect on how they learned what they currently know, they'll tell you: 'We learned most all we know from and with each other.' That takes social intelligence, not just cognitive ability. Many people have trouble because they don't understand how you become part of a human situation, part of a relationship. It's easy to focus on cognitive ability and ignore social intelligence. But it's when you bring those together that you can create magic."

At Xerox Corporation's legendary Silicon Valley R&D facility, which Brown directs, he tells me, "Everything is done collaboratively, like everywhere in today's high-tech world. There are no lone geniuses anywhere. Even Thomas Edison was a brilliant knowledge manager. We traffic in human capital; ideas don't come from a lone head, but from collaboration in a deep sense."

Social intelligence matters immensely for success in a world where work—especially research and development—is done in teams. "One of the most important skills in management is the ability to read the human context, to be aware of what's in play," says Brown. "Power in management is the ability to make things happen. But how do you let the world do some of the work for you? It takes what amounts to organizational judo—being able to read the situation, the human currents, and move accordingly. The more we operate in less controlled environments, the more we need to be able to read human energies."

Brown continues, "There are some people who are blind to the dynamics of a group. I'll walk out of a meeting with one researcher, and he won't have a clue about what went on, while another researcher will have read the dynamics in the room perfectly: knowing when to step in, how to put things, what matters. That person can carry ideas beyond work out into the world."

The art of "making an impact through people," Brown adds, "is the ability to pull people together, to attract colleagues to the work, to create the critical mass for research. Then, once you've done that, there's the next question: How do you engage the rest of the corporation? And then, how do you get the message out and convert the rest of the world? To communicate is not just a matter of pushing information at another person. It's creating an experience, to engage their gut—and that's an emotional skill."

Team Advantage: The Group Mind

In today's workplace, this is a fundamental fact: Each of us has only a part of the information or expertise we need to get our jobs done. Robert Kelley, of Carnegie-Mellon University, has been asking people working at a wide variety of companies the same question for many years: What percentage of the knowledge you need to do your job is stored in your own mind?

In 1986 the answer was typically about 75 percent. But by 1997 the percentage had slid to between 15 and 20 percent.[10] This no doubt reflects the explosive growth of information. More knowledge has been generated in the twentieth century, it is said, than in all of history before, and the rate of increase continues to accelerate as we enter the twenty-first.

Given this fact, the network or team of people to whom we can reach out for information and expertise is increasingly vital. We've come to depend on the group mind as never before.

"My intelligence does not stop at my skin" is how Howard Gardner, the influential Harvard theorist, puts it. Rather, he points out, it encompasses his tools, such as his computer and its databases, and, just as important, "my network of associates—office mates, professional colleagues, others whom I can phone or to whom I can dispatch electronic messages."[11]

There's no doubt the group mind can be far more intelligent than the individual; the scientific data on this point is overwhelming. In one experiment, students studied and worked in groups while taking a college course. For their final exam, they first took a portion of the exam individually. Then, after they turned in their answer sheets, they were given an additional set of questions to answer as a group.

Results from hundreds of groups showed that 97 percent of the time the group scores were higher than those of the best individuals.[12] This same effect has been found over and over again, even for extremely short-lived groups, ones that were formed solely for the purposes of an experiment. When teams of strangers listen to a narrative about the ups and downs of someone's career, the more people on the team, the better their collective memory: Three people did better than two, four better than three, and so on.[13]

"As a math major, I believed that the whole is equal to the sum of its parts—until I worked with teams," Chuck Noll, the legendary former coach of the Pittsburgh Steelers, told me. "Then when I became a coach I saw the whole is never the sum of its parts—it's greater or lesser, depending on how well the individuals work together."

Lubricating the mechanisms of the group mind so that it can think and act brilliantly demands emotional intelligence. Superb intellect and technical talents alone do not make people great team members.

That was shown in a compelling series of experiments at a business school at Cambridge University. Researchers there put together 120 simulated management teams to make decisions for a mock business. Some of the teams were composed entirely of people who were highly intelligent. But despite this obvious advantage, the high-IQ teams performed worse than other teams whose members were not all so brilliant.[14] And observation of the teams in action tells why: High-IQ members spent too much of their time in competitive debate, and the debating became an unending session of academic showmanship.

Another weakness of the high-IQ teams was that all the members opted for the same kind of task: applying their critical abilities to the intellectually intriguing parts of the job at hand, engaging in analysis and counteranalysis. No one got around to other necessary parts of the job: planning, collecting and exchanging practical information, keeping track of what had been learned, coordinating a plan of action. Everyone was so busy trying to be the intellectual star that the team flopped.

The Group IQ

They're lost on a desert, the sun beating down mercilessly, mirages shimmering, not a recognizable landmark in sight. Their water is running low, and they have no compass or map. Their only hope is to set out in search of rescue—but their supplies are too heavy. They have to choose what to take and what to leave in order to survive.

It's a life-and-death scenario, but not life-threatening—it's a simulation used to test the teamwork skills of participants. The scenario allows each person to be rated on his or her individual choices, and for those choices to be compared to those made by the group as a whole.

The conclusion, from hundreds and hundreds of trials, is that groups fall into one of three performance levels. At the worst, frictions within the group make it fail as a team, with performance that is *poorer* than the average individual score. When the team works reasonably well, the group score will be greater than the *average* individual score. But when the team has real synergy, its score far exceeds even the *best* individual score.

For example, in terms of technical expertise and experience, the members of the management team at the auto division of one of Europe's largest automakers outmatched those on the equivalent team in the truck division. Yet the management group for the truck division operated better as a team.

"It made no sense when you looked at the profiles and backgrounds of the individuals in the truck division—you'd think they would be mediocre compared to that other team," the management consultant who worked with the teams told me. "Yet when they operated as a unit, they were superb."

What makes a team perform better than the best person on it? That question is key. Outstanding team performance raises the "group IQ"—the sum total of the best talents of each member on a team, contributed to their fullest.[15] When teams operate at their best, the results can be more than simply additive—they can be *multiplicative,* with the best talents of one person catalyzing the best of another and another, to produce results far beyond what any one person might have done. The explanation of this aspect of team performance lies in the members' *relationships*—in the chemistry between members.

In a classic study of group IQ by Wendy Williams and Robert Sternberg at Yale, the interpersonal skills and compatibility of the group members emerged as key to their performance (a result found time and again).[16] Williams and Sternberg found that those who were socially inept, out of tune with others' feelings, were a drag on the whole effort—especially if they lacked the ability to resolve differences or communicate effectively. Having at least one high-IQ member was essential for good performance but not sufficient; the group had to click in other ways, too. Another potential liability was the "eager beaver," a member who was too controlling or domineering to allow the full contribution of the others.

Motivation mattered greatly. If members cared and were committed to the goals, they tried harder and so did better. All in all, the *social* effectiveness of the group predicted how well it would do, more than did the individual IQs of its members. The conclusion: Groups perform better when they foster a state of internal harmony. Such groups leverage the full talent of their members.

A study of sixty work teams in a large American financial services company found that many elements mattered to some extent for the teams' effectiveness. But the single dimension that mattered most was the human element—how members interacted with each other and those the team connected with.[17]

■ ■ ■

Several competencies of star performers are rooted in the basic human talents for social coordination:

- *Building bonds:* Nurturing instrumental relationships
- *Collaboration and cooperation:* Working with others toward shared goals
- *Team capabilities:* Creating synergy in working toward group goals

■ BUILDING BONDS ■

Nurturing Instrumental Relationships

People with this competence

- Cultivate and maintain extensive informal networks
- Seek out relationships that are mutually beneficial
- Build rapport and keep others in the loop
- Make and maintain personal friendships among work associates

Jeffrey Katzenberg is furiously making connections. Three headset-wearing secretaries function as his antennae, probing and searching the entertainment industry for his next point of contact—incessantly ringing people to arrange times, calling back to reschedule or with a reminder of the upcoming call—all so that Katzenberg can be continuously on the phone during any and all free moments, reaching out to the hundreds of people he stays in touch with as a matter of routine.[18]

Katzenberg, one of the three founders of the Hollywood creative company Dreamworks SKG, is a networker without equal. The motive for his manic flurries of calls is, mainly, just to stay in touch—not explicitly to "do business." But his telephone routine primes these relationships, keeping them fresh, so that when the business need comes along, he can call on them seamlessly: make a proposal, pin down a deal.

In the entertainment industry, relationships are the key to doing business, because the projects—a film, a TV series, an interactive CD-ROM— are all short-term, goal-focused, and time-limited. They require knitting together an instant organization, a pseudofamily of director, producers, actors, and production people, all of whom dissolve back at the end into a loose network of potential players. Katzenberg keeps a weblike thread of connection out to everyone so that he can reel them in as needed.

This talent for connecting epitomizes stars in almost every kind of job. For instance, studies of outstanding performers in fields like engineering, computer science, biotechnology, and other "knowledge work" fields find the building and maintenance of networks crucial for success.[19] Even in fields like technology, the networks are linked the old-fashioned way, face-to-face and by phone, as well as through e-mail.

But what cements a connection is not physical proximity (though it helps) so much as *psychological* proximity. The people we get along with, trust, feel simpatico with, are the strongest links in our networks.

The networks of top performers are not random; they are carefully chosen, with each person being included because of a particular expertise or excellence. These networks traffic expertise and information back and forth in an artful, ongoing give-and-take. Each member of a network represents an immediately available extension of knowledge or expertise, accessible with a single phone call.

People who work a network well also have an immense time advantage over those who have to use broader, more general sources of information to find answers. One estimate indicates that for every hour a star puts into seeking answers through a network, an average person spends three to five hours gathering the same information.[20]

The Art of Networking

Weblike connectivity is the secret of success in many industries where people spend less of their careers in a single organization and more in short-lived, high-intensity relationships. Entertainment is certainly one such field. But this pattern, some predict, will come to typify many or most fields in the years to come. In such a fluid reality, where virtual organizations form to do projects, then dissolve once the project is complete, the key to success is not whom you have worked *for* but whom you have worked *with*—and whom you are still in touch with.

The electronics industry offers a case study in the crucial role of human networks in entrepreneurship. One estimate of the growth in value of the personal computer industry from 1981 to 1990 puts it going from virtually nothing to nearly $100 billion—an immense accumulation of wealth spurred by the alliances forged between enterprising technical wizards and equally enterprising venture capitalists.[21] Two thirds of high-tech firms were backed by venture capitalists, a breed of investors that has had a symbiotic relationship with America's high-tech industry since its earliest days, long before banks, let alone financial markets, would invest a penny.

Venture capitalists in Silicon Valley do far more than just spot a promising idea and put money into the start-up—they stay involved with the company they invest in. Their involvement typically includes giving the fledgling company access to the people they know in management, finance, and the high-tech industry itself, and even helping recruit key talent.

For example, just about all of the start-ups funded by the venture capital firm of Kleiner Perkins Caulfield and Byers were sent to them by someone they knew and trusted. John Doerr, a lead partner at the firm, talks about this rich web of relationships this way: "Think of Silicon Valley as an effective system for getting people, projects, and capital together." Such a system of connections can spawn vast wealth—and the absence of such a system can take a dire toll, especially during hard times.

Social Networks, Personal Capital

I t was the 1980s on Wall Street, when just about anything went. He was only twenty-four, yet he managed a $3 billion money market fund, and his earnings were spectacular. But his investments were almost entirely in junk bonds, and the fund lost virtually all its value in the crash of October 1987. He lost his job.

"That was when he learned relationships are everything in business," his wife tells me. "There was no one there to protect him. He had gotten so cocky and full of himself, he hadn't bothered to cultivate the kind of friendships that might have led someone to say, 'Let's keep him.' Then, when he tried to look for a new job, he didn't know anyone who would help him find something at another company."

After six months—and five hundred fruitless phone calls—he finally landed another, far less prestigious job, from which he began to work his way up the ladder again. But his basic attitude has changed.

"Now he's the president of his local professional society, and he knows all the other key people in the business," his wife says. "The question we ask ourselves is, If he lost his job tomorrow, how many phone calls would it take for him to get a new job? Today it would take just one."

Networks of personal contacts are a kind of personal capital. Doing well in our jobs depends to a greater or lesser extent on the work of a web of others. As one executive put it, while it may *seem* that he has control over how well he does his job, "in reality, in addition to my direct subordinates, there are hundreds of people whom I have no direct control over but who can affect the performance of my job. At least two dozen of these people are crucial."[22]

One of the virtues of building relationships is the reservoir of goodwill and trust that arises. Highly effective managers are adept at cultivating such relationships, whereas less effective managers generally fail to do so.[23] This is particularly crucial for advancement from the lower rungs of an organization to the higher levels; these human links are the routes through which people come to be known for their abilities.

These networks may be quite distinct from the web of friendships we cultivate primarily for pleasure. Relationship building has a motive; these are friendships with a purpose. People skilled at networking often mix their private life and their work life, so that many or most of their personal friendships are made through work, though it takes clarity and discipline to keep work and private agendas from becoming entangled.

People who are shy, introverted, or reclusive are, of course, poor at cultivating such relationships. And people who merely accept the invitations they are extended but make none themselves or restrict their conversation to work matters do little to enlarge their web of relationships.

Another common failing is that people are too protective of their own work time and agendas, turning down requests to help or to work cooperatively; the result is often resentment and a stunted network. But people who can't say no whenever anyone makes a request of them are in danger of taking on so much that their own work suffers. Outstanding performers are able to balance their own critical work with carefully chosen favors, building accounts of goodwill with people who may become crucial resources down the line.[24]

Rapport building is central to developing strong, useful relationships. Rapport hinges on empathy and typically emerges naturally in the course of casual conversation about family, sports, children, and the stuff of life. Finally, the building of a close work friendship means establishing an alliance, a relationship that can be counted on. Those highly adept at relationship building, like Katzenberg or Doerr, can call on an extensive—and ever-expanding—network of friends.

Bring In the Relationship Managers

Marks & Spencer, the huge British retail chain, gives an unusual gift to its regular suppliers: a special key card that lets them into the chain's head offices anytime. Although they still have to make appointments, the key card makes them feel like members of the Marks & Spencer family.

That is exactly the point. The key card is part of an intentional effort by Marks & Spencer to nurture a relationship of trust and cooperation with its suppliers. That effort also includes trips with suppliers to trade shows and to other countries to visit sources of raw materials. The goal: to strengthen mutual understanding, as well as to spot new possibilities for products they can develop jointly.

The Marks & Spencer program exemplifies a trend among suppliers and retailers to build collaborative relationships, rather than simply playing one potential partner against another. That cooperative strategy has tangible payoffs: An analysis of 218 retailers carrying the products of a replacement auto parts manufacturer showed those retailers who trusted the manufacturer, compared to those who distrusted it, were 22 percent less likely to have alternative sources of supply, and to have 78 percent higher sales of the products.[25]

While links between such large organizations may seem abstract, they boil down to the day-to-day connections of sales reps, account managers, product managers, and the like. These people-to-people coalitions across companies have concrete benefits for both sides: They can share mutually important proprietary information and allocate people and resources to customize business. Those from one company can sometimes act as de facto consultants for another. For example, a sales team from Kraft Foods took it on itself to do a six-month study of a retailer's dairy case. The Kraft team then came up with recommendations for reorganizing shelf space and stocking new items that reflect recent buying trends. The result: Sales for the retailer—and of Kraft products to that retailer—increased by about 22 percent.[26]

Another example: Procter & Gamble used to pay its sales managers on the basis of the total amount of inventory they got retailers to take, even if that inventory ended up back in the warehouse. But that meant P&G salespeople were rewarded for a strategy that, in the end, hurt retailers and eroded business relationships. Now P&G has shifted its policy to compensate its salespeople for maximizing *both* P&G's results and those of the stores that sell its products.

Since a company-to-company relationship is nothing more than the ties between the people from each, the interpersonal chemistry is crucial. For that reason, Sherwin-Williams, the paint manufacturer, actually invites managers from Sears, Roebuck, one of its main retailers, to help choose the representatives who will handle the Sears account.

As Nirmalya Kumar, writing about this approach in the *Harvard Business Review,* put it, "The trust game has implications for the type of people that a company recruits to work with [its] partners. . . . Traditional manufacturers, salespeople, and retail buyers have had a volume or price focus. They need to be replaced by *relationship managers* with appropriate bedside manners."[27]

■ COLLABORATION AND COOPERATION ■

Working with Others Toward Shared Goals

People with this competence

- Balance a focus on task with attention to relationships
- Collaborate, sharing plans, information, and resources
- Promote a friendly, cooperative climate
- Spot and nurture opportunities for collaboration

Intel, the hugely successful computer processor manufacturer, had a paradoxical problem: Its success was, in a sense, killing it. An extremely task-focused organization, the company's concentration on product development, staying ahead of the curve in creating new technologies, and improving turn-around for new product introduction paid off in huge market share and profit. Yet for too many people, it just wasn't fun anymore.

That, at any rate, is how a consultant to a division at Intel, who was called in for some advice, put it to me.

"They wanted a workshop on how to attend to the relationship side of their business, because it was becoming increasingly unenjoyable," the consultant told me. "At the personal level they liked each other, but they were so intensely task-oriented, their working relationships were suffering. They needed to let supervisors know it's not enough just to get the job done if you destroy the relationships within the working group. They needed management to appreciate that neglecting the soft side has hard consequences."

This interpersonal crisis at Intel points to the value of a collaborative, cooperative spirit. Groups that have fun together—who enjoy being in each other's company, who can joke together and share good times—have the emotional capital not just to excel in good times, but to get through hard times as well. Groups who do not share this emotional bond are more likely to become paralyzed or dysfunctional or to disintegrate under pressure.

Even those who subscribe to the tough-minded business-is-war ideology and see no point in cultivating a humane tone may do well to ponder the immense effort put into cultivating esprit de corps at the platoon level in armies. The sophisticated understanding of what makes a unit work well under extraordinary pressures has always been that emotional bonds are crucial to morale, effectiveness, and the unit's very survival.

The Organizational Marriage

Everyone knew the meeting was a personal disaster for Al, a fledgling vice president at a large urban medical center. To be sure, all agreed the meeting was for a good purpose: to create a vision and strategy for a failing community program Al had been brought in to run. But Al sabotaged both himself and the meeting. As he admitted afterward, "I got my behind kicked."

Al's first mistake was calling the meeting of the hospital's already over-scheduled senior management group on too short notice, selecting a day when he knew the VP of the nursing unit—someone with a crucial contribution—was usually out of the hospital. The consultant to the management team also couldn't make it. Al's second mistake was failing to offer a pre-meeting briefing or preparation of any kind—he was winging it, even though this was his debut as a new vice president. His third and perhaps biggest mistake was to rebuff an offer from Sarah, his boss and the president of the medical center, to help design a meeting that would be lively and more effective.

As the meeting unfolded it was painfully evident to everyone that Al was unprepared and flustered, and those who came felt the session was a waste of their time. Sarah felt Al's disastrous performance reflected poorly on her judgment in bringing him into the job.

What went so wrong?

James Krantz, a professor at the Yale School of Organization and Management, who observed Al and Sarah on the job, says the failed meeting was yet another symptom of something deeply amiss in their working relationship.[28] With surprising rapidity, they had settled into a pattern that brought out the worst in each other. Privately, Al admitted to feeling that Sarah was overbearing and hypercritical of him, chronically dissatisfied with whatever he did; Sarah said Al seemed passive, inept, and sullen with her. At the emotional level, the two of them acted and looked like a couple trapped in a miserable marriage—except that this was work, not private life.

But, Krantz observes, it could happen anywhere—and with alarming ease. Any superior and subordinate can slip into a destructive emotional dynamic, because each needs the other in order to succeed. A subordinate can make a boss seem effective—or pathetic—to the boss's own boss, since the superior is accountable for how well the subordinate does. And, of course, the subordinate depends on the superior for promotions, raises, and simply keeping a job—all of which makes the subordinate emotionally vulnerable to the boss.

Therein lies the blessing or the curse. This interdependence ties a subordinate and superior together in a way that can become highly charged. If both do well emotionally—if they form a relationship of trust and rapport, understanding and inspired effort—their performance will shine. But if things go emotionally awry, the relationship can become a nightmare and their performance a series of minor and major disasters.

The Vertical Couple

The power of a subordinate to make a boss look good to *her* boss is, potentially, tremendous. But for Sarah, Al had become a magnet for some of her deepest anxieties about her own performance. She was embarrassed by the failure of the program Al had been brought in to run—she felt it reflected poorly on her own abilities as president and threatened her professional reputation. She now doubted Al's ability to save the unit—and thus her reputation—and so was angry about his performance.

Al, for his part, had been perfectly capable at his previous job, but the promotion to vice president left him unsure of himself. He feared the others on the management team would see him as incompetent; at his worst moments, he felt like an impostor. And, to make everything worse, Al sensed Sarah's lack of confidence in him, which only compounded his anxieties and his ineptitude.

Each secretly felt the other was the cause of their problems: Al saw Sarah as undermining his confidence by being overly controlling as well as doubting his competence. Sarah, for her part, had started to see Al (just as he feared) as lacking both the confidence and competence to do the job she needed him to do, and so she felt obliged to be responsible, even aggressive, for both of them. The result was a downward spiral in which Al became more passive, unsure, and inept, and Sarah micromanaged, becoming more critical and controlling, finally trying to do Al's job for him.

Krantz invokes a ponderous term for this dynamic between Sarah and Al: "projective identification." Each of them projected onto the other their worst fears and doubts in an emotional self-fulfilling prophecy.[29] Any close working relationship can take on such hidden undertones, though the one between a boss and subordinate is most prone to such emotional sabotage.

These unconscious agreements serve a rather sinister psychological function: They keep people from facing or even recognizing problems, bad news, or conflicts. If a boss can blame some defect of his own—and the resulting problems in the organization—on a subordinate, then he never needs to face the real source of trouble: himself. One symptom of this kind of projection—"the problem is with him, not me"—is a boss who can never find or name a replacement, even as retirement looms. No one is good enough; every candidate has fatal flaws.

Kiss Up, Kick Down

Sycophancy by subordinates, and a corresponding arrogance in the superior, is another all-too-common symptom of projection. The subordinates see the boss as having special power or ability; the boss buys into the projections and his sense of himself becomes inflated to the point where he feels the rules of decency no longer apply.

This pattern seems particularly common in some cultures. I'm told by Deepak Sethi, an expert in executive education, that in India, his country of origin, the rule is "Kiss up and kick down." As Sethi says, "There's a lack of empathy downward in most old-style Indian companies. You see it in bosses who are openly angry at people. There's no stigma to it; it's completely acceptable to yell at your subordinates there."

A major reason subordinates put up with it, Sethi says, is that so many Indian companies are privately held by powerful families, and there are many more highly qualified people than there are good jobs available, "So even if you're a professional manager, you're at the mercy of the owners."

An understandable result of the kiss-up–kick-down relationship is a large pool of resentment "that's never expressed upward, but passed on downward, in a chain of angry rudeness." This leads workers to sabotage the company's success in passive ways, like not getting things done on time—which, of course, makes the boss yell at everyone all over again.

That bitter cycle echoes the stalemate between Sarah and Al: Sarah felt she couldn't trust Al to do his job well enough, so she kept pushing him to do tasks while hovering over him, expecting the worst. This, in turn, made Al feel demeaned—and undermined his abilities.

The saga of Sarah and Al, fortunately, had a happy resolution. Sarah was acutely aware that something was off track in her relationship with Al, if only because it stood in such stark contrast to the effective ties she had to everyone else on the management team. Once the diagnosis was made, Sarah was able to stop micromanaging and show Al that she had some faith in his capabilities. She also clarified his responsibilities. No longer shadowed by the fear that she saw him as unfit for his job, Al was now able to take initiative and show his competence.

Their story is one with wide implications. Virtually everyone who has a superior is part of at least one vertical "couple"; every boss forms such a bond with each subordinate. Such vertical couples are a basic unit of organizational life, something akin to human molecules that interact to form the latticework of relationship that *is* the organization. And while vertical couples have all the emotional overlay that power and compliance bring to a relationship, peer couples—our relationships with coworkers—have a parallel emotional component, something akin to the pleasures, jealousies, and rivalries of siblings.

If there is anywhere emotional intelligence needs to enter an organization, it is at this most basic level. Building collaborative and fruitful relationships begins with the couples we are a part of at work. Bringing emotional intelligence to a working relationship can pitch it toward the evolving, creative, mutually engaging end of the continuum; failing to do so heightens the risk of a downward drift toward rigidity, stalemate, and failure.

■ TEAM CAPABILITIES ■

Creating Group Synergy in Pursuing Collective Goals

People with this competence

- Model team qualities like respect, helpfulness, and cooperation
- Draw all members into active and enthusiastic participation
- Build team identity, esprit de corps, and commitment
- Protect the group and its reputation; share credit

Teamwork is of utmost importance to companies like Owens-Corning, a building materials manufacturer, which found itself with about two hundred incompatible software systems, each tailored to a specific task like tracking shingle counts or invoices for insulation. To help their salespeople sell the company's whole line, rather than just insulation or roofing, Owens-Corning needed a single, unified software system.

So Michael Radcliff, their chief information officer, turned to SAP, a German industrial-applications software company, which installed a system at Owens-Corning that connects all the information in the entire operation. When a sales rep sends in an order, the system automatically allocates the raw materials for its manufacture, schedules its production and delivery, and takes care of billing—all with a single data entry.

But there's a risk—the SAP system is notoriously complex, and a small glitch can create company-wide chaos. Owens-Corning—and all SAP's other manufacturing customers worldwide—need to trust that they can rely on SAP to keep them running.[30]

"Before," an SAP account rep tells me, "I sometimes would have a hard time getting people from other divisions within our company to help me with a one-two punch—to come together with a unified solution for a customer's problem. After all, if our software goes down, they can't get their product out the door; they need to be assured they can count on us." Hence the formation of teamSAP, the shorthand term for the teams of SAP employees available to all their customers at all times.

Similar teams seem to be everywhere in business these days—management teams, task forces, quality circles, learning groups, self-managed work teams, and so on. And then there are the instant, ad hoc teams called into being over the course of a meeting, or as a short-lived virtual group working together on a one-time project. While people at work have always helped each other out and coordinated their efforts, the ascendance of work teams in large organizations puts a new premium on team skills.

About half the Fortune 1,000 companies in a General Accounting Office survey said they were using self-managed work teams, and expected to expand their use in coming years.[31] The advantages begin at the personal level—people feel the combination of cooperation and increased autonomy offered by a self-managed work team offers more enjoyment and fulfillment. When teams work well, turnover and absenteeism decline, while productivity tends to rise.[32]

Perhaps the most compelling strength of teams for business is their pure economic potential. Just as individuals who are superior performers can add tremendous financial value, so it is with teams. The top work teams at a polyester fiber plant achieved an astonishing productivity advantage when compared to teams doing the exact same work. Each of the top ten teams produced 30 percent more fiber per year—in total, about seven million pounds more.[33] At a market price of $1.40 per pound, that meant an economic value added of $9.8 million!

As analyst Lyle Spencer Jr. told me, "There's a huge leverage from better working teams. When you look at the economic value added, it's out of all proportion to the salaries of team members. Data like this give the lie to people who dismiss these competencies or things like team building as 'touchy-feely'—the benefits are quite real."

Spencer adds, benefits from high-performing teams at the top offer even greater payoffs. "At the highest levels, the scope of thinking is bigger—people are projecting five and ten years out—and the economic advantages of a high-performance executive team for a company can be vast."

Strong groups are essential in a climate of corporate upheaval. I visited AT&T in 1996, shortly after it had announced its intention to split into three separate companies and lay off forty thousand employees. An executive in a division that is now part of Lucent Technologies told me: "The pain is not being felt everywhere. In a lot of the tech units where people work in tight teams, and where they find great meaning in what they do together, they're fairly impervious to the turmoil."

He added, "Whenever there's a strong self-managed team, with clarity about its mission, high standards for its product, and a clear sense of how to do its work, you just don't see fears and uncertainty the way you do in other parts of the organization. Members put their trust in their teammates, not just in the organization or its leaders."

The Team Achievement Drive

A friend who manages a team of software engineers in Silicon Valley tells me, "With a single phone call, any of the people I work with could get a job across town for twenty thousand dollars more a year. But they don't."

Why?

"I keep it fun."

The ability to make everyone on a team love what they are doing together is at the heart of team building and team leadership. Studies of the highest-performing self-managing work groups find that a critical mass of their members love working in a group. This "team achievement" outlook is a combination of a shared competitive drive, strong social bonds, and confidence in each other's abilities. Taken together, these elements add up to what Spencer summarizes as "fast, focused, friendly, self-confident, fun teams."[34]

People on such teams tend to share a common motivational pattern. They are competitive and evenhanded in matching members to the best role for their talents. They have a strong affiliative need—they like people for their own sake—which makes them more harmonious, better able to handle conflicts and offer mutual support. And rather than seeking power that is purely self-interested, they wield power in the best interests of the group— they share a commitment to the group goal.

These are the kind of teams, Spencer notes, that are increasingly widespread in entrepreneurial high-tech organizations, where quick product development is vital to meeting the competitive pressure of an industry in which the shelf life of a product line is measured in weeks and months.

Just twenty years ago team skills were only threshold abilities, not a trait that defined outstanding leaders. In the 1990s, though, team skills are a defining quality of star performers. At IBM, 80 percent of the time a person's strength as a team leader predicts "whether someone is a top performer or just average," Mary Fontaine, of Hay/McBer, told me. "These are people who can create compelling visions, conceptualize their business in an exciting way, articulate it simply and emphatically," and so inspire others with enthusiasm in their work together.

In a study by the Center for Creative Leadership of top American and European executives whose careers derailed, the *inability* to build and lead a team was one of the most common reasons for failure.[35] Team skills, which had been of little consequence in a similar study in the early 1980s, had emerged as a key mark of leadership ten years later. By the 1990s, teamwork became the most frequently valued managerial competence in studies of organizations around the world.[36]

"The number one challenge for leadership here is getting the heads of our units to play together, to collaborate," an executive at a Fortune 500 company tells me. That is the great challenge at any level, in any organization. Team abilities come into play anytime people work together toward a common goal, whether in an informal group of three or in an entire corporate division. The demand for team skills will only grow in the coming years, as work revolves more and more around ad hoc groups and virtual organizations, around spontaneous teams that arise and dissolve as the need for them comes and goes—and as tasks become so complex that no one person has all the skills needed to accomplish them.

The Value of Star Teams

A s with individuals, so with groups: Emotional intelligence is key to excellence. Of course intellect and expertise matter—but what sets star teams apart has much to do with their emotional competence. Studies at companies like GE, Abbott Laboratories, and Hoechst-Celanese asked: What competencies distinguish highly effective teams from mediocre ones?[37]

To find that answer, Vanessa Drukat, now a professor at the Weatherhead School of Management at Case Western Reserve University, analyzed 150 self-managed teams at a huge American polyester fiber plant run by Hoechst-Celanese, the German chemical company (and where Spencer's data also came from). On the basis of objective performance data, she compared the ten most outstanding teams with average ones doing the same jobs.

These emotional competencies emerged as distinguishing capabilities of the ten star teams:[38]

- Empathy, or interpersonal understanding

- Cooperation and a unified effort

- Open communication, setting explicit norms and expectations, and confronting underperforming team members

- A drive to improve, so that the team paid attention to performance feedback and sought to learn to do better

- Self-awareness, in the form of evaluating their strengths and weaknesses as a team

- Initiative and taking a proactive stance toward solving problems

- Self-confidence as a team

- Flexibility in how they went about their collective tasks

- Organizational awareness, in terms of both assessing the need of other key groups in the company and being resourceful in using what the organization had to offer

- Building bonds to other teams

A case in point for how such competencies let teams work better can be seen in a study of strategic decision making in forty-eight top management teams at food-processing companies across the United States. CEOs were asked to identify the most recent strategic decision their company had made. Researchers then contacted the members of the management team who had been involved in that decision.[39]

Making team decisions presents a paradox: On one hand, the wisdom holds that the more freewheeling and intense the debate, the better the final decision; on the other hand, open conflict can corrode the ability of a team to work together.

Research on decision making in management teams shows that having people who possess the three qualities of high cognitive capabilities, diverse perspectives, and expertise leads to higher-quality decision making. But intellect and expertise are not enough; members also have to mix in a healthy interaction, one that furthers rigorous, open debate and critical examination of people's assumptions.

Achieving this level of openness can be a delicate, emotionally loaded matter. Too easy a consensus risks a low-quality decision, while too much contention results in a lack of unity and resolve. What allows a management team to argue heatedly but end up with a strong consensus? The presence of emotional intelligence.

And what makes a group go off track, with healthy debate devolving into open war? When disagreement is couched as personal attack, or when debate is in the service of political gamesmanship, or when a dispute triggers acrimony in a group member.

The central finding: If arguments become emotionally loaded, the quality of decisions suffers. As one consultant told me, "The image of the well-coordinated management team is a myth when amygdala hijacks, conflicts, and other undealt-with emotional static interfere with their abilities to plan, decide, and learn together." On the other hand, debate free of bad feelings—carried out in a positive spirit of mutual inquiry, with everyone feeling the process is fair and open, and holding a shared concern for the organization rather than their narrow self-interest—led to the best decisions.

In sum, there is a middle way: Teams can use intellectual battle to upgrade the quality of decisions, provided they keep debates free of the emotionality that might alienate or sabotage commitment to the decision by some team members. The key lies in emotional competencies such as self-awareness, empathy, and communication—that is, in how well team members argue.

The Glue People

The ability to keep a group working well together is a valuable talent in itself. Every high-functioning group almost certainly has at least one member with this talent. The greater the complexity of the group's task, the more crucial such people are to its success. This is most evident in science and technology, where the mission is to discover or create. Take neuroscience: "Biomedical research is increasingly interdisciplinary and high-tech; no one can know everything," says Dr. Jerome Engel, a neurobiologist and professor of neurology who directs the Seizure Disorder Center at UCLA. "It's all research teams now. People who are great motivators and collaborators, who are gifted in making a medical project work, are the glue that holds it all together. The future of research depends on having people like that on your team."

Yet, at least in the academic world, these skills are sadly undervalued. "When people come up for tenure review, the value of their contribution to the group gets no consideration," Dr. Engel adds. "These good collaborators tend to publish with other people, usually their supervisor, and tenure committees blindly assume it's the superior's work—though these people are key. It's a disaster. I find myself fighting for the reviewers to understand that the collaboration is in itself a skill worth keeping someone for—it's essential to biomedical research. But academics from disciplines like math and history, where research is a solitary pursuit, don't understand."

The result: "There's a counterreaction among younger researchers, who are sometimes afraid to collaborate because of this—which can mean they go off alone and do trivial or unimportant research," says Dr. Engel. "It's creating an atmosphere of paranoia, an unwillingness to share data or work together, that's undermining a scientific generation's ability to collaborate."

Where academia has been slow to recognize the value of a talent for cooperation and teamwork, business has not. Richard Price, a psychologist at the Institute for Social Research at the University of Michigan, calls these superbly nurturing types who are the cornerstone of strong work teams "health-engendering people," or HEPs. "They're crucial to a team," says Price. "It doesn't mean everyone has to be a social-emotional leader, but if one HEP is there, the team will work ten times better."

One legendary team, the engineering group at Data General whose efforts were memorialized in the best-selling book *The Soul of a New Machine,* had two HEPs on board.[40] The team's second in command, Carl Alsing, was everyone's confidant and emotional support. Alsing, who had planned to be a psychotherapist before heading into electronic engineering, became a group sounding board; everyone felt comfortable talking to him.

The second team nurturer was Rosemarie Seale, their secretary, who acted as a kind of den mother, seeing that everyone's material needs were taken care of and handling the minor crises of the day like a paycheck gone astray, or making sure people joining the team were shown around.[41] While such secretarial tasks may seem routine and mundane, they are crucial because they let people at work feel protected, supported, and cared for—and this, some say, is why secretaries or their equivalent will always be invaluable, despite technologies that would seem to render them obsolete.

The Competent Team Leader

An American pharmaceutical firm had an expensive problem: Once a new drug was identified and patented, testing and development took an investment of around $100 million and up to thirteen years to get the FDA approval that allowed marketing. Because the patent on a new drug's basic chemical compound lasts just seventeen years, that gave the company about a four-year window to recoup its investment and turn a profit before the drug became available as a generic.

A task force looking into the dilemma recommended a new structure: project teams focused on specific drugs, headed by project leaders reporting directly to the head of R&D—leaders who would be trained in the team leadership competencies. Such leaders could both be product champions within the company and bring entrepreneurial energy, enthusiasm, and collaboration to the team itself.

When these teams were compared three years later to others where the leaders had no such training, they not only had higher morale and esprit de corps, but had cut product development time by 30 percent, thereby doubling the time the company would have the drug exclusively.[42]

The designated leader is something like a parent in a family. Like a parent, leaders have to be sure that their actions are perceived by everyone on the team as fair, and, like a parent, a good team leader will look out for the team members, defending them—for example, when their reputation comes under attack—in the organization at large and providing for them by getting the practical support they need, in budgets, personnel, or time.

The best team leaders are able to get everyone to buy into a common sense of mission, goals, and agenda. The ability to articulate a compelling vision that serves as the guiding force for the group may be the single most important contribution of a good team leader. A charismatic leader can hold a team on course when all else fails.

Apart from molding the crucial emotional tone of a team, the leader provides coordination, which is the secret of cooperation and consensus. When people were put together in a leaderless group and told to work on solving a tough problem together, the more effective teams were those that spontaneously developed a structure where one person orchestrated their efforts, so they could solve a tough problem as efficiently as possible. Groups that operated in a leaderless mode, with everyone communicating with everyone else willy-nilly, were less effective.[43]

But strong team leaders do not act as the group's "brains," or autonomous decision makers, so much as consensus builders. When team leaders express their own opinion too early in a decision-making discussion, the group generates fewer ideas, and so makes poorer decisions. But when team leaders hold back, acting mainly as facilitators of the group's process without imposing their views, not expressing them until toward the end of a discussion, the outcome is a better decision.[44]

In this sense, team leaders lead best when they lead least. This is especially true for self-managed work teams, where the supervisors of the teams are not team members and the teams can perform autonomously.

In a study of self-managing customer service teams at a major American telephone company, the teams faltered when the supervisors gave suggestions and even "encouraging" advice.[45] The "advice" seems to have been read by the team in two ways: either as a demoralizing message that they were doing poorly and so needed extra help, or as meddling that got in the way of the team doing its best work.

The dynamic was very different in customer service teams that were self-managing but directly run by a supervisor. In these more traditional teams the supervisors' feedback had a positive effect on performance. The difference in the impact of supervisory control seems to revolve around the team's charter. When a team has a mandate to run itself, a supervisor, no matter how well-intentioned, may undermine team performance.[46] So when it comes to self-managed teams, the best leadership seems to be little or no leadership at all.

The Team and Organizational Politics

They've got these separate silos of authority and creativity, but no one talks across the boundaries," a consultant called in by one of America's largest food manufacturers tells me. "People who handle one brand won't cooperate with people who manage another, let alone try to innovate new products or marketing approaches together. But to stay competitive, they've got to create teams that transcend these boundaries."

Organizations of all kinds have come to the realization that the success of the whole demands that talents be orchestrated in teams that cut across traditional boundaries. This can be seen in ad hoc project teams and teams for planning, improving processes, developing products, and troubleshooting. All such teams are unified around a focused task, with members coming from discrete parts of the organization.

Such cross-functional teams are a special case, a kind of pseudo-team that brings together a mix of people who have their feet in two camps: their home base within the organization and their common meeting point as a team. Because they represent diverse parts of the organization, they have the potential for wider impact and coordination than would a team that is partitioned off. As these teams work together for the larger good of the organi-zation, each member remains beholden to a constituency back home.

But overallegiance to the home base can have disastrous effects for the team. At an American automaker, for example, a cross-functional steering committee working on a new prototype held a meeting to work out their mu-tual electrical needs. The car's electrical power serves twenty different sub-systems, including stereo, dashboard, headlights, and engine. The prototype for each of these subsystems, in turn, was being developed by a separate team, and when they met, they found that their combined solutions would consume 125 percent of the electrical power available. And since many members of the steering team were sent to the meeting with instructions from their own bosses to make *no* compromises, the meeting was a disas-ter.[47]

How can teams like this do their work effectively? An analysis of forty-three such teams at a global automaker—the same study that tracked the electrical power meeting—suggests several answers. The first lies in the or-ganizational context, in which resources and power are given to the team it-self and its members are rewarded based on the team's performance.

Another solution lies in raising the collective level of emotional intelli-gence. This might include delegating someone as a "process leader," who can track whether the group's work exemplifies collaboration, mutual re-spect, openness to diverse perspectives, listening, empathy, and the other hallmarks that raise a group's IQ. If the team process is on track, then mem-bers should feel the work is exciting, challenging, and important. Lacking these emotional intelligence team basics, the alternative is, as one member of a dysfunctional cross-functional team put it, "a fiasco."

The Team as Hero

The world's attention was captured for several weeks in 1997 by the spec-tacle of Sojourner, the spunky rover that sputtered along the rock-strewn landscape of Mars.

The television coverage of the tiny rover pluckily threading its way through Mars's jagged terrain like the Little Engine That Could was drama enough. But the real miracle was the remarkable team effort behind getting Sojourner there at all.

The project as originally conceived by NASA was a full-scale exploration of Mars. It suffered a near-fatal setback in 1992, when Congress froze funding, leaving barely enough to build a tiny, scaled-down demo model that had been planned only as a preliminary step in the larger plan.

So the project members were faced with converting what was to have been a nonworking scale model into a fully operational, miniaturized version of the probe.

Anthony Spear, the director of the Pathfinder project that delivered Sojourner, let Donna Shirley, the program manager, model a team on "Skunkworks," the name of the famed R&D team at Lockheed that sequestered itself and produced a stream of pioneering aviation prototypes, from America's first supersonic jet fighter to the Stealth bomber.

Shirley assembled a small, sleek team that would accomplish only the work necessary for the mission. Spear made the team even more efficient by doing away with layers of bureaucracy that had typified past NASA space projects. With the Pathfinder, one group would do everything, from design to operation.

The team shared the whole task, often in creative problem-solving sessions that wore on into the night. These were open forums, where everyone, no matter their ostensible rank, was given an equal hearing.

Though the challenge was daunting, the spirit was playful. Al Sacks, data systems manager, recalls someone asking for more money—yet again. So Sacks pulled a rubber dart gun from under the table and shot his teammate. "This was serious business," says Sacks, "but we turned it into fun."

The team had to be nimble; new challenges and surprises were constant. For instance, as Sojourner was being loaded into the Pathfinder spacecraft that would carry it to Mars, the engineers noticed—during a televised news conference, no less—that the large metal folding petals designed to protect the rover once on Mars were not shutting all the way. They were horrified.

Sending the press home, the team scrambled frantically to find the problem and solve it. Since they had never before put the whole rover together, they had not considered the possibility that the latches that closed the petals would sag under the weight of all the parts.

So team members pulled parts off an engineering model, made slight modifications, hand-carried them from their facility in California to the launch site at Cape Canaveral, and replaced them. It worked.

The team worked around the clock for six months before the launch. What kept everyone on track despite the grueling pace was the grandeur of their goal. Said Bridget Landry, deputy uplink systems engineer, "The idea that what we're building and testing right now will be used when we land on Mars was really exciting. I tried to think of that when the fourth revision in the last hour for the same sequence came in!" Yet, she added, "There are few jobs that are all glamour and no dirt; the good ones, like mine, are those where the glamour, excitement, and emotional rewards make up for the scut work."

That scut work produced a marvel. The six-wheeled rover had a surprisingly modest brain: While the best Pentium computers have more than five million transistors, there are under seven thousand in the rover's.

And when Sojourner was finally launched, the project was not only a spectacular success, it was also $7,000 under budget. The team had invented at least twenty-five new devices or processes and had produced a spacecraft in one fourth the usual time. While the Mars Observer, lost in 1991 before reaching the planet, cost $1 billion, Sojourner was successful and came in at a quarter of that cost.

As one team member says, "It was like we caught fire—nothing could stop us." The Sojourner team was in flow.

Group Flow

When I've asked seasoned executives and managers what it's like when teams they've been on or run have caught fire and outdone themselves—and achieved flow—the same characteristics come up time and again.[48]

■ *A daunting challenge or a noble mission.* "One of the reasons group goals often fail is they're too materialistic," a vice president of space launch systems at Lockheed Martin told me. "I look for superordinancy—goals big enough that the whole group can get behind them." Such work has compelling meaning and motivation; working toward something monumental deserves everyone's best effort.

The late Nobel Prize–winning physicist Richard Feynman remembered how differently people worked on the Manhattan Project before and after they knew what their effort was for. Originally strict security meant the whole team was kept in the dark, so they often worked slowly, and not always very well.

Then Feynman convinced Robert Oppenheimer to tell the team of technicians what they were actually working on—it was during the darkest days of World War II, and their project was a weapon that might stop the Axis enemy, who were at the time ascendant. From that point on, Feynman recalled, "*Complete* transformation. *They* began to invent ways of doing it better. . . ."[49] He calculated that their work went ten times as fast after they understood the goal.

■ *Intense group loyalty.* "When extraordinary teams talk about what made them so successful, you often hear them say it's because they really love and care about each other," says Daniel Kim, cofounder of MIT's Center for Organizational Learning, and now with Pegasus Communications. "If people were honest about what makes great teams in an organization, they'd say part of it is the emotional connections that allow both openness and caring."

■ *Diverse range of talents.* The stronger the array of capabilities a team brings to its task, the more flexible it can be in meeting changing demands. Diversity begins with technical demands, but extends also to emotional competence—including a "glue person."

■ *Trust and selfless collaboration.* People in successful teams feel they can count on each other. When Bob Taylor assembled the team at Xerox PARC that developed the prototype of the user-friendly computer (eventually the basis for the first Apple computer when Xerox failed to follow through), he looked for people who could work collaboratively, and encouraged everyone to help out with other people's work. "You could spend forty percent of your time working as 'hands' on somebody else's project," recalls Alan Kay, one of the first computer scientists asked to join.

■ *Focus and passion.* The demands of meeting a great goal inherently provide focus; the rest of life can seem not just mundane, but trivial by comparison. For the duration, the details of life are on hold. Focus can be sharpened by creating a working space for the group, separate from the rest of the organization, both in function and in place. The Manhattan Project was carried on at top-secret sites accessible only to project members; the Skunkworks at Lockheed was in a windowless, signless building that was off-limits to everyone else at the company.

■ *Work that is intrinsically fun and rewarding.* Such intense focus is in itself a kind of high. Members work less for external perks like money, promotion, or prestige than for the inner rewards of the work itself. Whether that thrill comes from the drive to achieve or a need to make an impact, there is an intense emotional payoff from outdoing all others as part of a group. As a member of the Data General software team put it, "There's a big high in here somewhere for me that I don't fully understand. . . . The reason I work is to win."[50]

The Team as Learning Lab: The Five Secrets

urt Swersey's bright idea came to him when an article I wrote for the *New York Times* back in September 1995 caught his eye. It was about the Bell Labs study in which stars in an engineering division seemed to owe their success more to emotional intelligence skills than to technical ones, and it inspired Swersey to try something new with his engineering students at Rensselaer Polytechnic Institute.

He started his class by telling them about the Bell Labs study and what he called the "five simple secrets of success": rapport, empathy, persuasion, cooperation, and consensus building. And, he announced, instead of spending the first day of class reviewing engineering basics, they would conduct a learning lab on the five secrets.

"How would you go about establishing rapport with someone you don't know?" Swersey asked.

As the class, somewhat baffled and tentative at first, offered suggestions, Swersey listed them on the blackboard: "Introduce yourself, look at the person while you talk, ask them a question about themselves, shake hands, tell them about yourself, listen carefully . . ."

"These sound like the right answers," Swersey told them. "Now pick someone you don't know and take three minutes to establish some rapport."

The students pitched in enthusiastically; the room was filled with their chatter and banter. Swersey had a hard time getting them to stop and focus on the next "secret," the art of being empathic.

Asking them what *empathy* meant, he wrote these answers on the board: "Caring, listening, being supportive . . ." A young man wearing a baseball cap backward, his feet on the desk, muttered, "Showing you give a damn."

"That seems to capture it pretty well," said Swersey. "Now I want you to come up with something in your lives you feel you need some support for, and tell it to your partner. Partners, your job is to empathize." The buzz in the room made it clear that this was going well, too.

So Swersey upped the ante: "Now make up something that directly negatively impacts your partner. If you're the listener, no matter how hard it is to take, resist the temptation to tear the person apart—just be empathic." So the role-playing began and students spun out earnestly enacted, antagonizing tales: "I smashed your car." "I killed your goldfish." "I slept with your girlfriend."

For the empathizers, Swersey insisted they go beyond a stoic "Okay" and put themselves in the shoes of their partner, saying something like, "I feel so bad for you; you must be so upset." That led to a classwide discussion of a more realistic situation: someone on an engineering team who fails to deliver their promised part of a project on time. The students talked about taking the other person's perspective—and began to understand the importance of being supportive rather than angry.

They went on to practice persuasion and consensus building, taking three minutes to decide as a group which was the single best flavor of ice cream in the world, and why (one consensus-building answer: Neapolitan, a combination of three favorite flavors).

The results of this small social experiment?

"These sections turned out to be the best teams I've had in years of teaching Introduction to Engineering Design," says Swersey now. "They not only worked better together than any students I've had, but they produced extremely ambitious, innovative devices. I attribute a good part of their success to the time spent working on the five secrets."

Swersey's humble experiment speaks to a larger problem in organizations, particularly ones that are laden with technical experts. "When I work with companies that have to manage engineers, the main problem in team building is that as a profession, engineers don't view people skills as relevant," Daniel Kim, formerly at MIT, tells me. "Now these companies are waking up to the cost of not having emotional competence."

That awakening can be seen, too, at professional schools like the Harvard Business School and the MIT Sloan School of Management. "These days more of the curriculum is becoming team based," Kim adds. "This is in response to criticism from companies that MBAs have been trained to excel as individuals, but they need to learn how to work well in teams, too."

What many team enthusiasts fail to see is that every team itself can become a learning lab for the very capabilities people need in order to perform better as team members. "Every member of a team brings unique strengths and skills to the group, some technical, some in emotional and social capabilities," observes Kathy Kram, a director of Boston University's executive MBA program. "It's a great opportunity for mutual learning, if the team can make that learning an explicit goal or part of their contract together."

That opportunity is typically wasted, she adds, "because too often a focus on how team members relate is seen as a distraction from achieving the team's goal, instead of a way to help them work better together. But using teams for learning team skills makes great sense, especially in team-based organizations."

And that brings us to the next point: Whether through a team or on our own, each of us can strengthen and develop any of these emotional competencies—if we know how.

4

················

A New
Model of
Learning

10

....

The Billion-Dollar Mistake

lready the country's fastest-growing major life insurance company, "We saw a way to do even better," says Jim Mitchell, president of IDS Life, American Express's insurance division. Mitchell saw an opportunity—a big opportunity. Despite clients' financial plans showing they should purchase life insurance, more than two out of three declined to buy it. This large loss of potential sales was no temporary blip; sales for several years running yielded the same conclusion.

The potential for more sales was so great that Mitchell, set up his own "Skunkworks" operation in order to find a "breakthrough that could make life insurance more compelling to clients."[1]

Their first step was an investigation of how planners and clients really felt about selling and buying life insurance. The answer, in a word: terrible.

The investigation tapped a startling outpouring of negative feeling from clients and planners alike. While the team expected to find some major flaws in the life insurance *products* the company was offering, they found instead that the problem was with the sales *process* itself. It boiled down to emotional incompetence.

Clients said they distrusted the sales relationship with advisors, that the prospect of buying insurance made them feel "powerless, uninformed, inadequate, and suspicious." The negativity was prevalent even among those clients who *did* buy insurance. The problem wasn't a fear of death, the expense, or any feature of the policies; in fact, clients said they were perfectly satisfied with the products offered. Rather, it was the sales interaction that soured them. Small wonder: Many advisors confessed feeling "unqualified, incompetent, untruthful, and selfish" while proposing life insurance. Some said a sense of pressure to "make the sale" led them to act in ways that challenged their personal ethics. They yearned to feel more confident and more principled. Many said that working under the general bad reputation of insurance salespeople and making cold calls was building up a reservoir of helplessness and depression.

When a client displayed anxiety or uneasiness, the common wisdom in the insurance industry held that the best response was not empathy but a rational argument. So the advisors were left trying to shut out the client's emotions as well as their own. "Our advisors had been taught that if there was an emotional reaction in a client, it was a form of resistance—so you needed to explain it logically, with more numbers, and ignore their feelings," explained Kate Cannon, who was a member of the Skunkworks team and who is now responsible for emotional competence programs at American Express Financial Advisors.

In short, the feelings roiling within clients and planners alike set a miserable emotional tone for their encounter; as a final report put it, "A mountain of emotional negativity stood between our sales process and our bottom line."

Advisors could set a more positive emotional tone, but they had to deal with their own rocky emotional state first. As one planner put it, "We can spend millions on product research and development, but if the delivery of these products is impaired due to our self-limitations, what have we accomplished?"

Remedying the Yuck Factor

The remedy began (as we saw in Chapter 4) with heightening the advisors' emotional self-awareness. And that unearthed what became known as the "yuck." "We analyzed the 'yuck' in the business—the emotional battles people faced daily that were distasteful and painful," Cannon told me.

The yuck list was formidable. Among the items:

- The rejections were demoralizing. A stream of rejections might lead to catastrophic thinking like "I can't do this—I'll lose my job. . . . I'll never be able to make a living."

- The sheer volume of information on products left some advisors overwhelmed.

- The entrepreneurial nature of the advisors' task, where their income depended on their sales, was scary for many advisors, who feared not being able to support themselves.

- Confusion about reconciling the needs of clients tormented some.

- The long hours needed to get a foothold in the business left a number of advisors anguished about the imbalance between work and family.

But for every emotional quandary there was a remedy—a skill to be acquired, an attitude to be changed. The solution was, in essence, to bolster the advisors' levels of emotional competence.

An emotionally competent advisor, in the words of one company analysis, "maintains confidence, has resilience in adversity, and acts from core principles and values." The rationale: Advisors who were driven by their own principles, not sales pressure, would relate to clients in a way that elicited trust. With their hearts in their work, they would be more convincing. And with better control over their own fears and frustrations, they would be able to persist despite setbacks. Sales would be a natural result of better meeting clients' needs.

Advisors themselves agreed; many said emotional competence was the hidden ingredient in their success or failure.

The evaluation team decided to focus on only a few emotional competencies at the outset. They knew advisors couldn't set the right tone or deal with their clients' emotions well until they could manage their own.

Building Emotional Competence—and Sales

'm a hothead," Sharmayne Williams, a financial advisor at American Express's Chicago office, confides. "I was extremely emotional—I'd take everything to heart and react strongly. It badly affected my relationships with people in the office: If they didn't see things my way, I'd get mad. It was my way or no way. I couldn't see it from their perspective, I wouldn't compromise."

That lack of emotional self-control worked against Williams. "It prevented me from moving up; it got in the way of making decisions," she told me. "If I was upset about something, I couldn't move on to the next project. It cost me money."

Williams had been a licensed stockbroker for eight years before joining American Express Financial Advisors, and when she had her first training session in emotional competence a year later, it was a revelation: "I'd never encountered anything like this before. This was the missing piece."

The program, she says, has changed her life. "I see how my emotions were controlling me. Now if something is bothering me, I talk it over with my business partner, write it in my journal, talk to my field vice president right away. I let them know I'm upset—I don't let it fester. I'm more accepting. I realize you can have all kinds of emotions, but you don't have to let them run you."

She has found ways to handle the tension. "Now when I feel it building up, I go to a ballet studio in my building and work out. The physical relaxation cools me out for days."

And now Williams, always a high performer, is doing even better. In her first year at American Express she made about $1,700,000 in sales. In her second year, Williams tells me, she reached $2,400,000, and is on track for advancement.

That improvement is just the point. In the first pilot of the emotional competence program, financial advisors who went through the training had sales gains of 8 to 20 percent over the previous year—significantly more than comparison groups who did not get the training, and more than the average company-wide.

"We were pleased enough with the outcome to make it part of our standard training for new salespeople, as well as offering it to managers and other people in leadership positions," Doug Lennick, an executive vice president at American Express Financial Advisors, told me. And it represents a personal triumph for Lennick, who championed the emotional competence program.

When Lennick became head of the American Express Financial Advisors sales force, he had the emotional competence program expanded and offered to a broader range of people. Now training covers two days—concentrating on self-awareness, interpersonal, and coping skills—with another three-day session a few weeks or months later. And the program is available to all incoming financial advisors and new supervisors, as well as to sales management teams and other team leaders and those directly under them.

For Lennick, the success of emotional competence training dovetails with a vision he has long held that the financial advisor's role should be less that of the traditional salesperson and more that of a trusted consultant in a long-term relationship.

"I never thought clients wanted a relationship with five or six advisors, but rather an ongoing relationship with one advisor," says Lennick. "The advisors with the best relationships with their clients do more than just help them achieve their financial objectives: They help with life planning. That's a radical revision of their role, encompassing not just helping the client stay financially fit, but also live in alignment with their sense of purpose."

Says Lennick, "We've proven that if you help people deal with their emotions, they will have more professional success without compromising their personal values."

As Sharmayne Williams puts it, "Being a trustworthy person and in control helps me with my clients." Emotionally intelligent relationships pay off.

The Good News

At Promega, a biotech company in Madison, Wisconsin, a group of scientists gather daily to practice mindfulness, a method for focusing and relaxing they learned in an eight-week training program. The scientists say they feel more calm, concentrated, and creative using the method.

Well and good. But even more impressive is that researchers documented positive changes in the scientists' *brain function* as a direct result of the mindfulness training. Their left prefrontal lobes—the brain area that suppresses amygdala hijacks and generates positive feelings—have become significantly more active than before the program.[2] The scientists' sense of greater alertness and relaxation is no mere illusion: It stems from an underlying change in the brain. This brain change duplicates that found in those individuals who are most resilient and adaptable under stress (as we saw in Chapter 5). The finding suggests that as a competence such as self-control strengthens, so do the corresponding circuits in the brain.

All emotional competencies can be cultivated with the right practice. Consider the people who did poorly on the empathy tests described in Chapter 2. They floundered when they were asked to read the feelings of videotaped men and women having spontaneous reactions—joy, rage, and so on—but with the words indistinct. But when they were given feedback after each of their guesses on what the people portrayed were actually feeling, their empathic accuracy improved markedly.[3] Even a small amount of immediate feedback on emotional accuracy has a surprisingly large carryover to empathy in other situations.[4]

The good news about emotional intelligence, then, is that—unlike IQ itself—*it can improve throughout life.* In a serendipitous fashion, life offers chance after chance to hone our emotional competence. In the normal course of a lifetime, emotional intelligence tends to increase as we learn to be more aware of our moods, to handle distressing emotions better, to listen and empathize—in short, as we become more mature. To a large extent, maturity itself describes this process of becoming more intelligent about our emotions and our relationships.

In a comparison of several hundred adults and adolescents by John D. Mayer, a University of New Hampshire psychologist who developed the pioneering theory of emotional intelligence with Yale's Peter Salovey, the adults were better at it across the board.[5] And an evaluation by Reuven Bar-On of emotional intelligence in more than three thousand men and women—ranging from teenagers to people in their fifties—found small but steady and significant increases as people go from age group to age group, with a peak occurring in the forties.[6] As Mayer concludes, "Emotional intelligence develops with age and experience from childhood to adulthood."

When it comes to cultivating emotional competence, maturity remains an advantage; it may be slightly harder to "teach young dogs new tricks." In a study of how well students in an MBA program were able to master new levels of emotional competence—with the age of students ranging from early twenties to fifties—the most improvement occurred in those twenty-nine or older, compared to those students under twenty-five.[7]

Whether that finding will generalize to other groups remains an open question. But it does show that, given the motivation, older workers can be as able or better than younger ones when it comes to mastering new levels of these capabilities.

Men and women seem equally able to increase their emotional intelligence. While women tend to be stronger in competencies based on empathy and social skills, with men doing better in those based on self-regulation, the same study of MBA students discovered that men and women can improve to the same extent, no matter where they start out on a given competence.

This improvement puts emotional intelligence in sharp contrast to IQ, which remains largely unchanged throughout life. While purely cognitive capacities remain relatively fixed, emotional competence can be learned at any point in life. No matter how insensitive, shy, hot-tempered, awkward, or tuned-out people may be, with motivation and the right effort they can cultivate emotional competence.

But how?

Understanding Is Not Enough

Consider Henry and Lai, who started out as electrical engineers at Bell Labs about the same time, with roughly the same credentials: Both had 3.8 grade point averages from top-flight universities with effusive recommendations from professors, and both had spent summers interning at computer companies.

But the moment they arrive at Bell Labs, all similarities fall away. Henry acts as though he hasn't left graduate school. He stays glued to his computer screen, voraciously devouring technical documents and learning new software programs. His new colleagues rarely see him except at staff meetings; he's a recluse. His thinking: "It's my technical proficiency that will matter most for me on this job."

Lai takes a different approach. She makes sure to devote adequate time to her work. But her spare time is dedicated to getting to know her coworkers, finding out about their interests, projects, concerns. When they need a helping hand, she offers one—when everyone needed to install a new, cumbersome software tool, for example, she volunteered to do it. Her thinking: "One of the best ways for me to be accepted into the team is to help out."

After six months on the job, Henry has done a slightly better job technically—but Lai is seen as someone who can work well on a team and take initiative, and is already marked for the fast track. Henry has failed to realize that building bonds is a crucial competence for his job; he's more comfortable as a loner. His coworkers see that he is technically adept, but they have little trust he can work well on a team.

Lai shows excellence in several emotional intelligence competencies—but if Henry's technical gifts are to be put to best use, he needs to master these competencies, too. How do you help someone like Henry change for the better?

Robert Kelley, of Carnegie-Mellon University, who offers this case study, points out that Lai has learned strategies typical of star performers, like building bonds and taking initiative.[8] But there is more to what she does than simply knowing about a winning strategy—the ability to *execute* a strategy such as networking and cooperation depends on the requisite emotional competence. For someone like Henry to make the necessary changes, it's not enough for him to have the *intellectual* understanding that they would be useful. Merely knowing that he should build relationships may not be enough to budge him from his cubicle—or to make him adept at it if he tries.

There is a crucial difference between *declarative* knowledge, knowing a concept and its technical details, and *procedural* knowledge, being able to put those concepts and details into action. Knowing does not equal doing, whether in playing the piano, managing a team, or acting on essential advice at the right moment.

A study of management training in a supermarket chain found very little correlation between managers' knowledge of the competencies they were trained in and how they actually behaved once back at their stores. Many trainees came out of the program with high levels of understanding about what they *should* do back on the job—they just failed to do it when they got there. Intellectual understanding of a competence may be necessary, but it is not sufficient in itself to result in behavior change.[9]

Having a cognitive realization about what to do says nothing about someone's readiness to begin to act differently, nor about his motivation or capacity to do so, nor about the method by which he can gain a new level of mastery of the new capability. Helping people master an emotional competence demands a new understanding of how we learn.

As one of the most frequently cited sources on training and development puts it, those who study training "have tended to consider all training the same, without regard to the purpose of the training or the type of learning involved."[10] For cognitive and technical competence, declarative knowledge may be sufficient—but not for emotional intelligence. It is time to stop lumping all training together; we need to use our new understanding of the brain's workings to make meaningful—and practical—distinctions and promote the real learning of emotional competence.

The Ultimate Test

Teaching *about* a competence—that is, having workers get an intellectual grasp of the concepts involved—may offer the easiest training approach, but compared to other approaches I'll discuss shortly, it has the least effect on actually changing performance. Intellectual understanding is a threshold process, necessary for learning, but not sufficient for lasting improvement.

Deep change requires the retooling of ingrained habits of thought, feeling, and behavior.

Consider Henry, the reticent engineer at Bell Labs who doesn't venture out of his office and engage his coworkers. Why does he behave this way?

Henry's isolation might be due to shyness, to social ineptness, or simply to being unskilled in the art of teamwork. Whatever the specific cause of his isolation, he is the victim of a learned habit. And what has been learned can be *un*learned—and a more effective habit learned instead—with effort and time. This unlearning and learning occur at the level of the brain connections themselves.

As we acquire our habitual repertoire of thought, feeling, and action, the neural connections that support this repertoire are strengthened, becoming dominant pathways for nerve impulses. While connections that are unused become weakened or even lost, those we use over and over grow increasingly strong.[11]

Given a choice between two alternative responses, the one that has the richer, stronger network of neurons will win out. And the more a response occurs, the thicker the neural pathways grow to support it. When habits have been well learned, through countless repetitions, then the underlying neural circuitry becomes the brain's default option—we act automatically and spontaneously.

Competencies can be seen as a coordinated bundle of habits—what we think, feel, and do to get a job done. When such a habit is dysfunctional, replacing it with a more effective one requires enough practice of the better habit—and inhibition of the poor one—that the neural circuitry for the old behavior finally withers (psychologists call this "extinguishing") and the circuitry for the better behavior grows stronger. Eventually the better habit will replace the old one as the automatic response in key situations.

The test of this kind of learning—of such rewiring—for an emotional competence lies in how a person automatically reacts in the salient moment. The proof of whether someone like Henry has mastered the fundamentals of making connections and cooperation comes in situations where he has a critical choice: either to remain in his cubicle grinding away alone or to consult several coworkers who have helpful information and expertise. If he spontaneously steps out of his cubicle to approach a colleague—and does so effectively—this would indicate that a new habit has been mastered.

A Different Model of Learning

A government researcher at the U.S. Office of Personnel Management is briefing me on the results of a massive analysis of the competencies required for a wide range of government jobs. "Training for the technical part of jobs is easy—but it's much harder to train people to be flexible, to have integrity, be conscientious, or be skilled interpersonally."

Technical training *is* easy compared to developing emotional intelligence. Our entire system of education is geared to cognitive skills. But when it comes to learning emotional competencies, our system is sorely lacking. Capacities like empathy or flexibility differ crucially from cognitive abilities; they draw on different areas of the brain.

Purely cognitive abilities are based in the neocortex, the "thinking brain." But with personal and social competencies, additional brain areas come into play, mainly the circuitry that runs from the emotional centers—particularly the amygdala—deep in the center of the brain up to the prefrontal lobes, the brain's executive center. Learning emotional competence retunes this circuitry.

Because intellectual learning differs from behavior change in fundamental ways, the models of education for each are significantly different. For intellectual skills, the classroom is an appropriate setting, and simply reading about or hearing a concept once can be enough to master it. Strategic thinking and computer programming can be taught effectively in this mode, removed from the give-and-take of life on the job. For behavior change, on the other hand, life itself is the true arena for learning, and this takes practice over an extended period of time.

Learning in school is, in essence, adding information and understanding to the memory banks of the neocortex. The neocortex learns by fitting new data and insights into existing frameworks of association and understanding, extending and enriching the corresponding neural circuitry.

But learning an emotional competence involves that and more—it requires that we also engage our emotional circuitry, where our social and emotional habits are stored. Changing such habits—learning to approach people positively instead of avoiding them, to listen better, or to give feedback skillfully—is a more challenging task than simply adding new facts to old. Emotional learning demands a more profound change at the neurological level: both weakening the existing habit and replacing it with a better one.

Understanding this difference in underlying brain function is crucial to designing ways to teach emotional competencies. One common mistake made by organizations is trying to instill an emotional competence like a service orientation or leadership, using the same techniques that effectively teach how to create a business plan. This is not enough: Changing a habit based on emotional intelligence demands an entirely new kind of learning strategy. Some schools, corporations, and even governments are finally beginning to understand this.

Many of the standard learning principles for training and development in organizations derive from trivial studies of college students practicing basic motor skills or engaged in simple cognitive tasks like memorizing lists of words.[12] But these principles are insufficient for the more complicated task of upgrading emotional competencies. Cultivating emotional competence requires an understanding of the fundamentals of behavior change. The failure to take this into account wastes an immense investment in development and training each year. As I write this, millions upon millions of dollars are being wasted on training programs that have no lasting impact—or little effect at all—on building emotional competence. It amounts to a billion-dollar mistake.

"Spray and Pray"

The CEO of one of America's leading pharmaceutical firms was impatient. He had seen a huge growth in training costs at the company and wanted to know one thing: What were they getting for their money?

A reasonable request—and, coming from the CEO, one that got an immediate response. Soon he was presented with a hastily drawn-up report—based on anecdotes.

That was not acceptable: The CEO, an M.D. by training with a Ph.D. in biomedical statistics, and a former research scientist himself, wanted hard data. So those involved went back to the drawing board and came up with a more thorough plan for evaluating the dollar value and long-term strategic worth of training. They called in outside experts—Charley Morrow, from the consulting firm Linkage, and Melvin Rupinski, of Tulane University. The result was a rarity in the organizational world: a rigorous, four-year project using the quantitative methods of science to assess whether the company's training actually justified its cost.[13]

That this is a rarity in the business world is itself a paradox. Despite the billions of dollars spent on corporate training programs globally, the effectiveness of these programs is rarely evaluated by the companies that pay for them—nor by anyone else. Estimates of the extent to which skills taught in company training programs carry over into day-to-day practice on the job are as low—and gloomy—as a mere 10 percent. But no one knows for sure what the true rate of improved job performance is, because the data are rarely collected.[14]

In October 1997 the American Society for Training and Development surveyed a select group of thirty-five highly regarded "benchmark" companies. Twenty-seven said they tried in some way to promote emotional competence through training and development.[15] But of these, more than two thirds had never attempted to evaluate the impact of their efforts. Those who did, for the most part, relied on soft measures like reactions to training sessions and employee opinion surveys.

A larger ASTD survey found that only 13 percent of companies evaluated their training in terms of on-the-job performance.[16] "The only hard measure we've had of development training is the number of bodies on chairs—we only know that people go through the training, not that they get anything out of it," the head of human resources at one of the world's largest financial services companies confided. "Sometimes we call it 'spray and pray': expose everybody to the training and hope it sticks to some."

The Bottom Line

The executives who gathered for a seminar in a secluded mountain resort were from the top tiers of management at a giant pharmaceutical company. The week focused largely on "people skills" and looking at ways to more effectively lead other managers in an increasingly competitive and dynamic business environment.

The topics included a range of emotional competencies, including how to model "effective people management," how to motivate subordinates and evaluate their strengths and weaknesses, and how to give performance feedback, manage teams, handle conflict, and lead innovation. There was also time set aside for some reflection on the executives' own behavior and its impact on the people they deal with.

It was a full five-day menu of development—one fairly representative of thousands of such executive and management courses given in organizations around the world. But was it worth the cost, as the CEO had wondered?

No.

Not only was there no improvement, but those executives who attended were rated by their bosses as, on average, *less* effective in these competencies than before the seminar. "Comparing pre- and postseminar ratings of their managerial behavior, there was a slight negative shift," one of the evaluators told me. "They were a little less capable."

This was one of the more disappointing among the dozen or so management programs evaluated by the pharmaceutical company's study. Overall, results were mixed; while some programs proved themselves definitely worth the effort, several did not.

The training programs were very different in focus, in audience, and in results. The competencies they aimed to bolster ranged from teaching top executives to motivate their employees, to helping managers communicate more effectively, resolve conflicts, and manage change, to improving supervisors' ability to give feedback and foster positive relations with workers.

All the programs were evaluated on the basis of their observable effects on the performance of those who went through them, with pre- and postprogram assessments by bosses, peers, or subordinates, as appropriate. A clever statistical technique allowed these results to be turned into calculations of return on investment, and the methods used offer a state-of-the-art model for such training evaluations—a model that should be widely imitated.[17]

The results of this very careful—and too-rare—evaluation are sobering, particularly for those in the business of management training. Three of the eleven programs focusing on interpersonal capabilities essential for management were found to be utterly worthless. These included the five-day mountain retreat, a training for lab chiefs in managing individual performance, and a program in team building.

Calculation of the time for these three programs to pay back their cost—that is, just to break even—showed it would take seven years for the team-building program to pay for itself, providing the effects could last that long (a dubious assumption). The time to pay back for the other two: *never.* Neither produced a strong enough impact on job performance to justify its cost!

Five of the eleven programs, the evaluation revealed, would take more than a year to pay for themselves, again assuming their results would last. Those five programs, so ineffective in retrospect, cost a total of nearly $700,000 for the 147 employees evaluated.

The news was better for the five other leadership and management trainings.[18] The return on investment for these ranged from 16 percent to 492 percent. And another program on time management (a stress-management skill that calls on impulse control and other self-regulation competencies) had a spectacularly short payback period—about three weeks—and a return on investment in the first year of 1,989 percent. In terms of return on investment, this home-grown course, developed in-house, outperformed a well-known time-management course by far—largely because it cost just $3,000, compared to $68,000 for the nationally prominent course.

In short, when programs work, they pay for themselves, most within the first year or so, and are justified by quantifiably improving on-the-job performance. When programs fail, they waste time and money.

Was the four-year project to evaluate training at the pharmaceutical firm worth the time and money? Undoubtedly. For one thing, it was a relative bargain: The entire effort cost $500,000—during a period when the company was spending $240 million on training. In other words, the evaluation represented only .02 percent of the training budget.[19]

Since then the company has completely revamped its training and development programs; none of the money-losing programs is offered anymore. And the study itself stands as a benchmark, setting the standard for how companies could go about getting an empirically sound reading of the value of their own training programs.

When the Hard-Nosed Become Soft

After searching far and wide for corporate training programs in emotional competencies that had been evaluated using impartial outcome measures and a comparison group—the golden mean of evaluation—Cary Cherniss, a psychologist at Rutgers University (and cochair with me of the Consortium for Research on Emotional Intelligence in Organizations), noted with amazement, "Few companies actually test the training programs they're making million-dollar bets on. When it comes to human relations, hard-nosed companies become very soft; they just don't insist on demonstrated results. There are lots of executives who don't seem to realize you can design studies to test the programs you are spending so much on."

Sometimes this is a result of naïveté, and sometimes organizational politics are at fault. Cherniss tells of a high-tech company that invested over a million dollars in a training program for working better in teams. Yet they made no attempt to evaluate its effectiveness. Why? "It was a pet project of an executive vice president. No one wanted to know if it *worked*—just if people liked it. Companies don't evaluate outcomes to see if the programs have any real impact on performance."

When they do, the results can be disturbing. "We just tried to assess the benefits of a training program we've used for years and spent millions of dollars on," an executive at a Fortune 100 company lamented. "We've found zero correlation with productivity on any measure."

Too often the only real effect of training, no matter what it's for, is that people get a short-term "buzz" of energy that lasts no more than a few days or weeks, after which attendees fall back into whatever their habitual mode was before the training. The most general effect of training seminars—no matter the ostensible content—is that they increase people's self-confidence—at least for a while.[20]

But if all that has been boosted is the trainee's confidence, then these expensive programs are like the magic feather in the old Disney cartoon *Dumbo.* When the timid baby elephant with the huge ears gets a magic feather from his mentor, a wily field mouse, he clutches it tightly in his trunk, flaps his ears—and starts to fly.

Of course, Dumbo loses his feather one day, and learns he still can fly. For emotional competencies it's not always that simple. While enthusiasm and a can-do spirit are helpful, they can only work to the degree that people have the underlying skills and learn the competencies to *make* them work. If you don't have empathy or are socially inept, or haven't learned to manage conflict or take a customer's perspective, sheer enthusiasm is no replacement—and can lead to well-intended blunders.

The world of training seems prone to whims and infatuated with fads. So laments a review of the current state of training and development, which concludes that too many programs are "adopted on the basis of a persuasive salesperson, a slick brochure, or testimonials from previous participants."[21]

When it comes to evaluation, rigor gives way to impression. Hard-nosed evaluations like the ones done at the pharmaceutical firm are extremely rare. Rather than an objective assessment of the effects of training, the typical evaluation comes in the form of "happy sheets," feedback from participants about whether trainees liked the program, and what about it they liked the most—a rating system that patently favors slick, fun experiences over substantive ones. Having a good time becomes the mark of excellence, a valuing of entertainment over education.

This lack of data feeds the endless waves of "hot" programs that sweep through the corporate seas. In the 1960s and early 1970s companies sent thousands of employees off to "encounter groups" and "sensitivity training"—unstructured sessions where people vented their rawest feelings (an often futile exercise in emotionality, as opposed to being intelligent *about* emotion). They did so despite the lack of any evidence that such sessions helped people in their jobs, and in the face of emerging data that such groups, when poorly led, could have negative repercussions.

Emotional Competencies: Guidelines for Learning

When heads of development at Fortune 500 companies were asked what makes it difficult for them to evaluate their own training programs, the most common complaint was the lack of standards and yardsticks available for training in the so-called soft skills like emotional competencies.[22]

To help change this, I cofounded the Consortium for Research on Emotional Intelligence in Organizations, a coalition of researchers and practitioners from business schools, the federal government, consulting firms, and corporations.[23] Our consortium has searched the scientific findings on behavior change and studied exemplary training programs, to create basic guidelines for the best practices in teaching competencies based on emotional intelligence.[24]

The resulting guidelines are summarized in Table 2. Two key points:

- Each element is necessary for effective learning, but not sufficient by itself.

- The impact of each element increases to the degree it is part of a process that includes the others.

TABLE 2

Guidelines for Emotional Competence Training

....

Assess the job. Training should focus on the competencies needed most for excellence in a given job or role.

Caveat: Training for irrelevant competencies is pointless.
Best Practice: Design training based on a systematic needs assessment.

Assess the individual. The individual's profile of strengths and limitations should be assessed to identify what needs improving.

Caveat: There's no point in sending people for training in competencies they already have or do not need.
Best Practice: Tailor training to the individual's needs.

Deliver assessments with care. Feedback on a person's strengths and weaknesses carries an emotional charge.

Caveat: Inept feedback can be upsetting; skillful feedback is motivating.
Best Practice: Use emotional intelligence in delivering initial evaluations of a person's emotional competence.

Gauge readiness. People are at differing levels of readiness.

Caveat: When people lack readiness, training is more likely to be wasted.
Best Practice: Assess for readiness, and if someone is not yet ready, make cultivating readiness an initial focus.

Motivate. People learn to the degree they are motivated—for example, by realizing that a competence is important to doing their job well— and making the competence a personal goal for change.

Caveat: If people are unmotivated, training will lack effectiveness.
Best Practice: Make clear how training will pay off on the job or for the individual's career, or be otherwise rewarding.

Make change self-directed. When people direct their learning program, tailoring it to their needs, circumstances, and motivation, learning is more effective.

Caveat: One-size-fits-all training programs fit no one specifically.
Best Practice: Have people choose their own goals for development and help them design their own plan for pursuing them.

Focus on clear, manageable goals. People need clarity on what the competence is and the steps needed to improve it.

Caveat: Poorly focused or unrealistic programs for change lead to fuzzy results or failure.
Best Practice: Spell out the specifics of the competence and offer a workable plan to get there.

Prevent relapse. Habits change slowly, and relapses and slips need not signal defeat.

Caveat: People can become discouraged by the slowness of change and the inertia of old habits.
Best Practice: Help people use lapses and slip-ups as lessons to prepare themselves better for the next time.

Give performance feedback. Ongoing feedback encourages and helps direct change.

Caveat: Fuzzy feedback can send the training off track.
Best Practice: Design into the change plan feedback from supervisors, peers, friends—anyone who can help coach, mentor, or give appropriate progress reviews.

Encourage practice. Lasting change requires sustained practice both on and off the job.

Caveat: A single seminar or workshop is a beginning, but not sufficient in itself.
Best Practice: Use naturally arising opportunities for practice at work and at home, and try the new behaviors repeatedly and consistently over a period of months.

Arrange support. Like-minded people who are also trying to make similar changes can offer crucial ongoing support.

Caveat: Going it alone makes change tougher.
Best Practice: Build a network of support and encouragement. Even a single buddy or coach will help.

Provide models. High-status, highly effective people who embody the competence can be models who inspire change.

Caveat: A do-what-I-say-not-what-I-do attitude in superiors undermines change.
Best Practice: Encourage supervisors to value and exhibit the competence; make sure trainers do, too.

Encourage. Change will be greater if the organization's environment supports the change, values the competence, and offers a safe atmosphere for experimentation.

Caveat: When there is no real support, particularly from bosses, the change effort will seem hollow—or too risky.
Best Practice: Encourage change that fits the values of the organization. Show that the competence matters for job placement, promotion, performance review, and the like.

Reinforce change. People need recognition—to feel their change efforts matter.

Caveat: A lack of reinforcement is discouraging.
Best Practice: Be sure the organization shows it values the change in a consequential way: praise, a raise, or expanded responsibility.

Evaluate. Establish ways to evaluate the development effort to see if it has lasting effects.

Caveat: Many or most development programs go unevaluated, and so mistakes or pointless programs go unchanged.
Best Practice: Find measures of the competence or skill as shown on the job, ideally before and after training, and also several months (and, if possible, a year or two) later.

Teaching the Skills That Matter

S he was an accountant in the health care industry—and she had a real problem. She couldn't take criticism; when she felt her ideas—or her character—were being attacked, her anger flared and she said things she felt ashamed about later.

But she was determined to do something about it. Now enrolled in an executive MBA program, she had an opportunity to cultivate emotional self-control, a competence she knew she needed to improve.

Her plan for doing so was multipronged:

- Learn and master steps for better self-control, such as anticipating hot-button situations and preparing herself so that she won't "lose it." Remind herself that what she sees as "criticism" or an "attack" is most often feedback that is meant to be helpful.

- Practice those responses at every opportunity. Mentally rehearse them twice a month.

- Recruit fellow students to role-play troubling situations with her so she can try out new self-control strategies.

- Have a fellow member of her learning team agree to signal her when he sees her being stubborn, inflexible, or otherwise overreacting, to remind her to exercise self-control.

This set of learning tactics, so well-suited to cultivating emotional intelligence, may seem out of place in an MBA program. But they are part of the curriculum at the Weatherhead School of Management at Case Western Reserve University in Cleveland, a leader in preparing its students in these crucial capabilities.

Weatherhead took to heart a number of common criticisms of MBA graduates—including that they are too analytical and lack interpersonal, communication, and team skills. So the school embarked on a plan to reinvent business education, developing an innovative course, Managerial Asessment and Development, that incorporates many (if not most) of the Consortium guidelines.[25]

The course, spearheaded by Richard Boyatzis, an associate dean, offers students tools for lifelong learning: methods for assessing and developing the personal abilities they need for management throughout their career.

Since 1990 it has been offered to several different groups of students. Most are men and women in their twenties and thirties who have decided to go back to business school for an MBA after several years on the job. It is also offered to physicians, lawyers, and other professionals, most of them in their forties and fifties, who attend a special one-year, nondegree program at Weatherhead.

The course begins with a period of self-examination during which students reflect on their values, aspirations, and goals. They then go through a range of assessments of their competencies, identifying their strengths and weaknesses.

The course provides a map of the emotional competencies similar to Table 1 in Chapter 2.[26] From this map, and in light of their own assessment results and their career needs, each student chooses a set of competencies to strengthen. Instead of the one-size-fits-all approach so familiar in organizational training, students construct an individualized learning plan for themselves.

The class meets for one three-hour session a week. The first two weeks focus on assessment; the next seven weeks reflect on the results. Only then, when the assessments and their implications have been fully digested, do students spend up to five weeks developing their learning plans—like that of the hot-tempered financial advisor, who needed to cultivate self-control.

Does it work? To find out, successive graduating classes of Weatherhead students have been put through a set of rigorous assessments, using objective measures common in industry.[27] Compared to similar ratings on entering the school, they showed improvement in 86 percent of the abilities assessed. And follow-ups three years after they had finished the program showed these gains holding on the job.[28]

The moral for business education: Students can master the emotional intelligence capabilities the working world demands—if they are given the right tools for learning.

Getting Back to Work

One of the more innovative workplace applications of emotional intelligence training is not to be found in any company: It's a program for people who have *lost* their jobs, and it's designed to help them cultivate the inner resources that will help them find a new one.

Because people are shaken after losing a job, uncertain about their future, frightened about finances, and haunted by self-doubt, the job search it-self can be made easier by boosting their emotional competence. That was the strategy used in a strikingly successful reemployment project, the Michi-gan JOBS program, set up by a group at the University of Michigan after a wave of job cuts in the state's auto industry.

The program was a huge success—and another model application of the Consortium guidelines. People who went through the program got jobs about 20 percent more quickly—and higher-quality jobs—than did compa-rable people who had not.

"This works for everyone—the laid-off vice president as well as the guy who used to empty the VP's ashtrays," says Robert Caplan, head of the or-ganizational behavior program at George Washington University and co-founder of the JOBS program with Richard Price, a psychologist at the University of Michigan.

The underlying principle is simple: Many of the same emotional com-petencies that make people excel at work also make them more adept at finding a new job. Helping people boost those competencies helps them get back to work sooner—and do better once they're there.

"If you're shy, as well as pessimistic and depressed after losing your job, you're in double jeopardy," Caplan says. "It's a paralyzing combination."

Yet the JOBS program found that job seekers who faced the worst odds in finding new employment benefited the most from the training. "This works even for those who are clinically depressed, as many people are after they've lost their job," Caplan asserts.

JOBS instills two sets of abilities in job seekers: practical skills (like identifying marketable talents and networking to hear about opportunities) and the inner resiliencies that let them capitalize on their marketability.

In a simple five-session format, two trainers work with groups of fifteen to twenty participants, most recruited through corporate outplacement pro-grams.[29] The sessions focus on action learning, employing tools like mental rehearsals, dramatizations, and role-playing of key skills.

One of these skills is optimism. Given the uncertainties and setbacks that job seekers confront, they need an inoculation against defeatism in the face of failure. Rejections are an inevitable part of any job search. Discour-agement can bleed into hopelessness and despair. And despair is not a mar-ketable attitude.

Small wonder depression, drinking problems, and marital strife escalate among those who remain out of work—and abate once the person finds a re-warding job.[30] In the program, people are taught to anticipate rejection and rehearse what they should tell themselves when it happens. Anticipating such difficult moments and having a workable internal response lessens the emotional toll and speeds up the bounce-back time.

Among other capabilities the program bolstered:

■ Perspective taking, to help job seekers think like an employer

■ Self-confidence, the crucial sense that one can succeed, which is critical to making the effort in the first place

■ Networking, since most jobs are found through personal contacts

■ Decision making for career management—the first offer that comes is not necessarily the one to take, and any job needs to be measured against a person's values and career goals

■ Emotional self-control, so that distressing feelings don't overwhelm and paralyze the person, making it difficult to put in the hard effort that is needed

All these emotional intelligence capabilities, of course, are likely to pay off *after* landing a job as well. That's what happened with JOBS: Midway into their second year of working, JOBS grads outearned similar job seekers who did not go through the program by $6,420 (and had estimated lifetime earnings that were $48,000 greater).[31]

The JOBS program, like those at Weatherhead and American Express, offers a model of how to help people strengthen emotional competence.

11

....

Best Practices

ince the 1995 publication of my book *Emotional Intelligence,* programs bearing the same title have taken their place in the lineup of trendy trainings. I regularly get reports from various parts of the world that someone or other is offering a program in what purports to be "emotional intelligence"—often only a repackaging or slight remodeling of a program they had offered before under another name.

If such programs follow the guidelines outlined here, well and good. If not, let the buyer beware.

All too often development programs for emotional intelligence are poorly designed, executed, and evaluated—and so have disappointingly little impact on people's effectiveness back on the job. Thus the need for the guidelines elaborated on in this chapter.

Though almost every program includes at least a few of these "best practices," optimal impact comes from their added potency when used in combination.

It will be tempting for those involved in training and development to read through the guidelines with a mental checklist in mind, ticking off those they already follow. More helpful—and challenging—however, is to highlight those that are *not* part of the routine at one's own organization, and to consider including them.

Few, if any, training programs follow every one of these guidelines, but to the degree a program follows many or most, it should be discernibly more effective in producing on-the-job performance improvements.

The goal: to use this new understanding of best practices to put the entire enterprise of improving "soft skills" on a sounder, more scientific footing. These guidelines offer a state-of-the-art blueprint for teaching—and learning—emotional intelligence.

Assess the Job

One basic question needs to be asked and answered before any training is undertaken: What does it take to do this job superbly? The answers to that question are not always readily apparent.

Take strategic planners. The going theory holds that the sharper the intellect of a strategic planner, the better the performance; planning, after all, is a purely cognitive task—or so the thinking goes. And when experts—strategic planners themselves, or those executives they report to—were polled, they pretty much agreed that the single key for successful planning is "analytic and conceptual thinking."[1]

True, a strategic planner can't do the job without the requisite cognitive skills, but it turns out there's more to success as a planner than brainpower. Emotional skills are essential as well.

Studies reveal that the *outstanding* strategic planners are not necessarily superior in their analytic skills. Instead, the skills that raise them above the crowd are those of emotional competence: astute political awareness, the ability to make arguments with emotional impact, and high levels of interpersonal influence.[2]

The "experts" had overlooked a simple fact of organizational life: Everything is political. A more objective analysis revealed that planners' effectiveness depended on knowing how to involve key decision makers in the planning process at every step, making sure these people bought into the plan's assumptions and goals and were therefore willing to adopt it.

No matter how brilliant a strategic plan is, without allies and supporters it is doomed, given the politics of organizational life. And even the smartest strategic planners can be blind to the true role of emotional competence in their success.

When Coopers & Lybrand, one of the Big Six accounting and consulting firms, decided to offer their partners training in the key skills for their role, they did not assume they knew what that training should focus on. Ever methodical, in the style of their firm, they wanted data.

"Our charge was to identify the competencies required for success in our firm," said Margaret Echols, the senior manager in charge of competency development at the time, who directed the initiative at Coopers & Lybrand. "So we started by creating a competency model for partners."

Their team started out by having partners nominate those among them who were outstanding in their performance. Once that pool of standouts was identified, they and a comparison group of average performers were studied in depth, using structured interviews in which, for instance, they were asked to describe in detail "critical incidents"—occasions when they had done superbly, and some where their performance had been disappointing.

Transcripts of those interviews were then coded and analyzed to detect common themes and the patterns of thinking, feeling, and acting that were at the heart of their success. From those results, the list of competencies that mattered most were identified. Then these competencies were tested to see if they actually distinguished average from star performers, to be sure they held up. In short, Coopers & Lybrand followed a state-of-the-art methodology for developing a competence model.[3]

Such a systematic, objective method is needed to get a true picture of the competencies that matter most for a given role. That's why assessing the competencies that make someone outstanding at a particular job has become something of a mini-industry, with practitioners using a range of well-validated methods to tease out the ingredients of star performance.[4]

Training strategies also need to take into account the ways one set of capabilities supports another. People rarely need to improve just one competence; emotional capabilities are interwoven, not independent. And, as we have seen, many higher-order competencies like change catalyst or leadership are actually constructed from others.

There are some elements of emotional intelligence that are so basic as to constitute "meta-abilities," which are essential for most other competencies. These basics include self-awareness, self-regulation, motivation, empathy, and social skills. These primary capabilities are essential for supporting the emotional competencies that flow from them. For instance, a manager who tries to shift his or her leadership style may also need to improve in self-awareness in order to make the other change.

In studies of a European airline, what set apart superior flight attendants were two clusters of emotional intelligence attributes: a self-mastery cluster, including emotional self-control, achievement, and adaptability, and an interpersonal cluster, including influence, service, and teamwork.[5] So when an American airline asked me and my colleague, Thérèse Jacobs-Stewart, to help design a training program for them, we focused on self-management and on handling people well.

But we added two supporting emotional intelligence capabilities, each of which makes people better at those needed competencies. One is self-awareness, which helps people recognize when they are about to become victims of an amygdala hijack—and so become better able to short-circuit the hijack before they find themselves out of control. The other is empathy, which allows them to do the same for someone else—pick up the early warning signs of irritation, frustration, or anxiety that mark a person as being at risk for a hijack. The reason is simple: The best strategy for avoiding destructive encounters is to prevent them.

The flight attendants also needed empathy training with an international twist. Every culture puts a unique stamp on how people express emotions; the less familiar we are with a given group, the more likely we are to misinterpret their feelings. So we focused on developing empathy with a diverse range of people.[6]

Assess the Individual

Are we the best judge of our own strengths and weaknesses? Not always. Consider an irony about empathy. When you ask people how accurate they are at reading other people's feelings, there is no correlation between their answers and how well they actually perform on objective tests.[7] In contrast, when people who know them well rate someone on empathy, there is a very high level of accuracy. In short, there are many ways in which other people know us better than we know ourselves—particularly when it comes to how adept we are in our relationships.

In general, the ideal evaluation relies not on any one source but on multiple perspectives. These may include self-reports as well as peer, boss, and subordinate feedback. The "360-degree" evaluation method offers feedback from all these sources and can be a powerful source of data targeting the competencies that need to be improved. There are several 360-degree methodologies that assess at least some of the emotional competencies.[8]

Ideally, an evaluation would also include more objective indexes of work performance, such as the "assessment center" methods, which gauge how people do in simulations of work situations. While any method individually is fallible, used in combination they can paint a more accurate, if complex, picture of our profile of emotional competence. (See Appendix 5 for more on evaluation methods.)

As Susan Ennis, head of executive development at BankBoston, observes, "Multiple perspectives on yourself are extremely powerful ways to build self-awareness—and get you ready to do something about it."

At the Weatherhead School of Management, for instance, students get information on themselves from three very different sources. First they do a self-evaluation of their strengths and limits, as well as their values. Then there is feedback from others, including members of a working team they belong to as part of the course, peers and a boss at work, and family and friends. Finally they get results from a battery of assessment tests and simulation exercises.

They are forewarned, however, that none of these sources is in itself better or more accurate than any of the others, or less prone to distortion. Each simply adds different kinds of data and perspectives offering a different eye, ear, and voice. The students themselves—with guidance—interpret the data and from this find a path to self-development.

The JOBS program borrowed a method from the entertainment industry to assess the emotional competence of people they were screening to hire as trainers—they held auditions. "We wanted to observe them in a situation that would draw on all the social and emotional competencies they'd need as trainers," Robert Caplan tells me. "So we asked each one to come and teach us something—how to budget our money, how to interview, *anything*—for just fifteen minutes. You could see how competent people were from the very first few moments."

The auditions were telling, Caplan recalls. "One prospect would start in a businesslike way, passing out budget forms and putting up a slide, starting out by saying, 'I want you to put how much you spent in column A.' No engagement, nothing personal. Deadly. But one we hired started out in a very genuine tone, 'It's really good to see you here; I know what a difficult time this has been for you. I'd like to hear about each of you before I begin.' You immediately felt the empathy, that you liked and trusted this person."

Deliver Assessments with Care

A health plan in the Southwest decided to evaluate employees using the 360-degree method, and then have them coached as needed by their supervisors.[9] The trouble began when someone decided to simply send all the results to both the employees and their supervisors at the same time, with no warning or interpretation.

The result was a disaster: Some supervisors called employees in at once, before the employees had a chance to digest the evaluations, so many felt they were being called on the carpet rather than being helped. Some employees were enraged—especially when the supervisor's ratings were lower than those by peers—and went storming in to demand an explanation or even an apology.

Feedback is too often given ineptly, with predictably bad consequences. But used artfully, feedback on competencies can be a priceless tool for self-examination—and for cultivating change and growth. Used poorly, it can be an emotional bludgeon.[10]

"I don't hear good things from people about their experiences with 360-degree feedback," a manager at one company tells me. "The people giving the feedback lack empathy, self-awareness, and sensitivity themselves—so the experience can be brutal for those getting it."

Much better is the report from a computer software giant, where an executive development specialist tells me that he delivers 360-degree feedback results strictly in confidence, one-on-one. "No one else sees their results, and they never have to share them with anyone. I don't even keep a copy when I'm done with them. We want this to be a development tool, not a hammer for someone else to use."

A common mistake is simply devoting too little time to the feedback. "People will spend two or three days in an assessment center, going through complex simulations, taking inventory after inventory, getting all kinds of performance measures done on them," a consultant tells me. "Then, after it's all done, they'll spend an hour or two going over the results in what amounts to a data dump. People end up confused, not more self-aware."

If there ever was a task that called for emotional intelligence, giving people the results of 360-degree evaluations is it; empathy, sensitivity, and delicacy are essential. One common mistake is focusing on people's weaknesses and failing to note their strong points. This can be demoralizing rather than motivating.

"You've got to celebrate the strengths a person has, as well as show them where their limits are," Boyatzis says. "Too often the focus is on someone's deficiencies. But you want to help the person recognize the core of their strengths, to affirm what they value about themselves. For instance, people can gain much resolve from the belief that they have the capacity to change."

At Weatherhead, great care is taken to help students interpret the results of their competence evaluations and use the information to shape a genuinely helpful learning plan. The program for executive MBAs devotes four three-hour sessions, plus individual counseling, to interpreting and absorbing the data from the competence evaluations. Then four more three-hour sessions focus on using the information to create individual learning plans.

Gauge Readiness

A large number of people at our training seminars feel like prisoners of the human resource department," a management trainer at a multinational bank tells me. "They just don't want to be here. And their resistance is infectious."

Willingness is crucial, but many organizations pay no attention to whether the people they send for training really want to learn or change. The director of executive development at a Fortune 100 company remarked to me that trainees fall into three groups: the "eager beavers," who are ready to change; the "vacationers," who are happy to get out of work for a day or two; and the "prisoners," who were told by their manager they had to come.

One rule of thumb is that only about 20 percent of a group are ready to put in the work to change at any given point, though the vast majority of development programs are designed as though 100 percent are.[11] There is no reason to let that low percentage stand. Interest, motivation, and readiness to change—the prerequisites for attending and benefiting from training—can be assessed (see Appendix 5 for details); if people aren't really ready to change, then that fact itself can become a first focus for them. Anything else will be a waste of time. If people are not ready to take action, forcing them will lead to disaster: the sham of going through the motions only to satisfy others, resentment rather than enthusiasm, quitting.

To avoid such a waste of time and money, a first step is to help people assess their own readiness. There are four levels of readiness: obliviousness or outright resistance, contemplating a change at some vague point in the future, ripeness to formulate a plan, and readiness to take action.[12]

At American Express Financial Advisors, before a team comes for its training in emotional competence, one of the training staff meets with the team leader, who in turn discusses the program in team meetings to gauge how people feel about going through it. In addition, "Before they come to the first session we try to talk to each person about any concerns they might have," Kate Cannon says.

Those not ready may benefit from exploring their own values and vision for themselves, to see if they want to change at all. Which brings us to the next step.

Motivate

The feeling 'I can do it' is the motor that drives change," Robert Caplan says, and in the JOBS program this is visibly true. "When it comes to job seeking, if you don't make the call and keep the appointment, you won't get the job. And to get people to make the effort, you have to raise their expectation of success, pump them up."

That applies in general: People learn to the degree they are motivated. Motivation influences the entire learning process, from whether or not someone signs up to whether they actually apply what they've learned in their jobs.[13] And we are most moved to pursue change that fits with our values and hopes. As Weatherhead's Boyatzis puts it: "People have to be grabbed by their values, their goals, their dreams of what's possible for them. If you focus at the outset on people's values and visions, on what they want to do with their life, then they see themselves as using the training opportunity for their own development—not just the company's."

Windows of opportunity for development—moments when we are most motivated to upgrade our capabilities—come at predictable points in a career.[14]

- Added responsibility, like a promotion, can make a weakness in emotional intelligence glaringly apparent.

- Life crises, like trouble at home, career doubts, or a "midlife crisis" about direction, can offer a fruitful motivation to change.

- Job troubles, like interpersonal difficulties, disappointment with an assignment, or feeling unchallenged, can motivate efforts to boost competencies.

For most of us the simple realization that cultivating a given capacity will help us do better increases our enthusiasm. "Because people here realize these competencies matter for their performance, motivation for training is usually high," Kate Cannon at American Express tells me. When people understand that training can increase their competitiveness in the job market or within the organization—that is, when they see it as an opportunity—their motivation increases. And the more motivated people are to learn, the greater the effectiveness of the training for them.[15]

Make Change Self-Directed

The assembly-line approach, where everyone in a particular job or role at a company gets sent through an identical program, may work when the content is purely cognitive. But when it comes to emotional competencies, this one-size-fits-all approach represents the old Taylorist efficiency thinking at its worst. Particularly in this domain of education, tailoring—not "Tayloring"—maximizes learning.

We change most effectively when we have a plan for learning that fits our lives, interests, resources, and goals.[16] At American Express, everyone designs their own action plan. One financial planner working to boost initiative had a personal goal of making twenty cold calls a week. His plan included writing out the scenario of a successful call and rehearsing it before he dialed each number. "That method and focus worked very well—for him," says Cannon. "But I wouldn't advise all the planners to try it. It might be inappropriate or irrelevant."

Plans also need to be fine-tuned to the individual's level of development. "We've set it up so that each person can grow and develop from wherever their starting point is," says Cannon. "For example, some people simply don't realize that what you say to yourself—your thoughts about what you're doing—affects your results. Others have a more sophisticated understanding."

Ideally, trainees should be able to consult a menu of techniques and be encouraged to contribute ideas of their own. One weakness of many pre-packaged development seminars is their reliance on a single, generic approach.

"The standard training program, where everyone goes through a cookie-cutter experience, turns out to have the worst return on investment," Charley Morrow, of the consulting firm Linkage, tells me. From evaluation research he's conducted at Fortune 500 companies, Morrow concludes, "When people *have* to go, there are many kinds of problems. Some people may already have the skills they're being sent to learn, others don't need them. Others simply resent having to go, or are just unmotivated—they don't care."

Giving people the power to tailor their learning plans to their own needs and aspirations overcomes many of these problems. The guiding principle behind self-directed learning at Weatherhead, says Richard Boyatzis, is "You place control of the change process in the hands of the students. After all, they are in control anyway. This approach merely avoids the delusion of faculty control."[17]

Focus on Clear, Manageable Goals

He had moved to Ohio from the East Coast to participate in the Weatherhead MBA program, and he needed a part-time job. But he lacked self-confidence, particularly in approaching people he didn't know. At Weatherhead he was shown how to break his larger goal—developing this kind of self-confidence—into smaller, realistic action steps. The first, updating his résumé, was easy. But the next steps were more challenging, so he first made these promises to himself: "I will call the chairman of the University Finance Department by next month and request a meeting to discuss any available opportunities there. If not, I'll ask about other people to approach." He planned to do the same with his mentor, a local executive. On top of that, he committed himself to searching the local want ads and calling to apply for promising jobs. And he resolved, "I will be confident and assertive in these conversations." The concrete payoff of this strategy: He had a part-time job by the beginning of the next term.

The task seems mundane enough; thousands of people go through similar motions daily. But for this Weatherhead student, these methodical steps were part of a larger plan. They put him in situations that challenged him to practice self-confidence. And each completed step increased his confidence to undertake the next.

While a grand goal beckons, the practical focus needs to stay on the immediate, manageable steps—and the operative word is *manageable*. Those who attempt changes in whopping doses set themselves up for failure. Breaking goals into smaller steps offers easier challenges—and successes.[18]

Because we are buoyed by frequent small successes, we stay motivated and engaged, propelled by a growing sense of self-efficacy. And the more ambitious the goal, the greater the resulting change. A Japanese strategy takes these two principles into account: In *kaizen,* or continuous improvement, people start with goals that are only moderately difficult, and then gradually raise the challenge as the process continues. Making a change in such manageable steps lets us feel we are making at least a bit of progress toward our goal, and so keeps our spirits—and hope for success—high.[19]

Without clear goals, it is easy to wander off course. In the American Express program, seasoned psychologists work with each person to help them create clear personal goals for change. One common goal, for example, is to learn to handle distressing feelings better. But that goal is too global and fuzzy to be useful. "People start by realizing they need to take better care of themselves emotionally," Kate Cannon tells me. "But when they explore the trouble they have managing their feelings, they realize that it's due to being too stressed—and that often leads them to focus on specific helpful steps, like better time management."

But "better time management" is itself a fuzzy goal. It needs to be broken down into specifics: for example, spending twenty minutes a day meeting with subordinates to delegate responsibilities, eliminating time wasted watching junk TV, and setting aside three hours each week for relaxation.

Goal setting should also include the specific steps it will take to get there. For example, if the goal is to become more optimistic, taking setbacks and rejections in stride (an extremely useful competence for someone in sales), the analysis can be fine-grained: "You might start by noting your hot buttons, the events that trigger the unhelpful habit, and precisely what you think, feel, and do," says Kate Cannon. "You might identify pessimistic self-talk, like 'I can't do this,' 'This proves I'm not good at this.'" Or a pattern: First you get angry, then you withdraw, then you act up. You diagram the pattern or habit, familiarize yourself with what it is you do that you're trying to change and with the better way to think and act at those times. And each time you encounter one of those hot-button moments, you try to break the old pattern. The closer to the beginning you break it, the better."

In a sense, setting a goal defines what amounts to a "possible self": a vision of what we will be like after we have changed.[20] Just imagining this potential self has a certain power: Seeing ourselves as able to master the hoped-for change raises our motivation to take the steps to get there.

Prevent Relapse

Cultivating a new skill is gradual, with stops and starts; the old ways will reassert themselves from time to time. This is particularly true at the beginning, when the new habit feels strange and unfamiliar, and the old habit still feels natural.

Training can disintegrate—at least temporarily—in the face of stiff challenges. Such temporary lapses are only to be expected, and that fact can be used to advantage in relapse prevention.[21]

The key to using slips constructively is to realize that a step backward is not the same as a total relapse. People need to be warned at the outset of training that they are likely to experience bad days, when they revert to their old habits. Showing them how to learn valuable lessons from these slips provides a vaccination of sorts against despair or demoralization at such moments. Otherwise they might interpret the lapse with pessimism—as a total failure that means they are forever flawed and cannot change. Relapse prevention training prepares them to react like optimists, using slips in an intelligent way to gather critical information about their vulnerabilities and habits.

Take a manager who, under time pressure, slides back into dictatorial habits of leadership. He might learn that under pressure his own anxiety makes him susceptible to falling back on an autocratic style. Once the manager learns to recognize his trigger situations, he can prepare himself to act differently by rehearsing what to do—for example, asking for help instead of barking orders. This will up the odds that he will choose a better response, even under high stress.

Of course, developing such an early warning system requires self-awareness and the ability to monitor the incident (or, more likely, to do a postmortem afterward). Tracking the exact events that triggered the relapse, and the thoughts and feelings that went along with it, gives us added awareness of the moments in which we need to be particularly watchful and consciously recruit our new emotional competence.

Seeing the consequences of the lapse—a missed business opportunity, ruffled feelings in a colleague or customer—can also fuel our motivation to pursue change with more vigor.

Give Performance Feedback

A golf pro was prone to unpredictable rages that were ruining both his marriage and his career. While going through a program to reduce the intensity and frequency of his outbursts, he kept a "score" of sorts, tracking each time he got angry, how long it lasted, and how intensely he felt it.

Several months into the program, he blew up as intensely as ever, his rage completely out of control. The episode left him demoralized, despairing that all his efforts to change had led nowhere. But he was reinspired when he looked at his record. He realized that his rages had decreased markedly, from several times a week to just this one episode in the past two months.

Feedback lies at the heart of change. Knowing how we are doing keeps us on track. In its most basic form, feedback means that someone notices whether—or how well—the new competence is being used and lets us know.

When we are doing well, there can be a "feedforward" effect, where positive feedback buttresses our self-confidence to try out the emotional competence we are working to improve. This heightened self-confidence helps us do even better.[22]

When feedback is given poorly, too harshly, or not at all, it can demoralize and demotivate (as we saw in Chapter 8). The best results come when those giving feedback know how to do so productively and are encouraged or rewarded for doing so—and are open to feedback themselves on the quality of their feedback.

At American Express Financial Advisors, much of the feedback for emotional competence is woven into the fabric of work. "We pay as much attention to *how* you do your work as to how well you achieve goals," says Kate Cannon. "There are regular meetings with your direct supervisor. It's a relationship business—not just with our clients, but among ourselves. So people routinely get feedback about their emotional competence, even though it's probably called something else like teamwork or communication."

Encourage Practice

An international hotel chain was getting poor ratings from customers on the quality of staff hospitality. So they gave all employees who come into face-to-face contact with customers training designed to bolster their emotional intelligence. The training allowed them to practice being more aware of their feelings and showed them how to use that awareness to short-circuit their own amygdala hijacks. It also taught them how to tune in to the feelings of the hotel guests and influence their moods positively.

But the director of training and development complained that there was no benefit—that things even seemed to get a little worse.

How long did the training program last?

Just one day.

Therein lies the problem. Emotional competence cannot be improved overnight, because the emotional brain changes its habits over weeks and months, not hours and days. The old paradigm for development tacitly assumes change occurs dramatically and immediately: Send people through a two-day seminar, and—*voilà*—they are transformed. As a result of this misguided assumption, people are sent through brief trainings that have little lasting effect—and then may end up blaming themselves (or being blamed by supervisors) for some lack of will or determination when the promised improvements fail to materialize. A single seminar or workshop is a beginning, but it is not sufficient in itself.

People learn a new skill more effectively if they have repeated chances to practice it over an extended period of time than if they have the same amount of practice lumped into a single, intensive session.[23] Yet this simple rule of thumb is ignored time and again in training. Another mistake is to spend too much time merely talking about the competence, with not enough time devoted to actually practicing it in a controlled situation. In a study of training programs for managers and salespeople, Lyle Spencer Jr. and Charley Morrow analyzed how training time was divided between information about the competence learning, and actual practice. Practice sessions had double the impact on job performance as the presentation of concepts alone. And the return on investment for practice during training was *seven times* greater than for the didactic sessions.[24]

"If you use simulations to teach a competence like giving feedback—instead of just outlining the five principles of effective feedback without any opportunity for practice—the impact of training is far stronger," Spencer notes.

Reaching the point where a new habit replaces the old takes extensive practice. As one manager in a government agency put it, "People here get sent to a training, then go right back to work with no chance to try it out. So they revert to their old ways—the training never has a chance to transfer back to the job." But "overlearning," when people practice a new habit far beyond the point when they can do it well, greatly reduces the likelihood they will revert to the old habit under pressure.[25] Clinical studies of behavior change find that the longer people work at changing, the more durable the change will be. Weeks are better than days; months are better than weeks. For complex habits like emotional competence, the practice period for maximal effect may be three to six months, or longer.[26] (For more on practice issues, see Appendix 5.)

One rule of thumb for improving emotional competence: Capabilities that are being improved on or added to a person's repertoire—like becoming a better listener—can be developed in less time than is needed for remedial learning. Long-established habits, like having a short temper or being a perfectionist, are deeply ingrained. In such cases, we need to work both at *unlearning* the old, automatic habit and at *replacing* it with the new, improved one.

Exactly how long it will take a given person to master an emotional competence depends on a variety of factors. The more complex the competence, the longer mastery takes; time management, which draws on just a few competencies (self-control, which is necessary to resist the temptation of time-wasting activities, and achievement drive, which spurs a desire to improve by becoming more efficient, are two essentials for time management), can be mastered more quickly than, say, leadership, a higher-order competence that builds on more than half a dozen other competencies.

An effective program will encourage practice on our own time as well. Though we may have work reasons for cultivating a competence like listening, most are relevant in our private lives, too. Consider this provocative set of figures: Students in a two-year, full-time MBA program typically spend 2,500 hours in classes and doing assignments. But, assuming they average seven hours of sleep a night, they are awake about 10,500 hours during those two years. The question is, "What are they learning during the other 8,000 hours?"

That question was posed by Richard Boyatzis and the other designers of the Weatherhead course. It led to the proposition that self-directed learning can and should go on whenever and wherever the opportunity arises. Likewise, we don't spend all our waking hours at work (though it may *seem* we do). Especially when it comes to emotional competence, all of life can be the arena for change; life itself is the best classroom.

That attitude promotes "positive spillover," where the skills honed for work pay off elsewhere in life. A supervisor, for instance, learns to listen more effectively to employees, and brings it back home in talking with her kids. This positive spillover is seen as an explicit benefit at some companies, such as 3M, where a program designed to lower health costs purposely aims to bolster resiliency competencies for employees both at work and at home.

Arrange Support

A vice president at one of America's largest food companies had both a bachelor's degree in engineering and an MBA, as well as an IQ somewhere above 125. The president of the company would have liked to promote him. But this vice president had hit a ceiling: He wouldn't get the promotion unless he changed his style.

Unsociable and introverted, he was more comfortable sending e-mail or memos than dealing with colleagues face-to-face. In meetings he was often belligerent, combative, and dictatorial. "He would not get promoted unless he stopped doing this," recalled the executive coach brought in to help the otherwise promising vice president.

The coach went to work one-on-one with the VP. "I helped him to recognize his trigger points, so he can avoid situations where he's more likely to lose it. I taught him how to use self-talk, like athletes do, to prepare for situations where he's prone to get angry—he'll remind himself going in, 'I'm not going to let this happen to me, I'm not going to lose my temper.'

And I showed him a technique to short-circuit anger when he feels it build-ing in his body: tighten all the muscles in his body, then let go all at once. It's a quick muscle-relaxation method."

The coaching sessions continued for months, until the VP was finally able to manage his anger. Such one-on-one lessons in the essentials of emo-tional competence are increasingly common in American business, particu-larly for highly valued employees. Coaching is one of many forms that sustained support can take. Mentors can serve much the same purpose.

While the standard view of mentoring is that it's a way to foster career development, mentoring can also serve as a coaching forum for boosting emotional competence. As Kathy Kram, director of the executive MBA pro-gram at the Boston University School of Management, found in her land-mark study of mentors, people can get two kinds of benefits from mentors: help with their careers (such as protection, visibility, and sponsorship) and counseling and coaching.[27]

Much learning occurs in the natural course of relationships at work, whether it is deemed "coaching" or not. As Judith Jordan, a Harvard psy-chologist, points out, every relationship is an opportunity for both individuals to practice their personal competencies, and so grow and improve together.[28]

Such reciprocal learning can come naturally in peer relationships, where people can spontaneously alternate between the roles of mentor and learner, depending on their strengths and limits. "Some companies, like Bell At-lantic, have experimented with mentoring circles," Kathy Kram tells me. "They tried bringing together groups of midlevel women executives and at-taching them to a more senior executive, to talk over common problems at work. They would tell each other about their experiences, rehash how they could have been handled, and so widen their own repertoire of how to deal with those same situations. The net effect was to build up their social and emotional competence."

For those who lack a formal mentor, one strategy is to find a temporary coach, someone adept at a specific skill or competence who will consult for a limited time. This arrangement differs from full-fledged mentoring by virtue of its temporary, task-oriented nature. As Kram has found, any rela-tionship with someone who has greater experience or competence can be an opportunity for learning. And people who develop multiple relationships with a range of coworkers in varying areas of competence stand to improve the most.

As part of the American Express Financial Advisors emotional compe-tence training, participants often choose a "learning partner," someone who teams with them for continued encouragement over several months once back on the job. "People agree to offer mutual support, to meet regularly for lunch, or to call routinely," says Kate Cannon. "They can discuss whatever habit they're trying to change—like worrying too much about things, being more assertive. They update each other, give advice, cheerlead."

Such buddy systems increase the transfer of learned emotional intelligence skills to the job.[29] And coaching can be very helpful on the spot: "If your partner knows that a particular person pushes your hot buttons, he might help you by giving you a reminder signal to ready yourself just before you go into the encounter," says Cannon. Such on-the-spot support happens more readily when, as is the case at American Express, an entire work group goes through the training together.

Weatherhead students are grouped in teams of ten to twelve, each with a facilitator and a corporate executive who serves as advisor. In addition, each student gets a mentor who is a midlevel manager or advanced professional. The combination of peer group, advisor, and mentor at Weatherhead offers students a variety of people to turn to for support as they strengthen their target competencies.

Provide Models

In learning a new behavior, having access to someone who exemplifies the competence at its best is immensely helpful. We learn by watching others; if someone can demonstrate a competence, they create a living classroom for us.[30]

For that reason, those who teach emotional competence should embody it. Here the medium is the message: Trainers who merely talk about these competencies but act in ways that make it clear they don't possess them undermine the message. When it comes to teaching someone how to use a computer program, the trainer's warmth is of relatively little importance. But it's crucial when it comes to helping someone be more expressive and empathic in their dealings with clients, or to control their temper in management meetings.

In the JOBS program, "It was clear we needed trainers who embody social and emotional competence," Robert Caplan told me. "That was the basic principle that guided our selection of trainers as well as their own training. And to maintain their level of competence, we gave them ongoing evaluation and feedback on these competencies. It has to permeate the culture of the group giving the training."

In general, we pattern our behavior after high-status people in our organization—which means we can take on their negative habits as well as positive ones.[31] When workers are exposed to an intemperate supervisor—say, one who arbitrarily reprimands people—they tend to become less tolerant and more harsh in their own leadership style.[32]

At Eastman Kodak, a manager told me, "In the old days, everyone was in the same place, here in Rochester, sitting next to each other. You'd see someone every day, get to know their style, get mentored or just be exposed to good role models—people who knew how to establish rapport, listen well, build trust, be respected. But now people are scattered all over, isolated in smaller units. You don't have the same chance to learn these soft skills."

Because there is less chance for these competencies to be modeled and passed on, the manager adds, he feels the need to be more intentional in seeing that people in his unit learn them. "We have a development plan to be sure we groom people in the skills that make people successful, not just the technical or analytic abilities, but the leadership skills like self-awareness, persuasion, reliability."

Encourage and Reinforce

Take two aides at a nursing home. One was callous and brusque with patients, occasionally even to the point of cruelty. The other was a model of compassionate care.[33] The callous aide, however, always finished tasks on schedule and followed orders; the kind aide sometimes bent the rules to help a patient, and, largely because she spent more time talking with patients, often finished late. Supervisors gave the cold aide top ratings, while the caring one was frequently in trouble and her ratings were far lower. How could this be when the stated mission of the nursing home was to provide compassionate care?

Such gaps between the espoused mission and values of an organization and what actually goes on become glaring when people are being encouraged to cultivate emotional competencies that, in day-to-day practice, are simply not supported. The result is employees who are more emotionally competent than their jobs require or than is appreciated in their organization.

An organization can help people upgrade their emotional competencies not just by offering programs to do so, but by creating an atmosphere that rewards and even celebrates such self-improvement. After all, our attempts to change are most effective in an atmosphere that makes us feel safe.[34] To develop, a competence must be meaningfully flexed—and for that to happen, it needs to be valued at work, as reflected in the criteria for selection, job placement, promotion, performance review, and the like. That might mean, for example, rewarding people's efforts at mentoring, and building coaching and training in emotional competencies into the performance appraisal process; opportunities for 360-degree feedback and competency training.

A fledgling competence needs to be expressed during the actual situation at work in order to take hold. Lack of connection between the new learning and on-the-job reality means the learning will wither. As a "training high" evaporates, our enthusiasm for following through on what we've learned often fades. And whether or not an organization has a supportive climate is cited over and over by people going through training programs as determining the extent to which they can transfer what they learned to their job.[35]

Perhaps the optimal supportive climate for training occurs when an entire work group focuses on cultivating competencies together, as happens with some management teams at American Express Financial Advisors. In these teams everyone, including the leader, makes a commitment to emotional competence training. Feedback and support are built into staff meetings, and time is set aside to talk about how people are doing with their emotional competence goals.

In addition, the talent assessment for executives there uses a checklist that includes emotional competencies. "Each senior executive completes the checklist on those in a unit, and each vice president does the same on himself or herself," says Cannon. "Then they have a dialogue over those areas where they differ. The conclusions are presented to the company president. Things like relationship skills, motivating yourself and others, self-management skills, really matter here."

Shortly after taking the helm at Banker's Trust New York, the new chairman and CEO, Frank Newman, worked with a consulting firm to make top managers more aware of the human skills the company needed to stay competitive.[36] The result was a program showing it was no longer enough simply to focus on the bottom line: Management skills would matter as much as financial performance for promotions and compensation.

How could Newman get his bankers and traders to pay attention? He went to at least part of each training session himself, where members of the bank's management committee are among the teachers. As the bank's head of development puts it, "This way no one is saying, 'My manager told me it isn't important.' "

Evaluate

The recommendation: first, establish sound outcome measures, especially for the competencies that were targeted in training, and include job performance measures. The best designs use pre- and post-training measurements, plus a long-term follow-up several months after training ends, and control groups with participants randomly assigned. While this ideal may be hard to meet, there are alternatives, such as using people's baseline measurements in lieu of a control group, or comparing an individual's changes on targeted competencies with changes in those not targeted. And if a program falls short, that information should be used to improve the next round of training.

But almost nowhere are these simple principles followed. Instead, there is a distressing gap between what research shows should be done and how training is actually conducted and evaluated. A survey of Fortune 500 companies found that chief training officers believe the number one reason to evaluate training is to determine if there is a payoff. Yet there was little or no hard evaluation of their training programs.[37]

The most common source of data was student evaluation sheets, followed by continuing demand for the training—more like popularity polls than hard indicators of performance change. Research suggests no correlation between trainees' reports of satisfaction and their learning or demonstrated improvement on the job—as one review puts it, "Liking does not imply learning."[38]

The best method for evaluation—an objective pre- and post-training look at the impact on job performance—was not used routinely by a single corporation. Ten percent did report having used such a design on occasion, though many of those assessments focused only on people's change in attitudes rather than on any change in their on-the-job performance.

But this is slowly changing. One of the most ambitious training evaluation projects anywhere is under way at the Weatherhead School of Management.[39] There the students who have gone through the managerial skills training program are asked to become part of an ongoing follow-up research project to see what advantage, if any, the cultivation of these capabilities gives them in their careers. The project is envisioned to go on for the next fifty years.

5

·················

The
Emotionally
Intelligent
Organization

12

....

Taking the Organizational Pulse

At an international business conference I attended recently, people were asked, "Does your organization have a mission statement?" About two thirds raised their hands.

Then they were asked, "Does the mission statement describe the day-to-day reality of life there?" All but a few hands went down.

When there is a glaring gap between the espoused vision of an organization and the actual reality, the inevitable emotional fallout can range from self-protective cynicism to anger and even despair. Companies whose profitability is won at the price of violating the implicit shared values of those who work there pay an emotional price: a burden of shame and guilt, a sense of tainted rewards.

An emotionally intelligent organization needs to come to terms with any disparities between the values it proclaims and those it lives. Clarity about an organization's values, spirit, and mission leads to a decisive self-confidence in corporate decision making.

An organizational mission statement serves an emotional function: articulating the shared sense of goodness that allows us to feel what we do together is worthwhile. Working for a company that measures its success in the most meaningful ways—not just the bottom line—is itself a morale and energy raiser.

Knowing what those shared values are requires what amounts to emotional self-awareness at the organizational level. Just as each person has a profile of strengths and weaknesses in the different areas of competence and has a certain level of awareness of these, so with organizations. For any organizational competence, these profiles can be mapped at every level: division by division, and down through each smaller unit to each working team.

But few organizations take stock of themselves in this way. How many companies know where, for instance, blundering managers infect their people with rancor and fear, or where the pockets of enterprise are among their salespeople? Many organizations may *think* they are making these assessments through internal surveys of job satisfaction, commitment, and the like. But these standard tools may miss the mark.

Some of the most widely used organizational measures were assessed by the Personnel Resources and Development Center at the U.S. Office of Personnel Management, under the direction of Marilyn Gowing.[1] The question: To what extent do these surveys assess emotional intelligence at the organizational level?

There were, as Gowing puts it, "some amazing gaps" in what was measured. These gaps point to missed possibilities in thinking about what makes an organization effective—and to ways of diagnosing performance lapses. Among the most notable gaps:[2]

- *Emotional self-awareness:* Getting a reading of the emotional climate as it impacts performance

- *Achievement:* Scanning the environment for crucial data and opportunities for enterprise

- *Adaptability:* Flexibility in the face of challenges or obstacles

- *Self-control:* Performing effectively under pressure rather than reacting out of panic, anger, or alarm

- *Integrity:* The reliability that breeds trust

- *Optimism:* Resilience in the face of setbacks

- *Empathy:* Understanding the feelings and perspective of others, whether clients and customers or internal constituencies

- *Leveraging diversity:* Utilizing differences as opportunities

- *Political awareness:* Understanding salient economic, political, and social trends

- *Influence:* Adeptness at persuasion strategies
- *Building bonds:* The strength of personal links between far-flung people and parts of an organization

The importance for any organization of these competencies seems self-evident. As I write this, Microsoft's top executives are publicly bemoaning their organization's lack of political awareness, a deficit that has put them at a seeming disadvantage in their struggle with the Justice Department over charges of monopolistic practices.

Still, the extent to which each of these collective competencies predicts better organizational performance remains to be seen. But that is just the point: No one seems to be looking.

Imagine the advantage for companies that cultivate these competencies—and the problems for those that don't. Let me make my point by sketching the differences for organizations, for better and worse, that three kinds of competencies can make: self-awareness, managing emotions well, and the drive to achieve.

Blind Spots

At the beach on a hot August day a family of four has packed up their towels, toys, and beach gear and is trudging through the sizzling sand when the younger child, a girl of about five, starts whining, "I want some *water.* Gimme some *water.*"

Her father, annoyed at her whining tone, complains to the mother, "Where'd she learn to talk like that?"

Then, to his whiny daughter, he says curtly, "Nobody hears you when you sound like that"—and walks on, pointedly ignoring her plaintive plea.

Through countless exchanges like this—often more covert and implied—each of us learned in our family of origin a set of rules about attention and emotions.

The first rule: Here's what we notice.
The second: Here's what we call it.
The third: Here's what we don't notice.
The fourth: Since we don't notice it, we don't call it anything.

So it is with organizations. Each has a distinctive zone of collective experience—of common feeling and shared information—that goes unvoiced (or is spoken of only in private, not openly), and so falls into the abyss of what amounts to an organizational blind spot.

Those zones of inattention can harbor potential dangers. At the Barings Bank branch in Singapore, for example, the fact that a renegade trader was in charge of both the front and back office operations—and so had no one supervising his trades—allowed him to lose hundreds of millions of dollars, sinking the company. For Archer Daniels Midland, the agricultural giant, a high-level collusion winked at price fixing that, when exposed, resulted in indictments of several top executives.

The Organizational Family

The rules that tell us what we can and cannot express at work are part of the implicit contract each organization imposes. Honoring these rules is the cost of being a member of the organizational family. We won't notice, say, that the manager here is a washed-out alcoholic who years ago had a better position but was parked here to get him out of the way of top management. We'll just deal with his assistant (who actually does his job), the way everyone else does.

Fear—which is not unreasonable—binds people to silence. Take the fate of whistle-blowers, people in an organization who publicly reveal its misdeeds. Studies of whistle-blowers in business find they are typically motivated not by vengeful or selfish motives, but by a lofty one: loyalty to the ethics of their profession or to the organization's avowed mission and principles. Yet most are victimized by the organization—fired, persecuted, sued—rather than thanked.

They commit the ultimate sin: speaking the unspeakable. And their expulsion from the organization sends a tacit signal to everyone else: "Go along with the collusion here lest you, too, lose your membership." To the extent that such collusion keeps questions vital to organizational effectiveness from being asked, it threatens the organization's survival.

It also contributes to frustrating group charades, like this example from a study observing top executive decision-making meetings:

The subordinates were in agreement that too much time was spent in long presentations in order to make the president happy. The president, however, confided that he did not enjoy listening to long, and, at times, dry presentations (especially when he had seen most of the data anyway). However, he felt that it was important to go through this because it might give the subordinates a greater sense of commitment to the problem![3]

Business Is Business

In the early 1990s Carl Frost, an American business consultant, was meeting in Sweden with work teams at Volvo.[4] The talk was about the extra-long vacations everyone was anticipating that year. But Frost was disturbed by an ominous fact underlying the length of those days off: Vacations were being extended because sales were down. Volvo had a huge amount of excessive inventory on its hands, and with demand low, assembly lines were idle.

The managers, Frost found, were quite comfortable, even happy about the decision to extend their holidays. But Frost felt the need to raise questions, to bring to the surface facts that the people at Volvo seemed oblivious to. The fundamental fact was that Volvo was losing the race in global competition for the auto market: Volvo's manufacturing costs exceeded those of every other major automaker in the world, it took Volvo workers twice as long to make a car as it took Japanese autoworkers, and Volvo's overseas sales had shrunk in recent years by 50 percent.

The company was in crisis, its future—and the jobs of these workers—in jeopardy. And yet as Frost tells it, everyone acted as though nothing were wrong. No one seemed to see a connection between the vacations they were about to take and the troubled company's future.

This blasé attitude, Frost felt, was a sign of a troubling failure of communication, one that let workers at Volvo ignore any link between their situation and the larger fate of their company. This lack of connection, he claims, meant they took little responsibility for helping their company become more competitive.

The inoculation against such collusion entails making an organization more honest and more open in its internal communications. This requires an atmosphere that values the truth, no matter how anxiety-provoking it may be, and that seeks to hear all sides of a question. But such real debate is only possible if people feel free enough to speak their minds without fear of punishment, retribution, or ridicule.

In a Coopers & Lybrand survey of Fortune 500 companies, only 11 percent of CEOs believed that "messengers of bad news take a real risk in my company." But among middle managers in those companies, a third said bearers of bad news put themselves at risk. Among nonmanagement workers, about half felt there was real risk in bearing bad news.[5]

This disparity between those at the top and those most in touch with what is going on day to day means that top decision makers may labor under the illusion they are getting all the data they need, while those who have the data—especially troubling facts—feel too anxious to share it. Leaders who fail to set a tone that encourages people to bring up all their misgivings and questions, including unsettling news, are setting themselves up for trouble. Then, says William Jennings, who led the Coopers & Lybrand survey, "It is easy for employees to view internal controls as an impediment to productivity, and to jettison them in a misguided effort to 'make the numbers.'"[6]

Lore has it that some years back, whenever new executives were hired at PepsiCo, then-president Wayne Calloway interviewed them. He would tell them, the story goes, "There are two ways to get fired here. One: not meet your numbers. Two: lie. But the fastest way to get fired is to lie about your numbers."

"If you withheld information, especially about a business disaster, he was unforgiving," a former colleague of Calloway told me. "But if you were immediately forthcoming, he was very gracious. The result was a culture where people were very candid, very genuine and open about the truth."

Contrast that with what I'm told about one high-tech company by an executive: "Telling the truth around here is career-eliminating behavior."

Managing Emotions Well

One largely ignored pulse of an organization's viability can be read in the typical emotional states of those who work there. Systems theory tells us that to ignore *any* significant category of data is to limit understanding and response. Sounding the depths of emotional currents in an organization can have concrete benefits.

Consider a gas plant division at Petro Canada, the country's largest oil and gas refining company. "Guys in the gas plants were having a wave of accidents, some fatal," I was told by a consultant who was called in to help.

"I found that in the macho culture of the petrochemical industry, guys never acknowledged their feelings. If someone came to work hung over, preoccupied over a sick child, or upset by a spat with his wife, his workmates would never ask how he was doing that day or if he was okay enough to be sharp on the job. The result would be that the guy would be inattentive and cause an accident."

With this basic insight into the human cost of ignoring emotions on the job, the company initiated a series of workshops for crews "to get them to see that how they are feeling has consequences—that *this matters*. They saw that they had to look out for each other, and they were doing themselves and everyone else a favor if they checked in about how they were doing. If someone was off that day, they needed to say to him, 'I don't think I can work with you today.' And their safety record improved."

This is not to argue for making organizations a place where people simply bare their feelings or souls to each other, in some nightmarish vision of the office as a kind of emotional salon or ongoing sensitivity group. That would be utterly counterproductive, a blurring of the distinction between work and private life that itself signifies poor emotional competence.

From the perspective of work, feelings matter to the extent that they facilitate or interfere with the shared goal. The paradox, though, is that our interactions at work are relationships like any others; our passions operate here also. As leadership expert Warren Bennis put it: "People feel alone with their pain—the hurts, the loneliness, the closed doors, the things left unsaid and unheard. It's not permissible to discuss this."

In too many organizations, the ground rules that marginalize emotional realities guide our attention away from such emotional static as though it did not matter. These blinders propagate endless problems: decisions that demoralize; difficulty managing creativity and making decisions; ignoring the crucial value of social skill; the inability to motivate, let alone inspire; hollow mission statements and empty slogans of the day; leadership by the book, lacking zest or energy; drudgery instead of spontaneity; a lack of esprit de corps; teams that don't work.

Burnout? Blame the Victim

As one executive at a high-growth company—where the turnover rate was recently at 40 percent—told me, "People at the top work all the time; many are candidates for divorce. We get huge rewards, but if you don't do better each year than the one before, you get fired. Job security doesn't exist here."

Such plaintive reports are the new downside of a technological and competitive landscape that has escalated demands of every kind. "It's constant white water," I'm told by a manager at a hugely successful company. "There's so much turbulence today, just from the sheer complexity of the business environment. You used to be able to come home and rest, but if you work for a global company, now you have to be available twenty hours a day—calling Europe at four in the morning, Asia until midnight."

One way his company gets people to challenge themselves relentlessly is by making the rewards so great: They pay more than anyone else, with many employees getting huge performance bonuses. It's a winning strategy for the company, but it often carries a high personal cost. Companies like this one can turbocharge productivity—to a point. The most driven workers will reap benefits, but if they are kept at this frenzied level, their personal lives, their morale, or their health—or all of these—will surely suffer.

Few organizations address the extent to which they themselves generate the stress. More usual is a form of blaming the victim. "Burnout is really a problem for the individual," one CEO told researchers.[7] "It does not have any real impact on the organization's productivity. It's a soft problem, not a clear-cut matter of finance or strategic management. If people want to use the EAP program or take their vacation days to get a good rest, that's fine. That's what those things are there for. There's not much else the organization can do."

The CEO's glaring errors: assuming that there's little an organization can do, and that such emotional exhaustion has no effect on an organization's productivity. One of the defining signs of burnout is a drop in efficiency and the ability to accomplish even routine tasks. If that occurs not just in a few individuals but among broad swaths of employees, the organization's performance inevitably suffers.

A study of burnout among nurses makes the point. In a large medical center, the extent to which nurses on inpatient units had classic burnout symptoms like cynicism, exhaustion, and frustration with working conditions correlated with patients' reports of dissatisfaction with their hospital stay. The more content nurses were with their jobs, the better patients rated their medical care overall.[8] Since patients are consumers who make choices about where to spend their health care dollars, such human realities can make a large difference in the competitiveness of the hospitals those nurses work for.

Consider, too, the risk when things go wrong. In a study of twelve thousand health care workers, those departments and hospitals where workers complained most about on-the-job stress had the highest rates of medical malpractice claims against them.[9]

How to Lower Performance

Companies can do much to protect themselves—and their employees—from the costs of burnout. This is evident in a twenty-year series of studies of the causes of burnout in several thousand men and women, from hundreds of organizations.[10] While most studies of burnout focus on the individual, this one looked at the practices and patterns in the organizations the people worked for. It pinpointed six primary ways organizations demoralize and demotivate employees:

- *Work overload:* Too much work to do, with too little time and support. Job cutbacks require supervisors to handle more employees, nurses more patients, teachers more students, bank tellers more transactions, managers more administrative duties. As the tempo, complexity, and demands of work escalate, people feel overwhelmed. Escalating work erodes the downtime during which people can recover. Exhaustion accumulates, work suffers.

- *Lack of autonomy:* Being accountable for work but having little say in how to go about it. Micromanagement means frustration when workers see ways to do their work better but are held back by rigid rules. This lessens responsibility, flexibility, and innovation. The emotional message to workers: The company lacks respect for their judgment and innate abilities.

- *Skimpy rewards:* Getting too little pay for more work. With cutbacks, wage freezes, and trends toward contract work and cutbacks in fringe benefits like health coverage, people lose their expectation that their salary can increase as their career continues. Another loss of reward is emotional: Work overload combined with too little control and job insecurity robs work of its intrinsic pleasure.

- *Loss of connection:* Increasing isolation on the job. Personal relationships are the human glue that makes teams excel. Shuffled job assignments lower a sense of commitment to the work group. As relationships fragment, the pleasures that come from a sense of community with workmates erodes. That growing sense of alienation fuels conflict, even as it erodes the common history and emotional connections that can help heal such rifts.

- *Unfairness:* Inequities in how people are treated. Lack of fairness breeds resentment, whether due to unequal pay or workloads, disregard for grievances, or policies that seem high-handed. Rapid escalation of top executive pay and bonuses while salaries in the bottom tiers rise little or not at all undermines people's trust in those who run the organization. Resentments breed in the absence of honest talk. The result: cynicism and alienation, along with a loss of enthusiasm for the organization's mission.

- *Value conflicts:* A mismatch between a person's principles and the demands of their job. Whether this pushes workers into lying to make a sale, skipping a safety check to get things done on time, or simply using Machiavellian tactics to survive in a viciously competitive environment, the cost is to their moral sense. Jobs at odds with their values demoralize workers, leading them to question the worth of the work they do. So do lofty mission statements when belied by the day-to-day reality of operations.

The net result of these organizational malpractices is to breed chronic exhaustion, cynicism, and a loss of motivation, enthusiasm, and productivity.[11]

Now consider the advantages for a company of raising its collective emotional intelligence.

The Spirit of Achievement

The manufacturing company was losing a race with its competitors, who were getting price quotes for potential jobs to customers in twenty days, while those same quotes took this manufacturer forty days to get out the door.

So they reengineered. They changed the quote-generating process by adding more control points, computerizing parts of it, and making other such structural changes. Result: The turnaround time for quotes escalated from forty to fifty-five days.

Then they turned to outside expertise, bringing in consultants who were specialists in reengineering. The time for quotes ballooned to seventy days—and the error rate increased to 30 percent.

Desperate, they brought in experts in the methods of the "learning organization." Today the time it takes them to get a quote to customers is down to five days, and the error rate is down to 2 percent.

How did they do it? They changed their working relationships, not the technology or structure. "It's futile to try to solve with technology or structure a problem that is really a people problem," Nick Zeniuk, president of Interactive Learning Labs, who led the company through the learning process, tells me.

Zeniuk should know. He won fame in the world of learning organizations for his pivotal role in a triumph of the method when he, with Fred Simon, led the launch of the 1995 Lincoln Continental, and their case is cited as a classic success story by Peter Senge, of MIT's Learning Center.[12]

There's no question the redesigned 1995 Lincoln Continental was a spectacular success story. Independent ratings of quality and owner satisfaction pegged the '95 Lincoln at the top of the Ford line, better than every American car in its class, and on a par with the best foreign competition, from the Mercedes to the Infiniti. Customer satisfaction increased 9 percent, to 85 percent (Lexus, the highest-scoring car, had an 86 percent rating).

Equally impressive: Though the redesign effort started four months late, the car arrived on the market a month ahead of schedule. And on every metric of production success, the new Lincoln met or exceeded goals, a prodigious feat for a process that involved more than a thousand people, a core team of three hundred, and a budget of $1 billion.

The challenge could easily have been viewed as entirely technical—a cognitive puzzle par excellence that could be solved only by the smartest people with the most expertise. Auto design demands meshing hundreds of sometimes contradictory demands, from engine torque to braking, acceleration to fuel economy. The most intricate and difficult part of designing a new car is coming up with final engineering specifications for its components— a task akin to figuring out the size and shape of each piece of an immense jigsaw puzzle, and crafting the parts as you go, during the very act of trying to solve it.

Understandably, auto design teams typically have to backtrack and re- work many of their design specifications after a prototype is assembled, be- cause with the first prototype unanticipated problems become obvious. At this point—once hot metal has been poured to make a working model—such reworking is quite expensive: The job requires redoing the machine tooling for every part involved, typically at costs of millions of dollars.

Yet the Continental design team, with a budget of $90 million for these retooling needs, used only a third that amount, bucking an industry-wide trend to overspend the retooling budget. The design effort was as efficient as the Continental's engine itself: Engineering drawings for components were out a month early, rather than the usual three or four months late, with 99 percent of the parts in final shape rather than the standard 50 percent.

Hard Results, Soft Means

The challenge facing the Continental redesign team was to get hard re- sults—a better car—through approaches that many managers in the auto industry felt were just too soft to matter, like openness, honesty, trust, and smooth communications.[13] The culture of that industry traditionally disre- garded such values: It was hierarchical and authority-based, with the guid- ing assumption that the boss knows best and makes all key decisions.

Compounding this cultural problem was a dense emotional fog. There was a pervasive sense of frustration at starting four months late, and a host of barriers to trust and openness. One of the main roadblocks was at the very top of the team; Zeniuk recalls that the tensions between himself and the fi- nance manager were so great, he couldn't talk to him "in less than a high- decibel range." That tension was a symptom of a deep hostility and mistrust between those in charge of producing the new model and those whose duty was to control costs.

To tackle these problems, the core management team used many learn- ing organization methods, including one that helps people unlearn defensive habits of conversation.[14] The method is simple: Instead of arguing, the parties agree to mutually explore the assumptions that undergird their points of view.

A classic example of how people jump to conclusions is when you see someone yawn in a meeting, leap to the assumption he is bored, and then skip to the more damaging overgeneralization that he doesn't care about the meeting, anyone else's thoughts, or the entire project. So you tell him, "I'm disappointed in you."

In this learning organization method, that comment gets listed under a heading: "What Was Said or Done." The more critical data, though, is in another column, "Unspoken Thoughts and Feelings": that the yawn meant he was bored and doesn't care about the meeting, anyone else, or even the entire project. In that column, too, go our own feelings of hurt and anger.[15]

Once these hidden assumptions surface, they can be tested against reality by talking about them. For instance, we may discover the yawn was not from boredom but rather exhaustion due to getting up in the night with a cranky infant.

This exercise in learning to articulate what we are thinking and feeling—but not saying aloud—allows us to understand the hidden feelings and assumptions that can create otherwise inexplicable resentments and puzzling impasses.

Beyond requiring self-awareness to retrieve those hidden thoughts and feelings, this task demands other emotional competencies: empathy, to listen to the other person's point of view with sensitivity, and social skills, to collaborate productively in exploring the hidden differences—and loaded feelings—that surface.

In a sense, the *real* conversations are the inner ones, if only because they reveal how people actually think and feel about what's going on. The inner dialogue, especially if it is emotionally turbulent, often seeps out in a truculent tone of voice, say, or an averted gaze. But we can miss these signals, in others as well as in ourselves, when things move fast or we are pressured or distracted. The net result: The inner dialogue is ignored, even though it is rife with crucial information—misgivings, resentments, fears, and hopes.

As Zeniuk puts it, we don't know what to do with this real conversation, "So we ignore it. It's like toxic waste—what do you do with it? Dump it? Bury it? Whatever we do with this toxic waste is corrosive—it pollutes the conversation. If we confront people, they pull out their defenses." And so conversations at work go on as though there were no inner dialogue, even though everyone is utterly engaged in this mute exchange. The roots of conflict as well as the start of true collaboration are to be found in this deep level of discourse.

When used at the start of the Lincoln Continental project, the dialogue exercise revealed two bitterly opposed camps. The finance people thought those managing the program didn't care at all about controlling costs; the program managers thought the finance people "didn't have a clue" about what it took to build a quality car. The net result of this mutual exploration of hidden feelings and assumptions was to make glaringly clear that the project was hobbled by a lack of trust and openness. The core issues:

- Fear of being wrong led people to withhold information.

- The bosses' need to control got in the way of people on the team using their best capabilities.

- Suspicion was widespread—people saw each other as unhelpful and not to be trusted.

Here emotional intelligence becomes essential. To have a working group that can go beyond fear, power struggles, and distrust takes a reservoir of trust and rapport. The task ahead focused as much on strengthening the level of trust in the relationships between people as on surfacing their hidden assumptions. And that took a great deal of social engineering. As Fred Simon put it, "If I wanted to improve the quality of this car, my greatest leverage was in helping my team members develop better personal relationships and see each other more as people."

Starting at the Top

At first people had a deep resentment and despair about their inability to do the work they needed to—they started with a blame-the-bosses attitude," Zeniuk recalls. "But as the bosses engaged, really listening to what they had to say, it switched to 'Okay, I can do it. But leave me alone to do my job.' But no such thing: We're interconnected in our work, and we had to go the next step—learn to be interconnected. So the bosses became facilitators and coaches. The role of the leader was no longer just controlling and telling, but listening, providing resources and stewardship."

To facilitate these changes, the entire three-hundred-person design team was brought together in groups of twenty to work on the real problems they faced together on the job, such as reconfiguring the interior of the car. As they talked through their problems, facilitators like Daniel Kim, then at MIT, taught them the basic conceptual tools of collaborative learning. But the key was, as Zeniuk puts it, "emotional awareness, empathy, and building relationships. Fostering emotional intelligence wasn't a direct goal, but it evolved naturally as we tried to reach our goals."

Consider again the challenge involved: fifteen different design teams, each oriented around the parts of the car that performed a given function, like the car's chassis and power train, each working independently. But in the final design for the car, their efforts had to mesh seamlessly—yet they weren't talking enough to each other. Traditionally each team would work in isolation to produce what it considered the best design and then try to force designs for other parts to change to fit their own requirements. It was out-and-out turf warfare.

"If I make a design mistake in sheet metal and then have to go back and retool to correct it, that can cost nine million dollars," Zeniuk observes. "But if I spot the mistake before I get to the sheet metal–tooling stage, it costs nothing to fix. If something's not going to work, we need the bad news early."

In the typical design of a new model, there might be hundreds of small adjustments made to parts specifications down the line. That's why the Continental team had a budget of $90 million to cover the costs of these changes, a budget that usually is exceeded in the American auto industry. But in Japan, Zeniuk knew, most such changes were being made up front, before the specifications were set in the tooling machinery, when they would become so expensive to adjust.

"We found we didn't know about these changes up front because the engineers feared being embarrassed or attacked," Zeniuk tells me. "They'd hope someone else would admit the mistake first and take the blame. They'd think, 'Well, I can fix my dashboard mistake when they fix their side panel problem and no one will notice I goofed.' How do you get people to share the painful truth when they have such fear?"

But the crucial shift showed up, for example, in a new style for meetings. Says Zeniuk, "We made sure everyone had a chance to share what was on their minds" instead of letting the old habits take over, where "management walks into a situation thinking they have all the answers and are hesitant to admit when they don't know something." Instead, "We'd put out a decision and ask, 'How do you *feel* about this?'"

Rather than the usual political jockeying and trying to look good that so often sets the tone of group meetings, this more direct approach took hold, in effect raising the group's level of collective self-awareness. When someone was uncomfortable with a decision that was being made, they would stop the meeting and use the methods they had learned to engage in a careful, respectful inquiry into the feelings and assumptions that fed that unease.

"There is a high probability that there was a reason for that discomfort, and that reason could frequently change the entire decision," Zeniuk says. "It took a while for us to reach that level of honesty and openness."[16]

He notes one concrete payoff for this more emotionally intelligent approach: "We saw the teams stop competing to meet cost and quality objectives at the other guy's expense, and start working together. Instead of working in isolated islands, there was a constant back-and-forth. Once they saw the bigger picture, that my work is part of the other guy's, there were many, many trade-offs among the various teams. We even had some design teams give up part of their budget to let others add to the cost and quality of their part—something that just never happens in auto design."

The bottom line? "We got seven hundred changes in specifications eighteen months before production, instead of the usual wave of costly changes at the very last minute. That let us save sixty million dollars in retooling costs out of a budget of ninety million, and finish ahead of schedule by a month, despite starting four months late."

13

....

The Heart of Performance

ppliance sales at GE had slowed alarmingly, and the manager was dismayed. Studying a chart showing a steady dip in sales, he and his colleagues realized the appliance division was having serious trouble with marketing. The conversation quickly turned to seeking a solution. Should they concentrate on pricing? On advertising? On some other change in marketing?

Then someone from the company's financial services arm, GE Capital, displayed a chart showing that consumer debt was reaching saturation levels—it wasn't that the company was failing in its marketing, but that people were having more trouble paying for big-ticket items like appliances.

"Suddenly, everyone had a whole new angle on the problem," one meeting attendee noted. This fresh information led the discussion away from marketing to financing—searching for ways to help customers pay for such a large purchase.[1]

It was a moment when crucial information—a look at the bigger picture—arrived in time to avert the corporate equivalent of a minor shipwreck.

This example illustrates the way in which an organization as a whole has an "intelligence" of sorts, just as do the groups and teams within it.[2] *Intelligence,* in one of its most basic senses, is the capacity to solve problems, meet challenges, or create valued products.[3] In this sense, *organizational* intelligence represents that capacity as it emerges from the complex interplay of people and relationships, culture and roles within an organization.

Knowledge and expertise are distributed within an organization, and no one person can master all the information the group needs to run efficiently—the financial officer has one type of key expertise, the salespeople another, those in research and development still another. The organization itself will only be as "smart" as the timely and appropriate distribution and processing of these diverse elements of information.

Any organization is "cybernetic," which means being engaged in continuous and overlapping feedback loops, gathering information from within and without and adjusting operations accordingly. Systems theory tells us that in an environment of turbulent change and competition, the entity that can take in information most widely, learn from it most thoroughly, and respond most nimbly, creatively, and flexibly will be the most adaptive.

That principle applies to both the smallest corner business and the largest global firm. It points to the crucial role of information flow throughout an organization in determining its viability. Some discuss this in terms of how companies must use "intellectual capital": their patents and processes, management skills, technologies, and accumulated knowledge of customers, suppliers, and business practices. The sum of what everybody in a company knows and knows how to do gives a company much of its competitive edge—if it is mobilized well.

Maximizing the Organization's Intelligence

The "tech reps," who repaired copy machines for Xerox, were wasting huge amounts of time. Or so it seemed when Xerox analyzed how they went about doing their job.

They discovered the reps spent a good deal of time with each other rather than out helping customers. They'd regularly get together at the local parts warehouse and exchange stories from the field over a cup of coffee.

From an efficiency-minded perspective, this was an obvious waste of time. But that's not how John Seely Brown, Xerox's head scientist, saw it. Brown had sent a trained anthropologist to tag along with the reps, and this researcher believed the downtime was not wasted but rather was central to the reps' ability to do their jobs well.

As Brown puts it, field service "is a *social* activity. Like most work, it involves a community of professionals. The tech reps weren't just repairing machines; they were also coproducing insights about how to repair machines better."[4]

The reps are knowledge workers, and their conversations are where their knowledge is transferred and built upon. As Brown observes, "The real genius of organizations is the informal, impromptu, often inspired ways that real people solve real problems in ways that formal processes can't anticipate."

Both work and learning are social. Organizations, as Brown describes them, "are webs of participation." Key to successful performance with knowledge workers—with *any* workers—is instilling enthusiasm and commitment, two qualities that organizations can earn but not compel. "Only workers who choose to opt in—who voluntarily make a commitment to their colleagues—can create a winning company," says Brown.

That's where emotional intelligence comes into play. An organization's collective level of emotional intelligence determines the degree to which that organization's intellectual capital is realized—and so its overall performance. The art of maximizing intellectual capital lies in orchestrating the interactions of the people whose minds hold that knowledge and expertise.

When it comes to technical skill and the core competencies that make a company competitive, the ability to outperform others depends on the *relationships* of the people involved. In Brown's words, "You can't divorce competencies from the social fabric that supports them."

Just as maximizing the IQ of a small working group depends on the effective knitting together of the people within the group, so with organizations as a whole: Emotional, social, and political realities can enhance or degrade what the organization potentially can do. If the people in the organization cannot work well together, if they lack initiative, connection, or any of the other emotional competencies, the collective intelligence suffers as a result.

This need for smooth coordination of widely distributed knowledge and technical expertise has led some corporations to create a new role: that of "chief learning officer," or CLO, whose job it is to direct knowledge and information within an organization. But it's all too easy to reduce an organization's "intelligence" to its databases and technical expertise. Despite the ever greater reliance on information technology in organizations, it's put to use by *people*. Organizations that have such learning officers might do well to expand the CLO's (or *someone's*) duties to include maximizing the collective emotional intelligence.

Emotionally Intelligent Organizations: The Business Case

■ "We're a ten-billion-dollar-a-year telecommunications company, but our past leader was very autocratic; the group he left behind was like an abused family," a senior vice president confides in me. "Now we're trying to heal the organization, make it more emotionally intelligent—so we can grow another ten billion dollars."

■ "We've just gone through wrenching changes, and there will be more of them ahead," a director of a European airline reports. "We have an immense need for trust from our employees, and empathy and understanding from our managers—for a greater sense of 'we.' What we need throughout the company is emotionally intelligent leadership."

■ "Our company culture has its roots in engineering and manufacturing," a corporate director at a high-tech company observes. "We want to build an atmosphere of trust, openness, and teamwork that touches on people's ability to deal with emotions in a direct and honest way. But we find many of our managers are just not skilled in dealing with this emotional side. We need to make ourselves more emotionally intelligent."

The quest to make companies more emotionally intelligent is one more and more organizations are embarking on, whether they use the term or not. An organization's collective emotional intelligence is no mere soft assessment; it has hard consequences.

Mitchell Kapor, the founder and former CEO of Lotus Development Corporation, now an investor in high-tech start-ups, told me that before his group puts its money into any company, they try to determine the company's level of emotional intelligence.

"We want to know if anyone is angry or resentful toward the company, if they harbor a grudge against it," Kapor said. "Companies have styles, like people. If they've been arrogant or duplicitous to their vendors, employees, or customers, those karmic debts can come back to haunt them. The more people they've angered while starting up, the more likely they are to be sued once they become successful."

Perhaps the strongest argument for the economic advantage of emotional intelligence in organizations can be read in data generated by Jac Fitz-Enz at the Saratoga Institute, in a project sponsored by the Society for Human Resource Management. Since 1986 the institute has collected data from nearly six hundred companies in more than twenty industries, detailing policies and practices. They analyzed top companies, selected for profitability, cycle times, volume, and other similar indices of performance.[5]

Searching for what these outstanding companies held in common, the institute identified the following basic practices in managing "human assets"—their people:[6]

- A balance between the human and financial sides of the company's agenda

- Organizational commitment to a basic strategy

- Initiative to stimulate improvements in performance

- Open communication and trust-building with all stakeholders

- Building relationships inside and outside that offer competitive advantage

- Collaboration, support, and sharing resources

- Innovation, risk taking, and learning together

- A passion for competition and continual improvement

This list is intriguing because of the clear similarities between these organizational practices and the emotional competencies that typify top-performing individuals. The last, for example, describes a motivational competence, the achievement drive, described at the personal level in Chapter 6. Likewise with innovativeness, comfort with risk, collaboration, building relationships, open communication, trustworthiness, initiative, commitment—we've seen in earlier chapters how each of these emotional competencies is an ingredient of star performance in individuals.

But here these same capabilities have ended up on a list generated by observing top-performing *companies,* not individuals.[7] Just as with individuals, organizational competencies can be thought of as falling into three domains: cognitive abilities, in the sense of managing knowledge well; technical expertise; and managing human assets, which requires social and emotional competence.

But what does an emotionally intelligent organization look like? Consider the case of Egon Zehnder International, a global executive search firm.[8]

A Global Team

Victor Loewenstein had a dilemma—a global dilemma. Asked by the World Bank to locate a candidate for a newly opened vice presidency, he was told to search the world for the right person. It had to be someone with sophisticated financial expertise, of course—and because the World Bank was trying to diversify, preferably not an American, a nationality over-represented in the bank's ranks. And Loewenstein, managing partner of the New York City office of Egon Zehnder International, was planted squarely in midtown Manhattan.

Undaunted, Loewenstein called into action the firm's worldwide offices. "I sent a memo to about twenty different offices in the countries most likely to have pools of people with the required high level of expertise in finance—mostly in Europe, but also in Hong Kong, Japan, Singapore, and Australia."

From these offices Loewenstein received twenty profiles of possible candidates; he asked that the eight he saw as most promising be interviewed by people in those offices to see if they indeed had the requisite technical competence. This eliminated two more.

"Beyond professional qualifications," says Loewenstein, "the person needed personal qualities and competencies that would mesh with the unique environment of the World Bank—and as the one who had dealt with the bank, only I could make that final determination." So with the field winnowed to six, Loewenstein himself crisscrossed the globe to visit the remaining candidates.

"The World Bank is a highly collegial environment," he observes. "You need to be able to work in a team, make decisions by consensus, cooperate; you can't be a prima donna. One candidate, for instance, was an investment banker; he was aggressively ambitious for center stage—it just wasn't appropriate in such a collegial organization, so he was out."

The ultimate choice, from the Netherlands, was a senior partner of a major auditing firm—one of two candidates Loewenstein felt had the right mix of expertise and personal chemistry to be a winning fit with the organization. Had he been on his own, Loewenstein might well have never found him—but by calling on his worldwide web of connections, the search was a success.

The story typifies the operations of Egon Zehnder International, which has knit its far-flung partners into a single global working team, fluidly sharing contacts and leads. When a Japanese auto manufacturer wanted a car stylist from Europe, Egon Zehnder International's offices in the United

Kingdom, France, Germany, and Italy scoured the auto industries in those countries, with the Tokyo office coordinating the search. When a global firm with a European base asked Egon Zehnder International to find a new head of human resources, the most promising candidate was identified by someone from the New York office who was on assignment in Asia. So the candidate was interviewed by the Hong Kong office, and was finally presented to the client by the firm's London office.

One for All: The Economics of Collaboration

Such seamless collaboration is a watchword at Egon Zehnder International. Perhaps the key reason the firm can operate so smoothly as a worldwide collaborative team lies in an innovation made early on in its history: It treats the global firm as a single team, with everyone paid on the basis of overall performance. The hundred or so partners share a pool of profits distributed according to a uniform formula. A person's share is calculated the same way whether their contribution to the firm's earnings that year was great or little. The entire firm operates as a single profit center.

Most search firms tie compensation to a mix of firmwide, office, and individual performance; stars usually earn a direct percentage of the fees they generate. But this is not the case at Egon Zehnder International. Says CEO Daniel Meiland, "The strength of our firm is that we do not have a 'star' concept."

From this equality in earnings and power stems an all-for-one, one-for-all spirit. This stands in contrast to the industry as a whole, where "headhunters" live up to their nickname by operating on a bounty system, with the successful recruiter receiving a proportion of the salary of the post filled.

As one executive at another search firm put it to me, "I hoard my information and contacts, because I get compensated on the basis of my listings. If I find a hot candidate in the course of a search for one position, I tuck that name away to keep it for myself for another search instead of sharing it with a colleague. I don't even know if I'll be working with the same company in another year—why should I give away my resources?"

At Egon Zehnder International, people of thirty-nine different nationalities and eight religions in forty-eight offices spread across thirty-nine countries operate as a single unit. "The fundamental difference between our firm and others is that we find ourselves all on the same ship," says Loewenstein. "We don't have differing agendas or vested interests to pull business our way. Instead, the more we collaborate, the more efficient we are—and the sooner we can get on with the next assignment."

The compensation model was a radical departure for its industry when Egon Zehnder instituted it. And even now, only a handful of competitors have begun to imitate it. Also, the firm is owned equally and entirely by its partners (consultants typically are elevated to partnership after about six years). Even Zehnder himself, who at one time owned the firm entirely, now holds just one share, like every other partner.

"I understood that if I did that, I could retain the best partners," Zehnder tells me. "It made us all entrepreneurs together.

"How do we work so well together? Because we've decoupled individual performance from money," Zehnder says. "No one is being evaluated by how big a billing volume they have. So a partner in Germany taking the time to help a partner in Tokyo with a search counts as much as getting a new client. Nobody cares who gets the credit for a success, because there's a single profit center that everyone shares in equally. An office that loses money gets as much as the office that made the most."

"We work in networks, sharing our expertise and trust," says Claudio Fernández-Aráoz, of the Buenos Aires office. "From Argentina I'm happy to share anything with my colleagues anywhere in the world, and I know they would help me in the same way, because our earnings depend on the total profits of the firm."

The company's egalitarian payment scheme reflects an insight Zehnder had about the nature of teamwork. "I realized that people who didn't make placements but did other things, like trying to get a new client or running the Harvard alumni association of Germany, were worth as much as the one who happens to be lucky in placing someone. I don't want stars—I want everyone to help everyone else be a star."

A Need to Achieve

That team approach pays off; Egon Zehnder International's performance as a business is extraordinary. As an executive search firm that specializes in finding CEOs and others in the top tiers of the corporate ranks, it is the most profitable search firm per capita in the world. And as of 1997 Egon Zehnder International's profitability had increased each year for the last six in a row.

According to the Economist Intelligence Unit, in 1995 the average net revenue per consultant for the top twenty such firms worldwide was $577,000.[9] For Egon Zehnder International, however, the equivalent figure was $908,000—making the company about 60 percent more productive than the industry average for top firms. By 1997, despite having increased its staff of consultants 27 percent (it typically takes new consultants three to five years to become fully productive), the revenue had risen to more than $1 million per consultant.

Egon Zehnder International's service is of tremendous importance to companies. Apart from the costs of replacing top executives who fail (a minimum of $500,000 for a top executive search is one standard estimate), the real value has to do with the impact, for better or worse, of these executives on an organization's performance.

As we saw in Chapter 3, the higher the levels of a job's complexity and authority, the greater the impact of outstanding performance on the bottom line. The implication for selection is clear: The higher the level of job, the more it pays to put great care into searching for the right person for the position. "Time after time we see cases where a company's poor performance is a reason to come to us to look for a new CEO," Claudio Fernández-Aráoz tells me. "Once he or she takes charge, if the search was properly conducted, results typically change dramatically."

The changes are not just in improved profitability, but also in "hard" areas like productivity, increased sales, and lowered costs, as well as in "soft" areas like increased morale and motivation, greater cooperation, and lower turnover and loss of talent. In short, as he puts it, "top managers can add or destroy huge economic value, and the higher the level, the higher the leverage—so the stronger the impact."

Building with Integrity

Zehnder himself was instrumental in introducing the executive search industry to Europe, where his company is still the leading executive search firm. In the 1950s, shortly after he finished his MBA at Harvard, Zehnder joined the American search firm Spencer Stuart, setting up offices for them first in Zurich, then London, Frankfurt, and Paris.

Integrity is a hallmark of the firm's culture, a value reflected, for instance, in the change Zehnder made in how he charged clients after he left Spencer Stuart to start his own firm in 1964.

"I didn't like the system where you were paid a percentage of the current salary of the person you were searching for, and only got paid if you found someone the client hired," Zehnder explains. "That created a pressure to only 'find' people who would demand the highest salary, whether or not they happened to be the most qualified, so you'd get the biggest fee."

Zehnder restructured compensation to make sure a candidate's fitness for the job was the only criterion. From the beginning Egon Zehnder International has charged clients only a flat fee calculated up front on the basis of the complexity of the search.

Zehnder's fixed fees free its consultants to search for the most qualified candidate rather than the highest-paid one. Their fees also mean that, at times, they "leave money on the table," getting less than the client would ordinarily pay for a given search done by another firm. For CEO Daniel Meiland, that loss of revenue pays back in client trust. As he puts it, "Clients pay based on their trust in the consultant and the firm. But as a professional firm, we must be consistent. We can't have one policy for setting fees seventy percent of the time and another policy the rest of the time."

It also pays back in repeat business and long-term ties with clients. Lee Pomeroy, of the New York office, describes a search for director of research at a large American bank. The search was relatively simple, so the fee was $110,000. But the first-year salary for the position was over a million dollars—and so would have commanded a fee of over $330,000 from another firm.

Pomeroy commented, "While the fee was low compared with what we could have charged if we had gone by industry standards, we started getting more business from this bank and we charged fees of a hundred and fifty thousand dollars each for the next two searches, which were international and a bit more complex in nature."

The firm balances its quest for profit with contributions to society. Partners are encouraged to do pro bono searches for charitable groups, hospitals, universities, and governments. "Monetary reward cannot be the sole incentive or objective of the firm," Victor Loewenstein comments. As of this writing the New York office is undertaking the pro bono initiative of finding high-caliber minority candidates for its longtime customers.

There is an indirect payoff from such pro bono activities. In the course of such work, the firm's consultants are "helping in ways that demonstrate their personal competence as well as dedication to serve others," Egon Zehnder points out. "Nothing is more important for attracting new clients than to see top talent like ours contributing unselfishly."

That speaks to Egon Zehnder International's tactic for growing its business through a naturally expanding web of relationships. In ordinary terms, the business seems to lack a marketing strategy; the firm never advertises, and partners are often reluctant to be quoted in the popular press. But in lieu of standard promotional efforts, the partners and consultants build networks of contacts through their day-to-day business, as well as through work in their communities. The company's people are networkers par excellence.

The Cardinal Sin

Loyalty marks the relationship between Egon Zehnder International's people and the firm itself. The company has yet to close an office where earnings lag. In the early 1990s, for example, some smaller offices were underperforming, but the company kept them going as part of its general policy of not laying people off—a stark contrast to the rest of the industry, where layoffs in hard times are routine.

As Meiland puts it, "Other search firms drop lots of consultants when the market sinks. They come to our people and ask them to leave, but we don't ever recruit from them. We don't buy Rolodexes. So how do we keep our people? People here say, 'This is the nicest firm I could be with. I have a good feeling here.' It's safe here and people know it."

With security comes obligation. There is, of course, a danger in the combination of what amounts to job tenure and a compensation system that rewards everyone regardless of their specific efforts. That's why loafing is a cardinal sin. As Zehnder tells me, "The system only works if all of us give our all. The crime is freeloading, not lack of success if you're working hard."

In such a close-knit group, "peer pressure and embarrassment," in the words of one partner, offer a major prod for people who fail to do their share of the work. When people seem to be loafing, they are given a warning. "I can tell someone, 'You aren't showing commitment in the hours you're putting in, the number of clients you talk to,' " Meiland says.

If there is still no improvement, people are put on a kind of probation by having their pay rate docked. For a ten-year veteran, their share for the year might be brought down to that of a five-year veteran, pending improvement. If there is no improvement that year, then it might be lowered again to the level of a three-year partner. But it very rarely comes to this, because of what partners describe as an intense loyalty and sense of obligation to each other and to their shared enterprise.

Because people join the firm to stay, there is a palpable sense of the company as a family. As one partner put it, "We know that we will be working together for many years, and therefore we are prepared to invest time and effort into building relationships."

Relationship building is a focus at the twice-yearly meetings, where all partners and consultants gather, and in which newly hired consultants are introduced to the firm. That meeting begins with a ritual: a slide show of the life of each fledgling consultant, with photos and stories from their infancy onward. "This gives us all a start at getting to know them," explains Fernández-Aráoz. "That's crucially important—our people are our only asset."

All this builds emotional bonds. "The best billers don't leave us," says Zehnder. "They stay because they love the culture. It's like a family. We understand the difficulties partners have in their lives—the crises in their families, illnesses, worries about children."

When a consultant in the New York office took a maternity leave, several colleagues volunteered to take on and complete the assignments she had not yet brought to a close, "helping out a colleague and a friend," as one of them put it. When Victor Loewenstein had a serious illness requiring an emergency operation, the whole firm got daily updates on his condition. And when a newly hired consultant in Canada was diagnosed with cancer during his first physical before joining the firm, he was hired anyway and kept on the payroll during the three years he battled the disease, until his death.

"We all feel a high level of personal concern for each other," Fernández-Aráoz tells me. That concern applies, too, to the balance between work and the rest of life. While the firm performs at the top of its industry, its culture discourages out-and-out workaholics, whose relentless hours destroy any hope of a sane family life.

"Twenty or thirty years ago people were willing to give up everything—family, marriage, private time—for their company's success," Zehnder recounts. "Now if someone says they're willing to pay everything for success, that's the wrong answer."

The familylike tone of the company stems in part from the democratization of power. As one partner puts it, "What we do at the top is what we do at the bottom." That is, no matter how long a person has been there, or what their title may be, everyone does more or less the same work. This sharing of work "cements relationships vertically in a very strong way, while the stability and reward structure cements relationships horizontally," as Philip Vivian, of the London office, puts it. The company chart is more web than hierarchy.

When Help Is Wanted

The operating style of Egon Zehnder International requires an extraordinary level of collaboration and cooperation, open communication, a knack for leveraging diversity, and a talent for teamwork. Its strategy for growth relies on its ability to network and develop relationships, and its collective drive to improve performance.

The firm's egalitarian approach to salary works only if everyone acts with both integrity and conscientiousness. Its very business, finding just the right person for a company, demands skill at empathy, intuitive accuracy, and organizational awareness. And nurturing long-term relations with clients demands a continued orientation to their needs. Small wonder Daniel Meiland tells me, "In what we do, emotional intelligence is essential."

How does the explicit focus on emotional intelligence look in operation? Consider how the firm goes about hiring people. Its business centers on gauging the chemistry between an organization and a prospective consultant. And the care they put into assessing prospective employees offers an exemplar for taking emotional intelligence into account in hiring.

While search firms typically put a premium on recruiting people from other search firms who can bring in business from the start, for Egon Zehnder International this is irrelevant: They never recruit people who have worked for search firms. "When we recruit a new consultant, our principal criteria are their personal qualities, rather than their ability to generate revenue on day one," a consultant said.

Prerequisites start with intellect and expertise. As with any job involving such a high level of cognitive complexity, IQ matters. And everyone hired has a prior record of success in another industry and *two* advanced degrees (mostly MBAs and law degrees from top schools, though about 25 percent have Ph.D.s). No one lacking this level of qualification need apply—but this high hurdle for intellect and experience merely gets people into the candidate pool.

A Human Radar

Typically a prospective consultant is interviewed by twenty, and sometimes as many as forty, of the firm's one hundred or so partners, in up to five different countries. Zehnder himself meets with around 150 prospects a year. He has no special veto power, but says that once or twice he has vigorously objected to what otherwise seemed strong candidates after he met them.

"We need a radar in this business, but that only develops with experience," Zehnder observes. "Our people need to be diligent in doing their research and homework, but the intuition develops the more they evaluate candidates."

Each partner who meets with prospective consultants evaluates them on four major dimensions. The first is purely cognitive—abilities like problem solving, logical reasoning, and analytic capability. But the other three reflect emotional intelligence. These include:

- *Building working relationships:* Being a team player; having self-confidence, presence, and style; being empathic and a good listener; having the ability to sell an idea; maturity and integrity

- *Getting things done:* Being a self-starter, with drive, energy, and a sense of urgency that gets results; showing judgment and common sense; being independent, entrepreneurial, and imaginative; having leadership potential

- *Personal fit:* Having the qualities of a friend, colleague, and partner; being honest and adhering to one's values; being motivated; being sociable, with "sparkle" and a sense of humor; modesty; having a full personal life and outside interests; understanding the firm and its values

The bar here is high, for good reason. "It's like joining a family," says Fernández-Aráoz. "We have to think in the long term. We don't want someone hiring just anybody because there's a heavy workload in their office and they need help—we want people who could someday become partners."

Egon Zehnder is more blunt: "We only have places in our ranks for zealous family members." That is not hollow rhetoric; the record suggests that about 90 percent of those hired as consultants go on to become partners. The number of those who leave is around 3 percent, compared to about 30 percent for the rest of the industry—a field in which anyone with a Rolodex thick enough can quit to start their own company.

Says Zehnder, "I meet with every single consultant for a two-hour talk before they are hired. I want to see what's important to them. Do they go to the opera? What kind of books do they read? What are their values? Are they too willing to give in, not able to stand up for their values?"

There's a personal motive beyond this business objective. candid: "I want to have fun doing my work. I want the kind of people sit over dinner with on a weekend. In my profession you need to be able to trust your people. I want the kind of people I like in my heart—people who I can still like when I'm exhausted at three A.M."

Some Final Thoughts

An organization is like an organism, with a moment of birth, growth through several distinct stages of development, maturation, and finally an end. Companies have life spans; if the past is prologue to the future, forty years from now up to two thirds of Fortune 500 companies will no longer exist.[1]

The adept ones likely will survive. And the ingredients of an effective organization, as we have seen, include a healthy dose of emotional intelligence.

Of course, there are numerous pathogens that can prove fatal to a company: seismic shifts in markets, myopic strategic vision, hostile takeovers, unforeseen competitive technologies, and the like. But a failure in emotional intelligence can be crucial in rendering a company vulnerable to the others—the corporate equivalent of a weakened immune system.

By the same token, emotional intelligence can be an inoculation that preserves health and encourages growth. If a company has the competencies that flow from self-awareness and self-regulation, motivation and empathy, leadership skills and open communication, it should prove more resilient no matter what the future brings.

And that, in turn, places a premium on people who themselves are emotionally intelligent.

Old ways of doing business no longer work; the increasingly intense competitive challenges of the world economy challenge everyone, everywhere, to adapt in order to prosper under new rules. In the old economy, hierarchies pitted labor against management, with workers paid wages depending on their skills, but that is eroding as the rate of change accelerates. Hierarchies are morphing into networks; labor and management are uniting into teams; wages are coming in new mixtures of options, incentives, and ownership; fixed job skills are giving way to lifelong learning as fixed jobs melt into fluid careers.

As business changes, so do the traits needed to survive, let alone excel. All these transitions put increased value on emotional intelligence. The ratcheting upward of competitive pressures puts a new value on people who are self-motivated, show initiative, have the inner drive for outdoing themselves, and are optimistic enough to take reversals and setbacks in stride. The ever-pressing need to serve customers and clients well and to work smoothly and creatively with an ever more diverse range of people makes empathic capabilities all the more essential.

At the same time, the meltdown of old organizational forms from a hierarchical wiring diagram into the mandala of a web, along with the ascendance of teamwork, increases the importance of traditional people skills such as building bonds, influence, and collaboration.

Then there is the challenge of leadership supply: The capabilities needed for leaders in the next century will differ radically from those valued today. Competencies like change catalyst, adaptability, leveraging diversity, and team capabilities weren't on the radar a decade ago. Now they matter more each day.

Our Children and the Future of Work

How can we best educate young people for the new world of work? For our children, this includes an education in emotional literacy; for those already at work, it means cultivating our emotional competence. All this, of course, demands rethinking the notion of the "basics" in education: Emotional intelligence is now as crucial to our children's future as the standard academic fare.

Parents around the world are waking up to the need for a broader preparation for life than the traditional school curriculum has offered. The Collaborative for Social and Emotional Learning at the University of Illinois at Chicago reports that more than 150 different emotional literacy programs are being used today by thousands of American schools. And from all parts of the world—Asia, Europe, the Middle East, the Americas, Australia— comes news of similar programs springing up.

Perhaps the most visionary approach can be seen in pioneering coalitions among local governments, schools, and businesses aimed at boosting the collective level of emotional intelligence in the community. The State of Rhode Island, for example, has begun an initiative to boost emotional intelligence in sites as varied as schools, prisons, hospitals, mental health clinics, and job retraining programs.

Farsighted companies are realizing that they, too, have a stake in how well the schools are educating their future workers. I can envision coalitions of companies encouraging emotional literacy programs as both a goodwill gesture and as a practical investment. If schools fail to help students master these human fundamentals, then companies will have to do it remedially when those students become employees. Such a concerted focus on helping schools teach these capabilities can help improve both the civility of life in our communities and their economic prosperity.

Tomorrow's Company: The Virtual Organization

The premium on emotional intelligence can only rise as organizations become increasingly dependent on the talents and creativity of workers who are independent agents. Even now 77 percent of American "knowledge workers" say they decide what to do on the job, rather than being told by someone else.[2]

The rising popularity of telecommuting is accelerating this trend. Autonomy can work only if it goes hand in hand with self-control, trustworthiness, and conscientiousness. And as people work less "for the company" and more for themselves, emotional intelligence will be required to maintain the relationships vital for workers' survival.

Such free agents suggest a future for work somewhat akin to the functioning of the immune system, where roaming cells spot a pressing need, spontaneously collect into a tightly knit, highly coordinated working group to meet that need, and dissipate into free agency once again as the job finishes. In an organizational context, such groups, each with a specialized mix of talent and expertise, may arise within and across organizational boundaries as demands require, then cease to exist once their task is accomplished.

That mode already typifies the entertainment industry, where a pseudo-organization coalesces for the duration of a project, then disbands. This, many suggest, will be a standard mode for work in the future.

Such virtual teams can be especially agile because they are headed by whoever has the requisite skills, rather than by someone who happens to have the title "manager." Ad hoc project groups and task forces are proliferating within many organizations; other companies are creating the latent capacity for such groups by linking people together to chat and to share information and ideas.

The question for us all is whether the new world of work will become increasingly grim, with relentless job pressures and apprehensions robbing us of both a sense of security and a place in our lives for even the simple pleasures—or whether, even in the face of this new reality, we can find ways to work that excite, fulfill, and nurture us.

The Bottom Line

The good news is that emotional intelligence can be learned. Individually, we can add these skills to our tool kit for survival at a time when "job stability" seems like a quaint oxymoron.

For businesses of all kinds, the fact that emotional competencies can be assessed and improved suggests another area in which performance—and so competitiveness—can be upgraded. What's needed amounts to an emotional competence tune-up for the corporation.

At the individual level, elements of emotional intelligence can be identified, assessed, and upgraded. At the group level, it means fine-tuning the interpersonal dynamics that make groups smarter. At the organizational level, it means revising the value hierarchy to make emotional intelligence a priority—in the concrete terms of hiring, training and development, performance evaluation, and promotions.

To be sure, emotional intelligence is no magic bullet, no guarantee of more market share or a healthier bottom line. The ecology of a corporation is extraordinarily fluid and complex, and no single intervention or change can fix every problem. But, as the saying goes, "It's all done with people," and if the human ingredient is ignored, then nothing else will work as well as it might. In the years to come, companies in which people collaborate best will have a competitive edge, and so to that extent emotional intelligence will be more vital.

But apart from the emotional intelligence of the organizations we work for, having these capabilities offers each of us a way to survive with our humanity and sanity intact, no matter where we work. And as work changes, these human capacities can help us not just compete, but also nurture the capacity for pleasure, even joy, in our work.

Appendix 1

....

Emotional Intelligence

"Emotional intelligence" refers to *the capacity for recognizing our own feelings and those of others, for motivating ourselves, and for managing emotions well in ourselves and in our relationships.* It describes abilities distinct from, but complementary to, academic intelligence, the purely cognitive capacities measured by IQ. Many people who are book smart but lack emotional intelligence end up working for people who have lower IQs than they but who excel in emotional intelligence skills.

These two different kinds of intelligence—intellectual and emotional—express the activity of different parts of the brain. The intellect is based solely on the workings of the neocortex, the more recently evolved layers at the top of the brain. The emotional centers are lower in the brain, in the more ancient subcortex; emotional intelligence involves these emotional centers at work, in concert with the intellectual centers.

Among the most influential theorists of intelligence to point out the distinction between intellectual and emotional capacities was Howard Gardner, a Harvard psychologist, who in 1983 proposed a widely regarded model of "multiple intelligence."[1] His list of seven kinds of intelligence included not just the familiar verbal and math abilities, but also two "personal" varieties: knowing one's inner world and social adeptness.

A comprehensive theory of emotional intelligence was proposed in 1990 by two psychologists, Peter Salovey, at Yale, and John Mayer, now at the University of New Hampshire.[2] Another pioneering model of emotional intelligence was proposed in the 1980s by Reuven Bar-On, an Israeli psychologist.[3] And in recent years several other theorists have proposed variations on the same idea.

Salovey and Mayer defined emotional intelligence in terms of being able to monitor and regulate one's own and others' feelings, and to use feelings to guide thought and action. While they have continued to fine-tune the theory, I have adapted their model into a version I find most useful for understanding how these talents matter in work life. My adaptation includes these five basic emotional and social competencies:

- *Self-awareness:* Knowing what we are feeling in the moment, and using those preferences to guide our decision making; having a realistic assessment of our own abilities and a well-grounded sense of self-confidence

- *Self-regulation:* Handling our emotions so that they facilitate rather than interfere with the task at hand; being conscientious and delaying gratification to pursue goals; recovering well from emotional distress

- *Motivation:* Using our deepest preferences to move and guide us toward our goals, to help us take initiative and strive to improve, and to persevere in the face of setbacks and frustrations

- *Empathy:* Sensing what people are feeling, being able to take their perspective, and cultivating rapport and attunement with a broad diversity of people

- *Social skills:* Handling emotions in relationships well and accurately reading social situations and networks; interacting smoothly; using these skills to persuade and lead, negotiate and settle disputes, for cooperation and teamwork

Appendix 2

....

Calculating the Competencies of Stars

There are two levels of job competence, and so two kinds of job competence models. One assesses the *threshold* competencies, those that people need in order to get the job done. These are the minimal skills needed to carry out the tasks associated with a given position. Most organizational competence models I've seen fit into this category.

The other kind of job competence model describes *distinguishing* competencies, the capabilities that set star performers apart from average ones. These are the competencies people already in a job need in order to perform superbly.

For example, anyone in information technology needs a high level of technical expertise simply to do their job at all; such expertise is a threshold competence. But the two competencies that carry most weight in making someone outstanding in that field are the drive to improve and skill at persuasion and influence—and these are emotional competencies.

Lists of competencies in themselves do not tell exactly how much each of these ingredients contributes to outstanding performance, though they are good general indicators. The absolute best data comes from competence studies that analyze the *relative weight* each competence carries in distinguishing the stars from the average. That's because a single cognitive competence, say, might turn out to be three times as important as a given single emotional competence—or vice versa—in contributing to star performance.

To get a more precise understanding of the contribution of emotional competence to excellence, I turned to Ruth Jacobs and Wei Chen, researchers at Hay/McBer in Boston. They reanalyzed their own raw data from competence studies at forty companies to assess the relative weight of a given competence in setting star performers apart from average performers.

The results: Greater strengths in purely cognitive capacities were 27 percent more frequent in the stars than in average performers, while greater strengths in emotional competencies were 53 percent more frequent. In other words, emotional competencies were *twice* as important in contributing to excellence as were pure intellect and expertise.

That estimate fits my own finding (reported in Chapter 2), and I feel comfortable with that number as a conservative rule of thumb for the general value of emotional competence in star performance.

These findings on the importance of emotional competence fit a general pattern revealed in other empirical studies of on-the-job excellence. The data come from a multitude of sources. All suggest that, in general, emotional competencies play a far larger role in superior job performance than do cognitive abilities and technical expertise.

For example, a classic study of more than two thousand supervisors, middle managers, and executives at twelve different organizations was done by Richard Boyatzis, of the Weatherhead School of Management at Case Western Reserve University.[1] Of the sixteen abilities that distinguished stars from average performers, all but two were emotional competencies.

Those results were duplicated in a larger analysis of the distinctive qualities of star performers done by Lyle Spencer Jr., director of research and technology worldwide at Hay/McBer. Spencer's analysis includes competence studies at 286 organizations, two thirds in the United States, one third in twenty other countries. Jobs for which the competencies of star performers were analyzed included managerial positions, from supervisor to CEO; sales and marketing staff; scientific and technical professions; health care, government, and education—even religious organizations.

Of twenty-one generic competencies Spencer identified, all but three were based on emotional intelligence. Of the other three purely cognitive competencies, two were intellectual: analytic skills and conceptual thinking. The third was technical expertise. In other words, the vast majority—more than 80 percent—of general competencies that set apart superior from average performers depend on emotional intelligence, not on purely cognitive ability.

Marilyn Gowing, director of the personnel resources and development center for the U.S. Office of Personnel Management, oversaw a thorough analysis of the competencies deemed to set superior performers apart from barely adequate ones for virtually all federal jobs. Analyzing that data at my request, Robert Buchele, a labor economist at Smith College, calculated the ratio of technical competence to interpersonal skills that distinguished outstanding performers for jobs from lowest to highest levels.

For lower level positions (like purchasing clerks and clerical assistants), there was a higher premium on technical abilities than on interpersonal ones. But at higher levels (professional or managerial positions), the interpersonal abilities mattered more than technical skills in setting star performers apart. And for these upper level occupations, the more people advanced in their position, the more important became the interpersonal skills (but not the technical ones) in distinguishing superior from average performance.

At my request, another study of emotional competence in leadership was done at Hay/McBer in Boston by Lyle Spencer Jr. with Wei Chen. Their analysis of more than three hundred top-level executives from fifteen global companies showed that six emotional competencies distinguished stars from the average: influence, team leadership, organizational awareness, self-confidence, the drive to achieve, and leadership itself.

As was found with David McClelland's analysis of star performers at the highest executive levels (described in Chapter 3), these competencies represent strengths in a wide spectrum of emotional intelligence, from self-awareness and motivation to social awareness and social skill. The only emotional intelligence capability not represented was self-regulation—but adaptability, from this cluster, was 57 percent more common in stars (and, in other samples, has emerged as one of the distinguishing competencies, too).

While neither technical expertise nor intellectual ability distinguished stars from average leaders, one set of cognitive abilities—pattern recognition and "big-picture" thinking—was 13 percent greater among the stars. But deductive, if-then reasoning abilities were not strongly represented among the best leaders—they displayed it in their work 12 percent *less* than did average leaders. In other samples, big-picture thinking has also emerged as significant, as some researchers have noted.[2]

Appendix 3

....

Gender and Empathy

Women generally have had more practice at some interpersonal skills than men, at least in cultures like the United States, where girls are raised to be more attuned to feelings and their nuances than are boys. So does this mean women are more empathic than men?

Often—but not inevitably. The popular assumption that women are naturally more attuned than men to the feelings of others has a scientific basis—but there are two notable exceptions of particular significance for the workplace. For one, there is no sex difference in cases where people are trying to conceal their true feelings, nor is there one when the challenge is to sense the unstated thoughts of someone in an ongoing encounter.

A caveat about sex differences in general: Whenever large groups like men and women are compared on *any* psychological dimension, there are far more similarities between the groups than differences; the bell curves for the two groups have immense overlap, and an edge where they differ. This means, for example, that while on average women may be better than men at some emotional skills, some men will still be better than most women, despite there being a statistically significant difference between the groups.

Now, the data on empathy. The results from dozens and dozens of studies on the question are both mixed and clarifying.[1] For one, whether women do better than men depends on what is meant by "empathy." There is one sense in which women—at least in Western cultures—*are*, on average, more empathic: having the same feeling another person does—that is, when one person feels distress or delight, so does the other. The data shows women *do* tend to experience this spontaneous matching of feeling with others more than do men.[2]

Women are also better than men at *detecting* another person's fleeting feelings, as was shown in a test called the Profile of Nonverbal Sensitivity (PONS), which was developed by one of my professors at Harvard, Robert Rosenthal, with Judith Hall, now at Northeastern University. The test consists of dozens of short video clips in which someone is having an emotional reaction (having been told, for example, they just won a lottery, or that a beloved pet has just died). The clips are filtered, so that the words cannot be heard distinctly, though the facial expression and the tone of voice are clear. Through hundreds of studies, Rosenthal and Hall found that 80 percent of the time women performed better on average than men at the task of guessing what emotion the person was actually feeling.[3]

However, the gender gap in reading emotions closed when the clips included emotional cues that are less easy to control than facial expression. People are better at controlling their overall facial expression than their tone of voice, body language, or fleeting "microemotions" that flit across the face for just a split second. The more emotional leakage, the better men become at reading emotion in others. Being able to pick up such emotional leakage is particularly important in situations where people have reason to conceal their true feelings—a fact of life in the business arena. And so sex differences in empathy tend to disappear in many everyday business situations, like sales or negotiation, where most people simply cannot control all the body's channels for expressing emotion.

And when it comes to another dimension of empathy—being able to sense someone's specific thoughts—there appears to be no sex difference at all. This more complicated task, called *empathic accuracy,* integrates cognitive and affective skills. The experimental methods used to assess empathic accuracy go beyond showing a snippet of an emotional response and asking people to guess the emotion; rather, subjects watch an entire videotape of a conversation and evaluate a person's hidden thoughts—as well as feelings—throughout. Those guesses are then compared with the target person's own narrative. On this task women generally did no better than men in a series of seven different experiments—there was no evidence of a "female intuition" advantage.[4] The significant exception was in a special subset of tests in which women were subtly prompted to prove themselves empathic by the researcher's suggestion that empathy is a hallmark of feminine identity. With that prompt, the female advantage in empathy emerged once again. In other words, the motivation to *seem* empathic made women more so (presumably because they made more effort).[5]

Indeed, a major review of data on male-female sex differences argues that men have as much latent ability for empathy, but less motivation to be empathic, than do women. To the extent men tend to see themselves in terms of something like machismo, the argument goes, they have less motivation to seem sensitive, because that could be seen as a sign of "weakness."[6] As William Ickes, one of the main researchers on empathy, puts it, "If men appear at times to be socially insensitive, it may have more to do with the image they wish to convey than with the empathic ability they possess."[7]

Appendix 4

·····································

Strategies for Leveraging Diversity

There has been a backlash from some earlier well-intended diversification initiatives that put minority workers in high positions only to see them fail—in no small part, no doubt, victims of stereotype threat, as we saw in Chapter 7. But several approaches can help.

Claude Steele, the Stanford psychologist who studied the power of stereotype threat, offers some. From his understanding of the emotional dynamics that undermine performance in minority group members, Steele created a program of "wise strategies" that change those dynamics for the better. Results have been heartening—for example, black students at the University of Michigan who went through his ten-week program did far better in their freshman year than did comparable black students.[1] Here are some aspects of Steele's program that match strategies used by companies to make the workplace congenial for people of all kinds:

- *Optimistic leaders:* Mentors or supervisors affirm the ability of people who might otherwise suffer the stigma of threatening stereotypes.

- *Genuine challenges:* Challenging work conveys respect for the person's potential and demonstrates he or she is not seen through the lens of a debilitating stereotype. These challenges are calibrated to the person's skill and offer a manageable "stretch," not an overly daunting demand that is a setup for failure nor a too easy assignment that reinforces the worst fears of the stereotyped: that they are seen as unable to do the work.

- *Emphasis on learning:* Emphasis is placed on the idea that expertise and ability grow through on-the-job learning and that competence increases incrementally. This challenges the cruelest stereotype, that a person's inherent capacity is limited by virtue of their belonging to a certain group.

- *Affirming the sense of belonging:* Negative stereotypes create a sense of "I don't really belong here," casting doubt on one's suitability for a job. The affirmation of belonging, though, must be based on a person's true capabilities for the job.

- *Valuing multiple perspectives:* A variety of contributions are explicitly valued in the organizational culture. This tells those threatened by stereotypes that this is an organization where such stereotypes are not allowed.

- *Role models:* People from the person's own group who have been successful in this kind of job carry the implicit message that the threatening stereotype is not a barrier here.

- *Building self-confidence through Socratic feedback:* Instead of judgmental responses to performance, an ongoing dialogue helps direct the person, with minimal attention to whether they did well or poorly. This strengthens the mentor relationship while minimizing the emotional cost of early failures, a strategy that allows self-efficacy to build gradually along with successes large or small.

Appendix 5

....

Further Issues in Training

More On: Assessing Emotional Competence

No evaluation measure is perfect. Self-evaluations are vulnerable to skews from people wanting to look good. And when it comes to assessing emotional competence, there is the question of whether someone low in self-awareness can be trusted to accurately evaluate her own strengths and weaknesses. While self-evaluations can be helpful (and candid) if people trust that the results will be used for their own good, without this trust they can be less reliable.

Those who design self-evaluation tools usually build in a "lie scale," a series of questions that catch people who are trying to look "too good to be true"—for example, by agreeing with the statement "I never tell a lie." But here's the catch: While lie scales can usually catch intentional deception, they may not detect a *self*-deception due to a lack of self-awareness that makes people poor observers of themselves.

"The usefulness of self-evaluations depends on the purpose," Susan Ennis, head of executive development at Bank Boston, tells me. "One key question is, 'What's the company's role, and how will the data be stored and used?' The wish to look desirable is bound to influence people's answers. You want to look good."

Says Ennis, "When a self-evaluation is purely between you and your coach, confidential, not seen or kept by your company, then you'll be more candid, or as candid as you can be, given whatever other limit you may have on self-awareness."

On the other hand, evaluations by other people are susceptible to another set of skews. When office politics are involved, for example, 360-degree feedback may not always offer a pure reflection of the person being evaluated, since these evaluations can be used as weapons in office political wars or as a way for friends to exchange favors by giving inflated "grades" to each other.

Organizational politics can make it particularly difficult for executives in the topmost tiers to get candid evaluations, if only because the power they yield gets in the way—and, as we saw in Chapter 4, success itself can sometimes foster a narcissistic sense that one has no weak points. Executives tend to be insulated from evidence to the contrary partly because they are isolated, partly because subordinates fear offending them.

To some extent, any evaluation reflects the evaluator. For that reason, getting evaluations from multiple sources is a way to correct any distortions, since presumably one individual's emotional or political agenda would be balanced by other evaluations.

More On: Gauging Readiness

Extensive research (on more than thirty thousand people) by James Prochaska, a University of Rhode Island psychologist, establishes four levels of readiness people go through during a successful behavior change.

- *Oblivious:* As G. K. Chesterton, the British pundit, put it, "It isn't that they can't see the solution—they can't see the problem." People at this stage aren't ready at all; they deny they have any need to change in the first place. They resist any attempt to help them change—they just don't see the point.

- *Contemplation:* People at this stage see that they need to improve and have begun to think about how to do so. They are open to talking about it but not quite ready to pursue development wholeheartedly. Ambivalence is rampant; some wait for a "magic moment" of readiness, while others leap into action prematurely but meet failure because they are halfhearted. People at this stage are as likely to say they intend to take some action "next month" as they are to say they'll do it "in the next six months." Prochaska notes that it's not unusual for people "to spend years telling themselves that someday they are going to change." They substitute thinking for acting. Prochaska cites the case of an engineer who spent five years analyzing the factors that had made him passive and shy—but didn't think he understood the problem well enough to do anything about it.

■ *Preparation:* Here people have begun to focus on the solution— on how to improve. They are on the verge, eager to develop an action plan. They are aware of the problem, see that there are ways to solve it, and palpably anticipate doing so. People are sometimes propelled to this heightened stage of readiness by a dramatic event—a heart-to-heart talk with a supervisor, a disaster on the job, a crisis in their personal life. One executive was jolted into bolstering his self-control competence when the police stopped him on the way home from a business dinner and arrested him for driving drunk. At this point people are ripe for change; this is the time for formulating a specific, detailed plan of action.

■ *Action.* Visible change begins. People embrace the plan, start practicing its steps, and actually change how they act—their emotional patterns, the way they think about themselves, and all the other facets of transforming a long-standing habit. This stage is what most people think of as "making the change," though it builds on the earlier steps in getting ready.

More On: Practice

At the neurological level, cultivating a competence means extinguishing the old habit as the brain's automatic response and replacing it with the new one. The final stage of mastering a competence comes at the point when the old habit loses its status as the default response and the new one takes its place. At that point, the behavior change has stabilized, making a relapse to the old habit unlikely.

Generally, underlying deep attitudes and related values are harder to change than work habits. For example, an ethnic stereotype is less readily altered than is what a person says and does in the presence of someone from that group. Motives like the need for achievement and personality traits like affability can be upgraded or modified, but the process is lengthy.[1] So, too, with building underlying capacities like self-awareness, managing distressing emotions, empathy, and social skill.

Beyond the complexity of the competence being learned, the distance from the person's baseline behavior to the new matters immensely. For people who are already fairly empathic, learning to give performance feedback artfully or to attune themselves to customers' needs may come quite easily, since these competencies represent specific applications of a capability they already have. But for those who struggle to empathize, this mastery requires a more determined and lengthy effort.

Training programs that offer people a chance to practice the desired competence through well-focused simulations, games, role-playing, and other such methods can offer a strong beginning for practice. But with more complicated simulated job tasks, computerized business games, role-playing, team problem-solving exercises, and large-scale simulations of an entire organizational reality, the results tend to be mixed.

It is often unclear precisely what skills such simulations are meant to cultivate; there typically is little or no attention paid to exactly what competencies are being practiced. Moreover, merely taking part in a game or an exercise is not the same as learning. The overall recommendation for such simulations and games is that they be carefully planned, focus on specific competencies that are clearly described to participants, and end with a debriefing of the experience. They should also be used in conjunction with (rather than as a replacement for) coaching and feedback, reinforcement, and on-the-job practice.[2]

Computer-aided instruction, a current vogue in training, has limits when it comes to offering practice for emotional competence. While they have real promise in terms of individualized instruction, self-pacing, private opportunities for rehearsal and practice, immediate feedback on progress and remedial assistance, and the like, computer-aided techniques are generally better suited for training in technical skills than for developing personal and interpersonal capabilities.

"People say you can sit at your computer, assess yourself, and find out how to develop a competency," observes Richard Boyatzis, of Case Western Reserve University. "But you can't do this without relationships—you can't learn this in isolation."

Enthusiasm is high in many quarters for converting training to high-tech media like intelligent computer-based tutoring systems, virtual reality, interactive CD-ROMs, and so on. While these technologies may offer economies of cost by using machines instead of people as trainers, and more flexibility for the people who use them, there may be much of importance that gets lost if they are the only tool used. As one psychologist put it, "High-tech training media may have many virtues, but they tend to score rather low on emotional intelligence." To be sure, there may be a place for such high-tech teaching aids in the overall design of an emotional competence training program (one example might be for individual practice sessions with video segments for feedback on empathic accuracy). Another possibility might be on-line affinity groups, a kind of virtual support and coaching group.

But an overemphasis on technology at the expense of essential human contact—especially when it comes to practicing competencies—could be a great mistake. One review of training trends observes wryly: "It is often the mundane and low-technology factors of a training system that make the difference between a successful training program and wasted organizational resources"—and these low-tech factors are people with the essential competencies of emotional intelligence.[3]

Notes

....

Chapter 1 / The New Yardstick

1. Daniel Goleman, *Emotional Intelligence* (New York: Bantam Books, 1995). See Appendix 1 for details on the nature of emotional intelligence.

2. Emotional intelligence in men and women: Reuven Bar-On, *Bar-On Emotional Quotient Inventory: Technical Manual* (Toronto: Multi-Health Systems, 1997).

3. No sex differences: Reuven Bar-On, a pioneer in assessing emotional intelligence and the researcher who did the study, tells me he finds the identical pattern of strengths and weaknesses for men and women worldwide—among the Igbu in Nigeria and Tamils in Sri Lanka, in Germany, Israel, America—everywhere he's looked. Bar-On's conclusions are based on studying the emotional intelligence of more than fifteen thousand people in a dozen countries on four continents.

4. Four out of five companies surveyed: ASTD Benchmarking Forum, Member-to-Member Survey results, American Society for Training and Development, Alexandria, Virginia, October 1997.

5. Job search by the employed: data from Challenger, Gray, and Christmas, reported in Bob Herbert, "Separation Anxiety," *New York Times,* January 19, 1996.

6. Krugman: quoted in Stephen Lohr, "On the Road with Chairman Lou," *New York Times,* June 26, 1994.

7. The rise in average IQ scores: Ulric Neisser (ed.), *The Rising Curve* (Washington, DC: American Psychological Press, 1997).

8. The decline in children's emotional intelligence: Thomas Achenbach and Catherine Howell, "Are America's Children's Problems Getting Worse? A 13-Year Comparison," *Journal of the American Academy of Child and Adolescent Psychiatry,* November 1989.

9. Survey of American employers: The Harris Education Research Council, "An Assessment of American Education," New York City, 1991.

10. What employers seek in entry-level hires: Anthony P. Carnevale et al., "Workplace Basics: The Skills Employers Want," U.S. Department of Labor Employment and Training Administration, 1989. By 1996, employers said the three most highly sought-after skills in new hires are oral communications, interpersonal abilities, and teamwork abilities.

11. Karen O. Dowd and Jeanne Liedtka, "What Corporations Seek in MBA Hires: A Survey," *The Magazine of the Graduate Management Admission Council*, Winter 1994.

Chapter 2 / Competencies of the Stars

1. The study of foreign-service officers and the beginnings of the competence-testing movement are described by David C. McClelland in his introduction to Lyle M. Spencer Jr. and Signe M. Spencer, *Competence at Work: Models for Superior Performance* (New York: John Wiley and Sons, 1993).

2. See David C. McClelland, "Testing for Competence Rather than Intelligence," *American Psychologist* 46 (1973). McClelland's landmark paper has continued to stir debate even after a quarter century.

3. The two computer programmers: Spencer and Spencer, *Competence at Work.*

4. Academic tests failed to predict best diplomats: Kenneth Clark found that scores by applicants on the selection test for foreign-service officers did not predict success as rated by their later on-the-job performance evaluations. Results of this study are reported by D. C. McClelland and C. Dailey, "Improving Officer Selection for the Foreign Service," McBer, Boston, 1972.

5. The test is the Profile of Nonverbal Sensitivity, or PONS, developed at Harvard by Robert Rosenthal. See, e.g., Robert Rosenthal, "The PONS Test: Measuring Sensitivity to Nonverbal Cues," in P. McReynolds (ed.), *Advances in Psychological Assessment* (San Francisco: Jossey-Bass, 1977).

6. The higher estimate of IQ and job performance: e.g., John B. Hunter and F. L. Schmidt, "Validity and Utility of Alternative Predictors of Job Performance," *Psychological Bulletin* 96 (1984); F. L. Schmidt and John B. Hunter, "Employment Testing: Old Theories and New Research Findings," *American Psychologist* 36 (1981).

7. A more careful view of IQ and job performance: Robert Sternberg, *Successful Intelligence* (New York: Simon & Schuster, 1996).

8. Harvard graduates entrance exam scores and later-life success: Dean K. Whitla, "Value Added: Measuring the Impact of Undergraduate Education," Office of Instructional Research and Evaluation, Harvard University, 1975;

cited in David C. McClelland, "The Knowledge-Testing-Educational Complex Strikes Back," *American Psychologist* 49 (1994).

9. Originally called McBer, the firm was also founded with David Berlew, another of McClelland's former students.

10. IQ in professional and highly complex technical fields: Spencer and Spencer, *Competence at Work*. As they put it, cognitive abilities alone are not the mark of top performers, since "in higher level technical, marketing, professional, and managerial jobs, almost everyone has an IQ of 120 or above and an advanced degree from a good university. What distinguishes superior performers in these jobs is motivation, interpersonal skills, and political skills."

11. See Robert J. Sternberg and Richard K. Wagner, *Practical Intelligence: Nature and Origins of Competence in the Everyday World* (Cambridge: Cambridge University Press, 1986).

12. See Sternberg, *Successful Intelligence.*

13. Practical intelligence and managerial success: R. K. Wagner and R. J. Sternberg, "Practical Intelligence in Real-World Pursuits: The Role of Tacit Knowledge," *Journal of Personality and Social Psychology* 49 (1985).

14. Technical skills as threshold abilities: Spencer and Spencer, *Competence at Work.*

15. The tale of Penn and Matt is told by Robert Sternberg in *Successful Intelligence.*

16. The tale of the president was told by Ann Graham Ehringer, director of the Family Business Program at the Marshall School of Business at the University of Southern California.

17. The measure of capacity to handle cognitive complexity was developed by Elliott Jacques; see Elliott Jacques, *Requisite Organization* (Arlington, VA: Cason Hall, 1989).

18. The term "emotional competence" has been used in this sense by several other theorists and researchers; see, e.g., Carol Saarni, "Emotional Competence: How emotions and relationships become integrated," in R. A. Thompson (ed.), *Nebraska Symposium on Motivation,* vol. 36, 1988; Carol Saarni, "Emotional Competence and Self-regulation in Childhood," in Peter Salovey and David J. Sluyter (eds.), *Emotional Development and Emotional Intelligence* (New York: Basic Books, 1997). By highlighting emotional competencies, I do not mean to imply that expertise and cognitive abilities are irrelevant; these abilities are part of a complex system, and in any such interacting system all parts make their contribution. My aim is to give emotional competencies—so easily discounted or overlooked—their due.

19. There is a nascent effort to translate emotional skills into software that will "humanize" computers. See Roz Picard, *Affective Computing* (Cambridge: MIT Press, 1998).

20. Damage to the brain's cortex impairs our abilities to think and perceive; damage to key subcortical areas destroys our ability to register emotions. Damage to circuits centering on the amygdala have the most devastating impact on the ability to register emotion. (See Joseph LeDoux, *The Emotional Brain* [New York: Simon & Schuster, 1996].) Cutting central links between the brain's topmost layers and these same emotional centers sabotages the emotional competencies, all of which depend on the tight orchestration of thought and feeling. The specific circuitry between neocortex and subcortex that is crucial for integrating thought and emotion runs from the amygdala in the limbic system, the brain's subcortical center for emotion, and the ventromedial area of the prefrontal lobes, the brain's neocortical executive center. This circuitry is described in detail in Antonio Damasio, *Descartes' Error: Emotion, Reason, and the Human Brain* (New York: Grosset/Putnam, 1994). Damasio, a neurologist at the University of Iowa Medical School, has done the best research on the brain basis of competence. When I sent him the list of emotional competencies, his conclusion was that all of them (though not cognitive abilities) would be impaired in people who had brain damage that cut the connections between the crucial prefrontal and emotional centers. In the logic of neurology, the capacities impaired in people with damage to a particular brain site suggest that this same area of the brain regulates those capacities in people whose brains are intact. In other words, the underlying neural circuitry for emotional competence—as opposed to intellectual competence—connects the prefrontal area with the emotional centers. The main clue is that damage to these areas impairs the personal and social abilities that allow effective job performance, even though cognitive abilities are intact.

21. The term "emotional competence" includes both social and emotional competencies, just as Howard Gardner uses the term "personal intelligence" to subsume both intra- and interpersonal abilities.

22. This generic competence framework distills findings from: MOSAIC competencies for professionals and administrators (developed by the U.S. Department of Personnel, 1996); Spencer and Spencer, *Competence at Work;* Richard Boyatzis, *The Competent Manager: A Model for Effective Performance* (New York: John Wiley and Sons, 1982); and competence studies published in Richard H. Rosier (ed.), *The Competency Model Handbook,* Vols. 1–3 (Lexington: Linkage, 1994–1996).

23. The specific competencies for Blue Cross reps, shoe store managers, brokers, and life insurance sales: Walter V. Clarke Associates, "Activity Vector

Analysis: Some Applications to the Concepts of Emotional Intelligence," June 1996.

24. Political awareness: Ann Howard and Douglas W. Bray, *Managerial Lives in Transition* (New York: Guilford Press, 1988).

25. Job-specific competencies: these can account for as much as 20 percent of those needed for superior performance. See Spencer and Spencer, *Competence at Work.*

26. Spencer and Spencer, *Competence at Work.*

27. These emotional competencies are to a large extent applicable to top performance in virtually every job. One estimate is that generic competencies cover 80 to 98 percent of behaviors typical of star performers, depending on the specific job. That estimate includes three that are purely cognitive—analytical thinking, conceptual thinking, and job-specific expertise—and so do not fall among the emotional intelligence group. See Spencer and Spencer, *Competence at Work,* for a more detailed discussion.

Chapter 3 / The Hard Case for Soft Skills

1. The Lucent Technologies, University of Nebraska, and Amoco competence models: Richard H. Rosier (ed.), *The Competency Model Handbook,* vol. 1 (Lexington, MA: Linkage, 1994).

2. In the best of the competence models, average performers are compared with those who rank in the top of their field. The pool of top performers is typically chosen on the basis of sales or other hard criteria of excellence, or on the basis of confidential 360-degree ratings, where bosses, peers, employees, and customers all rate the performance of a given person. Each nominee—and a comparable pool of average performers—goes through a rigorous interview about their job performance, including, for example, detailed narratives of what they actually did in three incidents of great on-the-job success and three instances of failure or missteps. The narratives are then analyzed and coded for clues to the competencies the person displayed in these actual samples of their behavior. A less precise method, though one commonly used to save time and money, asks expert panels to generate the competencies they have found typify star performers.

3. The U.S. government competency models are in a CD-ROM, "Personnel Manager." Personnel Resources and Development Center, U.S. Office of Personnel Management, Washington, DC, 1997.

4. While the best leaders relied more on big-picture thinking, they relied less than other leaders on deductive, if-then reasoning abilities.

5. Patrick McCarthy, star sales associate: Robert Spector and Patrick D. McCarthy, *The Nordstrom Way* (New York: John Wiley, 1995).

6. The landmark study of the value of top workers: John E. Hunter, Frank L. Schmidt, and Michael K. Judiesch, "Individual Differences in Output Variability as a Function of Job Complexity," *Journal of Applied Psychology* 75, 1 (1990).

7. By contrast, for low-level jobs the top 1 percent compared to the average, showed an advantage of 52 percent more value, and for medium-level jobs the added value was 85 percent more—still impressive. See Hunter, Schmidt, and Judiesch, "Individual Differences."

8. See his landmark book, Lyle M. Spencer Jr. and Signe M. Spencer, *Competence at Work: Models for Superior Performance* (New York: John Wiley and Sons, 1993).

9. Computer programmers, the stars and superstars: J. Martin, *Rapid Application Development* (New York: Macmillan, 1990); C. Jones, *Programming Productivity* (New York: McGraw-Hill, 1986). Both were cited by Lyle Spencer Jr. in his presentation to the annual meeting of the International Personnel Management Association, Boston, June 25, 1996.

10. The value-added of sales stars: S. Sloan and Lyle M. Spencer, "Participant Survey Results," Hay Salesforce Effectiveness Seminar, Atlanta, 1991.

11. Top executives and competencies: The six or seven that made for the tipping point were from among a set of twelve (ten of which are emotional competencies) that were especially important for success at a specific company. David C. McClelland, "Behavioral event interviews as an alternative to traditional ability tests as a way to identify personal competencies associated with top executive success," *Psychological Science,* in press, 1998. McClelland shared additional data with me.

12. Turnover rates: Spencer and Spencer, *Competence at Work.*

13. Division presidents cost of turnover: Hay/McBer Research and Innovation Group, 1997; McClelland, "Behavioral Event Interviews."

14. The three cases: Hay/McBer Research and Innovation Group, 1997.

15. Executive derailment meant getting fired, being forced to quit, or reaching a plateau in a dead-end position. Done originally in the early 1980s by researchers at the Center for Creative Leadership, the study was updated in 1996 in interviews with sixty-two executives at fifteen Fortune 500 multinational corporations in North America or the equivalent in ten European countries. Jean Brittain Leslie and Ellen Van Velsor, "A Look at Derailment Today: North America and Europe," Center for Creative Leadership, Greensboro, NC, 1996.

16. Leslie and Van Velsor, "A Look at Derailment Today."

17. Strengths and weaknesses of the successful versus failed managers were first identified in the original data set, and largely confirmed in the follow-up in 1996. Leslie and Van Velsor, "A Look at Derailment Today."

18. Comparison of 23 failed executives with 227 successes in Latin America: Claudio Fernández-Aráoz, personal communication, 1997.

19. The studies of failed executives were done in Japan by Ken Whitney and Tomo Watanabe in the Tokyo office of Egon Zehnder International and in Germany by Horst Bröcker of the Munich office of Egon Zehnder International.

20. Managers who failed: Leslie and Van Velsor, "A Look at Derailment Today."

21. Patrick McCarthy: Spector and McCarthy, *The Nordstrom Way.*

22. Stephen Rosen is director of the Science and Technology Advisory Board in New York City, a project of the Alfred P. Sloan Foundation. See Stephen Rosen and Celia Paul, *Career Renewal: Tools for Scientists and Technical Professionals* (New York: Academic Press, 1997).

23. Emotional intelligence in scientific careers: Gregory J. Feist and Frank Barron, "Emotional Intelligence and Academic Intelligence in Career and Life Success," presented at the Annual Convention of the American Psychological Society, San Francisco, June 1996.

24. Ernest O. Lawrence: His comment was in a conversation to Alvin M. Weinberg, former director of Oak Ridge National Laboratory, who repeated it to me.

Chapter 4 / The Inner Rudder

1. Decision making in entrepreneurs: Ann Graham Ehringer, *Make Up Your Mind* (Santa Monica, CA: Merritt Publishing, 1995).

2. The circuitry of the extended amygdala, which I refer to simply as the "amygdala," is described in James D. Duffy, "The Neural Substrates of Emotion," *Psychiatric Annals,* January 1997.

3. The amygdala as the storehouse for emotional memory—if only in terms of the emotional valence (liking or disliking) of what we experience: See Joseph LeDoux, *The Emotional Brain* (New York: Basic Books, 1996).

4. Bad decisions: Gretchen Vogel, "Scientists Probe Feelings Behind Decision-making," *Science,* February 28, 1997. Like the brilliant lawyer, Damasio's other patients with prefrontal deficits made disastrous financial, professional, or ethical decisions, even though perfectly capable of describing the rational

pros and cons of a decision. They drifted in and out of marriages, squandered money in foolish financial decisions, and at work would inadvertently offend or antagonize their coworkers.

5. Top executives and decision making: Weston Agor, *The Logic of Intuitive Decision-making* (New York: Quorum Books, 1986).

6. Ehringer, *Make Up Your Mind.*

7. Nalini Ambady, "Half a Minute: Predicting Teacher Evaluations from Thin Slices of Nonverbal Behavior and Physical Attractiveness," *Journal of Personality and Social Psychology* 64 (1993). Almost the same level of accuracy has been found from brief observations in forty-four other studies, including one of people's interactions with bosses, peers, and subordinates: Nalini Ambady and Robert Rosenthal, "Thin Slices of Expressive Behavior as Predictors of Interpersonal Consequences: A Meta-analysis," *Psychological Bulletin* 111 (1992).

8. Gavin deBecker, *The Gift of Fear: Survival Signs That Protect Us from Violence* (New York: Little, Brown, 1997).

9. "Awareness of One's Emotional Experience," one of several emotional competencies identified at American Express Financial Advisors, was shared with me by Kate Cannon, director of leadership development there.

10. The new introspectionism: Stratford Sherman, "Leaders Learn to Heed the Voice Within," *Fortune,* August 22, 1994.

11. Richard Abdoo: Sherman, "Leaders Learn to Heed the Voice Within."

12. Satisfying work and outstanding performance: Robert E. Kelley, *How to Be a Star at Work* (Times Books, 1998).

13. The unhappy entrepreneur: Ehringer, *Make Up Your Mind.*

14. Engaging skills at work and heart disease: see Leonard Syme, "Explaining Inequalities in Heart Disease," *The Lancet,* July 26, 1997.

15. One of the main self-awareness methods Zuboff uses is "focusing," developed by Eugene T. Gendlin at the University of Chicago, and The Focusing Institute, Spring Valley, New York. See Eugene T. Gendlin, *Focusing* (New York: Bantam Books, 1981).

16. Mort Meyerson recants: Mort Meyerson, "Everything I Thought I Knew About Leadership Is Wrong," *Fast Company,* special edition, May 1997.

17. Joe Jaworski: quoted in Allen M. Webber, "Destiny and the Job of the Leader," *Fast Company,* June/July 1996.

18. The case of Harry: Robert E. Kaplan, *Beyond Ambition: How Driven Managers Can Lead Better and Live Better* (San Francisco: Jossey-Bass, 1991).

19. Lack of self-awareness and derailment: Morgan W. McCall Jr. and Michael Lombardo, "Off the Track: Why and How Successful Executives Get Derailed," technical report no. 21, Center for Creative Leadership, Greensboro, NC, 1983; A. M. Morrison et al., *Breaking the Glass Ceiling: Can Women Reach the Top of America's Largest Corporations?* (Reading, MA: Addison-Wesley, 1987).

20. Accurate self-assessment in managers: Richard Boyatzis, *The Competent Manager: A Model for Effective Performance* (New York: John Wiley and Sons, 1982).

21. Common executive blind spots: Kaplan, *Beyond Ambition.*

22. How others see us as a more accurate predictor of job performance: e.g., Dianne Nilsen, "Understanding Self-observer Discrepancies in Multi-rater Assessment Systems," presented at the annual meeting of the American Psychological Association, San Francisco, 1991.

23. A small, inventive step: James O. Prochaska et al., *Changing for Good* (New York: Avon, 1994).

24. Self-awareness and superior performance: Dianne Nilsen and David P. Campbell, "Self-observer Rating Discrepancies: Once an Overrater, Always an Overrater?" *Human Resource Manager,* Summer/Fall 1993.

25. Self-awareness in star performers: Kelley, *How to Be a Star at Work.*

26. Boyatzis, *The Competent Manager.*

27. Lee Iacocca, *Iacocca: An Autobiography* (New York: Bantam Books, 1984).

28. The tale of the shy lawnmowing entrepreneur: cited in David Leonard, "The Impact of Learning Goals on Self-directed Change in Education and Management Development," Ph.D. thesis, Weatherhead School of Management, Case Western Reserve University, 1996.

29. People can learn to become more self-confident: see, for example, Jerome Kagan, *Galen's Prophecy* (New York: Basic Books, 1994).

30. Self-efficacy: see Albert Bandura, *Social Foundations of Thoughts and Action* (Englewood Cliffs, NJ: Prentice-Hall, 1986); Albert Bandura, "Organizational Applications of Social Cognitive Theory," *Australian Journal of Management,* December 1988.

31. Self-efficacy and job performance in new accountants: Alan M. Saks, "Longitudinal Field Investigation of the Moderating and Mediating Effects of

Self-efficacy on the Relationship Between Training and Newcomer Adjustment," *Journal of Applied Psychology* 80 (1995).

32. Inner maps of self-efficacy: Daniel Cervone, "Social-cognitive Mechanisms and Personality Coherence: Self-knowledge, Situational Beliefs, and Cross-situational Coherence in Perceived Self-efficacy," *Psychological Science* 8 (1997).

33. Self-confidence early in career predicts success later at AT&T: Ann Howard and Douglas W. Bray, *Managerial Lives in Transition* (New York: Guilford Press, 1988). Study after study finds that self-confidence distinguishes successful, effective workers from those who perform poorly; see, for example, Boyatzis, *The Competent Manager.*

34. Self-confidence in high-IQ people and career success: Carole K. Holahan and Robert R. Sears, *The Gifted Group in Later Maturity* (Stanford: Stanford University Press, 1995).

35. Self-confidence and dissent in nurses: Louise E. Parker, "When to Fix It and When to Leave: Relationships Among Perceived Control, Self-efficacy, Dissent, and Exit," *Journal of Applied Psychology* 78 (1993).

Chapter 5 / Self-Control

1. The amygdala: the best description of the emotional role of the amygdala is Joseph LeDoux, *The Emotional Brain: The Mysterious Underpinnings of Emotional Life* (New York: Simon & Schuster, 1996).

2. More specifically, the release of CRF triggers another brain chemical, called ACTH, which in turn causes a flood of hormones known as corticosteroids; in humans the main one is cortisol.

3. Cortisol and working memory: see, for example, O. M. Wolkowitz et al., "Cognitive Effects of Corticosteroids," *American Journal of Psychiatry* 147, 10 (1990).

4. Stress shrinks the hippocampus: Bruce McEwen and R. M. Sapolsky, "Stress and Cognitive Function," *Current Opinions in Neurobiology* 5 (1995).

5. Cortisol and memory impairment: M. Mauri et al., "Memory Impairment in Cushing's Disease," *Acta Neurologica Scandinavia* 87 (1993).

6. Deluge of messages: Alex Markels, "Memo 4/8/97, FYI: Messages Inundate Offices," *The Wall Street Journal,* April 8, 1997.

7. Engineer: Robert E. Kelley, *How to Be a Star at Work* (Times Books, 1998).

8. For example, a man who had an injury to his prefrontal cortex when an exploding tire drove part of the tire rim into his forehead was suddenly

transformed from a pious churchgoer to someone who would hurl a glass of orange juice at a waitress because it was warm. People with frontal lobe damage are prone to such fits of explosive, uncontrollable impulse, their primal feelings of fear or rage unchecked; Vietnam veterans with frontal-lobe damage were found to be up to six times as violent and aggressive as similar vets without such damage. Such clinical reports are telling for the rest of us: Whenever injury to a neural circuit results in dramatic changes in behavior, it suggests that normal variations in the operation of that circuit cause parallel variations in that same range of behavior. I review the evidence for the role of the prefrontal lobe, particularly the orbitofrontal cortex, in inhibiting impulse in more detail in *Emotional Intelligence* (New York: Bantam Books, 1995).

9. Impulsivity: Gordon D. Logan et al., "Impulsivity and Motor Control," *Psychological Science,* January 1997.

10. As these inhibitory circuits calm the amygdala, they allow the intellect to operate more effectively, even under stress. For example, in one laboratory experiment, people were given a fairly good analogue of the stress operating in a wide variety of jobs: They had to solve tough arithmetic problems under ever-increasing time pressure. People whose cortisol levels remained the lowest had the most accurate answers, and stayed accurate longer despite the tension of the situation; those with high cortisol had the most anxiety, anger, depression, and fatigue—and the poorest intellectual performance. J. Lehmann et al., "Differences in Mental Task Performance and Slow Potential Shifts in Subjects Differing in Cortisol Level," *International Journal of Psychophysiology* 13 (1992).

11. Tense managers and poor store performance: Robert F. Lusch and Rapy Serpkenci, "Personal Differences, Job Tension, Job Outcomes, and Store Performance: A Study of Retail Managers," *Journal of Marketing,* January 1990.

12. The story of the fight that didn't happen was passed on to me by Roger Grothe, then manager of in-flight training at Northwest Airlines.

13. The marshmallow kids grow up: The data collection and analysis of the children in the teen years and twenties was conducted by Philip Peake, a psychologist at Smith College, who shared the findings with me.

14. As the people at the Educational Testing Service in Princeton, who make the test, told me, a 210-point advantage is as great as that seen between children from the wealthiest and poorest homes, or between children whose parents have no high-school diploma and those with a parent who has a master's degree or better.

15. The follow-up was directed by Philip Peake.

16. Emotional labor: Arlie Hochschild, *The Managed Heart: The Commercialization of Human Feeling.* Berkeley: University of California Press, 1983.

17. Identity and emotional labor: Blake E. Ashforth and Ronald H. Humphrey, "Emotional labor in service roles: The influence of identity," *Academy of Management Review,* 18, 1993.

18. The costs of emotional suppression: James J. Gross and Robert W. Levenson, "Hiding Feelings: The Acute Effects of Inhibiting Negative and Positive Emotion," *Journal of Abnormal Psychology* 106 (1997).

19. Spontaneity in supervisors, managers, and executives: Richard Boyatzis, *The Competent Manager: A Model for Effective Performance* (New York: John Wiley and Sons, 1982).

20. The tale of Bill Gates's tirade: Fred Moody, "Wonder Women in the Rude Boys' Paradise," *Fast Company,* June/July 1996.

21. Relaxation as a stress buffer: My own research at Harvard offered some of the first evidence for this effect; see Daniel Goleman and Gary E. Schwartz, "Meditation as an Intervention in Stress Reactivity," *Journal of Clinical and Consulting Psychology* 44 (1976). Many other studies have found the same effect in the years since; see Daniel Goleman and Joel Gurin (eds.), *Mind/Body Medicine* (New York: Consumer Reports Books, 1994).

22. Stress and strain: M. Afzalur Rahim and Clement Psenicka, "A Structural Equations Model of Stress, Locus of Control, Social Support, Psychiatric Symptoms, and Propensity to Leave a Job," *Journal of Social Psychology* 136 (1996).

23. Little control over job, more heart disease: see Leonard Syme, "Explaining Inequalities in Heart Disease," *The Lancet,* July 26, 1997.

24. Lack of job control and heart disease: R. Karasek and T. Theorrell, *Healthy Work: Stress, Productivity, and the Reconstruction of Working Life* (New York: Basic Books, 1990).

25. Colds and bad bosses: Sheldon Cohen, paper delivered at the Third International Congress of the International Society for Neuroimmunomodulation, Bethesda, MD, November 1996. Reported in *Science,* November 29, 1996.

26. Distressing feelings and the heart: E. C. Gullete et al., "Effects of Mental Stress on Myocardial Ischemia During Daily Life," *Journal of the American Medical Association* 227 (1997).

27. Higher cortisol levels in working mothers: L. J. Luecken et al., "Stress in Employed Women: Impact of Marital Status and Children at Home on Neurohormone Output and Home Strain," *Psychosomatic Medicine* 59 (1997).

28. Cortisol and immune suppression: see Christine Blank, "Anticortisols Can Help Many," *Drug Topics,* December 8, 1997.

29. Cortisol and work stress: Kathleen Fackelman, "The Cortisol Connection," *Science News,* November 29, 1997.

30. The stressed professor: Richard Lazarus, *Emotion and Adaptation* (New York: Oxford University Press, 1991).

31. The self-aware laid-off managers: James Pennebaker, personal communication.

32. The experiment on self-awareness and handling stress well: Peter Salovey, John D. Mayer et al., "Emotional Attention, Clarity, and Repair: Exploring Emotional Intelligence Using the Trait Meta-mood Scale," in James W. Pennebaker (ed.), *Emotion, Disclosure, and Health* (Washington, DC: American Psychological Press, 1995).

33. Officer Wilson: in Deborah Sontag and Dan Barry, "Disrespect as Catalyst for Brutality," *The New York Times,* November 19, 1997.

34. The unflappable traffic agents: Elizabeth Brondolo et al., "Correlates of Risk for Conflict Among New York City Traffic Agents," in Gary R. VandenBos and Elizabeth Q. Bulatao (eds.), *Violence on the Job: Identifying Risks and Developing Solutions* (Washington, DC, American Psychological Association, 1996).

35. Calm counselors are superior: Richard A. Boyatzis and James A. Burrus, "The Heart of Human Resource Development: Counseling Competencies," unpublished manuscript, July 1995.

36. Unflappable flight attendants: Lyle M. Spencer Jr. and Signe M. Spencer, *Competence at Work: Models for Superior Performance* (New York: John Wiley and Sons, 1993).

37. Self-control in managers and executives: Boyatzis, *The Competent Manager.*

38. Hardiness and stress resilience: Salvatore R. Maddi and Suzanne C. Kobasa, *The Hardy Executive: Health Under Stress* (Homewood, IL: Dow Jones-Irwin, 1984).

39. The inventor and the man with two sets of books: the story is told in Stanley Foster Reed, *The Toxic Executive* (New York: HarperBusiness, 1993).

40. Survey of unethical business practices: reported in Henry Fountain, "Of White Lies and Yellow Pads," *The New York Times,* July 6, 1997.

41. The assessment of 4,265 people is reported in "Activity Vector Analysis: Some Applications to the Concepts of Emotional Intelligence," Walter V. Clarke Associates, Pittsburgh, June 1996.

42. Ratings of football players: "Activity Vector Analysis."

43. Conscientiousness and outstanding performance: M. R. Barrick and M. K. Mount, "The Big Five Personality Dimensions and Job Performance: A Meta-analysis," *Personnel Psychology* 44 (1991).

44. Conscientiousness and appliance sales: Murray R. Barrick, Michael K. Mount, and Judy P. Strauss, "Conscientiousness and Performance of Sales Representatives: Test of the Mediating Effects of Goal Setting," *Journal of Applied Psychology* 78 (1993).

45. Lack of conscientiousness and firing: Murray R. Barrick, M. K. Mount, and J. P. Strauss, "Antecedents of Involuntary Turnover Due to a Reduction in Force," *Personnel Psychology* 47 (1994).

46. Overconscientiousness and critical attitudes: Dennis W. Organ and Andreas Lingl, "Personality, Satisfaction, and Organizational Citizenship Behavior," *The Journal of Social Psychology* 135 (1995).

47. Andrew S. Grove: Robert A. Burgelman, and Andrew S. Grove, "Strategic Dissonance," *California Management Review* 38, 2 (1996).

48. Reactions of top management to crises is like the stages of coping with catastrophe: These ideas are developed in Burgelman and Grove, "Strategic Dissonance."

49. The Schwinn saga: Judith Crown and Glenn Coleman, *The Rise and Fall of the Schwinn Bicycle Company, an American Institution* (New York: Henry Holt, 1996).

50. Managers and flexibility: Boyatzis, *The Competent Manager.*

51. Innovative solution at Levi Strauss: Stratford Sherman, "Levi's: As Ye Sew, So Shall Ye Reap," *Fortune,* May 12, 1997.

52. Internal constraints: Robert Sternberg (ed.), *Handbook of Human Intelligence* (Cambridge: Cambridge University Press, 1988).

53. Creativity killers: Teresa Amabile, "The Intrinsic Motivation Principle of Creativity," in Barry Staw and L. L. Cummings (eds.), *Research in Organizational Behavior,* vol. 10 (Greenwich, CT: JAI Press, 1988).

54. Gina Imperato, "Dirty Business, Bright Ideas," *Fast Company,* February/March 1997.

55. Factors that boost organizational creativity: Amabile 1988.

56. Innovators versus implementers in engineering R&D: E. B. Roberts and A. R. Fusfeld, "Staffing the Innovative Technology-Based Organization," *Sloan*

Management Review 22 (1981); C. M. Beath, "Supporting the Information Technology Champion," *MIS Quarterly* 15 (1991).

Chapter 6 / What Moves Us

1. The classic description of flow: Mihalyi Csikszentmihalyi, *Flow: The Psychology of Optimal Experience* (New York: Harper and Row, 1990).

2. The real rewards of work: based on a survey of 1,528 men and women who had been followed at five-year intervals or so through the course of their lives, into the 1990s. See Carole K. Holahan and Robert R. Sears, *The Gifted Group in Later Maturity* (Palo Alto, CA: Stanford University Press, 1995).

3. The brain in flow: Jean Hamilton et al., "Intrinsic Enjoyment and Boredom Coping Scales: Validation with Personality, Evoked Potential and Attention Measures," *Personality and Individual Differences* 5 (1984).

4. Flow at work and leisure: Judith LeFevre, "Flow and Quality of Experience During Work and Leisure," in Mihalyi Csikszentmihalyi and Isabella S. Csikszentmihalyi (eds.), *Optimal Experience: Psychological Studies of Flow in Consciousness* (Cambridge: Cambridge University Press, 1988).

5. Flow and outstanding performers: Robert E. Kelley, *How to Be a Star at Work* (Times Books, 1998).

6. Being fully present: William A. Kahn, "To Be Fully There: Psychological Presence at Work," *Human Relations* 45 (1992); William A. Kahn, "Psychological Conditions of Personal Engagement and Disengagement at Work," *Academy of Management Journal* 33 (1990).

7. The professor and the factory worker: Maria T. Allison and Margaret C. Duncan, "Women, Work and Flow," in Csikszentmihalyi and Csikszentmihalyi (eds.), *Optimal Experience.*

8. The neurochemistry of motivation undoubtedly entails many neurochemicals, since the brain is continually secreting larger or smaller amounts of the more than two hundred neurotransmitters. But the catecholamines have been most studied, and they figure prominently in the underlying brain chemistry of motivation. See, e.g., U. Lundberg, "Catecholamine and Cortisol Excretion Under Psychologically Different Laboratory Conditions," in J. Usdin, T. Kvetnanski, and D. Kopin (eds.), *Catecholamines and Stress: Recent Advances* (North Holland: Elsevier, 1980).

9. Eugenia Barton, the compassionate teacher: in Cary Cherniss, *Beyond Burnout* (New York: Routledge, 1995).

10. Affiliation: see Richard Boyatzis, *The Competent Manager: A Model for Effective Performance* (New York: John Wiley and Sons, 1982); Lyle M.

Spencer Jr. and Signe M. Spencer, *Competence at Work: Models for Superior Performance* (New York: John Wiley and Sons, 1993).

11. Managers low in affiliation: Spencer and Spencer, *Competence at Work.*

12. Managers and affiliation: Boyatzis, *The Competent Manager.*

13. In a series of studies in which underlying brain chemistry was assessed in people ranked high in various motives, David McClelland deduced that norepinephrine is involved when the need for power is aroused, while the need for affiliation—wanting to feel close and connected to people—seems associated with dopamine, a brain chemical involved in pleasure, among other moods (see David C. McClelland et al., "The Relationship of Affiliative Arousal to Dopamine Release," *Motivation and Emotion* 11 [1987]; David C. McClelland et al., "The Need for Power, Brain Norepinephrine Turnover, and Memory," *Motivation and Emotion* 9 [1985]). And the need to achieve seemed to involve, among other brain chemicals, a pituitary hormone, vasopressin (see David C. McClelland, "Achievement Motivation in Relation to Achievement Related Recall, Performance, and Urine Flow, a Marker Associated with Release of Vasopressin," *Motivation and Emotion* 19 [1995]). But such specific connections between motives and brain chemistry are highly speculative at this point.

14. Computers and emotion: see Roz Picard, *Affective Computing* (Cambridge, MA: MIT Press, 1998).

15. The amygdala and motivation: see James D. Duffy, "The Neural Substrates of Emotion," *Psychiatric Annals,* January 1997.

16. In an analysis of 286 studies from organizations in twenty-one countries, the achievement motive turned up as the single most frequent distinguishing competence among superior executives. Spencer and Spencer, *Competence at Work.*

17. In Gates's industry, software development, as in most other technical and professional specialties, the need to achieve distinguishes star performers from average more than any other competency. Spencer and Spencer, *Competence at Work.*

18. Qualities of the wealthiest: Michael Klepper and Robert Gunther, *The Wealthy 100: A Ranking of the Richest Americans, Past and Present* (New York: Carol Publishing Group, 1997).

19. The study of fifty-nine high-tech entrepreneurs: John B. Miner et al., "Role of Entrepreneurial Task Motivation in the Growth of Technologically Innovative Firms: Interpretations from Follow-up Data," *Journal of Applied Psychology* 79 (1994).

20. The enterprising workers at Donnelly: in Carl F. Frost, *Changing Forever: The Well-Kept Secret of America's Leading Companies* (East Lansing: Michigan State University Press, 1996).

21. Money as keeping score: Ann Graham Ehringer, *Make Up Your Mind* (Santa Monica, CA: Merritt Publishing, 1995).

22. Nathan Myhrvold: Ken Auletta, "Annals of Communication," *The New Yorker,* May 12, 1997.

23. The description of the concern for efficiency is based largely on Spencer and Spencer, *Competence at Work.*

24. The Herman Miller raise-the-plush weekend: Frost, *Changing Forever.*

25. Patricia Sueltz: quoted in *Fast Company,* October/November 1997.

26. Commitment to the organization and thriving under stress: C. S. Leong et al., "The Moderating Effect of Organizational Commitment on the Occupational Stress Outcome Relationship," *Human Relations,* October 1996.

27. Attachment makes good organizational citizens: see, for example, Arthur Brief and S. J. Motowidlo, "Prosocial Organizational Behaviors," *Academy of Management Review* 11 (1986).

28. Organizational support and loyalty: Robert Eisenberger et al., "Perceived Organizational Support and Employee Diligence, Commitment and Innovation," *Journal of Applied Psychology* 75 (1990).

29. The glory-sharing manager and the glory-seeking consultant: in Spencer and Spencer, *Competence at Work.*

30. The new shape of loyalty: Tom Peters, "The Brand Called You," *Fast Company,* August/September 1997.

31. Adam Werbach: "We Can Sit Here Bemoaning Beavis and Butthead or We Can Learn from Their Appeal," *Time,* June 27, 1997.

32. The enterprising shipping clerk: The tale is told by Spencer and Spencer, *Competence at Work.*

33. The PNC Bank computer savings: Kelley, *How to Be a Star at Work.*

34. The extended time horizon as a mark of success: Elliott Jacques, *Requisite Organization* (Arlington, VA: Cason Hall, 1989).

35. Initiative in government: Boyatzis, *The Competent Manager.*

36. Initiative in real estate sales: J. Michael Crant, "The Proactive Personality Scale and Objective Job Performance Among Real Estate Agents," *Journal of Applied Psychology* 80 (1995).

37. Deloitte & Touche Consulting competency model: in Richard H. Rosier (ed.), *The Competency Model Handbook,* vol. 3 (Boston: Linkage, 1996).

38. The hardworking salesman: cited in Spencer and Spencer, *Competence at Work.*

39. The whims of fate and difficulty in managers: Ferdinand A. Gul et al., "Locus of Control, Task Difficulty, and Their Interaction with Employees' Attitudes," *Psychological Reports* 75 (1994).

40. The tale of the too-brash vice president of marketing is told in Boyatzis, *The Competent Manager.*

41. Too-eager managers perform poorly: Boyatzis, *The Competent Manager.*

42. The case of the two executives refused a promotion is described in Salvatore E. Maddi and Suzanne C. Kobasa, *The Hardy Executive: Health Under Stress* (Homewood, IL: Dow Jones-Irwin, 1984).

43. The cases of Anne Busquet and Arthur Blank: Patricia Sellers, "So You Fail. Now Bounce Back," *Fortune,* May 1, 1995.

44. Martin Seligman's studies of optimism and pessimism among insurance sales agents are detailed in Peter Schulman, "Explanatory Style and Achievement in School and Work," in G. Buchanan and Martin Seligman (eds.), *Explanatory Style* (Hillsdale, NJ: Lawrence Erlbaum, 1995).

45. Superior managers: Boyatzis, *The Competent Manager;* Spencer and Spencer, *Competence at Work.*

46. Hope in human services: Spencer and Spencer, *Competence at Work.*

47. Hopefulness in caseworkers: Stuart Kirk and Gary Koeske, "The Fate of Optimism: A Longitudinal Study of Case Managers' Hopefulness and Subsequent Morale," *Research in Social Work Practice,* January 1995.

48. The utility of unrealistic optimism: Shelley Taylor and J. D. Brown, "Illusion and Well-being: A Social Psychological Perspective on Mental Health," *Psychological Bulletin* 183 (1988).

Chapter 7 / Social Radar

1. Empathy in couples: Robert W. Levenson and Anna M. Ruef, "Physiological Aspects of Emotional Knowledge and Rapport," in William Ickes (ed.), *Empathic Accuracy* (New York: Guilford Press, 1997).

2. The physiological mirroring found in married couples has a paradoxical wrinkle. In couples who get along the least well, there is a strong tendency for

physiological linkage during the viewing of the video of their disagreement: The spouse viewing the video gets upset along with the spouse being viewed. This amygdala tango does not help the marriage, however, because though spouses have high empathy for what the other is feeling, they do not act on that knowledge in a constructive way. Though they have a raw empathy with their partner, they lack full empathic accuracy, in that they are clueless about what caused those feelings, what to do about them to make things better, and how to keep them from recurring in the future. See Robert Levenson and Anna Ruef, "Emotional Knowledge and Rapport," in William Ickes (ed.), *Empathic Accuracy* (New York: Guilford Press, 1997).

3. The physiological linkage was strongest for the high-arousal negative emotions, like anger, fear, disgust, and contempt. When partners were in rapport with positive emotions, the empathic physiological stance was to have low heart rate, an indicator of an amygdala in equipoise rather than in attack mode.

4. The insensitivity effect increases to the extent one's own strong emotions differ from those of the person one is with. Two angry people can still resonate with each other, but not an angry person and a sad one. See Levenson and Ruef, "Emotional Knowledge and Rapport."

5. Tuning in to one's own feelings as basis for empathy: Richard Boyatzis and James Burrus, "Validation of a Competency Model for Alcohol Counselors in the U.S. Navy," McBer, Boston, 1977.

6. The silent synchrony: Elaine Hatfield et al., *Emotional Contagion* (New York: Cambridge University Press, 1994).

7. Seeing an emotional face evokes the corresponding feeling in us: the data is reviewed in Hatfield et al., *Emotional Contagion.*

8. Coordination leads to emotional attunement: Hatfield et al., *Emotional Contagion.*

9. Neurons in the amygdala automatically register the emotions in the people around us. Studies with primates show that they have amygdala neurons that fire only in response to specific emotional expressions, like a grimace of fear or a threatening baring of teeth. See Leslie A. Brothers in *Science News,* January 18, 1997; and her "A Biological Perspective on Empathy," *American Journal of Psychiatry* 146 (1989). People with damage to the amygdala fail to display or register emotional distress, whether anger or fear, and have trouble recognizing cues for happiness and sadness. Ross Buck and Benson Ginsburg, "Communicative Genes and the Evolution of Empathy," in William Ickes (ed.), *Empathic Accuracy* (New York: Guilford Press, 1997).

10. The temperamental designer: William A. Kahn, "Psychological Conditions of Personal Engagement and Disengagement at Work," *Academy of Management Journal* 33 (1990).

11. Empathic physicians: Howard Friedman and Robert DiMatteo, *Interpersonal Issues in Health Care* (New York: Academic Press, 1982).

12. Interruptions by physicians: H. B. Beckman and R. M. Frankel, "The Effect of Physician Behavior on the Collection of Data," *Annals of Internal Medicine* 101 (1984).

13. Doctors who are sued don't listen: Wendy Levinson et al., "Physician-Patient Communication: The Relationship with Malpractice Claims Among Primary Care Physicians and Surgeons," *Journal of the American Medical Association,* February 19, 1997.

14. Empathic design: Dorothy Leonard and Jeffrey F. Rayport, "Spark Innovation Through Empathic Design," *Harvard Business Review,* November/December 1997.

15. Product development and customer service: Spencer and Spencer, *Competence at Work.*

16. Listening: Anthony P. Carnevale et al., *Workplace Basics: The Skills Employers Want* (American Society for Training and Development, Arlington, VA, and U.S. Department of Labor, Washington, DC, 1989).

17. Empathy limits sales: R. B. Marks, *Personal Selling* (Boston: Allyn and Bacon, 1991).

18. Sales and empathy: Bruce K. Pilling and Sevo Eroglu, "An Empirical Examination of the Impact of Salesperson Empathy and Professionalism and Merchandise Salability on Retail Buyers' Evaluations," *Journal of Personal Selling and Sales Management,* Winter 1994.

19. Extroverted glad-handing does not make for better sales: see also Murray R. Barrick, Michael K. Mount, and Judy P. Strauss, "Conscientiousness and Performance of Sales Representatives: Test of the Mediating Effects of Goal Setting," *Journal of Applied Psychology* 78 (1993).

20. Machiavellians lack empathy, those who trust have it: Mark Davis and Linda Kraus, "Personality and Empathic Accuracy," in Ickes, *Empathic Accuracy.*

21. Sam's emotional tone deafness: Hatfield et al., *Emotional Contagion.*

22. Avoiding empathy to resist caring: Laura Shaw et al., "Empathy Avoidance: Forestalling Feeling for Another in Order to Escape the Motivational Consequences," *Journal of Personality and Social Psychology* 67 (1994).

23. Managers who care too much: see, e.g., Richard Boyatzis, *The Competent Manager: A Model for Effective Performance* (New York: John Wiley and Sons, 1982).

24. Empathy and the collective good: C. Daniel Batson et al., "Empathy and the Collective Good: Caring for One of the Others in a Social Dilemma," *Journal of Personality and Social Psychology* 68 (1995).

25. The powerful don't empathize: see, for example, Hatfield et al., *Emotional Contagion*.

26. The GE plant closing follow-up: Deborah Sholl Humphreys, "Decline as a Natural Resource for Development," presented at the annual meeting of the Academy of Management, 1987.

27. Developing others is the second most frequent managerial competence: Spencer and Spencer, *Competence at Work*.

28. Sales managers and developing others: Spencer and Spencer, *Competence at Work*.

29. Competence of counselors: Richard Boyatzis and James Burrus, "The Heart of Human Resource Development: Counseling Competencies," unpublished manuscript, 1995; also Boyatzis and Burrus, "Validation of a Competency Model."

30. Developing others—supervisors, managers, executives: Boyatzis, *The Competent Manager*.

31. Career coaching pays off: Christopher Orpen, "The Effect of Mentoring on Employees' Career Success," *Journal of Social Psychology* 135 (1995); David Laband and Bernard Lentz, "Workplace Mentoring in the Legal Profession," *Southern Economic Journal,* January 1995.

32. Coaching by top executives: David Peterson et al., "Management Coaching at Work: Current Practices in Fortune 250 Companies," presented at the annual conference of the American Psychological Association, Toronto, August 1996.

33. Teaching superiors: Spencer and Spencer, *Competence at Work*.

34. Silence damages self-confidence as much as negative feedback: Paulette A. McCarty, "Effects of Feedback on the Self-confidence of Men and Women," *Academy of Management Journal* 29 (1986).

35. The low-performing sailors: K. S. Crawford et al., "Pygmalion at Sea: Improving the Work Effectiveness of Low Performers," *Journal of Applied Behavioral Science* 16 (1980).

36. Socratic coaching: Mark Lepper et al., "Motivational Techniques of Expert Human Tutors," in S. P. Lajoie and S. J. Derry (eds.), *Computers as Cognitive Tools* (Hillsdale, NJ: Lawrence Erlbaum, 1993).

37. Too much coaching, too little managing: Boyatzis, *The Competent Manager.*

38. Sandoz Pharmaceuticals: in Richard H. Rosier (ed.), *The Competency Model Handbook,* vol. 2 (Boston: Linkage, 1995).

39. Empathy in successful sales: Donald McBane, "Empathy and the Salesperson: A Multidimensional Perspective," *Psychology and Marketing* 12 (1995).

40. The helpful manager: Spencer and Spencer, *Competence at Work.*

41. The tale of Nancy Cohen: Jennifer Steinhauer, "Whatever Happened to Service?" *The New York Times,* March 4, 1997.

42. Customer service orientation: for more details, see Spencer and Spencer, *Competence at Work.*

43. Yankelovich survey of customer satisfaction: reported in Steinhauer, "Whatever Happened to Service?"

44. Flaws in *The Bell Curve:* The book ignores data showing that the black-white difference found in IQ scores among Americans does not hold in Caribbean cultures, where blacks are not an oppressed group, and that in every society where there is a privileged class and an oppressed group the same spread in IQ scores is found as that between American blacks and whites, suggesting the effect is due to economic and social conditions, not race. The book also neglects to mention data showing that when members of an oppressed group migrate to a culture where they are not victims of oppression, the IQ difference disappears in a single generation. See Ulric Neisser (ed.), *The Rising Curve: Long-Term Gains in IQ* (Washington, DC: APA Press), 1998.

45. Stereotype threat: Claude M. Steele, "A Threat in the Air: How Stereotypes Shape Intellectual Identity and Performance," *American Psychologist,* June 1997.

46. Reasons women are prevented from advancing to corporate leadership: "Women in Corporate Leadership: Progress and Prospects," *Catalyst*, New York, 1996.

47. Workplace prejudice against women leaders: The research by Alice Eagly, at Northwestern University, was reported in *The American Psychological Association Monitor,* August 1997.

48. Women in math, engineering, and science: N. M. Hewitt and E. Seymour, "Factors Contributing to High Attrition Rates Among Science and Engineering Undergraduate Majors," report to the Alfred P. Sloan Foundation, 1991.

49. Managers: Boyatzis, *The Competent Manager.*

50. People have more difficulty reading a person's emotions when that person is from a group they are not so familiar with. For example, when people from other nations try to read emotions from Americans on the PONS, they do more poorly the more dissimilar their own culture is from that of the United States: Robert Rosenthal, Judith Hall, et al., *Sensitivity to Nonverbal Communications: The PONS Test* (Baltimore: Johns Hopkins University Press, 1979).

51. David A. Thomas and Robin J. Ely, "Making Differences Matter: A New Paradigm for Managing Diversity," *Harvard Business Review,* September/October 1996.

52. Thomas and Ely, "Making Differences Matter."

53. Thomas and Ely, "Making Differences Matter."

54. The politically aware diplomat is described by David McClelland in his introduction to Spencer and Spencer, *Competence at Work.*

55. Key to the sale: Spencer and Spencer, *Competence at Work.*

56. Objective perception in superior managers and executives: Boyatzis, *The Competent Manager.*

57. The oil executive and the silent Chinese group: told in Richard Rosier, *The Competency Model Handbook,* vol. 3.

Chapter 8 / The Arts of Influence

1. Transmission of mood over two silent minutes: Howard Friedman and Ronald Riggio, "Effect of Individual Differences in Nonverbal Expressiveness on Transmission of Emotion," *Journal of Nonverbal Behavior* 6 (1981).

2. Sigal Barsade. "The ripple effect: emotional contagion in groups." Working paper, Yale School of Management, 1998; Sigal Barsade and Donald E. Gibson, "Group emotion: A view from the top and bottom," in D. Gruenfeld et al. (eds.) *Research on Managing Groups and Teams* (Greenwich, CT: JAI Press, in press, 1998).

3. Smiling the most contagious facial expression, and simply smiling primes happiness: Robert Levenson and Anna Ruef, "Emotional Knowledge and Rapport," in William Ickes (ed.), *Empathic Accuracy* (New York: Guilford Press, 1997).

4. Pathway of emotional transmission: Hatfield et al., 1994, op. cit.

5. Emotional adeptness and impact: Howard Friedman et al., "Understanding and Assessing Non-verbal Expressiveness: The Affective Communication Test," *Journal of Nonverbal Behavior* 6 (1981).

6. The rep who would not translate: Cited in Richard H. Rosier (ed.), *The Competency Model Handbook,* vol. 3 (Boston: Linkage, 1996).

7. Deloitte & Touche competency model for top-performing management consultants: In Rosier (ed.), *The Competency Model Handbook,* vol. 3.

8. Impact on supervisors, managers, and executives: Richard Boyatzis, *The Competent Manager: A Model for Effective Performance* (New York: John Wiley and Sons, 1982).

9. Quality services: Boyatzis, *The Competent Manager.*

10. The dramatic service call: Lyle M. Spencer Jr. and Signe M. Spencer, *Competence at Work: Models for Superior Performance* (New York: John Wiley and Sons, 1993).

11. The oil executive and the leisurely cup of coffee: cited in Rosier (ed.), *The Competency Model Handbook,* vol. 3.

12. Rapport in sales: Spencer and Spencer, *Competence at Work.*

13. Use local leaders: Sander Larkin, reply in *Harvard Business Review,* September-October 1996.

14. When strategic decisions are ignored: Paul C. Nutt, professor of management, Ohio State University, reported in *Fast Company*, October/November, 1997.

15. Power at the expense of others is a negative: Spencer and Spencer, *Competence at Work.*

16. Jerry Kalov's open phone line: Michelle Conlin, "The Truth," *Forbes,* February 10, 1997.

17. Poor communications: *Newsweek,* August 12, 1996.

18. Listening and effective communication: John Haas and Christa Arnold, "An Examination of the Role of Listening in Judgments of Communication Competence in Co-workers," *The Journal of Business Communication,* April 1995.

19. Self-regulation and communication: Walter V. Clarke Associates, Pittsburgh, April 1997.

20. The virtues of being an emotional clean slate for social interaction: see Ralph Eber et al., "On Being Cool and Collected: Mood Regulation in Anticipation of Social Interaction," *Journal of Personality and Social Psychology* 70, (1996).

21. "Away": Goffman cited as the primary example of someone who is away people with mental illness, who display their private moods in public places. Irving Goffman, *Behavior in Public Places* (New York: Free Press, 1963).

22. The universal appreciation of composure: see S. M. Lyman and M. B. Scott, "Coolness in Everyday Life," in S. M. Lyman and M. B. Scott (eds.), *The Sociology of the Absurd* (Pacific Palisades, CA: Goodyear, 1968).

23. Effective communicators are composed: "Activity Vector Analysis: Some applications to the concepts of emotional intelligence," Walter V. Clarke Associates, Pittsburgh, June 1996.

24. Extroversion not an asset in all settings: Greg L. Stewart and Kenneth P. Carson, "Personality Dimensions and Domains of Service Performance: A Field Investigation," *Journal of Business and Psychology* 9 (1995).

25. Charlene Barshefsky in negotiation: Elsa Walsh, "The Negotiator," *The New Yorker,* March 18, 1996.

26. Negotiation as cooperation: Herbert Kelman, "Negotiation as Interactive Problem-solving," *International Negotiation* 1 (1996).

27. Vendor-retailer relations and negotiation style: Shankar Ganesan, "Negotiation Strategies and the Nature of Channel Relationships," *Journal of Marketing Research,* May 1993.

28. The confrontation in Harlem: Linda Lantieri and Janet Patti, *Waging Peace in Our Schools* (Boston: Beacon Press, 1996).

29. The twin tales of Ronald W. Allen and Gerald Grinstein: Martha Brannigan and Joseph B. White, "Why Delta Air Lines Decided It Was Time for CEO to Take Off," *Wall Street Journal,* May 30–31, 1997; Phyllis Berman and Roula Khalaf, "Sweet-talking the Board," *Forbes,* March 15, 1993.

30. Lou Gerstner: quoted in Stephen Lohr, "On the Road with Chairman Lou," *New York Times,* June 26, 1994.

31. The power of Ronald Reagan's smile: G. J. McHugo et al., "Emotional Reactions to a Political Leader's Expressive Displays," *Journal of Personality and Social Psychology* 49 (1985). There was a downside to Reagan's emotional intelligence capabilities, as he displayed a certain lack of self-awareness, if not outright self-deception. At times he seems not to have known the difference between films he had seen or stories he heard and the actual facts. Reagan once brought tears to the eyes of Yitzhak Shamir, then prime minister of Israel, with a story about his days with the U.S. Signal Corps recording the atrocities of the German death camps at the end of World War II. The problem: Reagan spent the entire war in Hollywood recruiting for the army's film units. He had, however, seen footage from the liberated camps and, apparently, convinced himself he'd been there. See Michael Korda, "Prompting the President," *The New Yorker,* October 6, 1997.

32. Positive leader, positive group mood: J. M. George and K. Bettenhausen, "Understanding Prosocial Behavior, Sales Performance, and Turnover: A Group Level Analysis in a Service Context," *Journal of Applied Psychology* 75 (1990).

33. Expressiveness: Howard S. Friedman et al., "Understanding and Assessing Non-verbal Expressiveness: The Affective Communication Test," *Journal of Nonverbal Behavior* 6 (1981).

34. Sincerity and charisma: Patricia Wasielewski, "The Emotional Basis of Charisma," *Symbolic Interaction* 8 (1985).

35. In my (unweighted) analysis of leadership competence models from organizations around the world, the proportion of emotional intelligence-based competencies listed to cognitive abilities and expertise was about 80 percent. But in many corporate competence models for leadership, 100 percent of the ingredients listed derive from emotional intelligence. A weighted analysis, done by Hay/McBer, puts the value of emotional competence in contributing to outstanding leadership at just below 90 percent. See Appendix 2.

36. Cross-cultural comparison of CEO competencies: Lyle Spencer Jr. et al., *Competency Assessment Methods: History and State of the Art* (Boston: Hay/McBer, 1997). CEOs studied were in Japan, China, the Philippines, Canada, the United States, Mexico, Venezuela, the United Kingdom, Belgium, France, Germany, Spain, and Italy. This recipe for excellence in leadership seems roughly the same worldwide; differences from region to region are in nuances of how the competencies play out in a given culture.

37. Robert E. Kaplan, *Beyond Ambition: How Driven Managers Can Lead Better and Live Better* (San Francisco: Jossey-Bass, 1991).

38. Commands in the U.S. Navy: Wallace Bachman, "Nice Guys Finish First: A SYMLOG Analysis of U.S. Naval Commands," in Richard Brian Polley et al. (eds.), *The SYMLOG Practitioner: Applications of Small Group Research* (New York: Praeger, 1988).

39. Navy command emotional style: Polley et al. (eds.), *The SYMLOG Practitioner.*

40. The manager who put his foot down: Spencer and Spencer, *Competence at Work.*

41. Self-control and managers: David C. McClelland and Richard Boyatzis, "The Leadership Motive Profile and Long-term Success in Management," *Journal of Applied Psychology* 67 (1982).

42. Self-control and organizational goals: Boyatzis, *The Competent Manager.*

43. John Patrick's epiphany at IBM: the tale is told in Eric Ransdell, "IBM's Grassroots Revival," *Fast Company,* October/November 1997.

44. Self-confidence and flourishing in change: Jane Howell and Bruce Avolio, "Transformational Leadership, Transactional Leadership, Locus of Control, and Support for Innovation: Key Predictors of Consolidated-Business-Unit Performance," *Journal of Applied Psychology* 78 (1993).

45. Transformational leadership: M. B. Bass, *Bass and Stodgill's Handbook of Leadership: Theory, Research and Applications,* 3rd ed. (New York: Free Press, 1990).

46. Transformational leadership: see the discussion in Blake E. Ashforth and Ronald H. Humphreys, "Emotion in the Workplace: An Appraisal," *Human Relations* 48 (1995).

47. Transformational leadership marshals greater efforts: R. J. House et al., "Charismatic and Non-charismatic Leaders: Differences in Behavior and Effectiveness," in J. A. Conger et al. (eds.), *Charismatic Leadership: The Elusive Factor in Organizational Effectiveness* (San Francisco: Jossey-Bass, 1988).

48. Test of transformational leadership at a Canadian financial services company: Howell and Avolio, "Transformational Leadership."

49. Management versus leadership: John Kotter, "What Leaders Really Do," *Harvard Business Review,* May/June 1990.

Chapter 9 / Collaboration, Teams, and the Group IQ

1. The 1982 meeting: John Markoff, "The Soul of a New Economy," *New York Times,* December 29, 1997.

2. John Doerr: interviewed by Michael S. Malone, "John Doerr's Startup Manual," *Fast Company,* February/March 1997.

3. The need for cooperation as a force in shaping the brain in evolution was perhaps first proposed by Alison Jolly in "Lemur Social Behaviour and Primate Intelligence," *Science* 153 (1966).

4. The main theorist here is David S. Wilson, "Incorporating Group Selection into the Adaptationist Program: A Case Study Involving Human Decision-making," in J. Simpson and D. Kendrick (eds.), *Evolutionary Social Psychology* (Hillsdale, NJ: Lawrence Erlbaum, 1997). While some evolutionary psychologists focus on the human ability to deceive others as a source of competitive advantage, they slight the larger benefits accrued to the survival of a group by the more widespread acts of cooperation and mutual help that are essential to the group's very survival.

5. The evolutionary advantage of cooperation in human evolution can be glimpsed among chimpanzee bands; Jane Goodall reports those females who have particularly strong cooperative alliances with other females have a higher rate of infant survival, faster maturing daughters, and produce offspring most rapidly. Anne Pusey, Jennifer Williams, and Jane Goodall, "The Influence of Dominance Rank on Reproductive Success of Female Chimpanzees," *Science,* August 8, 1997.

6. Cooperation and a radar for selfishness: described in Bruce Bower, "Return of the Group," *Science News,* November 18, 1995.

7. The human brain evolved to handle the challenge of group life: The main proponent of this theory is Denise Cummins, an evolutionary psychologist, and author of *Human Reasoning: An Evolutionary Perspective* (Cambridge, MA: Bradford/MIT Press, 1997).

8. Neocortex is larger the bigger the group: T. Sawaguchi and H. Kudo, "Neocortical Development and Social Structures in Primates," *Primates* 31 (1990).

9. Social pressures drove brain evolution: see Cummins, *Human Reasoning.*

10. What percent of knowledge is stored in your own mind?: Robert E. Kelley, *How to Be a Star at Work* (New York: Times Books, 1998).

11. Intellect not in my skin: Howard Gardner, *Frames of Mind* (New York: Basic Books, 1993).

12. Groups outscore individuals: G. W. Hill, "Group Versus Individual Performance: Are N+1 Heads Better Than One?" *Psychological Bulletin* 91 (1982).

13. Collective memory in teams: Roger Dixon, *Interactive Minds* (New York: Cambridge University Press, 1996).

14. Simulated management teams: R. Meredith Belbin, *Management Teams: Why They Succeed or Fail* (London: Halstead Press, 1982); R. Meredith Belbin, *Team Roles at Work* (London: Butterworth-Heinemann, 1996).

15. The concept of group IQ was first developed in Wendy M. Williams and Robert J. Sternberg, "Group Intelligence: Why Some Groups Are Better Than Others," *Intelligence* 12 (1988). They define group intelligence as "the functional intelligence of a group of people working as a unit."

16. The classic study: Williams and Sternberg, "Group Intelligence."

17. Critical elements for effectiveness: Michael A. Campion et al., "Relations Between Work Team Characteristics and Effectiveness: A Replication and Extension," *Personnel Psychology* 49 (1996).

18. Jeffrey Katzenberg, as observed by Nathan Myhrvold of Microsoft, and described in Ken Auletta, "The Microsoft Provocateur," *The New Yorker,* May 1997.

19. Knowledge workers and networks: Kelley, *How to Be a Star at Work.*

20. Time saved through good networks: Kelley, *How to Be a Star at Work.*

21. The power of the alliance between high-tech start-ups and venture capitalists: "Venture Capitalists," *The Economist,* January 25, 1997.

22. People on whom performance depends: quoted in John Kotter, *Power in Management* (New York: AMACOM, 1979).

23. Superior managers effective at building bonds: Richard Boyatzis, *The Competent Manager: A Model for Effective Performance* (New York: John Wiley and Sons, 1982); Robert E. Kaplan, *Beyond Ambition: How Driven Managers Can Lead Better and Live Better* (San Francisco: Jossey-Bass, 1991).

24. Carefully chosen favors: Kelley, *How to Be a Star at Work.*

25. Marks and Spencer and other retailers are forging bonds of trust with suppliers: Nirmalya Kumar, "The Power of Trust in Manufacturer-Retailer Relationships," *Harvard Business Review,* November/December 1996.

26. Kraft Foods: Ken Partch, "Partnering: A Win-Win Proposition . . . or the Latest Hula Hoop in Marketing?" *Supermarket Business,* May 1991.

27. Kumar, "The Power of Trust."

28. The working relationship as a "couple": James Krantz, "The Managerial Couple: Superior-Subordinate Relationships as a Unit of Analysis," *Human Resource Management,* Summer 1989.

29. Projective identification: The best work on this insidious process is the classic by Thomas Ogden, *Projective Identification and Psychotherapeutic Technique* (New York: Jason Aronson, 1991).

30. Owens Corning and SAP: "Owens Corning: Back from the Dead," *Fortune,* May 26, 1997.

31. Self-managed work teams: cited in Lawler et al., *Employee Involvement and Total Quality Management: Practices and Results in Fortune 1,000 Companies* (San Francisco: Jossey-Bass, 1992).

32. Advantages of self-managed work teams: Richard Moreland et al., "Training People to Work in Groups," in R. S. Tinsdale (ed.), *Applications of Theory and Research on Groups to Social Issues* (New York: Plenum, 1997).

33. The value of a top team in a polyester fiber plant was 31 million pounds per year, while average teams produced 24 million pounds per year. The value of

the fiber from average teams was $33.6 million, that from superior teams $43.4 million. The total salary for a team was just $270,000. Source: Lyle Spencer Jr., presentation at International Family Business Programs Association, Northampton, MA, July 1997.

34. Team achievement profile: Lyle Spencer Jr. et al., *Competency Assessment Methods: History and State of the Art* (Boston: Hay/McBer, 1997).

35. Jean Brittain Leslie and Ellen Van Velsor, "A Look at Derailment Today: North America and Europe," Center for Creative Leadership, Greensboro, NC, 1996.

36. Team leadership most frequent competence in managers: Lyle M. Spencer Jr. and Signe M. Spencer, *Competence at Work: Models for Superior Performance* (New York: John Wiley and Sons, 1993).

37. The team studies were presented by Lyle Spencer Jr. and Charles Morrow at the International Conference on Competency-based Tools and Applications to Drive Organizational Performance, London, October 1997.

38. There were different ways teams could translate their competencies into team effectiveness; not every star team excelled in every one. One winning combination, for example, combined the drive to improve with a strong interpersonal focus, ensuring the team was cohesive and harmonious in working together. Another way to excel combined the drive to improve with an external outlook, emphasizing serving the needs of and building bonds with other parts of the company.

39. Strategic decision making in management teams: Allen C. Amason, "Distinguishing the Effects of Functional and Dysfunctional Conflict in Strategic Decision Making: Resolving a Paradox for Top Management Teams," *Academy of Management Journal* 39 (1996).

40. The Data General engineering team: Tracy Kidder, *The Soul of a New Machine* (Boston: Little, Brown, 1981).

41. The analysis of the Data General team: Lee Bolman and Terrence E. Deal, "What Makes a Team Work?" *Organizational Dynamics,* vol. 23, 1992.

42. The pharmaceutical R&D teams: Richard E. Boyatzis et al., "Entrepreneurial Innovation in Pharmaceutical Research and Development," *Human Resource Planning* 15 (1990).

43. The de facto leader: See Wilson, "Incorporating Group Selection."

44. Team leaders need to hold back: see, for example, L. E. Anderson and W. K. Balzer, "The Effects of Timing of Leaders' Opinions on Problem-solving Groups: A Field Experiment," *Group and Organizational Studies* 16 (1991).

45. Self-managing work teams: Susan G. Cohen et al., "A Predictive Model of Self-managing Work Team Effectiveness," *Human Relations* 49 (1996).

46. A meta-analysis of studies with hundreds of self-managing teams found that those without supervisors performed better than those that had supervisors: R. I. Beekun, "Assessing the Effectiveness of Sociotechnical Interventions: Antidote or Fad?" *Human Relations* 47 (1989).

47. The disastrous cross-functional meeting: Daniel R. Denison et al., "From Chimneys to Cross-functional Teams: Developing and Validating a Diagnostic Model," *Academy of Management Journal* 39 (1996).

48. The signs of group flow are seen in what Warren Bennis calls "Great Groups" in his landmark study of a half dozen remarkable teams. These groups display the hallmarks of people in a collective state of flow. That figures; flow is the state exhibited by people who are outdoing themselves, and so emerges with truly outstanding groups. Warren Bennis and Patricia Ward Biederman, *Organizing Genius: The Secrets of Creative Collaboration* (Reading, MA: Addison-Wesley, 1997).

49. Feynman quoted in Bennis and Biederman.

50. "I work to win.": Kidder, *The Soul of a New Machine.*

Chapter 10 / The Billion-Dollar Mistake

1. The case study of emotional competence at American Express was made available to me by Kate Cannon, director of leadership development at American Express Financial Advisors.

2. Brain changes at Promega were measured by the state-of-the-art method, a functional MRI before and after training. Those who went through the training were compared to a randomized control group of peers who had not yet had the training. The data was collected by Richard Davidson, director of the Laboratory for Affective Neuroscience at the University of Wisconsin. The mindfulness training was given by Jon Kabat-Zinn, director of the Stress and Relaxation Program at the University of Massachusetts Medical School in Worcester.

3. Training in empathy: see, for example, H. J. Smith et al., "Just a Hunch: Accuracy and Awareness in Person Perception," *Journal of Nonverbal Behavior* 15 (1991). While women on average do better than men on some tests of empathy, what gender differences exist can be erased by training men to be as accurate in reading emotions as women; see William Ickes (ed.), *Empathic Accuracy* (New York: Guilford Press, 1997).

4. Empathy training carryover: William Ickes et al., "Studying empathic accuracy in a clinically relevant context," in Ickes (ed.), *Empathic Accuracy.*

5. Adults are better at emotional intelligence than adolescents: John D. Mayer, David R. Caruso, and Peter Salovey, "Emotional Intelligence Meets Traditional Standards for an Intelligence," unpublished manuscript, 1997.

6. Emotional intelligence increases with age: Reuven Bar-On, *Bar-On Emotional Quotient Inventory: Technical Manual* (Toronto: Multi-Health Systems, 1997).

7. Most improvement in those over twenty-five: Ronald Ballou et al., "Fellowship in Lifelong Learning: An Executive Development Program for Advanced Professionals," unpublished manuscript, Weatherhead School of Management, 1997.

8. The case of Henry and Lai: Kelley, *How to Be a Star at Work* (Times Books, 1998).

9. Little correlation between knowledge of competence and on-the-job behavior: Bruce Tracey et al., "Applying Trained Skills on the Job: The Importance of the Work Environment," *Journal of Applied Psychology* 80 (1995). A more general review of correlations between what people learn in training programs and what they actually take back with them to daily life found that more than half of reported correlations between learning and behavior were disappointingly low—that is, it is common for people not to execute what they have learned. See G. M. Alliger and E. A. Janak, "Kirkpatrick's Levels of Training Criteria: Thirty Years Later," *Personnel Psychology* 42 (1989).

10. Consider all training the same: Scott I. Tannenbaum and Gary Yukl, "Training and Development in Work Organizations," *Annual Review of Psychology* 43 (1992).

11. Habits strengthen neural pathways: Gerald Edelman, *Neural Darwinism: The Theory of Neuronal Group Selection* (New York: Basic Books, 1987).

12. Learning principles based on trivial experiments: Tannenbaum and Yukl, "Training and Development."

13. The enlightened CEO's demand: Charley C. Morrow et al., "An Investigation of the Effect and Economic Utility of Corporate-wide Training," *Personnel Psychology* 50 (1997).

14. The gloomy estimate of transfer of skills to the job in corporate trainings: Timothy T. Baldwin and J. Kevin Ford, "Transfer of Training," *Personnel Psychology,* 41 (1988).

15. Two thirds of companies did not evaluate the impact of emotional competence training: Benchmarking Forum member-to-member survey results, American Society for Training and Development, Alexandria, Virginia, October 1997.

16. The ASTD survey: Laurie J. Bassi et al., "The Top Ten Trends," *Training,* November 1996.

17. The state-of-the-art training evaluation: see Morrow et al., "An Investigation of the Effect."

18. Two programs for managers were on cognitive or technical topics, not emotional competence.

19. While the pharmaceutical company evaluation cost was a trivial part of the total training budget, it did not evaluate all the trainings given there. However, as a pilot effort it established methods for ongoing evaluation that presumably could be adopted as a routine practice at a much lower cost.

20. The main effect of corporate training seminars is to increase self-confidence: Richard Boyatzis, "Consequences and Rejuvenation of Competency-based Human Resource and Organization Development," *Research in Organizational Change and Development* 9, 1993.

21. The current review of training and development: Robert Dipboye, "Organizational Barriers to Implementing a Rational Model of Training," in M. A. Quinones and A. Ehrenstein (eds.), *Training for a Rapidly Changing Workforce: Applications of Psychological Research* (Washington, DC: American Psychological Association, 1996).

22. Survey of Fortune 500 companies: William H. Clegg, "Management Training Evaluation: An Update," *Training and Development Journal,* February 1987.

23. The Consortium for Research on Emotional Intelligence in Organizations can be reached through my cochair, Dr. Cary Cherniss, in the Graduate School of Applied and Professional Psychology, Rutgers University, Piscataway, New Jersey 08855–0819.

24. The final report from the Consortium can be obtained from Dr. Cary Cherniss (see note 23), or the website: Http://www.EIConsortium.org

25. The Weatherhead initiative and details of the Managerial Assessment and Development course are detailed in Richard Boyatzis et al., *Innovation in Professional Education: Steps on a Journey from Teaching to Learning* (San Francisco: Jossey-Bass, 1995).

26. The competencies include self-confidence, initiative, flexibility, self-control, empathy, persuasiveness, networking, negotiating, team leadership, and developing others, among others. Analytic and technical skills are also included.

27. Assessments: Boyatzis et al., *Innovation in Professional Education.*

28. Three-year follow-up: Ronald Ballou et al., "Fellowship in Lifelong Learning"; Richard Boyatzis and Robert Wright, "Competency Development in Graduate Education: A Longitudinal Perspective," presented at First World Conference on Self-Directed Learning, Boston, September 1997.

29. Details of the JOBS program: J. Curran, *A Manual for Teaching People Successful Job Search Strategies* (Ann Arbor: Michigan Prevention Research Center, Institute for Social Research, University of Michigan, 1992).

30. The toll of the job search: Richard H. Price, "Psychosocial Impact of Job Loss on Individuals and Families," *Current Directions in Psychological Science* 1 (1992).

31. JOBS program: Robert Caplan, A. D. Vinokur, and Robert Price, "Field Experiments in Prevention-focused Coping," in George Albee and Thomas Gullotta (eds.), *Primary Prevention Works* (Thousand Oaks, CA: Sage, 1997).

Chapter 11 / Best Practices

1. Strategic planning is a purely cognitive task: see, for example, Chris Argyris and S. A. Schon, *Theory in Practice: Increasing Professional Effectiveness* (San Francisco: Jossey-Bass, 1974).

2. Strategic planners need competence beyond intellect: David C. McClelland, "Assessing Competencies Associated with Executive Success Through Behavioral Interviews," unpublished manuscript, 1996.

3. State-of-the-art methodology: the methods are detailed in several sources, e.g., Lyle M. Spencer Jr. and Signe M. Spencer, *Competence at Work: Models for Superior Performance* (New York: John Wiley and Sons, 1993).

4. Assessing competence models: see, for example, Spencer and Spencer, *Competence at Work;* David Dubois, *Competency-Based Performance Improvement: A Strategy for Organizational Change* (Amherst, MA: HRD Press, 1993).

5. Flight attendant competence study: Spencer and Spencer, *Competence at Work.*

6. Empathic accuracy for people very different from ourselves, like any other emotional competence, can be learned. We included training in reading feelings from faces of people from cultures that flight attendants were unfamiliar with. We also adapted the way empathy was approached to fit the cross-cultural realities of the job. The result: six months later, the attendants at a large overseas hub who had had the worst record of passenger complaints now had none.

7. People are poor evaluators of their own level of empathy: Mark Davis and Linda Kraus, "Personality and Accurate Empathy," in William Ickes (ed.), *Empathic Accuracy* (New York: Guilford Press, 1997).

8. One measure of the full spectrum of emotional intelligence capabilities I've co-developed is the Emotional Competence Inventory—360 (ECI-360), available from Emotional Intelligence Services, Sudbury, MA, 01776, e-mail: EISGlobal@AOL.com.

9. The Southwest health plan: in Mark R. Edwards and Ann J. Ewen, *360° Feedback* (New York, AMACOM, 1996).

10. Using 360-degree feedback as an emotional bludgeon: see, for example, "Performance Review Input by Peers Catches on at More Firms," *Los Angeles Times,* April 17, 1997.

11. The 20 percent rule is based on data from a wide range of behavior change programs, but its conclusion seems apt for development and training in organizations. See James O. Prochaska et al., *Changing for Good* (New York: Avon, 1994).

12. Questions to gauge readiness: In Prochaska et al., *Changing for Good.*

13. Motivation: Miguel Quinones, "Contextual Influences on Training Effectiveness," in M. A. Quinones and A. Ehrenstein (eds.), *Training for a Rapidly Changing Workforce: Applications of Psychological Research* (Washington, DC: American Psychological Association, 1996).

14. Windows of opportunity: Ellen Van Velsor and Christopher Musselwhite, "The Timing of Training, Learning, and Transfer," *Training and Development Journal,* August 1986.

15. Motivation and effectiveness of training: see, for example, Miguel Quinones, "Pretraining Context Effects: Training Assignment as Feedback," *Journal of Applied Psychology* 80 (1995).

16. Adapting training to the individual: see, for example, Scott I. Tannenbaum and Gary Yukl, "Training and Development in Work Organizations," *Annual Review of Psychology* 43 (1992).

17. Boyatzis: Richard Boyatzis et al., *Innovation in Professional Education: Steps on a Journey from Teaching to Learning* (San Francisco: Jossey-Bass, 1995).

18. Break large goals into smaller goals: C. R. Snyder, *The Psychology of Hope* (New York: Free Press, 1993).

19. Keep hopes high: Snyder, *The Psychology of Hope.*

20. Possible selves: Hazel Markus and Peter Nurius, "Possible Selves," *American Psychologist* 41 (1989).

21. The basic principles of relapse prevention are in Alan Marlatt and Judith Gordon (eds.), *Relapse Prevention* (New York: Guilford Press, 1985). The adaptation for organizational training and development is described in Robert D. Marx, "Relapse Prevention for Managerial Training: A Model for Maintenance of Behavior Change," *Academy of Management Review* 7 (1982) and Robert D. Marx, "Improving Management Development Through Relapse Prevention Strategies," *Journal of Management Development* 5 (1993).

22. Positive feedback enhances self-confidence and transfer of skills to job: Quinones, "Contextual Influences on Training Effectiveness."

23. Practice better when extended through time: F. N. Dempster, "The Spacing Effect: A Case Study in the Failure to Apply the Results of Psychological Research," *American Psychologist* 43 (1990).

24. Power of practice: Lyle Spencer and Charley Morrow did the analysis of data, reported in Lyle Spencer, "Competency Assessment Methods: what works; assessment development and measurement" (Hay/McBer, 1997).

25. Overlearning: See, for example, Timothy T. Baldwin and J. Kevin Ford, "Transfer of Training," *Personnel Psychology* 41 (1988).

26. Much of the research on the benefits of longer periods of effort in behavior change has been done by Kenneth Howard, a psychologist at Northwestern University. See, for example, Kenneth Howard et al., "The Dose-Effect Relationship in Psychotherapy," *American Psychologist* 41 (1986); Kenneth Howard et al., "Evaluation of Psychotherapy," *American Psychologist* 51 (1996).

27. Kathy E. Kram, "A Relational Approach to Career Development," in Douglas T. Hall and Associates, *The Career Is Dead—Long Live the Career* (San Francisco: Jossey-Bass, 1996).

28. Judith Jordan et al. (eds.), *Women's Growth in Connections* (New York: Guilford Press, 1991). As the title suggests, the relational mode of mutual learning comes more readily to women than men (at least in the United States).

29. Buddy systems: see, for example, R. K. Fleming and B. Sulzer-Azaroff, "Peer Management: Effects on Staff Teaching Performance," presented at the Fifteenth Annual Convention of the Association for Behavioral Analysis, Nashville, Tennessee, 1990. Cited in Tannenbaum and Yukl, "Training and Development."

30. Models: there is a rich documentation of the power of positive models in behavior change, dating from Albert Bandura's pioneering work. See, for example, Albert Bandura, "Psychotherapy Based on Modeling Principles" in

A. E. Bergin and S. L. Garfield (eds.), *Handbook of Psychotherapy and Behavior Change: An Empirical Analysis* (New York: John Wiley and Sons, 1971).

31. Imitation focuses on high-status people: see, for example, H. M. Weiss, "Subordinate Imitation of Supervisor Behavior: The Role of Modeling in Organizational Socialization," *Organizational Behavior and Human Performance* 19 (1977).

32. Taking on bad habits of the high-status person: Charles C. Manz and Henry P. Sims, "Beyond Imitation: Complex Behavioral and Affective Linkages Resulting from Exposure to Leadership Training Models," *Journal of Applied Psychology* 71 (1986).

33. The callous and compassionate aides: cited in Cary Cherniss, *Beyond Burnout* (New York: Routledge, 1995).

34. Psychological safety: David Kolb and Richard Boyatzis, "Goal Setting and Self-directed Behavior Change," *Human Relations* 23, 1970.

35. Supportive climate determines transfer: see, for example, Van Velsor and Musselwhite, "The Timing of Training."

36. Banker's Trust New York: reported in *Business Week,* October 20, 1997.

37. Survey of training evaluation in Fortune 500 companies: William H. Clegg, "Management Training Evaluation: An Update," *Training and Development Journal,* February 1987.

38. Liking does not imply learning: Tannenbaum and Yukl, "Training and Development."

39. The Weatherhead follow-up is under the direction of Richard Boyatzis.

Chapter 12 / Taking the Organizational Pulse

1. Analysis of organizational assessment surveys: Mary York, U.S. Office of Personnel Management, unpublished report, November 1997. Among the assessment instruments and models for high-performing organizations included in this analysis: S. M. Arad and M. A. Hanson, "High Performance Workplaces: A Construct Definition." Presented at the Twelfth Annual Conference of the Society for Industrial and Organization Psychology, St. Louis, MO; David Campbell, *The Campbell Organizational Survey: For Surveying Employee Attitudes about Organizational Issues.* National Computer Systems, 1988; James Collins and J. I. Porras, *Built to Last: Successful Habits for Visionary Companies.* (New York: HarperCollins Publishers, 1994); D. R. Denison, *Organizational Dynamics: Bring Corporate Culture to the Bottom Line.* (New York: American Management Association,

1984); D. R. Denison and A. K. Mishra, "Toward a Theory of Organizational Culture and Effectiveness," Organization Science, vol. 6 (2), 1995; D. R. Denison and W. S. Neale, *DENISON: Organizational Culture Survey, Linking Organizational Culture to the Bottom Line.* AVAIT, 1994; Jac Fitz-enz, *The 8 Practices of Exceptional Companies: How Great Organizations Make the Most of Their Human Assets*, (New York: American Management Association, 1997). D. J. Kravetz, *The Human Resource Revolution: Implementing Progressive Management Practices for Bottom-Line Success.* (San Francisco: Jossey-Bass Publishers, 1988); United States Office of Personnel Management, *Building a Model Agency: Changing OPM's Culture to Support Workplace Partnership and Diversity Initiatives, Organizational Assessment Survey,* (Washington, DC: US Office of Personnel Management, 1995).

2. Gaps: in the preliminary analysis, only one—or, more often, none—of the lists of key dimensions for organizational effectiveness matched on emotional competence at the collective level.

3. See Chris Argyris, "Interpersonal Barriers to Decision Making," *Harvard Business Review,* March/April 1966.

4. Volvo and the workers' vacations: Carl F. Frost, *Changing Forever: The Well-Kept Secret of America's Leading Companies* (East Lansing: Michigan State University Press, 1996).

5. Bearing bad news: William Jennings, "A Corporate Conscience Must Start at the Top," *New York Times,* December 29, 1996.

6. Jennings, "A Corporate Conscience."

7. The CEO and burnout: Christina Maslach and Michael P. Leiter, *The Truth About Burnout: How Organizations Cause Personal Stress and What to Do About It* (San Francisco: Jossey-Bass, 1998).

8. Nurse burnout and patient satisfaction: Michael P. Leiter et al., "The Correspondence of Nurse Burnout and Patient Satisfaction," *Social Science and Medicine,* in press, 1998.

9. Stress and malpractice: John W. Jones et al., "Stress and Medical Malpractice: Organizational Risk Assessment and Intervention," *Journal of Applied Psychology* 73 (1988).

10. The study of organizational factors in burnout: Michael P. Leiter and L. Robichaud, "Relationships of Occupational Hazards with Burnout: An Assessment of Measures and Models," *Journal of Occupational Health Psychology* 2 (1997); Maslach and Leiter, *The Truth About Burnout.*

11. Net result: Maslach and Leiter, *The Truth About Burnout.*

12. Peter Senge et al., *The Fifth Discipline Fieldbook: Strategies and Tools for Building a Learning Organization* (New York: Doubleday Currency, 1994).

13. Much of my account of the emotional turmoil faced in the 1995 Lincoln Continental launch, and how these problems were solved, comes from the documentation by George Roth and Art Kliener in "The Learning Initiative at the AutoCo Epsilon Program, 1991–1994," distributed by the Center for Organizational Learning at MIT, 1995. While the document describes how the principles of the learning organization were implemented, it also inevitably describes the emotional and social dynamics at work, since the two streams are intimately intertwined in life.

14. For more on the method, see Chris Argyris, *Overcoming Organizational Defenses* (New York: Prentice-Hall, 1990).

15. For more on the two-column method, see Peter Senge et al., *The Fifth Discipline Fieldbook.* While the two-column method is always explained as bringing to the surface hidden thoughts and feelings, in practice the emotions that accompany hidden thoughts seem often to be ignored, though in theory they are as important as the thoughts.

16. Zeniuk, in a presentation with Fred Simon to the Council for Continuous Improvement, "Learning to Learn: A New Look at Product Development," 1996.

Chapter 13 / The Heart of Performance

1. The meeting at GE is described in L. B. Ward, "In the Executive Alphabet You Call Them C.L.O.'s," *New York Times,* February 4, 1996.

2. The seminal article on organizational intelligence: Mary Ann Glynn, "Innovative Genius: A Framework for Relating Individual and Organizational Intelligences to Innovation," *Academy of Management Review* 21 (1996). Glynn offers this somewhat cumbersome definition: "Organizational intelligence is an organization's capability to process, interpret, encode, manipulate, and access information in a purposeful, goal-directed manner, so it can increase its adaptive potential in the environment in which it operates."

3. This definition of intelligence is a variant of that offered by Howard Gardner in his groundbreaking book *Frames of Mind* (New York: Basic Books, 1993).

4. The tech reps' rap sessions: John Seely Brown and Estee Solomon Gray, "The People Are the Company," *Fast Company,* November 1995.

5. Top 25 percent of companies: Jac Fitz-Enz, "The Truth About Best Practices: What They Are and How to Apply Them," *Human Resources Management,* Spring 1997.

6. Practices: Jac Fitz-Enz, *The Eight Practices of Exceptional Companies* (New York: American Management Association, 1997).

7. Of course, the collective emotional intelligence is but one set among the innumerable complex forces at play in determining business performance.

8. Egon Zehnder International: in addition to helpful sources at the firm, I have used the Harvard Business School case study done of the firm, "Egon Zehnder International," by Eunice Lai and Susan Harmeling under the direction of Professor Michael Y. Yoshino, Harvard Business School (N9–395–076), November 2, 1994.

9. Egon Zehnder International data: Nancy Garrison-Jenn, Economist Intelligence Unit, 1996.

Some Final Thoughts

1. Death rate of Fortune 500 companies: of those companies listed in 1955, 325 had disappeared by 1995. See Charles J. Bishop, 1995 annual report of the Industrial Research Institute, cited in Philip H. Abelson, "The Changing Frontiers of Science and Technology," *Science,* July 26, 1996.

2. The survey of American knowledge workers: this study was done by Michael Hair of Frank N. Magid Associates, Los Angeles, and reported in Dudley Buffa and Michael Hair, "How knowledge workers vote," *Fast Company,* October/November 1996.

Appendix 1

1. Multiple intelligence model: see Howard Gardner, *Frames of Mind* (New York: Basic Books, 1983). In addition to the standard cognitive abilities like mathematical reasoning and verbal fluency (as well as intelligences in domains like movement and music), Gardner proposed that there are "personal intelligences": one for managing oneself and another for handling relationships. But in Gardner's descriptions of the personal intelligences, he emphasized the cognitive elements of these personal intelligences, little exploring the crucial role of emotions in these realms.

2. Peter Salovey and John D. Mayer, "Emotional Intelligence," *Imagination, Cognition, and Personality* 9 (1990).

3. Reuven Bar-On's theory of emotional intelligence first appeared in his doctoral dissertation, which with further research was summarized in Reuven Bar-On,

"The Development of a Concept and Test of Psychological Well-being," unpublished manuscript, 1992. In essence, his model describes emotional intelligence as "an array of personal, emotional and social abilities that influence one's ability to succeed in coping with environmental demands and pressures." The fifteen key abilities fall into five general clusters: intrapersonal capacities (the ability to be aware of one's self, to understand one's emotions, and to assert one's feelings and ideas); interpersonal skills (the ability to be aware of and understand others' feelings, to be concerned about people in general, and to establish emotionally close relationships); adaptability (the ability to verify one's feelings, to accurately size up the immediate situation, to flexibly change one's feelings and thoughts, and to solve problems); stress management strategies (the ability to cope with stress and to control strong emotions); and motivational and general mood factors (the ability to be optimistic, to enjoy oneself and others, and to feel and express happiness).

Appendix 2

1. The classic study of competence among supervisors, managers, and executives: Richard E. Boyatzis, *The Competent Manager: A Model for Effective Performance* (New York: John Wiley and Sons, 1982).

2. Top leaders need more conceptual thinking: see, for example, Elliott Jacques, *Requisite Organization* (Arlington, VA: Cason Hall, 1989).

Appendix 3

1. Scientific studies of sex differences in empathy: see, for example, Tiffany Graham and William Ickes, "When Women's Intuition Isn't Greater than Men's," in William Ickes (ed.), *Empathic Accuracy* (New York: Guilford Press, 1997).

2. Women match emotions better than men: Graham and Ickes, "When Women's Intuition Isn't Greater than Men's."

3. Women better than men at decoding emotion: see Judith Hall, *Nonverbal Sex Difference* (Baltimore: Johns Hopkins University Press, 1984).

4. Men did as well as women in empathic accuracy: Graham and Ickes, "When Women's Intuition Isn't Greater than Men's."

5. Women become more empathic when motivated to be so: Graham and Ickes, "When Women's Intuition Isn't Greater than Men's."

6. Empathy as a sign of nurturance—or weakness: Graham and Ickes, "When Women's Intuition Isn't Greater than Men's."

7. Ickes, quoted in *Science News,* March 23, 1996.

Appendix 4

1. The remedial program for threatening stereotypes: Claude M. Steele, "A Threat in the Air: How Stereotypes Shape Intellectual Identity and Performance," *American Psychologist,* June 1997.

Appendix 5

1. Rules of thumb: adapted from Lyle Spencer Jr. et al., *Competency Assessment Methods: History and State of the Art* (Boston: Hay/McBer, 1997).

2. Simulations: Scott I. Tannenbaum and Gary Yukl, "Training and Development in Work Organizations," *Annual Review of Psychology* 43 (1992).

3. High-tech should not replace basic guidelines for training: Miguel Quinones, "Contextual Influences on Training Effectiveness," in M. A. Quinones and A. Ehrenstein (eds.), *Training for a Rapidly Changing Workforce: Applications of Psychological Research* (Washington, DC: American Psychological Association, 1996).

Index

Contacting Daniel Goleman

....

This book represents an ongoing exploration for me into emotional intelligence and its practical implications. I welcome thoughts, stories, and reactions from readers, though I am not always able to respond to every letter. My personal e-mail address is: goleman@javanet.com

For those people in organizations seeking to implement the ideas presented here, development tools, media products, and services are available through my consulting group, Emotional Intelligence Services. Among the tools EIS offers is the "Emotional Competence Inventory," which profiles the entire spectrum of emotional competencies. The ECI can be used as a needs assessment tool, or in a "360" form as a first step in developing emotional competence—both as a motivator for self-development and for targeting the competencies most in need of improvement. Other services include design and implementation of development programs in emotional competence, and training of trainers for organizations. To contact EIS:

Emotional Intelligence Services
142 North Road
Sudbury, MA 01776
Phone: (978) 371–5922 Fax: (978) 371–5903
e-mail: EISGlobal@AOL.com
website: www.EISGlobal.com

For a complete copy of the technical report on the development guidelines described in Chapter 11, visit the website of the Consortium for Research on Emotional Intelligence in Organizations: http://www.eiconsortium.org

About the Author

....

DANIEL GOLEMAN, Ph.D., is CEO of Emotional Intelligence Services in Sudbury, Massachusetts. For twelve years he covered the behavioral and brain sciences for *The New York Times*, and has also taught at Harvard (where he received his doctorate). In addition to *Emotional Intelligence*, his previous books include *Vital Lies, Simple Truths; The Meditative Mind;* and, as co-author, *The Creative Spirit*.